The Mississippi Territory
and the Southwest Frontier
1795–1817

The Mississippi Territory
and the
Southwest Frontier
1795–1817

Robert V. Haynes

The University Press of Kentucky

Scholarly publisher for the Commonwealth,
serving Bellarmine University, Berea College, Centre College of Kentucky,
Eastern Kentucky University, The Filson Historical Society, Georgetown
College, Kentucky Historical Society, Kentucky State University, Morehead State
University, Murray State University, Northern Kentucky University, Transylvania
University, University of Kentucky, University of Louisville, and Western Kentucky
University.
All rights reserved.

Editorial and Sales Offices: The University Press of Kentucky
663 South Limestone Street, Lexington, Kentucky 40508-4008
www.kentuckypress.com

14 13 12 11 10   5 4 3 2 1

Library of Congress Cataloging-in-Publication Data

Haynes, Robert V.
  The Mississippi Territory and the Southwest frontier, 1795–1817 / Robert V.
Haynes.
    p. cm.
  Includes bibliographical references and index.
  ISBN 978-0-8131-2577-0 (hardcover : alk. paper)
  1. Mississippi—History—To 1803. 2. Frontier and pioneer life—Mississippi.
3. Mississippi—History—19th century. 4. Frontier and pioneer life—Southwest,
Old. 5. Southwest, Old—History. I. Title.
  F341.H39 2010
  976.2–dc22   2009053115

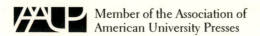   Member of the Association of
                       American University Presses

Contents

Acknowledgments

No authors, and most especially historians, ever work alone, and I have been blessed by never meeting a librarian or archivist who was not only gracious in offering assistance but also extremely knowledgeable. This assistance was crucial because of the wide dispersal of documents pertaining to the development and growth of Mississippi Territory. Staffs at the Library of Congress and the National Archives in Washington, D.C., as well as those at the Mississippi Department of Archives and History were especially helpful. A number of extremely capable historians have written extensively on various aspects of the Old Southwest, and I have relied heavily upon their excellent work.

While the names of those who assisted me over a span of three decades are too numerous to mention, I wish to single out a few who were both extremely supportive and influential in my development. Several are no longer with us, but I still want to acknowledge the late William H. Masterson and William B. Hesseltine, who taught me how to do research and sharpen my writing skills. I have benefitted enormously from a lifetime friendship with John D. W. Guice, whose support of my work has been unwavering for more years than I can count. Finally, I wish to acknowledge the financial support from the two institutions where I have had the pleasure to teach and at times to serve as an administrator—the University of Houston and Western Kentucky University. I particularly wish to thank my colleagues at Western Kentucky, especially Dick Troutman, Marion Lucas, and Richard Weigel, for reading portions of this manuscript and offering helpful suggestions, and to acknowledge the firm support and friendship of Dean David Lee and Robert Dietle. Without the persistent encouragement of my wife, Martha, this study might never have been completed. I dedicate this book to our children, the three Cs, who every day make us proud of their accomplishments and grateful for their love.

Prologue

In 1798, when Congress created Mississippi Territory, the United States was a young nation, struggling to forge unity at home and respect abroad. President John Adams was in his second year of office, having succeeded the much-admired and beloved George Washington, who had placed the country on a promising footing by resolving its internal fiscal problems and by pursuing a policy of neutrality toward foreign belligerents. Lacking his predecessor's charisma and political acumen, Adams tossed the nation into an undeclared naval war with revolutionary France, and polarized the public. In response, he persuaded Congress to embark on a costly preparedness program and acquiesced in the tightening of internal security by signing the controversial Alien and Sedition Acts. These measures and others divided the populace into two warring factions or embryonic parties (Federalists and Republicans) and forced a few to threaten nullification of the repressive acts.[1]

Conditions were not much better in the emerging western country. Officials worried about the loyalty of settlers there, separated as they were from the east coast by the rugged Appalachian Mountains and blocked from the seas by Spanish control of the lower Mississippi Valley. Americans had always been westward-looking, and none more than Washington, who was not alone in believing that America's future lay in the West.[2]

After the Revolution, immigrants poured across the mountains into the future states of Kentucky, Tennessee, and Ohio, encroaching on lands long held by Native Americans and arousing suspicions of the British in Canada and the Spanish in Louisiana. To ward off any potential threat, both European nations renewed their friendship with the Indians, and Spain craftily regulated commerce on the Mississippi to dis-

1

courage further American penetration. These and other impediments to western progress spawned separatist movements during the 1780s, particularly in Kentucky and Tennessee, that alarmed prominent figures in Philadelphia like George Washington, and caused others to doubt the commitment of westerners.

During the early 1790s, rumors of disunion reemerged, fueled by a tax revolt against the hated whiskey excise of 1791 and by French efforts to enlist frontiersmen in filibustering expeditions against Spanish possessions. Then, in the mid-1790s, two fortuitous developments gave impetus to another western surge. First, an American army commanded by Gen. Anthony Wayne defeated a coalition of Indian tribes at Fallen Timbers, freeing most of modern Ohio for American pioneers. Second, U.S. minister Thomas Pinckney negotiated a favorable treaty with Spain that reopened the Mississippi River by granting Americans free deposit at New Orleans and set the southern boundary at the thirty-first parallel of north latitude.[3]

Yet these favorable events did not completely erase western inquietude. In 1798, reports surfaced that Senator William Blount of Tennessee had conspired with the British and local Indians to wrest Florida and possibly Louisiana from Spain.[4] Even more disturbing was the decision of the Georgia legislature in 1795 to grant for a second time its vast western land claims (modern states of Alabama and Mississippi) to four land-speculating companies for a mere pittance. After it was discovered that all the legislators but one were participants themselves, the outcry was so loud that the next session rescinded the so-called Yazoo grants, but not before the original recipients had sold their claims to unsuspecting third parties.[5] In the aftermath, landholders were left in a state of anxiety, and "Yazoo" became a watchword for scandal and greed.

It was in the midst of such unsettled times that possession of the modestly settled and long-disputed district known as Natchez, after the vanished Indian tribe of the same name, passed to the United States. Although Congress had incorporated all lands between the Chattahoochee and Mississippi rivers, north of the thirty-first and south of the thirty-second parallels, into Mississippi Territory, the only portion of interest to federal officials was the elongated Natchez District. Not only was this district located in the remote southwestern corner of the country, rendering it open to foreign intrigue, but it was also populated mostly by wary Native Americans and former British Loyalists. At the time, the only concentrated settlement was in and around the boat landing at Natchez. The rest of this odd, triangular-shaped district covered an expanse of territory along the eastern bank of Mississippi River between the thirty-first parallel northward to the mouth of the Yazoo River. Its eastern border was protean and irregular, depending upon the extent of Indian settlement, which, in a few instances, came within thirty miles of the Mississippi. Except around Natchez, white settlements were sparse and scattered, extending only a few leagues into the backcountry, which, in contrast to other frontiers, lay east instead of west of populated centers.

Two small, navigable rivers as well as several creeks and bayous intersected the district, providing easy access to New Orleans and beyond. The rivers were Big Black to the north and Homochitto in the south. The small streams from north to south consisted of Bayou Pierre, Coles, Fairchild's, Second, Sandy, and Buffalo creeks and Bayou Sara. According to Andrew Ellicott, U.S. commissioner for marking the southern boundary between the United States and Spain, "the quantity of vacant land in the district to which the Indian claim has been extinguished cannot be very large," covering "but about 2,464,000 acres, the one half of which at least has been appropriated."[6]

Like the nation as a whole, Natchez District had already weathered a period of unrest and chaos before it fell under American control. The first permanent settlers were British, although the French had tried and failed to establish an outpost there earlier in the century. In 1763, at the Treaty of Paris ending the Seven Years' War, the British acquired Spanish Florida, which they immediately divided into two provinces, East and West Florida. Except for European settlements at Mobile and Pensacola, West Florida was home to some thirty thousand Indians, divided into three loose-knit confederations—Choctaw, Chickasaw, and Creek.[7] Only after 1770 did the British attempt to settle Natchez District by negotiating removal of Choctaw rights and introducing rudimentary governmental services there. To bring some semblance of protection and order, they replaced the abandoned French fort (Rosalie) with Fort Panmure.

To populate the far-flung district, isolated from the capital at Pensacola by more than three hundred miles of unspoiled wilderness, the British relied primarily upon private entrepreneurs, who acted as both speculators and promoters. Consisting mostly of former military officers and court favorites, they frequently received gigantic tracts of the best lands. Uninterested in settling themselves, they nonetheless realized that, to return a profit, they would have to entice immigrants in the form of buyers, tenants, or renters. While this scheme never worked to perfection, it brought in farmers and laborers who raised crops and sometimes exported them to distant markets and encouraged others to follow. At first, growth was slow due to the district's remoteness, its vulnerability to Spanish influence, and Indian chariness. It grew apace, however, in the late 1770s once word of its rich alluvial soil, temperate climate, and proximity to the wide Mississippi became better known.[8]

A majority of early residents, who came mostly from the southeastern colonies of Virginia, the Carolinas, and Georgia, were predominantly of English or Scottish stock. Like other American frontiers, the region attracted the usual number of displaced individuals, including desperate debtors, criminals of various sorts, bigamists, spouses of broken marriages, and youngsters of dysfunctional families, most of whom were forced initially to become squatters. More likely to be poor and rural than wealthy and urban, they nevertheless proved to be energetic and resourceful. A sizable number were Loyalists escaping Patriot wrath before and during the Revolution. A few were yeomen farmers eager to join the planter class or small merchants seeking new opportunities in a place they hoped would be a new Canaan, a land flowing with milk and honey. Some of these brought along their slaves or purchased them on arrival, implanting that odious institution that was to become synonymous with the sunny South.

To be sure, land was the magnet that pulled families by the thousands to the unruly frontier, but its acquisition proved more difficult than middling farmers and landless migrants anticipated, creating opportunities for the unsavory as well as the enterprising. Moreover, confusion over land titles granted by a succession of previous governments (France, Britain, and Spain, as well as the state of Georgia) attracted a host of lawyers, not to mention speculators and swindlers. It was these conflicts, which unnerved many but pleased others, that were to color territorial development to statehood and beyond.

Hardly had the British established a solid foothold in the district before the American Revolution evolved from a local rebellion into an international conflict. In 1778, France allied itself with the American rebels, and the next year Spain joined France in the war against England, expecting to recover Florida and other territories lost in earlier eighteenth-century conflicts. This diplomatic revolution was to have an immediate and lasting impact on the Natchez District.

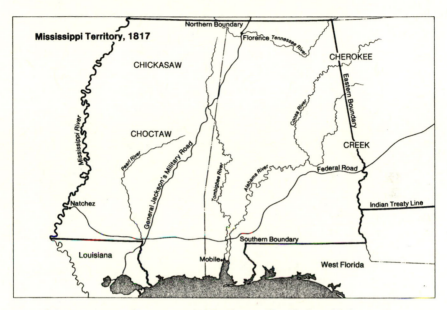

Map of the Mississippi Territory in 1817 (Thomas D. Clark and John D. W. Guice, *Frontiers in Conflict: The Old Southwest, 1795–1830* [Albuquerque, N.M., 1989]).

CHAPTER 1

From Province to Territory

Late on the evening of March 29, 1798, U.S. commissioner Andrew Ellicott learned through a "confidential channel" that Spain planned to evacuate Natchez. After a restless night, Ellicott awoke at four o'clock the following morning; dressing quickly, he hurried to Fort Panmure in time to witness the last contingent of Spanish soldiers marching toward the river. Finding the gate to the fort open, he entered and climbed to the parapet, where he observed "the pleasing prospect of the gallies and boats" sailing downstream toward New Orleans. Before daylight, they were out of sight. Later that day, Ellicott watched gleefully as American troops took possession of the abandoned fortification.[1]

In such routine fashion, Spain relinquished control of the fertile Natchez District, almost three years after conceding American claims to the region in Pinckney's Treaty of 1795. If removal of Spanish troops from Natchez in 1798 appeared prosaic, Spain's protracted rule left a legacy of bitterness and discord that would be indelibly stamped on the region. In the ensuing aftermath, the ruling class of landholders and merchants separated into two hostile camps, with one side favoring a government in the hands of a small elite with plenary powers and the other wanting the people to have a meaningful voice. This bitter division, which had intensified during the late 1790s, was to shape early territorial politics for a decade or more.

Spanish possession dated from early October 1779, when a motley military force under Bernardo de Galvez, Spanish governor of Louisiana, seized the British fort at Baton Rouge in a swift attack. The British commander not only surrendered Baton Rouge but ordered his counterpart to relinquish Fort Panmure as well.[2] Later, Spanish officials placed both districts under the governor of Louisiana. Yet Spanish occupation of Natchez was only one of several events that, during the American Revolution, interrupted the otherwise humdrum lives of these settlers.

The ravages of revolution had first come to Natchez in February 1778 in the form of a party of American raiders led by Capt. James Willing. A former Natchez merchant who, out of personal and financial failure, had left the district in 1777, Willing returned next year, intent upon taking possession in the name of the "United States of America." Younger brother of Thomas Willing of the Philadelphia firm of Morris and Willing, James used his influence with Congressman Robert Morris to have himself commissioned a naval captain and outfitted at Fort Pitt with a small riverboat named the *Rattletrap* and manned by twenty-four sailors. On his way down the Ohio and Mississippi rivers, Willing added a hundred or so adventurers to his party. Upon landing at Natchez, Willing forced the inhabitants, few of whom were avowed Tories, to take an oath of neutrality. He also gathered additional recruits, seized the property of several personal enemies, and took hostage Anthony Hutchins, the district's most notorious Loyalist.[3]

Willing's raiders then departed for New Orleans. En route they engaged in widespread plundering and wanton destruction of property. They indiscriminately laid waste to settlements on both sides of the Mississippi from Point Coupee to Manchac, a tiny port (at the mouth of the Iberville River) near the Louisiana border. Although Willing established ties with Spanish New Orleans, the relationship was short-lived, and he turned a majority of Natchez settlers against the United States.

His exploits also emboldened Anthony Hutchins, who, after escaping the clutches of Willing, returned to Natchez, where he persuaded several inhabitants to break their vow of neutrality and reaffirm allegiance to England. Willing sent a small detachment to Natchez to prevent the British from regaining control, but Hutchins was waiting. He surprised and defeated the American rebels in a brief but bloody skirmish. Afterward, Hutchins proudly informed his superiors that "the American colors were soon torn down and . . . those of the Britannic Majesty most splendidly appear in triumph."[4]

Hutchins's triumph was ephemeral, and Spain easily reasserted its authority in 1779. Two years later, in what was to become known as the Natchez Rebellion of 1781, a combination of footloose Americans and British Loyalists led by John Blommart, a restless gristmill owner, recaptured Fort Panmure. The surrender of Pensacola to the Spaniards a few weeks later compelled the insurgents to return the fort, putting an end to British presence in Natchez District.[5] Even though Spain ruled the area for the next nineteen years, the composition of the population, which was largely English and Celtic, remained unchanged despite a steady influx of immigrants.

During the Spanish period, which lasted from 1779 to 1798, Natchez District continued to grow and assume the trappings of a cultured society. To the surprise of Anglo settlers, Spanish rule was less despotic than expected, and Spanish officials lured "respectable" families by confirming existing land titles and issuing new ones, discouraging speculation, and preventing vagabonds, drifters, and "undesirables" from lingering in or around Natchez. They allowed immigrants to import personal belongings free of duty and extended them liberal commercial privileges in New Orleans. A royal order of 1788 offered religious toleration to Protestants as long as they practiced their beliefs in private and refrained from proselytizing. The following year saw the arrival of the first Spanish governor, Manuel Gayoso de Lemos, who quickly ingratiated himself with Natchez aristocrats by entertaining them lavishly at night and seeking their counsel by day.[6]

Two planters who profited from Spanish beneficence were William Dunbar and Stephen Minor. Possessed with a fine intellect, an insatiable interest in natural science, and polished manners unusual in the backcountry, Dunbar rose to prominence and developed a close relationship with Governor Gayoso, who rewarded him with choice land grants, including a plot in Natchez, and a handful of offices.[7] Minor was also adept at currying favors, due to his undivided loyalty during and after the American Revolution. In 1798, he succeeded Dunbar as Spanish commissioner for drawing the southern boundary.[8]

More than Minor or Dunbar, prominent residents such as Bernard Lintot, John Ellis, John Bisland, and William Vousdan typified the behavior of planters during the interlude. While they were careful not to disparage Spain, and occasionally to flatter her officials, they never adjusted comfortably to life under a Catholic monarchy. Eschewing politics, they devoted themselves to amassing land and slaves, raising children and marrying them off to promising spouses, and producing tobacco or indigo.[9]

Others like Daniel Clark Sr. and Peter Bryan Bruin were more calculating. As long as Spain possessed the district, they refrained from criticism and resorted to sycophancy in hopes of winning favor. Prior to 1798, Clark remained on good terms with Governor Gayoso, who, in his frequent journeys to and from Natchez, either stopped at Clark's landing on the Mississippi River, just north of the international border, for a visit or "fired a swifel" in salute as he passed. By late spring of 1798, Clark, delighted by the prospect of American rule, was expressing satisfaction with no longer being "the Subject of a Despotic monarch in a remote Province where Tyranny flourishes and where the inherent Rights of Man are not known."[10]

In contrast to Clark, who came to the district while it was British, Bruin was a newcomer, arriving at Natchez on June 10, 1788, in the company of sixty-five others. After settling on a Spanish grant at the confluence of Bayou Pierre and the Mississippi River, approximately forty miles north of Natchez, Bruin spent his time planting tobacco and placating officials. In 1792, when that notorious land speculator Doctor James O'Fallon sought to enlist him in a scheme to settle families along the Big Black River, Bruin dutifully reported the overtures to Gayoso, while keeping on good terms with the Irishman. In appreciation of Bruin's apparent loyalty, Gayoso named him alcalde of Bayou Pierre and colonel of the Natchez volunteers.[11]

Bruin also collaborated with a few notorious adventurers, like the infamous Philip Nolan, without severing his Spanish ties. Consequently, when Andrew Ellicott arrived in early 1797, he contacted Bruin, who furnished him with information about influential inhabitants and Spanish policies.[12] Bruin, ever the opportunist, was adroit at straddling the fence in times of uncertainty. Regardless of which nation—Spain or the United States—emerged supreme, Bruin prepared to befriend it.

While most residents were outwardly loyal to Spain, there were two notable exceptions. The first consisted of a small band of ardent pro-Americans led by Col. Thomas Green, a transplanted Virginian who had served with Gen. George Washington during the American Revolution. Infuriated that apathetic inhabitants had "allow[ed] a few incrohen tyrants [Spaniards], to take the most valuable places in this country," Green sought Georgia's assistance in driving out the despised dons.

By virtue of its colonial charter, supplemented by the Treaty of 1783, Georgia claimed the region between the Chattahoochee and Mississippi rivers north of the thirty-first parallel. In 1784, Green asked that state to place Natchez under its protection, and in 1785, the Georgia legislature established Bourbon County to include the entire Natchez District and dispatched four commissioners, one of whom was Green, to cajole the Spaniards into withdrawing and to organize a county government. The project was aborted after Spain refused to recognize Georgia's jurisdiction and the United States opposed the effort.[13]

Moreover, the commissioners themselves nearly came to blows when the truculent Green threatened to lead a party of Indians against the Spaniards. Two of the commissioners opposed the use of force and denounced Green's aggressiveness. In fact, Green misjudged the Americans who favored independence and not subservience to Georgia. Even those who supported the project worried lest Georgia refuse to sanction their land titles. At least one settler preferred "Spanish government to the American, for the taxes give me the headache whenever I think of them."[14]

Although Green continued to reside in the district after the Bourbon scheme collapsed, Spanish officials carefully monitored him. In 1792, when the Indians again became aggressive, Gayoso banished him to Baton Rouge and advised the governor there to keep him under surveillance. Yet Green's distrust of Spaniards was not shared by all Natchez residents, many of whom viewed his antics with detached amusement.[15]

A second group opposed to Spanish rule was a small cadre of Loyalists whose spokesman was Col. Anthony Hutchins, a British pensioner and former officer. Following the Natchez Rebellion of 1781, in which he participated, Hutchins fled the district until the governor of Louisiana permitted him to return unmolested. Although Hutchins behaved himself during the early 1790s, he was never a Spanish favorite, and always discontented. One reason for Hutchins's disenchantment was Spain's erratic economic policy. In 1789, in an effort to attract American settlers, Spain relaxed its traditional mercantilistic policy, granting them commercial privileges and subsidies for tobacco. These policies stimulated production, resulting in a bumper harvest for district planters in 1789, when they marketed a total of 1,402,725 pounds of tobacco. Anthony Hutchins, Thomas Green, and Daniel Clark exported at least 20,000 pounds each.[16] In late 1790, the Spanish government abruptly reduced its purchase of tobacco from 2 million to 40,000 pounds due to a glut in the world market. This curtailment was especially disastrous for those Natchez planters who had mortgaged their properties to buy more land and slaves in anticipation of continued prosperity.[17]

Although Spanish officials in Madrid offered planters some relief for their 1790 crops, the next year they made the reduction permanent, throwing both planters and creditors into dire economic straits. Rather than fostering closer cooperation, the ensuing hardships drove planters and merchants apart. Planters accused the merchants of trying to recoup their losses by charging outrageous prices for goods and extracting exorbitant interest rates payable in "silver dollars." Unless "equitable prices were charged," they declared, "the time is not very far distant when the planter must destroy the merchant or the merchant must destroy the planter." Sympathetic to these pleas, Gayoso convinced the Spanish government to grant Natchez planters a three-year grace period, beginning in 1792, on payment of their debts and to restrict interest charges "to the rate of five per centum only."[18]

But Natchez merchants accused planters of not taking advantage of the moratorium to discharge their debts. In 1795, when the three-year period was to expire, they implored Gayoso not to extend it. "A very large majority of the Debtors, so far from exerting their endeavors, to extricate themselves from their difficulties," read a petition, and "having no longer the Dread of the Law before their eyes, have become Indolent, Dissipated, and Deaf to the calls of their Creditors."[19]

Realizing that the district's economy rested on agriculture, Gayoso renewed the moratorium until 1800. Unhappy creditors then charged debtors with shirking their financial obligations. "It is well known," they argued, "that if payments are to depend upon the Justice, Discretion, and promise of these men, the whole of the Debt may be considered a total loss." Agreeing with the merchants in this case, Gayoso lectured debtors on the necessity to "comply with their engagement."[20]

Happily, planters proved resourceful enough to discover a new cash crop—cotton—to replace tobacco. Cotton had been raised in the district for some time, but the effort and expense required to remove the seeds from the boll by hand made it unprofitable. This disadvantage ceased in 1795, when John Barclay, a Natchez debtor-planter returning from a visit to South Carolina, where he saw Eli Whitney's crude gin in operation, constructed, with the assistance of Daniel Clark, one of his own. Shortly afterward, other gins began to pop up, and at least one pub-lic gin was in operation on a Selsertown plantation as early as 1796.[21]

Fortunately for Natchez planters, cotton commanded a high price after 1795 due largely to reduced exports from the French West Indies, where a slave insurrection had brought production to near standstill. Pro-duction in Natchez of a generally dry and good-quality cotton steadily rose from 36,351 pounds in 1794 to more than 1.2 million pounds in 1800. According to Ellicott, Natchez planters in 1798 sold approxi-mately four thousand bales of cotton in the New Orleans market at forty dollars per bale. Dunbar voiced the planters' excitement. "We continue to cultivate cotton with very great success," he wrote; "it is by far the most profitable crop we have ever undertaken in this country."[22] Although prosperity had returned to Natchez District by 1798, divisions between planters and merchants were hardly healed.

In addition to the persistent conflicts between creditors and debtors, differences in religious preference, political persuasion, national origins, and social standing separated the citizens, although none was pervasive enough to create lasting cleavages. Next to the planter-merchant dichot-omy, conflicting land claims were the most disturbing. The earliest set-tlers had received their grants from the British government while recent immigrants held Spanish titles. Although Spanish officials recognized the validity of British grants upon which settlers had made improvements, they were not hesitant to grant vacant lands to newcomers even where there were prior claimants. Furthermore, Spain ignored the claims of the State of Georgia to lands in Natchez District and treated the Yazoo grants as nugatory.[23]

It was against this backdrop of a variety of competing interests that the transfer of the district from Spanish to American rule began on February 22, 1797. Two years after Pinckney's Treaty ceding Natchez to the United States, Andrew Ellicott, accompanied by a small military guard, a hand-ful of attendants, and two dozen woodsmen, reached Bayou Pierre, the district's northern extremity. Ellicott had orders from President Adams to accept evacuation of the Spanish military posts of Natchez and Wal-nut Hills (present-day Vicksburg) and to cooperate with Spanish offi-cials in drawing the international boundary. At the request of Governor Gayoso, Ellicott halted his military escort at Bayou Pierre. But, two days later, without notifying Gayoso, he proceeded to Natchez, arriving there on February 24, accompanied by local residents Peter Bruin and Philip

Nolan. Irritated by Ellicott's unauthorized presence, Gayoso treated the American coolly, refusing to evacuate until the arrival of vessels appropriate for transporting the men and supplies to New Orleans.[24]

Ellicott, who by nature was overly suspicious, incorrectly interpreted Gayoso's icy reception as evidence of a calculated scheme to "delay or evade from one pretence or another" execution of the treaty. An impatient Ellicott pressed Gayoso for an exact date when marking the boundary was to commence. Eventually Gayoso relented, agreeing to May 19, 1797.[25]

Although Baron de Carondelet, governor of Louisiana, considered the terms of Pinckney's Treaty overly generous, he instructed Gayoso to prepare for departure and destruction of the forts at Walnut Hills and Natchez. After hearing rumors of British designs on Upper Louisiana, Carondelet decided to transfer the troops and material from the two lower forts upriver to St. Louis. Although Gayoso too had misgivings about the treaty, he prepared to execute Carondelet's orders.[26]

In the midst of these developments, Carondelet received furtive orders directing him to delay evacuation of the Spanish forts in the Southwest, and he assiduously moved to comply. On March 22, 1797, Gayoso had the cannon, which he had already hauled to the Natchez landing, returned to the fort. Ellicott, who watched these developments in disbelief, saw them as proof of Spanish intransigence. He had earlier resented Gayoso's instructions to prevent American military forces encamped at Bayou Pierre under Lt. Piercy Smith Pope from entering Natchez on the specious grounds that the presence of U.S. troops during evacuation of the forts would imply that Spain was acting under duress.[27]

Spain's abrupt change of plans was the result of two developments. First, Spanish officials realized that the attempt to wean the United States from Great Britain by negotiating a favorable treaty was futile; the Federalist administration in Philadelphia remained firmly wedded to the British. Second, Spain's previous efforts to sell Louisiana to France were unsuccessful largely because the French refused to pay the high price demanded by Spanish officials. As long as Louisiana remained in Spanish hands, her officials were hardly eager to have Americans at their doorstep.

Again Spanish strategy reaffirmed Ellicott's suspicions that Spain planned to delay, if not evade, evacuation of Natchez District. In late March, Spanish officials compounded the confusion by offering a rash

of new excuses, none satisfactory to Ellicott. Aware of Tennessee senator William Blount's alleged scheme to seize, with British aid, Louisiana and West Florida, Spanish officials employed it to justify continued
possession of Natchez District. Carondelet also insisted that the ambiguity of certain treaty clauses necessitated postponement until the two
governments resolved them. These included pacification of the Indians,
navigation rights on the Mississippi River, confirmation of land titles,
and condition of the forts at the time of transfer.[28]

If Gayoso was eager to delay execution of the treaty, Ellicott was
determined to oust the Spaniards immediately. By the end of March,
he resorted to intrigue with a small clique of pro-American and anti-
Spanish inhabitants to accomplish his assignment. He persuaded Lieutenant Pope to encamp his troops near Natchez, where they could better
protect Ellicott's surveying party and reaffirm America's intention to
take the district.

As Ellicott hoped, the military's presence instilled courage in the
pro-American inhabitants, who vowed allegiance to the United States
and denounced Spanish officials for their past misrule. "Some [of the
inhabitants] have been already torn away from the bosom of agricultural
life, and conveyed to prison with every indignant epithat that malevo-
lence could invent," they charged. "Scouts are crossing the country in
various directions, breathing threats of vengeance against those who had
unguardedly thrown aside the mask of duplicity."[29]

On March 29, Gayoso, anxious to quell the uproar, attempted to
counteract the activities of those who had "made it their business to
dazzle the public with false notions." He pledged not to depart until
"the real property of the inhabitants [was] secured," nor disturb planters in preparing crops for market "on account of depending debts," and
never to molest anyone because of "religious principles or in their private meetings."[30]

While acknowledging the ingenuity of Gayoso's appeal to property
holders and debtors, Ellicott still believed that "nine-tenths" of the inhabitants, who were "more numerous" than he expected, were "warmly
attached to the interests of the United States." Despite the strong ties
to Spain among the Indians, who frequently roamed through his camp
"with drawn knives," Ellicott was confident that a thousand American
troops could take the district within weeks. As a result, he became bolder
in his behavior and more bellicose in his statements.[31]

After the arrival of Pope's detachment of thirty-six men at Natchez on April 24 and Spain's subsequent decision in early May 1797 to reinforce Fort Nogales at Walnut Hills with forty men and "a company of grenadiers," tensions rose noticeably. Ellicott recorded in his journal that "the public mind might be compared to inflammable gas; it wanted but a spark to produce an explosion."[32]

The spark was ignited on June 9, 1797, when Barton Hannon, an itinerant Baptist minister who was then inebriated, accosted Governor Gayoso, seeking revenge for the "sound thrashing" given him by some angry Irish Catholics in the lower part of Natchez while he attempted to convert them. Gayoso found Hannon's behavior so obnoxious that, after warning him to desist his tirades, he ordered the fiery evangelist incarcerated "to preserve the peace." On his way to Fort Panmure, where he was to be placed in stocks, Hannon passed by Ellicott's camp and spotted several Americans. "Help me, fellow Americans," he yelled, as he tried to escape. Reacting quickly, the Spanish guards recaptured Hannon and threw him in jail.[33]

As soon as news of Hannon's arrest spread, a number of infuriated inhabitants approached Ellicott with wild schemes of retaliation. Hutchins wanted to seize Gayoso and whisk him off to the Chickasaw Nation. Others favored capturing Gayoso and ransoming him for Hannon. For days, rumors circulated that angry settlers intended to seize the fort, which Gayoso had hastily reinforced with a detachment of Loyalists. Armed inhabitants roamed the countryside, blocking roads and threatening to plunge "cold steel" into the fort's defenders. Meanwhile Gayoso pleaded with Carondelet to send more troops, while Lieutenant Pope, in an address to "the citizens of the Natchez District," promised to protect them "at all hazards . . . from every act of hostility" and urged them to "come forward and assert your rights" by repelling any attempt to reinforce the Spanish garrison.[34]

In response to Pope's plea for assistance, several men rode through the countryside collecting signatures to a pledge of cooperation with American troops. On June 12, some three hundred armed men gathered at William Belk's tavern to foment rebellion, but upon learning that Gayoso had refortified the fort, they suddenly lost a taste for valor. Nevertheless, at Pope's instigation, a few tested Gayoso's resolve by occupying a rise of ground near the fort, but brisk Spanish fire drove them back.[35]

Although Pope, widely known to be unstable—he was frequently referred to as "crazy"—was eager for a showdown, cooler heads prevailed. Gayoso, in a demonstration of good faith, released Hannon from prison and promised to take no punitive action against the insurgents. Meanwhile, Ellicott broke with Pope and agreed to meet Gayoso in the hope of arranging a settlement.

On June 20, the leading inhabitants of the district, including Pope, Ellicott, and Hutchins, met the insurgents at Belk's tavern and elected a citizens' committee consisting of such prominent men as Hutchins, Isaac Gaillard, and Cato West, Thomas Green's son-in-law. By unanimous vote, they later added Pope and Ellicott to the committee, which drew up a list of conditions that Gayoso accepted on June 22. He agreed to respect the "neutrality" of the district, pending resolution of the controversy, summon the militia only in case of Indian attack or civil riot, and refrain from transporting prisoners out of the district for trial on "any pretext." In return, the citizens pledged to respect Spanish laws.[36]

Although no further violence occurred during the summer of 1797, a few firebrands on Coles Creek continued "to be troublesome," and they consented to uphold the agreement only after the committee threatened them. Ellicott described the rowdies as "that class who have nothing to lose and therefore something to expect"; but, he reported, their prejudice was so obvious as "to render their influence inconsiderable."[37]

Ellicott soon found Lieutenant Pope equally troublesome. Never very perceptive about people, Ellicott failed to appreciate Pope's talent for mischief or Gayoso's displeasure with his antics. He became equally distressed when Pope declared that "by the Great Jehovah no man shall speak at Natchez but him[self]." Upon learning that Pope's replacement, Capt. Isaac Guion, was already "on the River," both Gayoso and Ellicott rejoiced. The Spaniard had told Ellicott that he was willing to accept "any man who is not absolutely mad," and Ellicott asked Secretary of State Pickering to assign him any military officer "possessed of sobriety, talents, and prudence." It was necessary, he insisted, "to send officers to this country who are not mad."[38]

Yet, before Guion's arrival in Natchez, Gayoso received the assignment he had always wanted, the governorship of Louisiana. On July 29, 1797, he departed Natchez for New Orleans, leaving affairs in the hands of Stephen Minor.[39] Gayoso's promotion convinced everyone that the days of Spanish occupation were numbered. Thereafter inhabitants began to refocus attention from personalities to what form of government should be established. Three considerations informed their discourse—cumbersome debts, conflicting land claims, and identification of officials to administer the new regime. Differences over these matters split them into two warring factions, with Andrew Ellicott and Anthony Hutchins as the principal spokesman of each.

On July 13, the Ellicott faction, with the concurrence of Gayoso before he departed, had established the "Permanent Committee." Its members, including Peter Bruin, represented the merchant-creditor faction, and wished for a government capable of rewarding them and protecting their interests.[40] Convinced that Ellicott intended to appoint his friends to the important offices, Hutchins devised a strategy to thwart him. First of all, he tried to undermine the Permanent Committee's authority, insisting that it was unrepresentative and established only "to promote peace and to cooperate in acts of duty with the Spanish government." According to Ellicott, hardly an unbiased observer, Hutchins barged into a meeting of the committee and, after "some preliminary observations," proclaimed that he was there to dissolve it. "I am the Organ and Oracle of the people," Hutchins exclaimed; "you are no committee. I will issue circular letters, and have another elected which shall be the Committee of the People."[41]

Recognizing the need to establish a legitimate base of power from which to counteract Ellicott's influence, Hutchins secured permission from Acting Governor Minor to hold a special election on September 2 so that the "people" might elect "a Committee of Safety" and "an able and trusty man as Agent, to communicate with Congress." According to Hutchins, the Permanent Committee could hardly speak for the people after some members had "held the Election, took the Polls, and returned themselves elected" and then proceeded to "push themselves on you as your Committee." He warned "the Planters, Mechanics & Labourers of Natchez" that unless a trusted agent "of your own likeness" informed Congress of "a true & perfect state" of the origin of their debts "as contracted on the paper system," they would be ruined financially and permanently mired in poverty. Also, he reminded them, agents of land companies were already in the district seeking to purchase from Indians "the most valuable body of Land."[42]

Hutchins and his friends aimed their abuse against those Ellicott supporters who, in their opinion, were likely to receive public office under the new government. Although they accused Dunbar of being a Spaniard in disguise, Bruin was their favorite target. "The torrent of abuse, which has pour'd in upon me, from all quarters has been as great as it has been unmerited," Bruin bemoaned. "I am one day a Frenchman, another a Spaniard, at all times a Turk & not infrequently a Devil." At one tense moment, he even feared for his life.[43]

Afraid that Hutchins might mobilize the people because of uneasiness over debts and land titles, the pro-Ellicott faction mobilized. In a secret meeting, some seventy-five inhabitants protested the upcoming election. They questioned its legality, denounced it as a dangerous precedent designed to sow "seeds of anarchy," and objected to allowing eighteen-year-olds to vote.

While a second group of protesters along Buffalo Creek and Bayou Sara was gathering, the first group quietly circulated a petition. Their efforts were amazingly successful. Even at Coles Creek, stronghold of the Hutchins faction, nearly half of the residents signed the petition, including every prominent citizen "except for five or six."[44]

Leaving nothing to chance, Ellicott persuaded Lieutenant Pope, still in charge of the military detachment, to deliver a circular letter to the ten persons designated by Hutchins as supervisors, warning them against participating in the illegal summer election. The result was a smaller than expected turnout in some districts and a complete breakdown in others. Still, the few participants chose an eight-person Committee of Safety led by Thomas Marston Green (Thomas Green's son). This committee, proclaiming itself the true representative of the people, commissioned Anthony Hutchins to draft a memorial asking for extension of popular government to the district, resettlement of merchants' accounts and relief for impoverished debtors, and validation of all lands in possession of actual settlers.[45]

At the same time, the Permanent Committee persuaded Governor Minor to censure Hutchins for his "barking, insolent inflammatory" circular letter and to designate the Permanent Committee as "the true and sole representatives of the inhabitants." It also delegated Ellicott to lay before President Adams "our present situation" and to take whatever "other measures he deems conducive to the welfare of this country." Later Minor thanked Ellicott, Pope, and the Permanent Committee for preserving the "happy state of neutrality" and preventing it from being "polluted by the unhallowed hands of faction."[46]

In an effort to discredit Hutchins, Ellicott sought to link him to the British and William Blount. He collected affidavits proving that Hutchins was still a British pensioner, that he had commanded "the party which massacred the Americans at the [White] Cliffs" during Willing's raid in 1778, and that he was leader of the Natchez Rebellion of 1781, which sought to regain the district for "the Crown of Great Britain."[47]

Ellicott accused Hutchins of heading what he derisively called the "party of British interest" and of "keeping up an unnecessary commotion" in support of Blount's conspiracy. He characterized Hutchins, whom he once described as "Squeaking Tony, long and bony," as the "most inveterate anti-American in the district."[48] Ellicott even hinted that Governor Gayoso had encouraged Hutchins's efforts in order to furnish Spain an excuse for sending additional troops to Natchez. Infuriated, Hutchins threatened to expose the story about "Old Ellicott, young Ellicott and a housekeeper."[49]

The unexpected arrival of Gen. George Mathews and Judge Arthur Miller, both avid land speculators, magnified the people's anguish, especially those like Hutchins who held British grants. As governor of Georgia, Mathews had signed the notorious Yazoo grants of 1795. Mathews and Miller were in Natchez partly in anticipation of being named governor and secretary of the territory, respectively, and partly as agents of the New England and Mississippi land companies, two associations of speculators who had purchased claims from the original Yazoo grantees. Although they promised not to interfere with claims recognized by the Spanish government, most inhabitants were not reassured. Even Acting Governor Minor was suspicious. He invited Mathews to dinner, after which they "pushed about the bottle," but Minor extracted no useful information from the wily general. "I believe all the wine I have," he bemoaned, "could not make him drunk." Hutchins, however, could hardly help but notice Mathews's close friendship with Ellicott, and his anxieties were hardly relieved by Miller's departure in late 1797.[50]

One reason for the vitriolic exchange was the Committee of Safety's success in securing signatures to a petition requesting Congress to remove Ellicott or restrict his duties to "Latitude and Line." In a secret clause omitted from the public memorial, Hutchins and his friends accused Ellicott and Pope of inciting the June insurrection that had hurled the district into chaos and the inhabitants into confusion.[51]

To expose Hutchins's perfidy, Ellicott's friends plotted to intercept the memorial before it reached Philadelphia. Fortunately for them, Hutchins delayed sending the packet containing the petition and his letter to Secretary of State Pickering, when James Stuart, the express rider, was taken ill. He eventually sent Daniel Burnet instead. On November 20, Burnet, who according to Ellicott was "well known in the State of Georgia for his dexterity in Negro stealing," set out for Philadelphia by way of Nashville. As he rode along the Natchez Trace, two armed gunmen, later identified as James Truly and Silas L. Payne, overtook him at gunpoint and seized the saddlebags containing the controversial documents.[52]

According to Hutchins, the two "Ruffians" offered the packet to Pope, who "refused to countenance the unwarrantable act." They then delivered it to Ellicott, who, "having fallen among thieves and Robbers," treated them with "refreshments and marks of hospitality." In addition to charging Ellicott with armed robbery, Hutchins accused him of using his office to engage in land speculation and informing Congress "that all the inhabitants of the district were in favor of the abolition of slavery."[53]

Ellicott angrily denied the charges. He insisted that Truly and Payne gave Burnet a receipt for the packet and notified the public of their actions. Later he implored signers of the memorial to meet at Belk's on November 25, where a throng of more than one hundred settlers, equally divided between adherents of Ellicott and Hutchins, conducted a mock trial to clear the air. According to Ellicott, Hutchins's followers, "who consisted of enemies to all government, refugees and plunderers," came armed while his supporters did not. Hutchins spoke first, followed by Payne, who explained that he took the packet in order to prove that Hutchins was "deceiving the people." According to Hutchins, a majority of the crowd, unswayed by Payne's diatribe, "rescued" the memorial and "acknowledged it to be the act and will of the people."[54]

The uproar continued for weeks as both sides threatened the district "with all the horrors of plunder, rapine, and murder." William Vousdan, Hutchins's son-in-law, reported a plot to assassinate the old man. "If Col. Hutchins is murdered," Vousdan warned Minor, "I am induced to say that Mr. Ellicott may be the next victim, for retaliation will have no bound when once begun." Minor sent word to Gayoso in New Orleans that "the People are getting heartily tired of all party business, and American politics is now becoming an old thing." In fact, he stated, several inhabitants favored reestablishing Spanish rule. "God send a speedy determination of things," he lamented; "otherwise they will all run mad, with memorials, certificates, circular letters & ca."[55]

The announcement in early November that Col. Carlos de Grand-Pre was to replace Minor as governor of Natchez District added more fuel to the controversy. Most inhabitants considered Minor a perfect caretaker. Ellicott's friends appreciated Minor's willingness to cooperate with them, and they wanted nothing to upset the state of "neutrality" established by the articles of June 22. The Permanent Committee fired off a strongly worded protest, warning Governor Gayoso that the citizens regarded Grand-Pre's appointment as "a breach of the neutrality." Gayoso wisely kept Grand-Pre in Baton Rouge and Minor in nominal authority.[56]

Meanwhile, Capt. Isaac Guion, whose troops had been lingering for months at Chickasaw Bluffs (modern Memphis), finally received orders to proceed downstream in late November 1797. Guion's appearance in Natchez on December 6 seemed to please everyone. Hutchins expected him to put an end to Ellicott and Pope's arbitrary rule. Ellicott believed his presence would guarantee order "by awing the turbulent and rendering the possession of the country more certain." Dunbar hoped that "protection will not be wanting against the unruly parts of our Society." While the Permanent Committee offered its congratulations, it politely reminded Guion that it "had acted as 'Guardians' of the inhabitants whose duty it is . . . , to watch over and preserve the advantages," derived from "the articles of agreement or convention with Spanish officials," and that it expected these arrangements to continue.[57]

Unfortunately, Guion was in poor health, suffering from what he called a "severe undescribable inflammation . . . [of] the head." Ellicott was less kind. Guion "was much indisposed by an inflammatory complaint on one side of his head, and face," Ellicott reported, "that evidently had an effect upon his understanding." In this condition, he fell victim to the wiles of "a number of unworthy characters, who . . . prejudice[d] his mind against the permanent committee." What really displeased Ellicott was Guion's refusal to play favorites. He intended to obey Gen. James Wilkinson's instructions. Recently assigned command of American forces in the West, Wilkinson had cautioned Guion "to conciliate all parties to the government of our country by every means in your power, avoiding at the same time, every just cause of offense to the Spanish authorities."[58]

News in January 1798 of Spain's plans to remove her troops from Natchez and Walnut Hills set the stage for the final demise of Spanish rule. Although Ellicott was skeptical, less suspicious individuals treated the reports as true. The two factions instantly maneuvered to fill the vacuum occasioned by departure of Spanish officials. The Committee of Safety, now dominated by the Greens (Thomas, his son Thomas Marston, and his son-in-law Cato West), called a public meeting for February 5 at Belk's tavern, where the citizens adopted resolutions critical of what they styled "the coalition," which, in addition to Ellicott, consisted of "the titular Governor," the Permanent Committee "formed to cooperate with the Spanish officers," and "a few other designing persons." They denounced "Ellicott and the rest of that coalition" for recommending the establishment of a government in Natchez District identical to that of Northwest Territory, accused Spanish officers of violating the neutrality by refusing to prosecute Silas L. Payne, and asked Congress to abrogate all agreements made by Ellicott and his friends with Georgia agents respecting Natchez lands and not to appoint as governor or secretary of the territory anyone affiliated with the Yazoo lands. Finally, they urged all male inhabitants of voting age to reassemble on February 26 and to elect a committee that would occasionally meet on "matters of safety" and appoint "Judicious men to act as magistrates."[59]

The Permanent Committee was hardly idle. On February 1, 1798, it had queried Captain Guion if he were "empowered . . . to exercise any authority among us" after the Spanish evacuated. Answering in the negative, Guion pledged to cooperate with those who wished "to continue the tranquility and good order." The committee then called for election of a convention, "under the protection and with the concurrence" of Captain Guion, to assume "operation at the withdrawing of the Spanish Jurisdiction" and to continue until "arrival of [American] officers."

Captain Guion, his health improved, was determined to restore peace and end the petty bickering between factions. He grew increasingly protective of his prerogative, which he believed Ellicott was usurping, particularly after the commissioner excluded him from negotiations with Gayoso for drawing the boundary line. For his part, Ellicott interpreted Gayoso's effort to include Guion as another "finesse" by the Spaniards to delay execution of the treaty.[60]

Guion's patience, never extensive, was soon exhausted. One evening, he barged into Ellicott's house, where he found Minor, Isaac Gaillard, a member of the Permanent Committee, and the commissioner conferring with one another. After "Inquiring by what authority they met," Guion firmly informed them "that it was improper" and that he planned to dissolve the committee. "He knew better than to be made a cypher of," he roared, "and by God [he] would rule the district with rod of iron." He left by declaring that "you may all kiss my A**e; I will be harder upon you than ever Hutchins was."[61]

The rift between the commissioner and the captain continued to widen throughout February and March as Guion tightened his control and Ellicott continued to watch the Spaniards with an expectant but wary eye. Then, on April 9, as Gayoso had earlier promised, a relieved Ellicott met him on the boundary line. With Ellicott's departure, Guion was unofficially in charge of affairs, which he exercised with the approbation of the Green-Hutchins faction and the disapproval of Ellicott's coalition.[62]

By early May, the turmoil began to subside. Most inhabitants displayed more interest in repairing public roads, establishing slave patrols, banning the sale of spirits to Indians, and establishing regulations for the recovery of debts than in incriminating one another. This changed attitude was confirmed when the Green faction attempted to call another election for the purpose of notifying Congress of its choice for public officials. Guion took this occasion to inform the citizenry for the first time that Congress had authorized a permanent government for Natchez District. In wake of this welcome news, Thomas Green, who apparently had expected to be chosen governor, suffered public humiliation when he was soundly defeated in a mock election by an obscure chair maker from Coles Creek. A dejected Hutchins left the meeting, promising never to "meddle again in public affairs." As one observer gleefully reported, "I had the satisfaction of seeing Col. Green move off the field under the shouts of boys and the lower class of men; they were not shouts of applause but of derision." In fact, the situation appeared so depressing to Hutchins and others that they applied to Gayoso "for lands below the line." Only the governor's refusal to assent "from a knowledge of their turbulent dispositions" prevented their leaving the district.[63]

By the summer of 1798, the district was more tranquil than at any time since early 1797. Several factors contributed to the peace. Ellicott's departure on April 9, 1798, deprived the district of its most talented troublemaker. When he left for the demarcation line, he took along two of his cohorts—Stephen Minor and William Dunbar—and their absence contributed significantly to the welcome tranquility.[64] Finally, Hutchins retired from politics upon learning that Secretary of State Timothy Pickering had summarily refused to submit the Committee of Safety's memorial to Congress because of its offensive "style" and "the numerous invectives" against respectable inhabitants.

As Guion reported, Congress indeed had incorporated not only Natchez District but also everything east of the Chattahoochee into Mississippi Territory. Applying the same principles to this territory that its predecessor had to the Northwest Territory in 1787, Congress, under the first stage of territorial government, centralized power in the hands of five officials—a governor and secretary and three judges—all appointed by the president for specified terms and subject to removal at his discretion. Treating new territories as nurseries for transforming lawless and licentious frontiersmen into virtuous and law-abiding citizens, Congress gave the people almost no role in local government. It authorized the governor and any two of the three judges to adapt but not make laws for the territory and to ensure their proper execution. By consolidating power (executive, legislative, and judicial) in the hands of a few officials, Congress effectively eliminated all checks and balances to their authority. While this arrangement was appropriate to the largely unsettled Northwest Territory, it was less genial to a better-established and more mature society like that of Natchez District. Indeed, it was a recipe for confrontation and controversy.

Furthermore, without a well-functioning federal patronage system or a president knowledgeable about conditions in the Southwest, appointment of the first officers proved challenging. Dependent upon others for advice, Adams was faced with choosing between those who saw western posts as a stepping-stone to advancement or those who sought them for personal gain. Still, he was never short of advice or likely candidates. Also, he needed to placate local residents like Anthony Hutchins, who was already dissatisfied since the governing act contained several provisions contrary to those he and the Committee of Safety had recommended. Hutchins's displeasure soon hardened into bitterness after Pickering's insulting dismissal of their memorial became public knowledge. One of Hutchins's enemies announced with satisfaction that the old man was "quite chop fallen."[65]

Word that President Adams had withdrawn the nominations of Gen.

George Mathews and Judge Arthur Miller as governor and secretary was welcome news to settlers who feared that these appointments might jeopardize their land titles. Opposition to Mathews had peaked during the spring and summer. Even Ellicott's friend Lewis Evans, a silversmith and merchant of Natchez, was not displeased. "The would be Governor," he satirically wrote, "has decamp'd to some Sequester part of the country in Imitation perhaps of the love Sick Shepherd . . . to pour out his complaints to the woods & rocks." Ellicott, too, was relieved. Mathews, he reported, would have been a "very unpopular Governor," largely because he had supported "some irregularities by the military."[66]

By July 1798, inhabitants of Natchez District eagerly awaited the first American governor, who reportedly was on his way down the Ohio and Mississippi rivers in the company of General Wilkinson and expected to arrive in early August.[67]

CHAPTER 2

"His Yankeeship"

On Monday, August 6, 1798, as the boat bearing Winthrop Sargent, first governor of Mississippi Territory, docked at Natchez landing, a throng of curious people waited to get a glimpse of "his Yankeeship." Despite Sargent's wish to make a favorable impression, he was too ill to disembark, and for two days he remained on board not sure whether he would survive.[1] Peter Bruin and Captain Guion then escorted Sargent to Concord, the fashionable mansion of former Governor Gayoso, where he spent another week convalescing.[2]

Whether the sick and exhausted Sargent recognized it or not, he faced a daunting assignment. He was not only left with the immediate task of reconciling the antagonistic factions created by Ellicott's machinations, but he also had to steer a precarious path amidst unfriendly and distrustful Indian and Spanish neighbors. In the end, it was a burden too heavy for someone with his prejudices and shortcomings to overcome.

Nevertheless, Sargent seemed to possess several essential traits that at least gratified President Adams and Secretary of State Timothy Pickering. Like them, he had grown up in New England, where he absorbed the sturdy tenets of Puritanism. Son of a middling Gloucester merchant, Sargent graduated from Harvard in 1771 and fought, without distinction, in Henry Knox's artillery regiment during the American Revolution.[3]

Emerging from the war penniless, without training in a profession, and feeling "ill used," Sargent joined other disillusioned New Englanders who ventured west in search of fame and fortune. Appointed, in short order, a surveyor for and secretary of the Ohio Company, Sargent settled in Marietta before becoming secretary of the Northwest Territory under Governor Arthur St. Clair. For the next ten years, he gained valuable administrative experience during St. Clair's frequent illnesses and protracted absences. Participating in St. Clair's disastrous Indian campaign of 1791, where he was wounded twice, Sargent acquired firsthand knowledge of frontier warfare. Pickering thought it essential that the governor of Mississippi Territory be a "man of energy, of application to business, and a <u>military</u> character," and Sargent qualified on all counts.[4]

More noteworthy, Sargent, a staunch Federalist, believed in government by the elite, favored a strong executive, regarded local interests as subordinate to national welfare, and viewed with alarm any sign of excessive democracy. "Better face relentless opposition," he wrote, "than stoop to gain peace and popularity by the cheap methods of the demagogue." While acknowledging that he possessed "an inordinate passion for fame," he refused to become a "Machine of the Multitude."[5]

Yet the same traits that excited Pickering made Sargent anathema to western settlers, who judged his stiff mannerisms and unapproachable temperament repugnant. Sargent's disdain for democracy particularly annoyed Anthony Hutchins and others, who found him as loathsome as they had Andrew Ellicott. Furthermore, Sargent rarely concealed his strong distaste for western manners and morals. As a Puritan, he was obsessed with public morality and misinterpreted frontier exuberance for lawlessness and profligacy. Finding conditions along the riverfront shameful, he railed against the people's failure to keep the Sabbath holy. "Natchez," he complained, "from the perverseness of some of the people and the ebriety [sic] of Negroes and Indians on Sundays, has become a most abominable place." He agreed with one petitioner who described it as a place "where every Blasphemy, Adultery, and Fornication, as well as other vices, have by long custom, become so common and fashionable as to escape public censure or legal punishments, and where such vices, if prohibited by law, have still been fully tolerated."[6]

Unable to fathom the lifestyle of frontiersmen, he labeled them lawless and licentious and, not a few, as "the most Abandoned Vilians who have escaped from the Chains and Prisons of Spain and been convicted of the Blackest of Crimes." Although a compassionate person in private, he thought it a sign of weakness to display effete characteristics publicly. Still, he appeared aloof even to friends, excessively formal in public, and "rigidly observant of etiquette." Taller than most men (five feet eleven), he stood "almost painfully erect." He proudly exhibited an appearance of being "angular and military all over." These traits hardly endeared him to carefree frontiersmen, who saw him as "a haughty, over-bearing man."[7]

Even Sargent's friends considered his temperament a liability. To longtime Natchez residents, the contrast between him and Gayoso was striking. Where Gayoso was gracious and affable, Sargent was austere and condescending. People viewed Gayoso as their friend; Sargent, on the contrary, was insouciant at best and cantankerous at worst. Since Gayoso had "lived on a very familiar footing with the people at the Natchez," Pickering admonished Sargent not to appear aloof and cautioned him that "condescending manners toward our fellow citizens of all degrees are very compatible with self respect and official dignity." William Dunbar, hardly an egalitarian, found Sargent's "phlegmatic and austere disposition" disgusting and wondered if "a man so frigid and sour" could please "a free people."[8]

On the other hand, some of Sargent's problems were not his fault. He had purposely delayed his departure from Cincinnati, hoping the territorial judges would be present when he arrived, but he was disappointed. Except for Bruin, the other two were slow to arrive, loath to remain, and eager to depart. Unfortunately, Sargent and Bruin were both without legal training, and neither possessed a set of the laws of the United States or one of the states to consult as a model. Though anxious to adopt a code of laws, Sargent remained powerless without a second judge.

Furthermore, the act establishing Mississippi Territory was hopelessly flawed. It contained no provisions for resolving conflicting land claims or clarifying the status of Yazoo claimants. By prohibiting the importation of slaves into the territory from foreign countries, Congress inadvertently angered those planters who owned lands in both Spanish and American territories and who customarily transferred their bondsmen from one plantation to another.[9]

Aware of his limitations, Sargent, in his first address on August 18, promised "to promote the peace and good order of society." Choosing to deliver his inaugural speech in the solemnity of a local church, the bewhiskered governor, whose voice was "rather harsh and unpleasant," tried to assuage the better element by emphasizing the need for "a concise and clear code of laws" administered in a firm and uniform manner. In making appointments, he declared, "merit only can entitle a man to office," and he pledged to favor only those who possessed "strong and evident marks of attachment to the United States and good government, and a disposition to preserve the peace and order in society and harmonize contending sentiments." He also vowed to establish a "well ordered militia" when he had "due information of characters suitable to commission."[10]

Recognizing the importance of defense in an isolated wilderness surrounded by unfriendly Indians and hostile Spaniards and a nation on the verge of war with France, Sargent was determined to organize the militia and to appoint officials bent on upholding the law. Following Pickering's advice, he waited until he had consulted Ellicott and his associates before making his choices. In late August, Sargent, accompanied by Judge Bruin, met with Ellicott, Dunbar, and Minor. Aware that Spanish officials were closely monitoring him, Minor was circumspect and uncooperative, but Ellicott, flattered by the attention, was forthcoming. Not surprisingly, Ellicott stressed the merits of his friends, but he cautioned Sargent to include a few "Hutchinites." Ellicott later defended his recommendations, which included Anthony Hutchins's son Samuel, by reminding his critics that principle should not be "carried too far for whenever it is it produces that evil it was intended to cure."[11]

But the loudest outcry came from those who expected the commissioner's influence to wane once he had left Natchez. Sargent's pilgrimage to Ellicott's shrine rekindled the flames of discord and restored the commissioner's prestige among those who looked to him for advantage. "Now it matters not what you recommend," a friend wrote Ellicott; "it is Said it is a law and this current of opinion is that G— was ordered to your camp for his instruction how to act."[12]

On September 8, Sargent disclosed his plans for organizing the militia and the names of his appointees. He divided Natchez District into two legions and required all free males between the ages of sixteen and fifty to enroll in a horse or foot company. To command the upper or northern legion, Sargent selected Cato West, son-in-law of Thomas Green. He left the southern position unfilled until he persuaded Daniel Clark to accept command. For the northern district, Sargent named Narsworthy Hunter "Major of Horse" and John Girault "Major of Foot." The same positions in the south went to Benijah Osmun and Sutton Banks.

Initial reaction to the appointments was mixed. Clark, for one, was not pleased, despite his own appointment. "The Consiliatory System which our Seemingly worthy Sargent is fond of adopting," he wrote, "will not suite those implacable spirits that have lately been the Terrorists and anarchists of Natchez." Although less distressed than Clark, Minor winced at the choices of Osmun and Hunter.[13]

Sargent's solicitation of Ellicott's advice was sufficient to repel some appointees, while others found the governor's staid personality and prejudicial attitudes offensive. Hunter, Joseph Calvit, and a handful of other nominees declined their commissions immediately. It took Cato West longer to decide, but in early 1799 he too resigned, taking along a few companions. Blaming Hutchins for the rash of resignations, General Wilkinson surmised that it would "turn out to be the Effects of the Old Hell Cats Intrigues, and if it should, he will have prepared work for Himself during the residue of his natural Life."[14]

Sargent also thought it essential to fill temporarily a few civil offices since Judge Bruin alone was unable to handle "the many Misdemeanors which are Complained of" daily. For the coveted posts of sheriff, he chose Lewis Evans for the southern and William Ferguson for the northern district. As conservators of the peace in the lower district, he appointed Daniel Clark, William Dunbar, Isaac Gaillard, John Ellis, James McIntosh, and Joseph Calvit, while appointments in the upper district went to Cato West, Samuel Gibson, and Tobias Brashear. Except for West, all were friends of either Ellicott or Bruin.[15]

More controversial was Sargent's decision to create a probate court to administer estates; grant letters of administration; appoint guardians for orphans, lunatics, and the poor; and record last wills and testaments. Sargent asked Dunbar to assume the duties on an interim basis so that the flood of "applications . . . upon the subject of interstate Estates" could be processed faster. The choice was unpopular. Not only was Dunbar distrusted by some, but he was also vested with limitless power to investigate decedent estates, authority that many considered an invasion of privacy. Dismayed by these arbitrary measures, some murmured that "Royalty could do no more."[16]

While an organized militia was essential to defend the territory against rival nations and distraught Indians, Sargent exaggerated its value in combating internal dangers. Alarmed by the number of "Foreigners who have taken refuge within our Domains" and worried lest the district become "an Asylum for Criminals[,] . . . abandoned men, and dangerous aliens of every description," Sargent often overreacted to perceived dangers, a tendency evident in his reaction to Zachariah Cox's arrival in Natchez on August 11, 1798.

Cox's reputation for speculation and intrigue was legendary. In 1791, he and several of his Yazoo associates, who earlier had formed the Tennessee Company, attempted to establish a colony at Muscle Shoals on the Tennessee River. Although thwarted by the combined efforts of the federal government and Cherokee Indians, Cox was not easily discouraged. In 1796, he established the Mississippi-Mobile Commercial Company with plans to link Muscle Shoals and Mobile by water via the Tombigbee River. Then, in early 1797, with approval of the Kentucky and Tennessee governors, Cox laid out Smithland, a small settlement on the Ohio between the mouths of the Tennessee and Cumberland rivers. Later, he tried to plant a second settlement at Muscle Shoals, but again the Indians, with encouragement from Indian Superintendent Benjamin Hawkins, blocked it.[17]

Finally, in 1798, a frustrated but persistent Cox led an expedition of some hundred men down the Mississippi River, ostensibly to settle in Spanish territory. Sneaking past Spanish Walnut Hills under cover of darkness, Cox and his band reached Natchez on August 11. Meanwhile, on August 1, Wilkinson had arrived at Fort Massac, where he learned of Cox's movements. Immediately, he warned officials of Cox's approach at the head of "an armed rabble" and urged them "to seize this chief actor and to hold him in safe custody," before he could launch his "extensive confederacy," which was allegedly to extend from "Georgia to the Monongahela" and to unfold in December.[18]

The fact that Dr. James White and Gen. George Mathews, two notorious speculators linked to the Yazoo scandals, were also in Natchez convinced Sargent that Cox was up to no good. He ordered Captain Guion to place Cox "in close confinement," pending instructions from the president, and put his thirty-five cohorts under surveillance. Although White insisted that Cox was "seeking refuge for his friends in the Dominion of Spain," Sargent believed he was there "to assume the government for the state of Georgia."[19]

After several futile attempts by his friends and himself to secure his release legally, Cox, presumably with connivance of Lieutenant Pope, made his escape on September 26, shortly before Wilkinson arrived in Natchez.[20] Two days later, Sargent notified Gayoso that Cox was heading for New Orleans and requested him to return the fugitive to Natchez under military guard. Wilkinson warned Gayoso that Cox planned to plunder Spanish settlers along the way.

Instead of arresting Cox, Gayoso treated him cordially. After listening attentively to his proposal for a "mercantile establishment," he concluded that while "his projects [were] very wild," they were harmless. Believing that Cox wished to "justify himself" to Sargent, Gayoso granted him safe conduct to Tennessee. But Cox was no fool. He headed straight for Mobile and with the assistance of friendly Indians, reached Nashville in late 1798.[21]

Annoyed by these developments, Sargent had several of Cox's accomplices, including James White, arrested. He offered a three-hundred-dollar reward for the elusive Cox. Upon learning that Cox was returning to Tennessee through the Tombigbee settlements, Sargent instructed Indian agents to intercept him while Wilkinson hastily collected depositions to prove that Cox had uttered "seditious calumnies . . . against the Government," traded illegally with Indians, and trespassed on their lands. These efforts were fruitless. Cox eluded his captors, aware that the evidence collected by Wilkinson was insufficient to sustain the charges. In fact, Sargent appeared so arbitrary that a few anxious inhabitants followed White's advice and moved to Spanish territory to escape the clutches of an oppressive governor.[22]

Despite Sargent's suspicions, White was not a party to Cox's scheme. Instead, he was acting as a Spanish agent to encourage Mississippi settlers, uneasy about land titles, to migrate into Louisiana and Florida under promises of free land, protection of property (including slaves), and noninterference in private religious matters. Although White had little success, Sargent justified his confinement on the ground that "the few scattered inhabitants of the Territory, are every day thinning by the Machinations of a Doctor White . . . and other malcontents."[23]

Another result of the Cox affair was to reopen the issue of conflicting land claims. In addition to the gargantuan and fraudulent Yazoo grants, Great Britain had made numerous grants to settlers and speculators alike. While the claims of actual residents were never in doubt, grants to court favorites and military officers, most of which were neither occupied nor cultivated, were both extensive and of doubtful validity.

Beginning in 1788, Spanish officials had added to the confusion by luring newcomers with generous grants of lands, most of them layered over British claims. Between late 1796 and early 1798, they promoted another wave of speculation by rewarding favorites with land titles that they carefully predated, giving them the illusion of legitimacy. With land claims overlapping like shingles on a roof, uneasy settlers pressed Sargent for validation of their titles. Meanwhile, new arrivals had either to purchase lands at inflated prices or squat on vacant lands until land offices opened. Unfortunately, Governor Sargent was helpless to act except against intruders on public or Indian lands since only Congress could unravel the mess, and more pressing matters commanded its attention. As a result, the troublesome land question remained unresolved.[24]

The prevalence of inquisitive Indians in and around Natchez irritated Sargent and frightened inhabitants. With adroit diplomacy, Gayoso had virtually eliminated Indian depredations by cementing friendships with neighboring tribes through treaties and annual gifts and annuities. But Spanish departure left the principal Indian nations—Choctaw, Chickasaw, Cherokee, and Creek—fearful lest the United States discontinue these practices.

Nearby Choctaws displayed their apprehensions by stealing food and livestock from the scattered and defenseless inhabitants of the countryside. Sargent reported that "a number of families" who resided along roads traversed by Indians had been "literally eaten out of house and home by them." Sizeable delegations of Choctaws periodically visited a perturbed but polite Sargent, whose inability to speak their language severely hampered communication. Eventually Sargent uncovered two individuals who spoke Choctaw, one a white man who demanded forty dollars a month for his services and the other Stephen Minor's slave Cesar. In the interest of economy, Sargent set aside his racial misgivings and retained Cesar for "fifteen dollars per month and two Rations," while critics denounced his choice as an insult to "a free and independent people."[25]

Confusion about his responsibilities as superintendent of Indian affairs further complicated Sargent's life, and Pickering was no help in clarifying them. He suggested nothing more practical than closer consultation with the knowledgeable Indian agent Hawkins and nearby military commanders. Sargent's pleas to Secretary of War James McHenry for clarification of his duties and for funds to purchase blankets and other provisions for the Indians, promised earlier by Ellicott, went unanswered. Confronted with disgruntled Indians, Anglo indifference to militia service, a restless slave population, an apathetic and inaccessible federal government, and Indian agents resentful of executive meddling in their affairs, Sargent complained bitterly that "I am the veriest Slave in the World." Since he was unable "even to offer a Pipe of Tobacco to the Indians," settlers were left to pacify the Indians themselves. Sargent, who sympathized with the settlers' plight, urged the federal government to dispense goods to the Indians only at military posts located some distance from white settlements in order to keep them away from populated centers.[26]

Rumors that the Spaniards were enticing Choctaws to molest white settlers and Creeks to wipe out Ellicott's party marking the southern boundary intensified Sargent's anxieties. Gayoso's stern warning that Spain would treat an attack upon the American boundary commissioners as a declaration of war was largely responsible for saving Ellicott's party from annihilation.[27]

More ominous were reports that Spain had re-ceded Louisiana to France. Sargent was so disturbed that he proposed raising a makeshift force of American volunteers from Tennessee, Kentucky, and Northwest Territory to prevent French occupation of New Orleans. Otherwise, he feared, Spanish Creoles and their black slaves, together with allied Indians, might become formidable neighbors.

Relations with Spanish Creoles, however, noticeably improved after Sargent, following a whirlwind courtship of six weeks, married a wealthy Natchez widow, Mrs. Maria McIntosh Williams, whose complexion was "dazzlingly fair" and whose eyes were "the blue of heaven." One of Sargent's friends described her as "an Elegant woman with a large fortune" and Sargent himself as "a man of Discernment." Since Williams's daughter was Gayoso's godchild, Sargent and his Spanish counterpart began a cordial correspondence that spanned a range of interesting topics from flowers to fugitives.[28]

Meanwhile, Sargent's "deplorable" situation improved in early January 1799, with the arrival of Judge Daniel Tilton. Under the first stage of territorial government, the governor and two of the three judges were to "adopt and publish . . . such laws of the original states, Criminal and Civil, as may be necessary," provided they did not interfere with the disposal of public lands or private title to the soil. Chief Justice William McGuire, the only judge with legal training, did not arrive in Natchez until summer. In the interim, Sargent and Judges Bruin and Tilton enacted a legal code based on the only set of laws they possessed, those of Northwest Territory, which, Sargent acknowledged, were not "a very good Basis." Consequently, they had to formulate rather than adopt laws as the ordinance specified. In late February, the three officials enacted nine laws, four of which legalized or enlarged upon measures Sargent had already adopted. These included rules and regulations for organizing the militia, establishing a territorial judicial system, and authorizing a probate court.[29]

While these acts aroused modest opposition, stronger protests followed passage of the territory's first criminal code, principally because of its harsh punishments. For example, a person convicted of perjury was to pay a fine not exceeding sixty dollars, to receive up to thirty-nine lashes on the bare back, to stand in the pillory for no longer than two hours, and to be barred from testifying in court. Treason was punishable by death and forfeiture of all property, real and personal, while arsonists were to suffer loss of property, a public whipping (not to exceed thirty-nine stripes), confinement in the pillory for no more than two hours, and a jail term of three years or less. If death resulted from an act of arson, the offender could be hanged. Punishments for burglary or robbery were equally severe, and anyone convicted of either was assessed triple the value of the property taken, one-third of which went to the territory and the rest to the injured party or parties.[30]

The severity of punishment reflected Sargent's belief that the territory, populated by individuals of "a refractory and turbulent Spirit . . . who have run wild in the recess of Government," was in a "state of Anarchy." He agreed with Lewis Evans that there were not "three men in the district that are sincere friends" of order. "Law is the crie," he wrote, but "all are unfitted for it as a Bride is generally for the first night or two of her marriage."[31]

A similar attitude influenced the enactment of laws dealing with maiming, defalcation, marriage, and taverns and other places of entertainment. Individuals like Sargent raised in a sedate society were ill-equipped to appreciate western frontiersmen who fought viciously, drank excessively, and often engaged in such brutal practices as eye gouging, tongue extraction, or biting off the nose or ear of a combatant. By imposing stiff fines, Sargent's code attempted, with meager success, to curb such displays of masculinity. In addition to prohibiting the sale of liquor to Indians and slaves, the code required tavern keepers to pay the governor eight dollars and the country clerk twenty-five cents for a license. The governor also received ten dollars for every marriage contract, fees which many found excessive, surpassing "anything ever heard of."[32]

Laws alone were insufficient to bring tranquility and order to a society that, according to Sargent, was characterized by shameless immorality and unbridled violence. Courts, jails, judges, sheriffs, constables, justices of the peace, and other officers of the law were essential. As a first step, Sargent divided the Natchez District at Fairchild's Creek into two counties, Adams to the north and Pickering to the south. He then reappointed those who had accepted temporary commissions as county officials and filled the remaining vacancies.

With these appointments, Sargent initiated another round of resignations. Henry Green returned his commission because he was to command an infantry instead of a horse company. Considering a coroner's position beneath his dignity, William Vousdan asked the governor to bestow it upon another. "I think it would be infinitely more agreeable to me," he wrote, "to judge about the living than about the dead." Thomas Calvit found it "inconvenient" to accept any offer, and Thomas Burling declined to perform the duties of a justice of the peace because he was too old and "ignorant of the business."[33]

Location of county seats was another of Sargent's headaches. While Natchez was the obvious choice for Adams County, no consensus existed in Pickering County. Contest for the county seat began in 1798 when John Foster donated that portion of his plantation, "within two hundred yards of" Ellicott's Spring, "for the use of public buildings." He asked Ellicott "to use your influence" with the governor "to have the town of Washington (for so I call it) made a County town."

Union Town quickly made a counteroffer. In addition to free land, residents there agreed to erect a temporary jail and courthouse "by private Subscription," pending construction of permanent structures. Instantly, Cato West and his friends protested. Not only was Union Town, located just six miles from the Adams County line, inconvenient for most residents of Pickering, but critics, aware that its promoters included the commercial establishment, were appalled that "the purses of the merchants of Natchez should have any influence in a matter so momentous." Yet Sargent's eventual choice of Villa Gayoso, located on Coles Creek, was more than a desire to humor his critics. Economy was a major factor since Villa Gayoso, which had previously been the seat of

Spanish government, contained enough buildings to accommodate the needs of county government.[34]

Sargent, whose penchant for frugality was boundless, ran into unexpected difficulty when he tried to obtain possession of the public buildings at Natchez and Villa Gayoso. Upon evacuating the district, Spanish officials had transferred all public property to General Wilkinson, who refused to relinquish control without the War Department's approval. But finding the buildings at Villa Gayoso too expensive to maintain, Wilkinson relinquished them before Sargent was ready to move in. Meanwhile, Thomas Green insisted that the village belonged to his son Everard, and Sargent feared the Greens might seize the buildings before he could take possession.[35]

Wilkinson was less accommodating with respect to public buildings in Natchez. Sargent planned to use one of the houses, located in the town's square, as the Adams County courthouse until permanent quarters were erected. Even after Sargent produced a letter from Secretary Pickering authorizing him "to take charge of the Public Buildings," Wilkinson refused to comply, forcing postponement of the county court's May meeting. Finally, on July 1, as he left for Philadelphia, Wilkinson transferred the public house but not the hospital.[36]

During the summer of 1799, Congress authorized a customs district on the lower Mississippi River. At the request of President Adams, Sargent queried several prominent citizens about a proper place for "the Port of Entry and Delivery" and a suitable person for collector. Recommendations for the location were divided evenly between Natchez and Loftus Heights. To no one's surprise, Hutchins and Thomas Green wished to deprive Natchez of this advantage. Although Sargent finally chose Natchez, he tried to please everyone by naming two additional sites, one "at Clarksville, near the international boundary, and another at the Bayou Pierre." On the other hand, Sargent rejected both nominees for collector. He dismissed Hutchins's recommendation of Narsworthy Hunter, and Dunbar's nomination of Sargent's brother-in-law James McIntosh embarrassed him. Eventually, he selected John F. Carmichael, an ex-army surgeon, recommended by Federalist Senator James Ross of Pennsylvania.[37]

Until the summer of 1799, however, Sargent faced no sustained or systematic opposition, although he encountered occasional outbursts from malcontents like Daniel Burnet. An inveterate opponent of Ellicott, Burnet despised Wilkinson and blamed the government for not confirming land claims. Burnet supposedly remarked that he wished "every one of them [the Americans] coming to this country might be massacred or forced to return with the loss of his scalp." Angered by the riposte, Sargent acted decisively if unwisely. He ordered Judge Bruin to arrest "that Incendiary Burnet." Shocked by the governor's vindictiveness, Burnet denied uttering the remarks and apologized to Sargent and Wilkinson. Yet Sargent's decisiveness pleased one local resident, who thought him "a damned clever fellow." "In short," he wrote, "we find firmness to be his leading principle[,] no encroachment on his prerogative his motto and justice to all without distinction the standing order of the day."[38]

The first sign of organized opposition appeared in the summer of 1799, when Cato West, in collaboration with other prominent citizens, launched an assault upon Sargent's policies. West's rise to leadership resulted from Hutchins's illness and division of the district into two counties. During the previous spring, Hutchins had suffered a severe stroke from which he was not expected to recover. "Our worthy friend Anthony," a gleeful Wilkinson wrote, "will soon cease to pester mankind and be eased of his worldly strifes—for I am informed he languishes on His Death Bed." While Hutchins's quick recovery disappointed his enemies, he never regained a zest for politics, preferring to leave such matters to his youthful relatives. Public exposure of the fact that he was still a British pensioner also dampened his ardor for remaining in the limelight.[39]

More importantly, division of Natchez District into two counties weakened Hutchins's influence since he resided in Adams County, where Sargent's friends outnumbered his opponents. On the other hand, the Greens were dominant in Pickering, where they behaved like country squires. Yet the change of command was not displeasing to "old Tony" since the two families were united by marriage as well as by politics. Indeed, family ties were so pervasive that even the sensational and sordid divorce of Elizabeth, daughter of Thomas M. Green, and John Hutchins failed to loosen the alliance, although the scandal kept tongues wagging for months. John accused his mother-in-law of promoting a clandestine relationship between Elizabeth and a carpenter named Norwood in order to secure alimony for her daughter.[40] In addition to this short-lived marriage, Mary Hutchins, Anthony's daughter, was wedded to Thomas Green's son Abner. Cato West, who migrated to Natchez District with Thomas in the early 1780s, had married one of Green's daughters in Virginia. William Vousdan, another of Ellicott's foes, was the husband of Celeste Hutchins.

Despite Hutchins's ostensible retirement from politics, Sargent "believe[d] him capable of any mischief" and carefully monitored his every move, while trying to win over West and the Greens. By summer of 1799, Sargent realized that he had misjudged his three nemeses — Hutchins, West, and Thomas Marston Green, son of the patriarch Thomas.[41]

The emerging alignments followed county divisions. The Green-West faction was dominant in Pickering County, drawing support from the planter-debtor element that had opposed Ellicott so vigorously, long-term residents without antedated Spanish grants, and a host of disappointed office seekers. In addition to West and the Greens, this faction included a number of prominent planters like Thomas and Joseph Calvit and aspiring politicians like Ebenezer Dayton and Narsworthy Hunter.[42]

On the other hand, Sargent attracted a cadre of loyalists who were as powerful in Adams as his opponents were in Pickering County. Former friends of Ellicott generally gravitated to Sargent. In addition to Judge Bruin, merchant Cochran, and Dunbar, these included Daniel Clark Sr., loquacious squire of Clarkesville; Isaac Gaillard, member of Ellicott's Permanent Committee; and Lewis Evans, an outspoken and witty Natchez silversmith who by shrewd investments became one of Adams County's largest landowners.[43]

Through the steady application of patronage, Sargent also attracted a coterie of grateful followers consisting of William Ferguson, first sheriff of Pickering County; Capt. John Girault, veteran of George Rogers Clark's Illinois campaign during the American Revolution and former recorder for the Spanish government; Benijah Osmun, commander of the southern militia legion; John Ellis, son of a Tory settler who was made conservator of peace in Adams County and a major in the militia; Lyman Harding, native of Massachusetts, a recent immigrant from Kentucky and an ex-schoolmaster who found the practice of law more rewarding; and Abijah Hunt, a former army sutler who secured the territory's first mail contract and later became a wealthy Natchez merchant.

The earliest sign of organized political activity came from Sargent's

Pickering County opponents, variously called the Green-West faction, the West Junto, and radical Republicans. They reemployed the same tactics earlier used so effectively against Ellicott. They established local committees, proclaimed themselves the sole spokesmen of the people, and fired off petitions and remonstrances first to the governor and the judges, as mere formality, and then to Congress, where they expected to find a sympathetic reception. Second, they utilized the grand jury by converting presentments from a legal instrument to a political weapon. In June 1799, the grand juries of Adams and Pickering counties compiled lengthy lists of grievances against the territorial government.

In these ways, the governor's opponents effectively summarized their positions locally to the inhabitants in hopes of wooing converts and nationally to Congress in anticipation of relief. They strongly objected to the laws of 1799, which they cleverly styled "Sargent's Codes." Denouncing the manner in which the laws were enacted, critics contended that Sargent, Bruin, and Tilton had unlawfully assumed "the liberty of making laws" when empowered "only to adopt laws made in the original States as may best suit the circumstances of the Country."[44] Considering both the punishments and the methods of enforcement cruel and unusual, they denied precedent for either. Because territorial officials, except for Bruin, were new arrivals and unfamiliar with the district, petitioners considered them incapable of legislating in the people's interest. Finally they objected to the mingling of "the executive, legislative, and judicial authorities . . . in the hands of three or four individuals, who have but a partial interest in the Laws which have been made."

Raising anew the Revolutionary shibboleth of "no taxation without representation," they decried the lack of popular participation, reminding authorities that they too had "fought and bled in the cause of America." Insisting that the Revolution had established as a "fundamental Maxim of American politics . . . the birth right of every Citizen to have a Voice by himself or his representatives in the forming of Laws and imposing of taxes," they refused to abdicate authority to alien officials. They objected to paying taxes before completion of a census and for the maintenance of roads and bridges which could be "more easily effected and less burthensome by the manuel labor of the male inhabitants and negroes." They disapproved of letting sheriffs levy taxes for defraying the expense of incarcerating citizens in "common goals" or make arrests with insufficient evidence. These powers, they argued, were especially odorous when left in the hands of such Ellicott favorites as Girault of Pickering County and Evans of Adams County.

But their principal grievance was the uncertainty of land titles. They complained that "suspense on this account, diminishes the actual value of our properties, interrupts in some measure our peace and tranquility of mind, and checks the spirit of industry" and that apprehensions over land claims, together with prohibition of importing slaves from foreign countries, threatened to reduce the population when the territory's exposed position necessitated a rapid increase.[45]

The petitioners suggested two remedies. First, they demanded a change of territorial officials. The best method to accomplish this objective, they believed, was to accuse Sargent of appointing to "Posts of Profit, Honour, and Trust . . . persons well known to be hackneyed in Spanish duplicity and drudgery . . . [and] who only wish and wait for an opportunity of aggrandizing themselves on the ruins of their country."

Second, they wanted a stronger voice in territorial affairs. As a temporary solution, they proposed creation of a popularly elected council of citizens to advise the governor and judges. As a permanent answer, they asked Congress to elevate them to the second grade of territorial government, which would automatically allow eligible voters to elect a lower house and the president to appoint an upper house.[46]

The Green-West faction hardly limited its tactics to petitions and presentments. Recognizing the importance that Pickering and Sargent attached to a "well-ordered militia," opponents hoped to discredit the governor by disrupting its formation. In these efforts, they were aided by westerners' antipathy for military service. Specifically they called for the popular election of officers and implored disaffected officers to resign and the rank and file to harass those who refused.[47]

This strategy was successful because Sargent responded exactly as his enemies expected. By insisting upon his prerogative to appoint all officers and by threatening to prosecute those guilty of "Determined Systematic opposition to his Sovereign Will," Sargent played into their hands. His obstinacy put even loyal officers on the defensive. As Daniel Clark aptly stated, "officers will not serve if their men dislike them nor do they like to enforce the militia law by fining delinquent neighbors." By the spring of 1800, Girault reported that the Pickering County militia was "in a perfect state of disobedience."[48]

To stem the chaos, Clark demanded tougher militia laws, warn-

ing that if "an itererant calumniator, a Slanderer, Libeller, or Blackguard" could ridicule militia officers with impunity, then others would
"pass on and smile at their impotence and the feebleness of their legal
power." Although Sargent and the judges extracted harsher penalties for
insubordination and reduced the number of field and muster days, the
governor was less successful in establishing the militia than his critics
in disrupting it.[49]

Sargent's opponents also attempted to disrupt territorial courts. Overlooked in civil appointments, they could hardly resort to resignation as
an effective tactic. Instead, they searched for fortuitous circumstances
to embarrass the government. In early 1800, the governor's detractors
in Pickering County brought justice to a standstill. When inclement
weather forced a delay in holding the winter session of the Adams County
Court, Sargent postponed those in Pickering to avoid inconvenience to
anyone having business in both counties. The Pickering County justices
dutifully canceled the February term and called a special meeting of the
Court of Quarter Sessions of Peace for March 3, 1800.[50]

In response, attorney Robert Knox, an outspoken Sargent critic,
contended "in an inflammatious harangue" that the governor's proclamation should be ignored. Two of the three justices, after defeating Attorney General Lyman Harding's motion to open the court as a
regular session, voted to adjourn until the regular May term. Harding
was outraged. "These irregularities and violations of Laws," he fumed,
"must certainly tend to defeat every object of the administration of
Justice."[51]

This altercation ignited a new round of resignations, but this time
it was the governor's friends who deserted. In August 1800, Girault
reported that "our court is likely to stop in the busiest of its time for want
of justices." By September, both the militia and the courts of Pickering
County were dysfunctional. In desperation, Sargent supplied Girault
with blank commissions and instructed him to fill in the names of anyone he could cajole into accepting.[52]

The introduction of a printing press added new kindling to the political fires. As a veteran of frontier politics, Sargent understood the value
of a friendly press. Happily, his search for a printer coincided with the
efforts of Lt. Andrew Marschalk, then stationed in Walnut Hills, to capture the governor's attention. Marschalk made certain that his first printing, a ballad entitled "The Galley Slave," fell into Sargent's hands. In

late 1798, Sargent arranged with General Wilkinson to have Marschalk transferred to Natchez, where he put his considerable talents to excellent use.[53]

After setting up a press, Marschalk's penchant for independence disappointed everyone. Not only did he have to endure the sneers of jealous officers who accused him of shirking his military duties, but he also incurred the enmity of Sargent, who persuaded Wilkinson to relocate him at Walnut Hills, where he would pester no one. Since Marschalk was the only available printer, Sargent allowed him to publish the first thirty-five laws of 1799. Upon completion of this "herculean task" in late October 1799, Marschalk sold his press to Benjamin M. Stokes, who began printing the *Mississippi Gazette* in early 1800.[54]

After Sargent found Stokes's politics equally distasteful, he encouraged James Green to establish a rival newspaper, which he called *Green's Impartial Observer*. Expecting more financial support than Sargent was prepared to offer, Green became so disenchanted that he upheld the paper's name by opening its pages to persons of every persuasion. Green subsequently sold his press to a pair of newcomers, James Ferrell and Darius Moffatt, who briefly published the *Intelligencer*. Without dependable patronage from private or public sources, no paper could survive, and Stokes's *Gazette* folded in 1802.[55] In the battle of the printed word, Sargent emerged second best, since all of these short-lived newspapers found more to criticize than to praise.

Meanwhile Sargent's opponents secretly dispatched Narsworthy Hunter to Philadelphia, where he acted as a surrogate lobbyist. There he befriended two young western congressmen, William Charles Cole Claiborne of Tennessee and Thomas T. Davis of Kentucky, who sponsored legislation favorable to the West-Green faction. By 1800, this faction had narrowed its demands to two—extension of the second grade of territorial government and confirmation of all Spanish grants made before the actual date of the Pinckney Treaty.[56]

Although neither Claiborne nor Davis would tackle the thorny land scrabbles, both favored establishment of an elective assembly. With Hunter's inflated population figures and his exaggerated claims about the ability of the citizens to sustain a more expensive government, Claiborne guided through Congress a bill granting Mississippians the second grade of territorial government. In addition to an elected house of representatives, this act provided for a legislative council of five members, appointed by the president from a list of ten men nominated by the lower house, and for a nonvoting delegate in Congress.[57]

Still dissatisfied with this partial, though substantial, victory, Claiborne demanded repeal of the territory's criminal code as well as laws regulating taverns and setting fees for justices. Several western Republicans also sought to abridge the powers of territorial governors, a move aimed primarily at Sargent. Although the Federalist-dominated Senate blocked these efforts, Claiborne succeeded in appointing a House committee to investigate Sargent's conduct.[58]

While the House investigation was proceeding in Philadelphia, Sargent undertook the unpleasant task of conducting elections for the first General Assembly. The results reaffirmed Sargent's belief that Mississippians were "unfitted in every view of the matter for that second stage of order." Voters in Pickering and Adams counties chose eight (four from each county) of Sargent's harshest critics, including Anthony Hutchins, Thomas M. Green, and Cato West. From the recently created eastern (Tombigbee) county of Washington, the voters selected William McGrew, patriarch of an important Tombigbee family.[59]

A humiliated Sargent convinced himself that elections in Adams County were fraught with irregularities. He contended that Hutchins, as a British pensioner, was ineligible and that Sutton Banks lacked the necessary property qualifications.[60] Ignoring Sargent, the uncontested representatives seated both. Sargent also insisted that the election in Washington County was invalid since it was not held on the appointed date. The sheriff, on his own authority, had arranged a special election after the governor's proclamation arrived late. As a result, McGrew was absent when the legislature convened, and Sargent maintained that no official business could be conducted while a county was unrepresented.[61]

Although the representatives continued to meet, they were so engrossed in controversy over credentials that they failed to submit a list of nominees for the Legislative Council in time for the president to act before the session expired. After trading insults with his legislative critics, Sargent reluctantly forwarded the names of the five least objectionable nominees, and President Adams dutifully appointed them. Although the lower house remained in session, as the law required, through September 9, 1800, they realized that they could not legislate without an upper house.[62]

While Sargent was outwitting the legislature, his friends petitioned for restoration of the first grade of territorial government. They denied that "the hasty, ill-timed, and indigested representations made to Congress by the self-created committee and agent" reflected public opinion. The second grade, they warned, would require an unbearable increase in taxation, and the territory would soon be depleted of population, leaving the remnant at the mercy of vicious Indians and cunning Spaniards. Branding these predictions "nefarious and factious," legislators countered by promising not to charge "for their services." A scribbler for Sargent predicted that such a policy would result in control of the legislature by "rich nabobs" because it would exclude men of merit but moderate fortune.[63]

By late 1800, pro-administration forces had regained the momentum. They gathered an impressive list of signatures to a petition requesting Congress to delay extension of the second grade of government until it was clearly "the wish of a majority of the taxable citizens to have it applied." They predicted that "discontents, dissentions, accumulation of taxes with a disposition to resist regular government, and general confusion, will be a few of the evils." In submitting the memorial to Pickering, Sargent insisted that it confirmed his contention that "the former Petitions Praying for a <u>Change</u> in Government had been surreptitiously secured."[64]

Meanwhile, political changes following the national elections of 1800 were not to Sargent's liking. Voters not only repudiated President Adams but also elected a heavily Republican Congress. As long as Adams and Pickering were in control of his fate, Sargent felt secure, but Thomas Jefferson, the newly elected president, was another matter. Consequently, in early April 1801, Sargent hurried east to defend himself. First he went to Boston, where he arranged for publication of two pamphlets in his defense and then proceeded to the new federal capital, where he obtained an audience with Jefferson.[65]

Sargent left territorial affairs at home in the hands of Secretary John Steele, a nondescript politician from the Carolinas. Although poor health distracted his attention, Steele steered a middle course. On the one hand, he tried to placate his opponents. By offering them commissions as justices of the peace in Pickering County, he expected to gain "some advantage over them in the end." Unfortunately, this strategy failed when they promptly declined "on the score of incompetency."

On the other hand, Steele was as adamant as Sargent in refusing to summon the General Assembly. Steele argued that since Congress had fixed "the first Monday in December" as the date for convening a special session, he was powerless to change it. But on closer examination of the supplemental act of 1800, he acknowledged his error. "Probably," he wrote Sargent, "I may gratify them 'ere long."[66]

Meanwhile, members of the General Assembly met informally, primarily to solidify Narsworthy Hunter's role as their spokesman in Congress. Since 1799, Hunter had been acting as unofficial agent, but without a portfolio he received neither compensation nor franking privileges.

By early June 1801, the opposition's patience was exhausted. Hutchins informed Steele that the General Assembly planned to meet with or without his approval to elect a delegate to Congress. The secretary eventually caved in, believing that "nothing would more completely destroy their popularity [than] to allow them to Legislate." He issued two proclamations—authorizing elections in Washington County and summoning the legislature on July 20, 1801. Predictably, it chose Hunter territorial delegate, but accomplished little otherwise.[67]

Preferring to focus on frivolous or partisan matters rather than tackle weighty issues, the session lapsed into atrophy. Eager to deprive Natchez of the seat of government, they plotted to transfer subsequent sessions of the General Assembly to Washington, a small hamlet eight miles north of Natchez, by joint resolution of both houses, in order to bypass Steele. When Steele understandably objected, his opponents threatened to adjourn and reconvene a few days later in Washington. One of Hutchins's friends reminded the lawmakers that their enemies "would be malignantly gratified to find your Infant Legislature" adopting such a questionable course of action. "Indeed," he warned, "they would rejoice to see you do anything unconstitutional." Wisely, the legislators decided to wait for the new governor before transferring the capital.[68]

Meanwhile Thomas Green persuaded the assembly to draft articles of impeachment "against Winthrop Sargent, for maladministration of office" and to appoint "one or more persons as a commission" to take "depositions of witnesses in support of the . . . impeachment." The lower house not only endorsed Green's motion, but it added the names of Judges Bruin and Lewis to the indictment. These efforts aborted when the commissioners appointed to take depositions, Samuel Hancock and Lewis Moore, refused to comply because "the said order was unconstitutional" and begged the Speaker "to revoke or supercede" the motion.[69]

But Sargent's fate was not to be decided in Mississippi Territory. The elections of 1800 had already spelled his doom. Once in office, President Jefferson refused to make a clean sweep of Federalist appointees; instead, he announced a patronage policy based upon ability and competence and not upon rotation of office as his more ardent supporters wished. Nevertheless, Sargent's extremely partisan conduct as governor provided the president with the excuse he needed to satisfy the people's wishes and to reward W. C. C. Claiborne for faithful service. On May 25, 1801, Jefferson sent Claiborne a commission as governor of Mississippi Territory. As a demonstration of his moderation, Jefferson left John Steele in office.

CHAPTER 3

Frontier Democracy, Republican Style

Governor William Charles Cole Claiborne and his new bride, accompanied by her sister, arrived in Natchez on October 23, 1801. The journey from Nashville was longer and more tedious than the youthful governor of twenty-six had envisioned due to fierce winds and "the low state of the Cumberland, Ohio, and Mississippi Rivers," making navigation "somewhat difficult."[1]

The new governor's challenges were not those of Sargent. He needed to rally Mississippians behind the policies of the newly elected and popular President Jefferson and correct the mistakes of his despised predecessor. Unfortunately, it was a time of learning for a young and untried executive whose professed friends would prove as obstreperous as his pronounced opponents. His brief administration coincided with the territory's first significant international crisis, which unexpectedly provided Jefferson with an opportunity to rescue Claiborne from the difficulties into which his inexperience had taken him.

As the townspeople soon discovered, Claiborne was nothing like his predecessor. A seasoned administrator, Sargent was mature, obstinate and aloof, imbued with a heady dose of New England culture, a veteran of the American Revolution, and a staunch Federalist.[2] He held Washington and Adams in high esteem, and his dislike of Republicans hardened into bitterness upon learning that Jefferson had deliberately misled him. Although an experienced politician, Sargent had naively expected

Jefferson to retain him if he demonstrated that he had the support of the better class.[3]

Although Sargent remained optimistic upon returning to Natchez in late January 1802, his political career was over, a fact he and his supporters never acknowledged. His northern friends looked to vindicate Sargent by publishing a pamphlet entitled *Papers in Relation to the Official Conduct of Governor Sargent,* which they selectively circulated in the territory and among federal officials.[4] After settling down to the life of a gentleman planter, Sargent, like other victims of "the Jeffersonian avalanche of 1800," still expected to be recalled to public service. But to his credit, he never organized an opposition faction.

Claiborne, meanwhile, was an exuberant convert of the new Republican Party, devoted disciple of Thomas Jefferson, ardent expansionist, and tireless advocate of democracy. A Virginian by birth, Claiborne possessed the grace of a southern gentleman (his ancestors were among the first Europeans to settle the Chesapeake), a vaulting ambition to excel, and a determination to protect his honor. Unlike Sargent, he was neither surprised nor upset by frontier rowdiness, having survived the rough-and-tumble politics of East Tennessee, and he never questioned the institution of slavery.[5]

Claiborne's reputation as defender of democracy and disciple of Jefferson was appreciated by many. As a young congressman from Tennessee, he had championed the cause of Mississippians dissatisfied with Sargent's administration and had launched an investigation of Sargent's official conduct.[6] As a result, Claiborne won the undying enmity of Sargent's friends but only the ephemeral accolades of others.

Unlike Sargent, Claiborne never enjoyed the benefits of a honeymoon. He came to Natchez with a set of determined enemies and friends hungry for patronage. Indeed, he was dismayed to find Sargent's pamphlet "in general circulation." "In this production," he wrote Madison, the president's conduct "in relation to Mr. Sargent is assailed with no less acrimony than that of my own." Claiborne lamented that his appointment "should have tended to increase the torrent of calumny [against] the executive."[7]

Claiborne faced two immediate problems. The first was an exposed territory, surrounded by unfriendly Indians and uneasy Spaniards. Despite his best efforts, Sargent had failed to organize the militia after several prominent inhabitants refused to serve unless the rank and file was allowed to select the officers, and the militia soon fell apart.

Claiborne found the territory, except for the presence of a few regular troops at Fort Adams, "entirely defenseless," and the people destitute of arms and ammunition. Bordering "upon the Dominions of a Foreign Power [and] separated from the nearest State [Tennessee] by a wilderness of 600 miles," the territory was engulfed by "numerous Savage Tribes," and a "population of Negroes, nearly equal in number to Whites." To make matters worse, Claiborne learned that Spain had ceded "Louisiana and East and West Florida . . . to France."[8]

Fear of Indian unrest as well as an "Insurrection among the Negroes" prompted Claiborne to ask the legislature for a stronger militia law and to erect "a small Block-House, central to the population of the District, [as] a place of deposit for . . . spare arms." From General Wilkinson he procured a "Brass field piece and all its apparatus together with 40 Stand of Arms," which he used to shore up the district's defenses.[9]

In response to Claiborne's pleas, Jefferson dispatched five hundred rifles and three hundred muskets for sale to individual militiamen at a price the governor judged appropriate. The War Department advised Claiborne "to set prices so high as to prevent their being purchased for the purpose of speculation" and to sell them only to persons "actually belonging to the Militia."[10]

Claiborne erected a small temporary blockhouse of "about fourteen feet square" to store the arms before selling them and collaborated with Capt. Richard Sparks of the U.S. Army to select a suitable site on high ground near the Mississippi River for a permanent military installation, which he named Fort Dearborn in honor of the secretary of war. By locating the fort in Washington, near his own residence and out of Federalist Natchez, Claiborne sent a message to both friend and foe. John Foster, proprietor of the land where Claiborne placed the blockhouse, gladly offered the site "gratis," expecting to dispose of the property "upon very moderate terms," aware that the fort's presence, by attracting population, would enhance the value of his adjoining acreage.[11]

Eventually, Claiborne and Sparks determined upon another spot for Fort Dearborn. They placed it six miles from the river on a site that possessed "the advantage of excellent spring water . . . near the center of our population." After purchasing from Joseph Calvit forty-three acres of land at fifteen dollars per acre near the town of Washington, Claiborne constructed a permanent blockhouse to store arms and barracks to accommodate a company of regular troops.

Although Claiborne intended for Fort Dearborn to replace Fort Adams, located near the international border, as the major "military deposit" on the southwestern frontier, General Wilkinson had other plans. He considered "the frittering up of Military Corps into small detachments destructive of order and intelligence, subversive of discipline and in every view uneconomical." While he favored "a territorial Arsenal" and thought the town of Washington a "well chosen spot for the establishment," he refused to station federal troops there. Wilkinson regarded Claiborne an alarmist since he could not "discern the smallest cause of alarm from either" the Choctaw or enslaved blacks. Instead Wilkinson proposed a simple warning system as more efficient and economical. "A cannon or musket fire by militia captains could alert the citizens" to take cover at "a general rendevous" in case of Indian attacks or slave uprisings.[12]

The governor had better success in revamping the militia. In his first address to the legislature, Claiborne emphasized the need for an "energetic and efficient militia," and the legislature passed a comprehensive militia law designed to improve effectiveness and curtail exemptions. To counteract the mistakes of his predecessor, Claiborne permitted "the Different Militia Companies to nominate (by Election)" officers, and he promised "uniformly (unless some very cogent reason forbids) [to] comply with the wishes of the People." Thus Claiborne overcame one of the earlier objections to establishing a militia.[13]

Organization of the militia proceeded neither uniformly nor smoothly. For instance, in the spring of 1802, Claiborne had to rely on a small voluntary force and a detachment of federal troops when "a daring set of Pirates and Robbers," led by Samuel Mason and Wiley Harp, threatened shipping on the Mississippi River north of Walnut Hills and travel on the Natchez Trace. Also he was noticeably inattentive to the needs of Washington County due to persistent difficulties in creating the militia there.

Nevertheless, Claiborne was pleased with his accomplishments. By the end of July 1802, he boasted that the western counties had been "laid off into regiments, battalions and company Districts, officers appointed and the men enrolled." He was delighted that "a great degree of rivalship existed between the different corps." By late September, Claiborne considered the militia sufficiently organized to appoint Benijah Osmun, a "Captain in the New Jersey line" during the Revolution, brigadier general. In early 1803, an elated Claiborne informed Secretary of State Madison that the territory possessed "about two thousand Militia" who, if required, could seize New Orleans from the Spaniards. Fortunately, no one challenged his bold assertion.[14]

Another problem Claiborne inherited was an unwieldy judiciary, and he asked the legislature to inquire if the present system "admits of improvement" since citizens were "entitled to Justice in the most cheap, easy and expeditious manner, promptly and without delay, comfortable to the Laws." In requesting this review, Claiborne was oblivious of an acrimonious dispute that had recently polarized the legal community.[15]

It grew out of a controversial decision rendered by the territorial superior court. An enterprising and independent widow named Phoebe Calvit, inclined toward litigation, possessed a lot in Natchez based upon a Spanish grant. In 1800, Robert Moore, a Natchez merchant, brought suit to eject her, claiming an earlier-dated Spanish grant to the same property. She contended that since Spanish officials had fraudulently predated Moore's grant, it was invalid. When the case came before the Adams County Court of Common Pleas, the justices, mostly landed gentry who resented the Spanish practice of bestowing land upon favorites, allowed her attorney to introduce parol (oral) testimony to prove her contention, and the jury found in her favor. Moore thereupon appealed to the superior court, which overturned the lower court's decision by declaring parol testimony inadmissible.

This decision raised a storm of protest from landowners uneasy about the validity of their claims and from those who saw in the court's ruling evidence of the capricious nature of territorial justice. Phoebe Calvit petitioned the legislature for a law to permit parol testimony where chicanery was suspected, and the Adams County grand jury indicted Moore for fraud, despite the superior court's ruling. In a presentment by the Pickering County grand jury and a petition signed by fifty citizens, the public rallied to her aid. Indeed, legislators were ready to enact a law authorizing "parol testimony to invalidate certain Spanish grants" until Claiborne disapproved, afraid it "might lead to injurious consequences." While acknowledging that "Spanish agents were guilty" of issuing antedated Spanish grants, he found the proposed remedy too great "an Innovation upon the Laws of Evidence," an opinion shared by most lawyers.[16]

Nevertheless, the legislature in early 1802 succumbed to public pressure and conferred equity jurisdiction on the superior courts. Although Claiborne believed the act would not serve the intended purpose and that the legislature had acted more "against men, than upon principle," he signed it in the hope of restoring confidence in the judiciary and thwarting the impeachment of Chief Justice Seth Lewis. Curiously, public wrath fell not on Judge Bruin but on Lewis, who as an outsider lacked local support. Still, Lewis never understood why he was singled out for condemnation when Bruin and "the whole bar" of the territory had supported him.[17]

Nonetheless, critics blamed Lewis for what they viewed as "an unimpardonable usurpation of power," and they petitioned Congress for his removal. They also asked Congress to abolish the office of territorial judge and to allow the governor to appoint all judicial officers. In imitation of their Kentucky cousins, radical Republicans in Mississippi Territory sought as much local autonomy as possible. Finally, they also pressed for restricting territorial offices to permanent residents by excluding easterners, especially New Englanders, whose political predilections were incompatible with their own. Although Lewis felt vindicated when Congress failed to act, he still resigned in 1803.[18]

The resignations of Judges Tilton and Lewis allowed Jefferson to replace them with men whose political views were more attuned to Republican principles and whose background and training would give the territorial bench a more professional tone. Tilton's replacement was David Ker, a recent immigrant from North Carolina. A native of northern Ireland and of Scottish descent, Ker graduated from Dublin's Trinity College and founded the University of North Carolina, where he briefly served on its first faculty. While his legal training was meager, he brought respectability to the bench.[19]

More significant was the appointment of Thomas Rodney, a member of a distinguished Delaware family. His brother Caesar had signed the Declaration of Independence and his son Caesar Rodney Jr. later became a member of Jefferson's cabinet. Thomas Rodney himself had compiled a credible record of public service, serving as colonel in the Delaware militia during the Revolution, member of the Confederation Congress and the Delaware Assembly, and county and state judge. His firm commitment to republicanism, his prestige as one of the nation's founding fathers, and his engaging personality endeared him to a wide circle of friends and served, together with Ker's appointment, to restore confidence in the courts.[20]

Claiborne's greatest challenge was working with a contentious territorial legislature. While Federalists found solace in the sanctity of the common law and a traditional legal structure, Republicans looked to the legislature for improving government and rectifying grievances. Yet the partisan legislature continued its assault on the previous administration, and Claiborne realized that he could not suppress the rancor that he himself had aroused.

Before leaving Nashville for Natchez, Claiborne had tried to put the best interpretation possible on happenings in Mississippi Territory. "Affairs in that quarter," he naively wrote Madison, "wear a favorable aspect; the public mind is tranquil; and Party Spirit considerably subsided." Once in Natchez, however, he changed his tune, describing politics there as "This Tempest of popular Passions." He blamed the approaching territorial elections for the changes that, he admitted, had "greatly increased the flame of Party." The solitude "of this little society," he wrote, "is disturbed by party divisions, infinitely more rancorous than any I have ever witnessed in our Mother States."[21]

Claiborne experienced his first lesson in local politics when the legislature met in December 1801. While his focus on "strict adherence to the Federal Constitution" and frugality in the operations of government pleased most members, they were not as inclined as Claiborne to pursue a policy of moderation toward Federalists. Instead of revamping the judicial system to ensure "a prompt redress of wrongs and a speedy recovery of all just demands," as Claiborne requested, they renewed their attacks on Judges Bruin and Lewis.[22]

In other partisan moves, the legislature changed the name of Pickering County to Jefferson County, transferred the "next and all future sessions" of the legislature from Natchez to Washington, and adopted a resolution denouncing Sargent's pamphlet, charging that "the Legislature of this territory had been greatly traduced and the people grossly calumniated." Finally, they dismantled Sargent's Code, repealing or modifying eighteen of the twenty-five laws, retaining only such innocuous measures as those authorizing the establishment of ferries or erection of public buildings.[23]

These developments distressed Claiborne, who surmised that they had "increased still more, the flame of *party*, and rendered the restoration of entire harmony, to this Society, (for the present) without the reach of human Power." In fact, Claiborne became so frustrated that he contemplated resigning. Only his belief that "a resignation at this particular time would portray a want of firmness and perserverance and might be disagreeable to my friends" convinced him to stay.[24]

One result of the assault upon the judiciary was open warfare between the legal community and radical Republicans. Incensed by the reduction of legal fees, by new restrictions upon attorneys, and by an investigation into Chief Justice Lewis's conduct, the lawyers, joined by Sargent's friends, mounted a campaign to win control of the lower house in the upcoming elections. They hoped to block Congress from letting governors appoint territorial judges, to replace Hunter as delegate to Congress with Sargent, and to retain Secretary John Steele in office. The last aim particularly angered Claiborne, who accused Steele of using his office as "a place of rendevous for opponents to the second grade of government." Forced to keep information from him, the governor became his own secretary. "The Judges, the Secretary, Old Winthrop, the Federalists and the old Tories," Claiborne lamented, "will give me all the opposition in their power."[25]

The unexpected death of Narsworthy Hunter in March 1802 disrupted Federalists' plans to send Sargent to Congress. During a hastily called special session of the General Assembly in May 1802, the Green-West faction secured the election of Thomas Marston Green, a choice particularly galling to Natchez Federalists. Even Claiborne was less than excited. He described Green as a "respectable and wealthy Farmer, warmly attached to the United States, and to the principles of seventy-six, possessing a tolerable correct judgment, but without the advantage of a good Education."[26]

The results of the summer elections further alarmed Claiborne. He had expected friends of the late governor to gain a legislative seat or two, but the magnitude of their victory was disconcerting. In 1800, opponents of the second stage of government had boycotted the elections, but in 1802 they turned out in record numbers. Voters in Adams County, which included the town of Natchez, swept in a new slate of legislators, consisting of Dunbar; William Connor, a Natchez lawyer and friend of Seth Lewis; and William Gordon Forman, an early settler from New Jersey and staunch supporter of Sargent.

Even in Jefferson County, where the Greens held sway, opponents captured two of its four seats. In addition to Roger Dixon, a former member of the pro-Ellicott Permanent Committee, the voters chose the egomaniacal John Girault, who running initially as a Republican, broke ranks and joined the Federalists in first naming Dixon and later Connor speaker of the lower house. With opponents in firm control of the lower house, Claiborne's "hope for the return of a calm and happy political hemisphere" was shattered.[27]

Of the myriad problems besetting the territory, the most pressing was the tangled web of conflicting land claims. Prior to creation of Mississippi Territory in 1798, three European governments (France, Spain, and Great Britain) had at one time or another controlled portions of the territory, and all had granted lands to both actual and potential settlers. As a result, they left land titles in a chaotic state. Adding further confusion was Georgia's decision in 1795 to grant the same lands to several prominent speculators, known as the Yazoo claimants, who in turn quickly disposed of their claims to a second set of land jobbers. Then, in 1802, after years of protracted negotiations, the State of Georgia ceded its western lands to the federal government in exchange for partial guarantees to Yazoo claimants. Congress, however, balked at compensating them, and the Yazoo scandals hung over the early territory like the sword of Damocles until 1814.

Even if some of the territorial lands had fallen into the hands of speculators who had no intention of making improvements, most of the grants went to bona fide settlers. Nevertheless a number of early British grants were conditional, requiring improvements within a specified period, before receiving full title. More often than not, the stipulations were never met. While Spanish officials recognized the claims of actual settlers, they unknowingly or not granted to recent immigrants lands that overlapped prior British grants. Furthermore, Spanish officials, shortly before relinquishing the Natchez District, extended to court favorites grants that predated the signing of the Pinckney Treaty in order to give them the appearance of legality. These tainted grants, although few in number, became a major source of controversy.

Finally, both England and Spain laid out a complex process for converting warrants of survey into a legal patent. For one reason or other, many claimants had failed to complete the process, leaving them with an incomplete but universally recognized right of ownership. Therefore, incomplete and conflicting claims became the norm rather than the exception, forcing the federal government to devise some system for determining which were valid. To be sure, land ownership was a sign both of economic success and of social status. But without sufficient labor, land was a surer path to poverty than to riches and privilege. Consequently, as landowners turned more and more to cotton for profits and corn for substance, slavery became critical to the region's future. Despite a few early objections expressed by northern congressmen and federal officials like Andrew Ellicott, the majority of residents unthinkingly accepted chattel slavery as commercially essential. Even if white planters never asked the slaves what they thought of the institution, the planters' constant fear of insurrection indicates they knew without inquiring. Ironically, the people with the best claims to the land—the Creek, Choctaw, Cherokee, and Chickasaw Nations—were also the most disadvantaged. Unable to prevent white settlers from devouring their lands and dismantling their cultures, they had traditionally resorted to playing off one European intruder against the other in an effort to retain their ancestral inheritance. With the French and British removed from the Old Southwest and the Spanish becoming impotent, the Indians grew increasingly vulnerable to losing their lands to Americans who questioned their right to possess uncultivated soil.

In order to untie the knot of entangling claims, Congress recognized the need for some impartial board to review the evidence and set guidelines for confirming the legitimate and negating the fraudulent claims. To start with, federal officials required reliable information before devising a plan, and they turned to Governor Claiborne for assistance. Madison instructed him to collect data about the extent of lands free of Indian title or claimed by settlers under the Agreement of 1802 with Georgia. In accordance with these instructions, Claiborne posted handbills throughout the territory requesting settlers to register their claims with a county clerk before November 1802.

The results proved disappointing. Claiborne blamed the poor response upon ignorance or "inattention" on the part of some settlers and deliberate misrepresentation by others. Apparently a number of settlers believed reports, spread by "some designing men," that registration might jeopardize their claims. Others, assuming "an unaccommodating disposition," boycotted the process. Claiborne himself knew individuals with legitimate claims who refused to register them for one reason or another.[28]

Consequently, in submitting his response, Claiborne cautioned Madison that his findings were incomplete. Nevertheless, it constituted the first survey of territorial land claims and the best description of procedures used by previous governments in issuing them. Despite its deficiencies, Claiborne's summary alerted the government to several potential problems. Because England and Spain had treated warrants and orders of survey as proof of ownership, most settlers never bothered to secure a patent. Furthermore, anyone who had improved his holdings within three years was, "by custom," free to sell the property and convey a clear title. Claiborne urged federal officials to follow similar practices. He confirmed that most of the fertile lands along the Mississippi River were subject to overlapping claims. Without a quick resolution, he warned, settlers in these parts of the territory would remain uneasy.

In addition, a number of immigrants had illegally squatted on unoccupied lands during the interval between Spanish and American control. Because of confusion over which government legally possessed the region, few newcomers had applied for warrants of survey. Claiborne estimated that at least seven hundred families, comprising a total population of "upwards of two thousand," fell into this category. Unless these individuals were made secure in their possessions or unless the federal government planned to sell vacant lands "in this district upon moderate terms and in a small tract to actual settlers," Claiborne warned, they will leave "the Territory in disgust, to become subjects in a Country, where heretofore, the most flattering invitations have been offered to the poorer class of industrious citizens, by bestowing, upon every applicant, without price, portions of the richest lands, proportioned to the extent of his family." Claiborne also feared that "the present farms of the settlers would then probably fall into the hands of rich speculators either in this District, or from the United States," resulting in an increase of emigrants and a decrease of immigrants. The remaining population would be dominated by "a few wealthy characters, with a large increase of negroes," rendering the settlements "weak and defenseless."[29]

The data from Washington County (Tombigbee District) were both incomplete and confusing. None of those claiming lands under Spanish grants had secured a patent before October 27, 1795; instead, they held only an order of survey. Again, Claiborne assured Madison that this "kind of title after three years of occupancy was esteemed valid." In addition, he urged the government to extend "a right of preemption" to the estimated 180 "heads of families" who had "settled vacant land and made considerable improvements subsequent to 1795," and dispose of the rest "to actual settlers, as the only means of preventing a considerable immigration to Louisiana."[30]

On March 3, 1803, Congress enacted a comprehensive land act that incorporated most of Claiborne's suggestions. It confirmed the claims of residents holding a British or Spanish patent or a warrant of survey issued before October 27, 1795, provided they headed a family or were twenty-one years of age or older. It also donated up to 640 acres to bona fide residents with a tract of land under cultivation before October 27, 1795, and granted preemption rights to those who had settled in the territory between that date and March 3, 1803.

The act empowered the president to appoint two land commissioners and a register for each of two districts (one in Adams County for lands lying west of the Pearl River and the other in Washington County for lands east of that river) and to establish land offices for the sale at public auction of all unclaimed lands to which Indian title had been extinguished. The commissioners and register of each district were to act as a board of commissioners for resolving conflicting claims. In addition, the president was to appoint a surveyor general for the territory. Claimants had until the last day of March 1804 to submit evidence in support of their claims. The commissioners were to issue certificates to those holding valid and uncontested claims, but in cases where an adverse claim existed, settlers could receive title only after a favorable judicial decision.[31]

For commissioners, Jefferson turned to nonresidents. The controversy surrounding the selection of Edward Turner as register of the western district proved the wisdom of his decision. Otherwise, Jefferson's choices were well received. These included the recently named Judge Thomas Rodney and Robert Williams of North Carolina as commissioners for the western district and Ephraim Kirby of Connecticut and Robert Nicholas of Kentucky for the eastern district. He wisely omitted Georgians despite strong pressure from officials of that state. Joseph Chambers accepted the post of register for the eastern land office, and the affable Quaker Isaac Briggs proved a worthy choice for surveyor general. Briggs immediately set about marking the land into ranges and townships as had been done previously in Northwest Territory.[32]

Despite its comprehensiveness and the government's generosity, the

act disappointed several inhabitants. Spanish claimants objected to listing the entire chain of titles since the filing fee was based upon the
number of words. "In the habit of considering . . . a Warrant of Survey granted by the Spanish Government" as proof of a legal title to the
land, they saw no reason to require additional evidence. Under Spanish
law, these lands had "been permitted to descend by inheritance or to be
transferred by sale although no improvement or actual settlement had
been made," as the act of 1803 required. If strictly enforced, this provision would adversely affect claimants "who had improved and cultivated [their lands] for many years but who by the rotation of crops and
the necessary repose to be given to the soil, had judged it expedient to
discontinue the cultivation" in 1795. Others objected to the restriction
against minors, who, unless they were heads of a family, were not to
be confirmed in their claims. As one petitioner pleaded, "many elder
persons residing in this country have preferred making application [for
lands] in the names of their children," which the Spanish government
had allowed. Unless modified, Claiborne warned, it will "turn out to
beggary and misery, families which are now comfortably settled," resulting in a general disposition against filing claims with the board and further delays in resolving the land business.[33]

Those who had migrated to the territory after Spain had evacuated
(March 30, 1798) felt the act discriminated against them. Instead of
securing donation rights to a section of land (640 acres) as did residents
before October 27, 1795, they received only an option to purchase a half
section (320 acres) at a price not less than two dollars per acre. Finally,
the act made no provisions for settlers on "unappropriated lands" or
future immigrants.[34]

Still, patronage considerations, more than land conflicts, commanded Claiborne's immediate attention. In distributing both civil
and military offices, Claiborne, following his mentor, Thomas Jefferson, avoided wholesale removals and filled vacancies with Republicans.
Although Jefferson once lamented that few die and none resign, Claiborne was more fortunate since a number of Sargent's friends followed
Dunbar's example and refused to serve under a governor affiliated with
the West-Green faction. Other Federalists were less principled, willing to forsake political orthodoxy for public office. For instance, Benijah Osmun showed no qualm in remaining commander of the Adams
County militia.[35]

Also like Jefferson, Claiborne avidly employed the lure of office to entice moderate Federalists into Republican ranks. For instance, he not only rewarded Samuel Postlethwait, a prominent Natchez merchant, with office, but he also favored his mercantile firm in purchasing supplies. The governor's standing among the merchants noticeably improved after his brother Ferdinand resigned from the army and opened a mercantile establishment in Natchez.[36]

But Claiborne encountered more abuse from his fair-weather friends than his avowed enemies. The Greens of Jefferson County were particularly troublesome. Having led the opposition to Sargent, they expected favors from Claiborne, who, bothered by "clamors about the Greens getting all the offices to themselves," was cautious but obliging. He named Abner Green treasurer general and justice of the peace for Adams County, Henry Green justice of the peace for Jefferson County, and Thomas Green treasurer of Jefferson County. Jefferson then unintentionally added to the Greens' political strength by naming Cato West to replace John Steele as territorial secretary.[37]

To build better cohesiveness, the Greens organized the Mississippi Republican Society. As one founder explained, its purposes were to promote "Republican principles," disseminate "political information among the people by means of discussion and [by] circulating political pamphlets and newspapers," and to prepare the inhabitants for statehood. By locating the society at Greenville on Coles Creek, seat of Jefferson County, and by having Cato West and his son-in-law Edward Turner draft the constitution and bill of rights, the Greens made sure the society would serve their interests.[38]

Disturbed by this development, Natchez Federalists in 1803 chartered the Mississippi Society for the Acquisition and Dissemination of Useful Knowledge as a counterweight to the Republican Society. While partisan at its inception, the former society outlived its original purpose to become the principal intellectual beacon of the territory, largely because its members were more eclectic in politics, better educated, and more curious than their counterparts. Charter members included Dunbar, Rodney, Seth Lewis, Briggs, Girault, and John Ellis. Later they made the famous naturalist Dr. John Sibley of Louisiana a corresponding member.[39]

Newspapers were the centerpiece of partisan activities. Like all frontier settlements, Mississippi Territory was short of talented scribblers.

In 1802, the Federalists lured Andrew Marschalk back to Natchez, where he launched the territory's first newspaper, the *Mississippi Herald*. Unable to locate or attract a suitable editor, Claiborne employed two local printers, Darius Moffett and James Ferrell, to publish the laws and to strike off circulars and handbills. Col. Joshua Baker, on behalf of Anthony Hutchins, solicited William H. Beaumont of Kentucky to set up a newspaper, but it never materialized, apparently due to lack of funds. By 1803, the mercurial Marschalk was supporting Claiborne against both his Federalist critics and the Green-West faction.[40]

By late 1802, the Republicans had split into two factions—Claibornites and the Green-West junta—based more upon personalities than principles. Governor Claiborne broke with the radical Republicans who wanted the franchise extended to all free males and the legislative council to be elected. Opposing West's effort to transfer the territorial capital to Greenville, Claiborne rallied the Republicans of Washington and Natchez behind him. The Green-West faction denounced Claiborne for embracing his former enemies, and Edward Turner blamed Dunbar and Girault for the governor's apostasy. According to him, both were "deep designing men, of plausible manners, very capable of imposing upon those who are fond of flattery."[41]

Another bone of contention among Republicans was Jefferson College. Claiborne shared Jefferson's faith in the efficacy of education, and both agreed that preservation of a republican government depended upon an educated citizenry. "A People involved in mental darkness," Claiborne asserted, "become fit subjects for despotic sway, but when informed of their Rights, they will never fail to cause them to be respected by the Public Authority." He also predicted that unless the increasing wealth of the territory was used "to promote knowledge and rational refinement . . . , it may produce Luxury and Vice in the rising Generation, and became the means of corruption[,] both Public and Private."[42]

To guard against these, Claiborne admonished the citizenry to set up "Literary Institutions" in their communities and the legislature to charter "A Seminary of Learning," situated in "a spot central to the population of the Territory, fostered by the Government, and placed under the direction of a well selected Board of Trustees." The legislature responded by creating Jefferson College and selecting a board of trustees, composed of the territory's most prominent citizens, regardless of political persuasion. Unfortunately, it made no provision for permanent support of the college, and the board of trustees had to petition the federal government for assistance, which came in the form of land grants. It also tried to raise local funds through a lottery, but this effort floundered when most of the tickets went unsold. Private donations fared little better since those pledging contributions made them contingent upon locating the college at a particular site. For instance, John and James Foster promised to donate approximately fourteen acres of land (including "one half of Ellicott's Spring") near Washington. Mordecai Throckmorton offered "a tract of 20 acres adjoining Greenville" in Jefferson County.[43] Soon the dispute degenerated into a political contest between the governor, who wanted the college in Washington, and the Greens, who favored Greenville.

In their quest of the college, the Greens waited patiently for the right opportunity. At a poorly attended board meeting on March 14, 1803, David Ker pushed through a motion in support of Greenville. Claiborne and the Adams County trustees, most of whom were absent, cried fraud, charging that Ker and his friends stood to benefit personally from this decision. Consequently, at the next board meeting, they rescinded the previous action and authorized the governor to appoint a selection committee to pick a location convenient to the population.[44] In an attempt to please both factions, this committee recommended the neutral site of Selsertown, but the Claibornites refused to compromise, confident of legislative concurrence. Claiborne then persuaded a coalition of Federalists and Claibornites to locate the college in Washington.[45]

In retaliation, the Greens reneged on their earlier pledges of support for Jefferson College, forcing the board to rely upon a congressional grant of two lots in the town of Natchez plus an adjoining out lot, not to exceed thirty acres, to finance the institution. The governor was to select the specific lots and sell them "to the highest bidder." After Claiborne chose two lots on the public square, next to the courthouse, the City of Natchez immediately protested and appealed to Congress for redress.[46]

Selection of the outlying tract was also controversial. After Claiborne departed for New Orleans, acting governor Cato West, no friend of Natchez, chose the city commons, which abutted the river. Again the city council of Natchez objected, arguing that Gayoso had set aside the commons for public use and that erecting buildings on it would endanger the community's health. In addition, Dunbar claimed that Gayoso had given him the lots in lieu of payment for services rendered the Spanish government, although he acknowledged that if the city kept this site, "the poor college will be absolutely nipped in the bud." Congress subsequently confirmed the city's right to the contested lots, but the dispute continued in the courts until 1816, when Natchez won "permanent and clear title" to the commons and the college received six thousand dollars in compensation. These disputes delayed the opening of Jefferson College until 1817.[47]

Controversy over Jefferson College brought the schism between the two Republican factions into the open and shoved Claiborne into closer cooperation with the Federalists. In addition, the marriage of his brother Ferdinand to Magdalene Hutchins forged a closer link between the two families. Thereafter, political divisions assumed a decided sectional flavor, and Ker's contention that the Jefferson-Adams county line separated the factions was not far off the mark.[48]

The breach between Republican factions became more acrimonious after Claiborne's brother failed to be named register. Instead, Thomas Green captured the coveted post for Edward Turner, son-in-law of Cato West. It intensified when the legislature selected William Lattimore, a physician who dabbled in politics, to replace Green as territorial delegate. "Doctor Lattimore is a young man of promising Talents," Claiborne wrote Madison, "and a firm and genuine republican."[49]

Before the schism completely dismantled Republican unity, a new crisis diverted the territory's attention. On October 18, 1802, Juan Ventura Morales, acting intendant of Louisiana, had unexpectedly closed the port of New Orleans to foreign commerce and suspended the right (or "privilege," in Spanish opinion) "that the Americans had of introducing and deporting their merchandise and effects in this capital." Adding insult to injury, Morales ignored the American request that he allow "stores destined for Fort Stoddert to pass through the Spanish Territory free of duty." Morales also disregarded the stipulation in the Pinckney Treaty of 1795 that if Spain withdrew the deposit at New Orleans, it "must assign some other place on the Banks of the Mississippi for an Equivalent Establishment."[50]

This disturbing announcement unified the contentious factions behind the efforts of Governor Claiborne and President Jefferson to seek a peaceful resolution of the crisis. In conveying the news to Secretary Madison, Claiborne stressed the "considerable agitation" of Mississippians. "It has inflicted a severe wound upon the Agricultural and

Commercial Interest of this Territory," he wrote, "and must prove no less injurious to all the Western Country." He dispatched a strongly worded protest to the governor of Louisiana, reminding him of the treaty's provision requiring Spain to designate an alternate port. Spanish governor Manuel Juan de Salcedo was as surprised as Claiborne by the intendant's actions, and he pleaded that he was powerless to interfere in commercial matters and insisted that Morales had acted on his own authority. Few Americans, and certainly not Claiborne, accepted the Spanish governor's explanation. Initially, Claiborne believed the order had come either from officials in Madrid or by the hand of Napoleon. As early as the beginning of 1802, rumors were alive in New Orleans and Natchez that Spain had ceded both Floridas and Louisiana to France, and Morales's proclamation appeared to confirm them.[51]

Claiborne's conjectures were only partially correct. Spain indeed had ceded Louisiana, but none of Florida, to France in a secret treaty signed at San Ildefonso on October 1, 1800. Although the intendant insisted that he had acted alone, he was following "very secret" instructions from Madrid. While American officials suspected that Napoleon was responsible, in truth he was as bewildered by Morales's action as were Claiborne and Madison. Indeed, Napoleon partly justified his decision to sell Louisiana on the grounds that removal of the deposit made it impossible for him to occupy it peacefully. Conversely, Morales insisted that the only way he could stop the extensive contraband trade in Louisiana and the wholesale smuggling of specie was by closing the port of New Orleans to foreign commerce and by rescinding the American deposit. Still, he refused to admit that he acted under the king's directions.[52]

If removing the deposit was not enough to excite Mississippians, the news in early 1803 that France would soon be on their doorstep was more than sufficient. Indeed, Jefferson regarded impotent Spain a perfect custodian of the Floridas and Louisiana until the United States was ready to acquire them. In contrast, France constituted a serious impediment, since Napoleon's army, the finest in Europe, appeared invincible, making it difficult to dislodge the French from New Orleans. Others, especially Federalists, feared that France planned to use the Crescent City as a base for introducing its brand of radicalism into the American West. Claiborne's apprehension of Napoleon's military power, combined with French expansionism, led him to wish that "the United

States could possess themselves of East and West Florida, including the Island of Orleans."[53]

Publicly, Claiborne urged patience, calling on the federal government to take immediate measures to "promote and protect the general interests of our common Country, as wisdom shall dictate." Privately, he agreed with Daniel Clark Jr. and William E. Hulings, the two bellicose American "consuls" in New Orleans who favored grabbing New Orleans and Florida before the French took possession. Believing that a majority of people in both areas favored American occupation, Clark and Hulings argued that the United States could seize Louisiana "now without bloodshed." The local inhabitants, Clark argued, "cry out against our temporizing when our dearest interests imperiously call upon us to embrace the favorable moment for acting and they tremble when they see it pass and themselves on the point of falling under the lash of a Government they detest."[54]

In and out of Congress, Federalists joined the war chant. Hoping to lure westerners into their camp and embarrass the president, they pressed for immediate military action to restore free navigation of the Mississippi River and the right of deposit. While Alexander Hamilton called upon the government "to seize at once on the Floridas and New Orleans, and then negotiate," Senator James Ross of Pennsylvania introduced resolutions authorizing the president to call out fifty thousand militiamen from the western states and Mississippi Territory. Meanwhile, Claiborne advised Madison that he could take New Orleans with approximately six hundred of the two thousand militia under arms in Mississippi Territory, "provided there should be only Spanish troops to defend the place." There were, he said, "in Orleans and on the Coast, a number of inhabitants devoted to the American interest, and in the event of hostilities, would most certainly join the American standard."[55]

Despite a rash of remonstrances in favor of hostilities, Jefferson doggedly pursued a policy of peace and procrastination. First, he insisted upon separating the two issues of free navigation on the Mississippi River and the right of deposit. He and Madison effectively used the threat of hostilities to pressure the Spanish minister, Marquis de Casa Irujo, into advising his government to restore the American deposit at New Orleans. They also secured from the French minister a promise that his government would not interfere with this right.[56]

Jefferson was less sanguine about free navigation of the Mississippi short of permanent possession of New Orleans. Reasoning that a renewal of war in Europe was imminent, Jefferson believed that time was on his side. Consequently, he prevailed upon James Monroe to undertake a special mission to France in the hope of purchasing New Orleans and West Florida. In case France proved intractable, Monroe was to seek an alliance with Great Britain. If necessary, Jefferson was prepared "to marry ourselves to the British fleet and nation" in order to keep France out of the Southwest.

Fortunately, extreme measures proved unnecessary, and Jefferson's patience was rewarded with more success than even he expected. Claiborne and Clark proved less representative of local sentiment as most westerners endorsed Jefferson's course of action, especially his decision to send Monroe to Europe. They saw Monroe as their true friend and "one of their best and ablest advocates." To the chagrin of Federalists, a majority of congressmen defeated all efforts to veer the nation toward war, and remained unswerving in their commitment to republicanism.[57]

In addition, Mississippians and Louisianans realized that peace in Europe was more responsible for the economic depression that hit the western states and territories in the early 1800s than withdrawal of the American deposit. With the cessation of hostilities in Europe in 1801 came an immediate reduction in the demand for American produce by the major powers of Europe. Furthermore, revocation of the deposit had not closed the Mississippi River to American commerce; it meant only that Americans no longer had the convenience of storing produce at New Orleans and exporting it duty-free. If the deposit was restored, Americans realized that they would still be subject to the same 6 percent duty as were merchants of other nations.

Furthermore, no one prevented the Americans from descending the Ohio and Mississippi rivers in seagoing vessels and entering the Gulf of Mexico unmolested. Also Morales never intended to interfere with the existing practice of transferring western produce directly from flatboats to American ships anchored at New Orleans. In fact, during the seven-month closure, there were more oceangoing American vessels than flatboats in and around the port of New Orleans. Although Claiborne had predicted that "only a few American ships would enter the Mississippi River" and that "the number will be insufficient for the demand and [that] the surplus produce of the West will be lost to our Country and to the industrious farmer" forever, he reported a few months later that "many *vessels* [were] yet lying opposite to Orleans, waiting for return Cargoes."[58]

The firmness of the western states and territories in support of Jefferson's policies was crucial to the president's success. As a result of strong pressure from Irujo and other Spanish officials who feared that the Americans might seize New Orleans at any moment, the Spanish government instructed Morales to reinstate the American deposit, which he did on May 17, 1803, some seven months after he had rescinded it.[59]

Although restoration of the deposit solved only one of Jefferson's problems, circumstances in Europe and the West Indies persuaded Napoleon to sell Louisiana, including New Orleans, to the United States. The renewal of hostilities in Europe, the bellicosity of western Americans, and France's failure to put down a slave rebellion on the island of St. Dominique informed Napoleon's decision. As a result of the purchase, Jefferson resolved permanently the vexing question of navigation rights on the Mississippi River and won the undying devotion of the West. The Legislative Council of Mississippi Territory expressed the sentiments of most westerners when it declared that "the knowledge of no occurance, except the establishment of American independence, has been more joyfully or more thankfully received, than the important cession of Louisiana."[60]

Both delighted and relieved by the turn of events in the Southwest, Claiborne received permission to take a much-needed respite from his duties, although Jefferson instructed him to remain in readiness at his home in Nashville. Shortly afterward, Jefferson appointed him to serve with General Wilkinson as one of two American commissioners to accept the transfer of Louisiana from France late in 1803. Claiborne considered the unexpected appointment "a great honor," even though he knew the assignment resulted more from his availability than from recognition of his abilities or accomplishments. Although Claiborne did not know it at the time, when he departed Natchez on December 2, 1803, to meet General Wilkinson at Fort Adams, he was leaving Mississippi Territory permanently.[61]

CHAPTER 4

An "Insidious Junto"

While the acquisition of Louisiana pleased some Mississippians more than others, residents of Natchez were especially elated. Hailing the purchase as the harbinger of a boundless future, they made plans to take advantage of the largesse, confident that it was no longer possible for a hostile nation to impose injurious duties upon their commerce or endanger their security. Moreover, the purchase laid the foundation for the district's cotton boom, ushering in an unprecedented period of peace and prosperity.[1]

On the other hand, residents along the Tombigbee River in the eastern half of the territory, known locally as the "Bigbee" District, were less enthralled since the purchase brought them neither long-range benefits nor immediate relief. Their principal commercial outlet was Mobile, not New Orleans, and Spain appeared determined to retain the Floridas whatever the cost. Although Jefferson insisted, with little justification, that the United States had acquired West Florida as well as Louisiana from France, most Bigbee settlers knew he was bluffing.[2]

These countervailing developments created serious tensions between the two separated settlements that, if not resolved, threatened to undermine the territory's future growth. The settlers in the Tombigbee were especially distraught. With New Orleans safely in American hands, they worried that federal officials might forget them. Based upon past precedent, their apprehension was not unreasonable. From the outset, the federal government had viewed the two settlements as distinctive, as in truth, they were.

71

Under Spain, Natchez had thrived, emerging from a backwoods settlement into a bustling river port and a prosperous agricultural community. Conversely, Tombigbee, because of its isolated and exposed position, lagged behind in population and prosperity, and neither government, territorial nor federal, displayed much interest in its plight.[3]

For example, fourteen months after ratifying Pinckney's Treaty, the United States still had not taken possession of the Spanish fort at St. Stephens, leaving the settlers under a disinterested government. The Spanish commandant grew so impatient with American procrastination that in early February 1799 he departed, handing the fort's keys to local inhabitants.[4]

Even after American troops took possession, Governor Sargent, more from negligence than malice, deferred setting up a civil government and allowed the military to stay longer than he should have. Finally, on June 4, 1800, Sargent established Washington County to encompass the region east of the Pearl River and north of the thirty-first parallel, an area twice the size of Natchez District, which then comprised four counties.[5]

Despite its vastness, Washington County contained only two pockets of Anglo settlement, both near forts erected by the Spaniards. The first was just north of the international border, where fewer than two hundred families resided around Fort Stoddert and along both banks of the Tensaw River. The other lay to the north on the western bank of the Tombigbee, "a fine clear navigable river, with the tide flowing up to St. Stephens," where approximately one hundred families resided.[6]

Directly across from Fort St. Stephens, on the fertile eastern bank of the Tombigbee, a few settlers cultivated lands by permission of the Choctaws, but they lived in constant fear of losing the privileges. Although not as "opulent and respectable" as those along the Tensaw River, the upper "piney woods" were more attractive to newcomers than the unhealthy, swampy lowlands of the Tensaw and Mobile rivers, where yellow fever and other diseases were omnipresent.[7]

In these circumstances, Washington County fell noticeably behind Natchez in economic and social development. Compelled to pay an exorbitant duty of 12 percent ad valorem on all exports passing through Mobile, the Bigbee settlers could not compete in foreign markets, and they had to sell their products, consisting mostly of livestock and grains, locally and cheaply.[8] As a result, these subsistence farmers could neither amass wealth nor acquire imposing estates.

Those attracted to Tombigbee were primarily poor, uneducated, hardscrabble farmers, most of whom were transients awaiting better opportunities elsewhere. Meanwhile, the insulated district became a haven for political refugees, fugitives from justice, and social outcasts of all descriptions. Before and during the American Revolution, a number of Tory sympathizers from the eastern states sought safety from persecution by fleeing to remote regions, and Tombigbee gained its share of these refugees. A visitor to the region complained that the settlers "had the audacity to calumniate in the most abusive terms" against the United States.[9]

If Sargent found the inhabitants of Natchez degenerate, immoral, and crude in behavior, immigrants and travelers to Tombigbee were equally appalled by the unsophisticated and backward residents there. Ephraim Kirby, the district's first resident official, was particularly carping. As long as the people remain "in their present condition," he reported, they will become "banditti, fugitives from justice, [and] disturbers of the peace, of our frontiers." Not until they obtained "that degree of moral or political virtue . . . essential to the existence of a free government" could they be productive citizens. Noting that "this section of the United States has long afforded an asylum to those who prefer voluntary exile to the punishments ordained by law for heinous offenses," Kirby characterized them as "illiterates, wild and savage, of depraved morals, unworthy of public confidence or private esteem, litigious, disunited, and knowing each other, universally distrustful of each other."[10]

Since he believed in the natural depravity of man, Governor Sargent had no trouble accepting Kirby's hyperbolic description, an attitude that hardly spurred him to appoint local officials. Capt. Bartholomew Schaumburgh, commandant of the small contingent of American troops garrisoning the district, aptly summarized Sargent's dilemma in locating qualified individuals. He informed the governor that "men in whom capability and integrity are united, are scarce" and that there were few "who are not either a principal or accessory to some criminality." In making selections, Sargent often had to choose between someone who wrote "a handsome hand and pretty correct" but who was too "fond of strong liquor" and one who was respectable and "honest" but illiterate and whose wife might "assume to rule the office, and pronounce sentence."[11]

Furthermore, few Bigbee settlers were pleased with being part of Mississippi Territory. Instead, they yearned for a separate government under which they could manage their own affairs. A number of factors, some real and others imagined, fed their thirst for independence. First, the district was unrepresented in the territory's first legislature after officials there failed to receive timely notice of the first territorial elections, and their representatives could not reach Natchez, a distance of some three hundred miles and requiring more than a week of arduous travel, before the legislature convened. While the oversight was unfortunate, it was hardly sinister or conspiratorial. The only important business transacted in the first session was to select nominees for the legislative council. Since the two Washington County nominees were acceptable to everyone, their complaints appeared more spirited than substantive, and no one objected when President Adams chose Flood McGrew instead of John Caller.[12]

A more serious grievance was the lack of a resident appellant judge, and even Sargent acknowledged the validity of that complaint. In June 1800, he dispatched Judge Tilton to give "due tone to judicial proceedings" there. Unfortunately, Tilton never arrived. After stopping briefly in New Orleans to transact personal business, he mysteriously disappeared, and his whereabouts were unknown until he officially resigned in 1802. It was late 1803 before Judge David Ker appeared to hear cases on appeal and to advise the governor of "the State of Public Affairs there."[13]

Meanwhile, President Jefferson, cognizant of the deficiency, persuaded Congress to establish a separate judgeship for the eastern district and named Ephraim Kirby, former governor of Connecticut, to the office, but he died before holding court.[14] Understandably, Bigbee settlers were distraught, but they erred in blaming officials rather than acknowledging the obvious—that a set of bizarre circumstances was responsible, not the administration.

To be sure, Jefferson's appointment of Harry Toulmin to replace Kirby pleased most people, although it initially disappointed two influential men in the district, Flood McGrew and James Caller, who backed a local favorite, Rodominick H. Gilmer. Nevertheless Toulmin was a prudent, if not always a popular, choice. Of the myriad territorial judges, none served longer than Toulmin, and only Thomas Rodney was more effective. Best of all, Toulmin was a survivor. Although he encountered harsh criticism and oftentimes bitter opposition, he was sufficiently resilient to best more than one determined adversary during a tenure spanning almost two decades.[15]

But more than anything, uncertainty of land claims disquieted the settlers. Like most western immigrants, they came to Tombigbee seeking good lands. Since a plethora of governments had previously ruled the area, all of whom had issued land grants of assorted types, some more valid than others and most with specific conditions and limitations attached, conflicts were the order of the day. A few settlers possessed British grants, but the vast majority held either some sort of Spanish claim or were squatters by virtue of "settlement and Occupancy."[16]

While all settlers wanted a clear title, none was more anxious than squatters who feared that lands they had cultivated might fall into the lap of speculators with ready cash. Consequently, they pushed the federal government to open land offices and grant them the right of preemption to some, if not all, of the lands they had improved.[17]

Shortage of good land free of Indian titles was a constant problem for frontiersmen, and for Bigbee settlers it was especially acute because of the high percentage of fertile lands still in Indian hands. For instance, settlers along the lower Alabama River had unsuccessfully solicited the federal government to purchase the triangular-shaped area between the Tombigbee and the Alabama rivers.[18] For seventeen years, Choctaws had allowed white settlers to cultivate these fertile and less flood-prone lands on the eastern side of the Tombigbee River, but anxious Anglos, who rarely trusted Indians, wanted the Indians eliminated. At the Treaty of Fort Adams, signed on October 17, 1802, the Choctaws ceded most of the area, freeing the federal government to remove its restrictions and paving the way for increased population.[19]

Nevertheless, Washington Countians wanted nothing so much as "division of the Territory" and formation of "a Separate Government . . . independent of that of the Mississippi Territory." According to them, the settlements of Tombigbee and Natchez were too incompatible to be united, "composed of people different in their manners and customs [and] different in their interests." Nature, they asserted, never intended "the two countries to be under the same government."[20] By 1804, the settlers had become ardent separatists.

As evident by their complaints, the acquisition of Louisiana still rankled, and they blamed the federal government for their plight. If "the free navigation of the Mobile[,] Tombecbee[,] and Alabama Rivers, [were] secured to the citizens of the United States," they declared, then "the amount of revenue arising from impost duties in this District, would exceed the necessary expenses in support of a separate Territorial Government."[21]

Even if Congress consented to splitting the territory, Jefferson was hardly prepared to pressure Spain into granting free navigation of rivers emptying into Mobile Bay as long as Great Britain refused to resolve its differences with the United States over impressment of seamen and maritime rights on the high seas. Jefferson was also unsuccessful in enlisting the assistance of the wily Napoleon in persuading Spain to recognize American claims to West Florida.[22]

Under the circumstances, settlers had one of three choices. They might wait patiently for favorable conditions abroad to improve their situation, pray that General Wilkinson's negotiations with Spanish officials in Louisiana were successful, or take matters into their own hands and dispel the hated dons. At least one prophetic official was certain that "a rude people, who have been in the habit of redressing themselves on all occasions," would not "under such circumstances continue quietly and peaceable."[23] Prudence, however, dictated that they adopt a wait-and-see policy.

Further west, along the Mississippi River, the mood was markedly different. While the fretful Bigbee settlers resigned themselves to a bleak future, inhabitants of the Natchez District were jubilant and buoyant. Their concern was not Spaniards or Indians, but who would be governor of Orleans and Mississippi territories.[24]

In late December 1803, as Claiborne departed for New Orleans, where he and General Wilkinson were to accept the transfer of Louisiana, Cato West could hardly believe his good fortune. Suddenly and unexpectedly, he was elevated into the position he had coveted since coming to Mississippi. Although the appointment was temporary, West expected it to become permanent shortly. Surely, he reasoned, Claiborne entertained thoughts of becoming governor of Orleans Territory, and if he succeeded, as his friends expected, Secretary West was in an ideal position to succeed him.[25]

With Claiborne momentarily out of the picture, West was not alone in recognizing the favorable circumstances. For the first time, he was in charge of his own destiny, and he aggressively seized the opportunity. A seasoned politician, he adroitly used his power of patronage to win converts and mollify incumbents. Among the talented and ambitious young immigrants he courted, three were to play active roles in territorial politics. The first was Dr. John Shaw, a native of North Carolina, who dabbled in medicine and read enough law to be licensed upon arrival in Mississippi. As a talented and vitriolic scribbler, he gravitated into politics, which quickly became his sole obsession. Another was young William B. Shields, who, like Judge Rodney, had been a Delaware attorney. Shields had come to the territory with Rodney, and he quickly established a close, avuncular relationship with him. Early on, Shields married into a prominent territorial family that propelled him up the social ladder and afforded him entry into local politics. Finally, there was Judge David Ker, the native of Ireland who had come to the territory in early 1801 from North Carolina, where he founded the state university.[26]

Additionally, West enjoyed the support of his own powerful and gargantuan family, the Greens of Jefferson County, headed in 1804 by Abner and Thomas Marston, sons of Thomas Green. Together, they formed a political faction fiercely loyal to West and dedicated to making him governor. Recognizing the value of a friendly press, West and his supporters persuaded the brothers Samuel and Timothy Terrell to set up the congenial *Mississippi Messenger*. They also made effective use of the Mississippi Republican Society, which they organized in 1802, to champion their cause and mobilize public opinion.[27]

Fortunately for West, the times were propitious. The euphoria over acquisition of Louisiana showed no sign of dissipating. Almost no one disagreed with West's exuberant pronouncement that the date of its transfer, December 20, would "doubtless be remembered & celebrated . . . as the greatest day in the annals of North America next to the 4th of July."[28] As everyone predicted, the acquisition paved the way for accelerated economic activity.

The cotton mania, which gripped the Natchez District, fed much of this spirit. As one new resident declared, "cotton is the rage of this country." Aided by a long growing season, lasting from early May to late September, and an adequate, if not abundant, rainfall, cotton flourished, yielding large and profitable crops that commanded excellent prices in a steadily expanding market. With the region showing signs of realizing its remarkable potential, a number of avid boosters who found the climate salubrious advanced glowing endorsements. The pace of immigration picked up. One traveler even boasted that the territory would "shortly be one of the most powerful and populous provinces of the United States," and there was evidence aplenty to convince even the most skeptical.[29]

The volume of trade at the bustling river port of Natchez increased exponentially, and the city's merchants, their numbers increasing monthly, were thriving as never before. Much of the commercial activity was due to the emergence of affluent planters with tastes for a variety of luxuries, some quite expensive, which Natchez merchants began to import in record amounts from Europe as well as from New York, Philadelphia, and Boston. The slave trade also grew as planters, both recent arrivals and established residents, purchased additional slaves in order to increase production.

The more affluent brought slaves with them or arranged to have them transported from the East shortly after settling in the territory. Entrenched planters and parvenus alike developed a keen, some said obsessive, interest in acquiring ostentatious furnishings, personal and household, which they equated with gentility. One immigrant was surprised to find "a good deal of Genteel company" in the territory, while a later visitor was amazed to discover a substantial community of planters who entertained him lavishly.[30]

Planters were not the only wealthy patrons. The merchants of Natchez too were beneficiaries of the prosperity. In fact, business activity grew at such a pace that the territorial legislature in 1805 petitioned the Bank of the United States to establish a branch in Natchez. Unfortunately, the bank directors were skeptical, but the rejection neither slowed the rate of growth nor stifled enthusiasm.[31]

Given the favorable conditions, West, not unreasonably, expected to keep his current office or persuade Jefferson to promote him. Unfortunately, he underestimated not only his own unpopularity but also the strength of his opponents. In fact, neither Claiborne nor West appreciated the importance Jefferson attached to the governorship of Orleans Territory.

Admittedly there were candidates aplenty for the office that Jefferson, with customary hyperbole, considered as second in importance only to his own. Besides Claiborne, aspirants included such well-known individuals as Daniel Clark Sr., longtime resident of the territory; Vice President Aaron Burr; and that intrepid Tennessean Andrew Jackson. However, none of the three enjoyed favor with Jefferson. Other lesser-known candidates were Thomas Sumner Jr. of South Carolina, William Lyman of Massachusetts, and Gen. Nathaniel Green's son-in-law, Fulwar Skipwith of Virginia, at that time the American consul general in Paris.[32]

Jefferson rejected all of these self-anointed candidates, preferring either the Marquis de Lafayette, whose valuable services in the American Revolution and international acclaim made him "peculiarly acceptable to the country at large," or Jefferson's own friend and protégé James Monroe, whose success in negotiating the Louisiana Purchase consolidated his popularity with westerners. Both declined. Lafayette was enjoying a revival of popularity in France, and Monroe opted to remain in his diplomatic posts at London and Madrid, leaving Jefferson no alternative except Claiborne.[33]

Meanwhile, Cato West had grown enamored with his role as interim governor, relishing the prestige and power it gave him. Taking advantage of a booming economy and a peaceful interlude, he began attracting new friends, including some of Claiborne's former supporters, who found him less distasteful than they expected. By enlarging his network of disciples through patronage, he built up a solid faction, which some called an "insidious junto." The clique sought, as one partisan put it, "to recall W. C. C. and appoint Cato" governor of Mississippi Territory.[34]

Converts included not only Judge Ker and Dr. Shaw but also a number of Adams County Federalists whose enmity for Claiborne was so embedded that they were willing, if only temporarily, to cooperate with anyone to rid the country of what one called "that nincompoop W. C. C." Indeed, Stephen Minor prayed for "God [to] send them good luck on both sides."[35] Together with the sizeable Green family, they represented a formidable force.

On the other hand, Claiborne was hardly without friends, and they rallied to his defense. With encouragement from Claiborne himself, they pressured Jefferson and Madison to name him governor of Orleans. Closer to home, they maneuvered to offset the adverse effect of anti-Claiborne petitions circulating in Jefferson County by encouraging friends in other counties to adopt remonstrances praising Claiborne's tenure as governor and calling for his return to Mississippi.[36]

Not content with limiting their entreaties to paeans of praise, Isaac Briggs and Robert Williams took advantage of a lull in the land business to set off for the nation's capital, where they planned to confront the president personally. Under the guise of suggesting modification of the Land Act of 1803, they hoped to protect themselves by keeping Claiborne in office.

On the way, Briggs and Williams paused in New Orleans to confer with Claiborne. The governor gave them a letter to Jefferson in which he described the machinations of "a small but aspiring Party" that sought to discredit him by insisting that he had lost "the confidence of the President" and by predicting that he would shortly be returned to Natchez "in disgrace."[37]

The delegates met with instant success in the nation's capital. On August 30, 1804, the president signed Claiborne's commission as governor of Orleans Territory, but, accepting Briggs's advice, he restricted it to an "interim" appointment.[38] Obviously Jefferson still entertained hopes of enticing a more prominent person for the post. As Jefferson rather clumsily explained, such an arrangement would allow Claiborne to acquire valuable experience while affording him the opportunity of resigning gracefully if he wished. But Jefferson neglected to clarify why he adopted such an unorthodox approach. Meanwhile, he continued to search for someone who at least spoke French and to prevail upon Lafayette or Monroe to reconsider.[39]

More than anything else, these personal conflicts demonstrated the importance of kinship ties in frontier Mississippi. Family connections explained much of the bickering and backbiting that characterized territorial politics. Political alignments were more likely to be based on familial relationships than political ideologies or economic interests. In an agrarian society like Mississippi Territory, family structures were more extended than nuclear. The importance of matrimonial alliances and blood relations was apparent in the contest between the Claibornes and Greens. Each group used political patronage to feed family ambitions more than to form political parties or to promote economic development. Affluent Mississippians proudly modeled themselves after Virginia planters and English gentry and not after incipient capitalists or a petite bourgeoisie, even if they sometimes behaved like British nabobs. For instance, the Claibornes feared that the Greens, in their obsession to monopolize territorial offices, might undercut their dominance, a belief that intensified as the influence of the once-powerful Hutchins clan began to wane. The rivalry between the Greens and the Claibornes was at its core a struggle over W. C. C. Claiborne's successor.[40]

The selection of a governor was uppermost in the minds of Briggs and Williams when they departed Mississippi for the nation's capital, but once there, they introduced a second issue, one in keeping with the true purpose of their visit. They wanted Edward Turner replaced as register of the western land office. As West's son-in-law, Turner was anathema to Claiborne, especially after the administration rejected the appointment of his brother Ferdinand. Due to the Greens' earlier success in securing offices, some of which they had received from W. C. C. himself, the Claibornites saw Turner's appointment as sinister, and they wanted him ousted. But Briggs and Williams were smart enough to realize that partisan arguments alone were insufficient for Jefferson, so they charged Turner with negligence of duties and malfeasance in office. Since Jefferson had consistently refused to tolerate incompetence or corruption, this tactic produced the desired result.[41]

Removal of Turner was one of several setbacks suffered by the Green-West faction in 1804. The unexpected death of Judge Ker was a particularly tragic blow, and the Greens could find no suitable replacement for him among their friends. Since the only residents with legal knowledge and experience were either Federalists or friends of Claiborne, West and his supporters urged Jefferson to appoint a nonresident of correct political views. They launched this effort with a memorial in the *Messenger*, under the signature of "John Shaw, Chairman," defending the record of Judge Ker and calling for the appointment of a staunch Republican without local connections.[42]

But, in their eagerness to win the president's approval, they committed a fatal error. In attempting to build a case for someone unfamiliar with local politics and with proper legal training, they overreached themselves by denigrating the two sitting judges. They accused Judges Rodney and Bruin of deficiency in judicial knowledge and of being without "that rigid fairness of character, indispensable to the impartial administration of justice." Rodney took immediate umbrage, responding promptly, if somewhat uncharacteristically, in kind. Under the pseudonym "Veritas," he penned a vicious attack on Shaw, whom he called a "quondam pill-maker late from the frog ponds of North Carolina." Rodney correctly predicted that the legislators, who had already "properly treated this libellous memorial . . . with marked reprobation," would again render Shaw's philippic "their severest censure." As for Shaw himself, Rodney continued, "the English vocabulary does not furnish terms sufficiently harsh by which to describe him. . . . He is capable of every meanness [and is] contemptible below all manner of conception;—versed in little villanies."[43]

While Rodney's satirical assessment of Shaw's character was more truthful than tasteful, Jefferson was largely oblivious to the controversy. Yet he met the usual difficulty in locating a qualified replacement. His first choice, Obadiah Jones of Georgia, declined. His second, George Mathews Jr., whose father was so deeply involved in the infamous Yazoo fraud that, when later offered a less controversial appointment to Orleans Territory, he readily accepted it, thereby depriving his defamers of opportunity to mount an opposition. Although the West faction voiced no public objection to either choice, its leaders could hardly be pleased. To compound the faction's misfortunes, Shaw's antics were so disgusting to legislators that in the summer of 1805 they forced his resignation.[44]

Despite a string of disappointments, the Green-West faction still expected Jefferson to retain West. As these hopes began to fade, West and his cohorts became so desperate that they tried to win Rodney's support by dangling the bait of office. They promised to support him for governor if he would desert the Claibornites, but he shunned the overtures, pleading inadequate compensation and poor health.[45] Meanwhile, the Federalists continued their strategy of playing one faction against the other as the best way of injuring Claiborne.

In the summer of 1804, Claiborne sought to dispel all rumors by announcing, through his brother Ferdinand, that he had no intention of returning to Mississippi Territory. His proclamation seemed to confirm prior reports that Jefferson had planned from the beginning to keep him in Orleans, but Jefferson's appointment of Ephraim Kirby as governor of Mississippi Territory sealed West's fate. Disappointed by his inability to resolve political differences in the Southwest and devastated by Kirby's subsequent death, a frustrated Jefferson took the easy way out by following Briggs's recommendation. He offered the Mississippi post to Robert Williams, who, with indecent haste, accepted it.[46]

If Williams was delighted, West was humiliated and embittered. Almost overnight West had watched his dreams sour. Only yesterday he had expected to be governor; now he was left only with his old subordinate position. The prospect of working with someone he had publicly traduced and did not respect him was unappealing. Likewise, the Greens' fortunes had collapsed. West's brief but turbulent tenure left territorial affairs in a shambles, and the Republicans hopelessly split into two warring factions. Many agreed with General Wilkinson's assessment that West's special talent was defiling governors. He "was instrumental in Sargent's removal," Wilkinson explained, and he "opposed Claiborne and would have turned out Williams or his God if he crossed the course of his ambition."[47] The sole beneficiaries in this strange turn of events were the Federalists, and they only momentarily.

CHAPTER 5

A Territory in Transition

By late spring of 1805, Robert Williams, never known for patience, became apprehensive as he awaited the arrival of his commission as governor. Rumors of his appointment were commonplace, but since he had heard nothing officially, he wondered if Jefferson had changed his mind.[1] He remained in a state of uncertainty until early May, when his commission arrived in the federal mails, well known, along the frontier, to be notoriously sporadic and frequently unreliable.[2]

Flattered by Jefferson's display of confidence, Williams accepted with two caveats, both relating to his work as land commissioner. First, he wished to remain commissioner for the western district. Second, he requested (for personal reasons) permission to visit his home in North Carolina once "the land business" was concluded. Jefferson, without the slightest hesitation, consented to both.[3] Despite the extra workload and the political risk of simultaneously holding two of the most influential positions, Williams was still excited.

In fairness to Williams, holding multiple offices by underpaid public officials on the frontier was the rule more than the exception. In Mississippi Territory, the practice was particularly widespread because of the high cost of living, especially in Natchez and Tombigbee District. For example, Thomas Rodney was both territorial judge and land commissioner, and Joseph Chambers once held as many as three appointments—register, Indian factor, and postmaster.[4]

But, in Williams's case, there was a significant difference. None of his predecessors had held multiple offices, an exception that opened

85

him to special criticism. Although his friends, especially Briggs, saw no "incompatibility between the duties of Governor and Commissioner," others did, viewing it as a conflict of interest.[5] Still, Williams did not wish to vacate his position as land commissioner for the District West of the Pearl River, the more controversial of the two boards, until its business was completed, which took until early 1807.

Although Jefferson's selection of Williams was more an act of desperation than deliberation, the new governor was not without qualifications or deficient in political experience. A longtime resident of staunchly Republican North Carolina, Williams served two terms in Congress, where he distinguished himself as the president's steadfast supporter.

In 1803, Jefferson, in recognition of his past loyalty, rewarded him with the important and highly coveted position of land commissioner for the western district, where he struck up a lasting friendship with surveyor Briggs and a cordial but hardly close relationship with his fellow commissioner Thomas Rodney.[6] More partisan and volatile than either of them, Williams developed, shortly after arriving in the territory, an instant dislike for his colleague Edward Turner as well as for the Greens. Later, he was instrumental in removing Turner as register because his connections with the powerful Green family precluded him from acting impartially.[7]

From the outset, Williams tried to solicit favor with the Clalbornites, but they found him more of a political liability than an asset. Irascible in personality and dictatorial in style, Williams was incapable of building a sustained friendship with anyone except Briggs or of instilling loyalty among his supporters. Instead, he attracted enemies as fast as honey draws flies.

Furthermore, it seemed as if, to function effectively, he needed an enemy, real or imagined, and if none existed, he had to invent one or more. Within weeks of assuming office, he managed to antagonize mildmannered Judge Rodney. Insisting that he needed additional space for his expanded administrative duties, Williams summarily evicted the Supreme Court from the Government House. "I believe," an incensed Rodney fumed, exuding more animosity than veracity, "that it is the first instance in America where the Governor has undertaken to dictate to a court of law."[8] But, unfortunately for Williams's sake, it was not the last.

As if his personality were not handicap enough, Williams assumed office as the Republicans were splintering, an outgrowth of the bitterly contested elections of 1804. Unfortunately, he failed to heal the rift, allowing it to fester and grow. Especially during these elections, party labels assumed greater importance than earlier. The Federalists in Adams County, campaigning on a unified ticket, captured three of its four seats in the lower house. Only the popularity of the governor's brother, Ferdinand L. Claiborne, prevented them from making a clean sweep. In Jefferson County, where the Greens reigned supreme, the reverse was true. There, as well as in the other river counties, the Republicans remained in the majority. On the other hand, political parties failed to develop in the Tombigbee District, where strong personalities and family ties, not party shibboleths, determined partisan differences.[9]

Once elected, however, they quickly discarded party labels, even those who had used them extensively in the previous elections. Instead, personal relationships and family connections more than party affiliations explained the bitter divisions that plagued the General Assembly during its third session, which began in December of 1804. Rather than rallying around common political principles, the Republican members split into two irreconcilable factions, one loyal to Cato West and the other to the Claibornes. As Briggs explained, "the republican interest altho' abundantly triumphant when united, is rendered totally inefficient by these unhappy divisions."[10]

The schism in Republican ranks momentarily gave the Federalists the balance of power in the General Assembly, and they exercised it to advantage. Cooperating with the West faction, they were largely responsible for broadening the franchise and reapportioning representation in the legislature. Both measures benefited the Federalists, although neither was a part of their normal political lexicon. In the process, the Federalists were able to forge a close if short-lived alliance with the West faction, who expected these reforms to strengthen the Natchez Federalists and undermine Republican efforts to seize control of Adams County.[11]

The brief resurrection of the Federalists was due more to the reputation of their leaders than to the appeal of party loyalty. Like their counterparts in the eastern states, these local Federalists tenaciously clung to those traditional and anachronistic principles of the original party, which had never gained much favor along the frontier and enjoyed only modest support elsewhere. Whatever respect the Federalists attracted in the territory was based primarily upon the wealth they possessed and the social prominence they commanded and not upon the principles they espoused.[12]

Rebirth of the Federalist Party was evident first during the lengthy and acrimonious legislative session of late 1804 and early 1805. Elections of the previous summer, when partisan differences resembled a melodrama, left the legislature hopelessly divided among three intractable factions: old-style Federalists, Claiborne Republicans, and the Green-West cabal. In fact, these factional divisions developed so suddenly and became so pervasive that the legislature soon reached an impasse.[13]

Because all four Federalists were members of the lower house, their influence in the General Assembly was greater than it might have been otherwise, but this advantage was quickly offset by controversies surrounding the elections in Adams County, where three of the four Federalists resided. According to several petitioners, the elections there were so replete with "intrigues and frauds" that the voice of qualified voters was silenced. They accused "a few designing men" with distributing "upwards of one hundred persons," most of whom were transients, fraudulent deeds, "usually made for 50 acres of land . . . with a view to the election of certain candidates." If the government countenanced such irregularities, they admonished, future elections would "be controlled by a few wealthy freeholders" because the timely and "accidental arrival of one or two hundred persons in our territory on their way to or from New Orleans will . . . always fix the fate of our elections." One outspoken critic, expressing the sentiments of a majority of the qualified voters, labeled it "an election pregnant with the blackest fraud."[14]

As acting governor, West had good reason to curry favor with Federalists, and he deftly ignored the pleas of the disaffected to nullify the results. But the General Assembly, spearheaded by the same Federalists that West was courting, moved to address two of the more serious issues exposed by the election results which West himself unwisely chose to ignore. Even the Claibornites, who otherwise had little to gain, acknowledged that reform was necessary.

All factions understood that Congress, by restricting the franchise to those who possessed "a freehold in fifty acres of Land," had inadvertently disfranchised "a very considerable part of its respectable citizens" (urban dwellers with town lots or homes) and thereby had encouraged the fraud that everyone was now condemning. As long as affluent residents of Natchez remained without an effective voice in county government, they had little reason to prevent the fraudulent voting.

Aware of the obvious connection between a restricted franchise and voting irregularities, the General Assembly petitioned Congress to extend the franchise to taxpayers who had resided in the district for at least one year. In addition, it sought permission to reapportion representation in the lower house to conform with recent population shifts, provided the total number of representatives did not exceed twelve (an increase of two members), a modification that benefited Adams County at the expense of Jefferson. Due to the growth of Natchez, the 1810 population of Adams County was nearly twice that of Jefferson County. No longer would Republican Jefferson County enjoy equal representation with Federalist Adams.[15]

This legislative session also had to address two other matters. The terms of the territorial delegate to Congress and the Legislative Council were due to expire shortly, and the General Assembly was to select suitable replacements. In the case of the Legislative Council, the lower house nominated a slate of ten (two each from the five counties) from which the president chose five.[16] In contrast to the conciliatory spirit that had characterized debates over the franchise and reapportionment, these two actions, because they involved personalities and patronage rather than principles, provoked prolonged controversy.

In selecting a slate of nominees, the three factions, according to Rodney, pursued a common strategy, that of "Endeavoring to exclude the favorites of each other." As a result, the assembly agreed upon a list of names few recognized and only a handful favored. As Rodney reported, "a good deal of dissatisfaction has been expressed out of doors at this Choice." Yet if no one was satisfied with the results, still the Assembly had averted a potential crisis. Under the conditions, the only alternative to recommending a list of nonentities was to adjourn, and few, if any, favored such a destructive course. Nevertheless, each nominee professed to be a Republican, a serious disappointment for those Federalists who had expected to benefit from Republican disunity. Again, according to Rodney, "the more respectable part of the Community [was] desirous that the President Should Select the Fittest of them to Compose the Legislative council."[17]

On the other hand, selecting a territorial delegate proved even more divisive. Unlike the previous debate, the assembly adjourned before reaching a decision because its members, divided immovably along factional lines, were unwilling either to compromise on a "dark horse" or to coalesce around one of the avowed candidates.[18]

As dictated by statute, the General Assembly, in selecting a delegate to Congress, met in joint session. In early balloting, the four Federalists rallied behind William Gordon Forman, patriarch of a large contingent of New Jersey Presbyterians who, after migrating to Natchez in 1790, settled along St. Catherine's Creek. On the other hand, Republicans divided equally between Edward Turner, son-in-law of Cato West, and the incumbent William Lattimore, a favorite of the Claibornites. After a third ballot ended with similar results, the Green-West faction switched to Cato West. Two factors informed this surprising decision. First, Turner's supporters had misjudged the extent of his unpopularity, and they realized belatedly that this obstacle was too much to overcome. Second, West himself acquired an interest in the position once he learned that Jefferson had offered the governorship to Ephraim Kirby.[19]

Instantly, West's enemies accused him of acting out of spite. According to Williams, West, "knowing that he could not be elected," entered the race "in order to prevent any appointment."[20] Nevertheless, Williams's hatred of West clouded his judgment since the legislative deadlock preceded rather than followed West's announcement. As many suspected, West was disinclined to disappear quietly. But, in recognizing that West's chances of winning were no better than Turner's, Williams was more perceptive. Because West's late entry perturbed more legislators than it placated, his last-minute heroics had no effect on the outcome. The stalemate continued.

After six fruitless ballots, Speaker Philander Smith, disgusted by the impasse and annoyed by "desultory conversation" among several members about whether to adjourn or not, terminated the balloting. Despite a boisterous chorus of objections from Lattimore's incensed supporters, Smith refused to budge.

The next day, after the House reassembled, a handful of "Claibornites" filed into the chamber, demanding another canvass, but the Speaker, emboldened by the favorable reaction to his prior ruling, ignored their presence and proceeded with business.[21] Nevertheless, the little fracas left the territory without a voice in Congress or an official liaison with the Jefferson administration. Meanwhile, a disgruntled West went into seclusion at his country estate near Greenville, taking along the official records. Governor Williams made several unsuccessful overtures to recover them, but West ignored his importunities while he clung to the secretary's office. In the end, his petulance brought more grief than gratitude, and even his friends grew tired of his juvenile antics. West soon realized that his enemies welcomed his aberrance in order to discredit him with Jefferson.[22]

Taking the only sensible option open left, West resigned before the president dismissed him. On the other hand, it required an act of the legislature to retrieve the territorial records. Afterward, West surprised everyone by withdrawing from politics, allowing Williams to enjoy a brief respite. West was not to hold public office again until after the War of 1812, when he served briefly in the territory's last Legislative Council and in the Constitutional Convention of 1817.[23]

By the summer of 1805, with an improving local economy, Williams had every reason to anticipate a successful administration. In fact, the public seemed to agree. On May 13, 1805, Williams's inauguration took place amid what Briggs described as "an uncommon degree of enthusiasm in the people." With West's departure, Williams's spirits rose accordingly. "Colonel West has had his political frolic," he informed Madison, "and all things are quiet." Briggs was equally sanguine. Insisting that West's "very small junto" would be hostile to anyone "outside of the clan," he assured Jefferson that West's resignation had improved the political climate immeasurably.[24]

Factors other than West's fortuitous retirement were responsible for the people's satisfaction and the governor's confidence. Most important was the region's reputation as a land of opportunity. Mississippi Territory was experiencing a wave of prosperity due largely to an unprecedented increase in population and to a highly favorable international market for cotton and the territory's other agricultural products.[25] The peaceful acquisition of Louisiana prepared the way for an influx of settlers by permanently opening the Mississippi River to western commerce and by removing any likelihood that an aggressive France might replace an impotent Spain at its doorstep.

The rage for cotton, if not in full bloom, was certainly in early blossom. With renewed peace in Europe following the Treaty of Amiens in 1802, demand for the white fiber soared, and the fertile soil and tropical climate of the Old Southwest were ideally suited for its cultivation. Even the outbreak of renewed warfare in Europe failed to dampen demand.

As a result, newcomers flocked into those parts of the territory free of Indian titles, sometimes squatting on vacant lands, in an effort to take advantage of the promising conditions.[26]

Immigrants were attracted by the glowing reports of travelers, surveyors, and other commentators as well as by a barrage of letters from territorial residents to relatives and friends back East. As early as 1802, Thomas Fenton, one of several surveyors who came to the Southwest seeking lands both for clients as well as themselves, instantly recognized the territory's potential. He predicted that the Natchez District would become "the garden of all America" as well as "a place of importance to the States." "The prospects of advancement to prosperity," he declared, were unsurpassed. He found "the soil fertile[,] the Climate genial and production" prodigious, largely because it was blessed with the presence of numerous streams, most of them navigable for some distance. "Every Creek of any size," Fenton reported, "is Navigable 3/4 of the year [for] a Distance of fifteen or twenty miles from the Mississippi which affords almost every Planter Navigation to his Door."[27]

Another recent traveler was equally enthusiastic. He described it as "the most important country that ever blessed the face of the Globe!" Ironically, Thomas Rodney, who complained incessantly about his meager salary and repeatedly threatened to return to Delaware, even tried to entice his son Caesar A. Rodney to the Natchez District. He described the climate as "delightful" and the soil as "more prolific than any to the Eastward." Land, he said, was "easy to acquire," and "lawyers make a fortune here."[28]

Lured by the glowing reports, newcomers came from everywhere, though predominantly from one of several southern states, and with varying backgrounds, though mostly of British stock. They also followed a variety of routes, some by sea or river and others along one of several trails or pathways (sometimes erroneously called roads) through Indian territory. A few came with slaves and fineries, but most traveled alone or in small family clans, bringing with them few possessions and little ready cash. Most expected to acquire land readily and cheaply; a few hoped to start a business or engage in some commercial venture; and all sought a better existence for themselves and their families.[29]

As long as good land was still available, more of the early settlers flourished than failed. Most successful were those who brought slaves or who could afford to purchase them in markets that sprang up in Natchez and nearby New Orleans. In fact, African Americans were the fastest growing portion of the population during the first decade of the nineteenth century. Their percentage of the population increased from 42 percent in 1801 to 47 percent by 1810, when they totaled 17,088, and their presence was a testament to the importance of cotton. Therefore, as early as 1810, at least the Natchez District acquired the attributes of a plantation economy, resembling a southern more than a frontier society.[30]

While favorable conditions were evident everywhere, the territory was not without problems, most of them beyond the governor's power to alter or ameliorate. Its prosperity was largely dependent upon continuation of American trade with western Europe, especially Great Britain, and Mississippians were aware that any interruption of commerce would have an immediate, and possibly disastrous, effect on their economy. Once the Napoleonic wars in Europe became a stalemate between an England dominant on the high seas and a France invincible on the continent, both belligerents resorted to commercial warfare to bring the war to a quick and favorable resolution.[31]

With this strategy in place, each belligerent tried to cripple its adversaries by regulating neutral trade between Europe and United States. Additionally, between 1807 and 1809, England, determined to retain dominance of the Atlantic trade, issued a series of Orders-in-Council requiring American vessels destined for the continent to pass through the British Isles, where the cargo was subject to oppressive duties and sometimes to confiscation. In retaliation, Napoleon ordered seizure of American ships complying with British restrictions. Happily, neither nation enforced its restrictions vigorously, since both remained dependent upon American commerce as long as war lasted. Nevertheless American merchants resented the interference, and American trade suffered as a consequence.[32]

Then, in the summer of 1807, the British added insult to injury by firing on the USS *Chesapeake* and removing four alleged deserters. Americans were exhausted.[33] Clamor for war rose from everywhere except New England, where the Federalists, for a variety of reasons, were less incensed. But Jefferson, rather than declaring war, persuaded a compliant Congress to clamp an embargo on American exports.

In deciding to adopt the same strategy as his European tormentors as well as to prove the Republican axiom that American commerce was so vital to the European belligerents that they would agree to respect American rights rather than risk losing its trade, Jefferson miscalculated. Instead of bringing England or France or both to heel, as he expected, the embargo brought chaos to the United States, and Mississippians, along with others, suffered severe hardship as bales of unsold cotton piled up in warehouses at Natchez and New Orleans while the cost of goods they had to buy either remained unchanged or rose slightly.[34]

Under these circumstances, numerous planters plummeted into debt and a few into bankruptcy while Jefferson and Madison steadfastly refused to abandon commercial coercion. Although Congress provided some relief to those who had purchased public lands on credit under the Land Act of 1800, it offered nothing to the legion of other debtors who had borrowed recklessly to acquire more lands and slaves in anticipation of flush times.[35] As a result, the territory's economy showed more signs of depression than prosperity, and beginning in mid 1808, the pace of immigration slackened considerably, trends that continued uninterrupted until the return of peace in 1815.

Although the increase in population between the acquisition of Louisiana in 1803 and the Embargo Act in late 1807 was impressive, it might have been larger except for confusion over land titles. In fact, until the federal government commenced the sale of public lands, it was incapable of accommodating incoming settlers reluctant to migrate to a region where land titles were subject to litigation and squatters to ejection.[36] Unfortunately, land sales could not commence until the two boards had finished their work and surveyor Briggs had divided the territory into ranges and townships.

Secretary of the Treasury Gallatin was not alone in realizing that the territory's most urgent problem was too much land and too few inhabitants, an unfortunate dilemma in an exposed region settled primarily by entrepreneurs and speculators and surrounded by hostile Spaniards and restless Indians. The shortage of population troubled both established and potential residents, as well as a Republican administration searching for an economical way of simultaneously preserving the peace and expanding westward.

Consequently, everyone (except the uneasy Indian nations) had reason to encourage immigration. The federal government, and especially Gallatin, welcomed anticipated revenue from land sales; speculators hoped to attract a bevy of avid buyers; apprehensive settlers found security in numbers; and entrepreneurs wished to augment business. There was also common agreement on the appropriate solution—promote settlement through treaties of cession with the Indians and the early sale of public lands.[37] Unfortunately, both solutions were easier to articulate than to accomplish.

In one respect, the territory was particularly blessed. The four Indian nations (Choctaw, Chickasaw, Creek, and Cherokee) that shared possession of the territory with the white and black settlers were more peaceful than bellicose. In contrast to the confederation of restless tribes in Northwest Territory, those in the Southwest gave the United States less cause to seize their lands by force. Except for a few incidents of petty stealing and an occasional murder, relations between the races were rarely strained seriously.[38] This was especially true of the two Indian nations—the Choctaw and the Chickasaw—occupying the western half of the territory.

The reasons for this passivity were as obvious as they were tragic. Over the years, both nations had become so dependent upon European goods and so heavily in debt to white traders that they could ill afford to antagonize the United States. Even among the more militant Creek, relations improved through the Herculean efforts of American agent Benjamin Hawkins, who encouraged them to take up husbandry and to embrace the "civilizing" policies of Jefferson. To a lesser extent, agents John McKee and Silas Dinsmoor served a similar purpose with the more pliable Choctaws and Chickasaws.[39] The Cherokee, who resided principally in northern and western Georgia and in the Tennessee Valley, were never a serious concern of Mississippians.

Known as the "Civilized Tribes," these four nations tried, in their own way, to accommodate the whites and to embrace, for a time, Jefferson's policies, even though it meant compromising or discarding some of their cherished cultural traditions. Although not everyone agreed, Jefferson's motive was more to satisfy the land hunger of white settlers than to promote Indian welfare. With respect to the Choctaw, who possessed more territorial lands than any of the other three tribes, Jefferson's policy paid handsome dividends. Because of their propensity for European goods, the Choctaw remained constantly in debt to foreign traders—first to the British firm of Panton, Leslie and Company and its successors and later to the American factories that the federal government had set up to wean them from the British. Under strong pressure from these creditors, the Choctaw were forced periodically to sacrifice their one remaining asset—land—in order to extinguish these debts, a process that would eventually culminate, during the 1820s and 1830s, in their removal to new lands in Arkansas and Oklahoma.[40]

Between 1801 and 1805, the United States, in a series of four treaties, purchased from the hapless Choctaw more than 6 million acres of choice farmland. In the last of these treaties, signed in 1805 at Mount Dexter, the Choctaw ceded the region between the Tombigbee and Pearl rivers. This cession particularly delighted the isolated eastern settlers who would no longer have to travel through hostile Indian country in order to reach the territorial capital.[41]

In contrast, President Jefferson was displeased. He had preferred a cession along the Mississippi River north of Walnut Hills, where the soil was richer and the settlers would enjoy unimpeded access to the sea rather than an interior one where the Spaniards would still extract a duty on both imports and exports. Rodney, for one, agreed with Jefferson's assessment. He once described this part of the country, also known as "the Yazoo land," as "the Garden of the Territories." Fearful that potential settlers would find the latter lands less attractive than those along the Mississippi, Jefferson refused to submit the treaty to the Senate until late 1807, when the threat of renewed hostilities with Spain made this acquisition strategically important.[42]

While negotiations with the Indians were progressing, the two boards of land commissioners, one meeting in the town of Washington in Adams County and the other at Fort Stoddert in Washington County, began their deliberations in late 1803. Expecting the registration of claims to take no more than a year, settlers proceeded to the territory in anticipation that land sales would begin no later than 1805. But nothing went as planned. Even the eastern board, where registrations were fewer and less controversial than those in its western counterpart, did not file its final report until September 21, 1805.[43] On the other hand, western commissioners encountered one problem after another, forcing postponement of its final report and delaying land sales far beyond the expectations of anyone.[44]

Under the provisions of the Land Act of 1803, the two boards were to invite landholders to come forward and file their claims with the register. The boards were then to record each claim, noting every conveyance that had occurred and, when appropriate, to interrogate claimants and other witnesses. In those cases where the board found a claim both valid and uncontested, it was to issue the applicant a certificate of confirmation under which the federal government surrendered all rights to the land. But in those cases where a claim conflicted with a prior British grant, the supplicant could receive a patent only by a favorable judicial decision.[45]

The claimants were allowed until the last day of March 1804 to present their evidence and the two boards until the end of the same year to submit a report to the secretary of the treasury, under whose jurisdiction the land office fell. Initially, both boards enjoyed a brisk business. By early April 1804, a pleased Kirby, commissioner for Washington County, reported that the work of the eastern board had "progressed very favourably."[46]

On the other hand, his western colleague Rodney was less optimistic. Although "nearly 2,000 claims" had been filed by the same date, he discovered that many of them were "adverse and Interferring," and he predicted that it would "take up much time to Examine and to determine with Justice and correctness" their validity. "We can't be through before October Next [1805]," he lamented, but even this pessimistic prediction was overly optimistic.[47]

Claimants and commissioners alike uncovered several deficiencies in the legislation and experienced considerable confusion as a result of complex procedures and ambiguous regulations. Moreover, the federal government failed to provide the commissioners with critical information, forcing them to improvise. For instance, they lacked copies of the treaties of 1783 and 1794 with England or the 1802 Articles of Agreement with Georgia, official documents essential to their work. Also, they quickly discovered the need for a Spanish translator and for a competent attorney to represent the government's interest, particularly in cases of antedated Spanish grants or other instances of suspected fraud.[48] Since many registrants could not produce written documentation in support of their claims because of their own carelessness or some natural catastrophe, the commissioners were forced to rely, more than was legally permissible, upon oral testimony of claimants and corroborating witnesses. Consequently, the western board, in the interest of fairness to distressed claimants, was compelled to function as a board of equity despite its inability to summon witnesses and compel their testimony.[49]

A more serious disruption stemmed from the frequent turnover of personnel. For the most part, the high rate was the result of unexpected deaths, sudden resignations, forced removals, or unauthorized and prolonged absences from the territory. For instance, Kirby died just as the eastern board was in the process of wrapping up its work; Williams and Briggs took off in early 1804 for an extended pilgrimage to the seat of government; another commissioner departed within a month of arrival; a register of the eastern district appeared briefly and left hastily; Jefferson dismissed Turner in the midst of the proceedings, and his replacement was suspected of speculating in British claims; and Rodney's duties as territorial judge conflicted with those of land commissioner, compelling him to neglect one or the other.[50]

These developments made it difficult not only for the board to find a convenient time to meet but also to obtain a quorum, causing additional delays and strained relationships among the commissioners. After the commissioners began deliberations on December 4, 1803, they were able to meet, for want of a quorum, only intermittently and rarely as a full board.[51]

Not all the delays were due to negligent officials or flawed legislation. Uneasy claimants also created problems. Many possessed what they believed were irrevocable grants based upon either Spanish patents or warrants of survey, only to learn that the land act had specifically validated only Spanish patents. Aware that most of the Spanish claims were patched over with prior British grants, more than a few feared that Jay's Treaty might give an unfair advantage to British claimants.[52] In fact, these anxieties reached fever pitch after the western board unintentionally created a "dreadful ferment." In an attempt to accommodate Judge Elihu Hall Bay of South Carolina, the largest of several British claimants, Rodney allowed him to survey his claim at Walnut Hills so that he might return home. It took all of Rodney's powers of persuasion to convince anxious Spanish claimants that allowing him to survey the land "made nothing in favor of Judge Bay's claim."[53]

In such an atmosphere, runaway speculation and favoritism were widespread, alarming newcomers and anxious claimants as well as the landless. Little wonder, then, that a number of uneasy settlers banded together and decided to boycott the proceedings. As a consequence, claims, which previously had flowed in steadily, began to trickle in or not at all. Meanwhile the western board sat bewildered and helpless, unable to make any decisions until all outstanding claims were filed.

Furthermore, the law required the commissioners, before they could issue a certificate of confirmation, to list every conflicting claim. Eventually, board members became as frustrated as claimants, blaming each other for the delays, which were both unnecessary and avoidable.[54]

The crisis turned serious when the best claimants—those possessing uncontested Spanish grants—objected to several provisions in the act. They were particularly annoyed by having to register anew lands previously confirmed by Spain and to resurvey, at their expense, lands that had been surveyed more than once. They were also required to record, paying a set fee for each hundred words, each past transaction, which, in a few cases, reached a dozen. Since the Agreement of 1802 with Georgia had validated most of these claims, it was hardly surprising that a sizeable number became so fearful of having their claims rejected by the board that they refused to file, bringing the work of western commissioners to a standstill.[55]

The federal officials not unreasonably assumed that the two boards and the surveyor for lands south of Tennessee would cooperate. As everyone recognized, claims could not be surveyed until the board issued a certificate of confirmation. No one better understood the problem posed by this restriction than surveyor Briggs. A devout Quaker and a dedicated public servant, he was also a close friend and confidant of Jefferson. In fact, Jefferson had such a high opinion of Briggs's abilities that he once proclaimed him "second to no man in the United States," comparing him favorably "in point of science, in astronomy, geometry, and mathematics" to the renowned Andrew Ellicott.[56]

Briggs's Quaker conscience encouraged him toward perfectionism, but he soon recognized that his penchant for precision put him at odds with Albert Gallatin's well-known passion for parsimony. Concerned more with economy than efficiency, he chided Briggs to keep his expenses within budget even at the expense of accuracy. On one occasion, a normally tactful Gallatin became so irritated that he fumed to Jefferson that "the degree of correctness contemplated by Mr. Briggs could not be obtained for five times the sum allowed by law."[57] On the other hand, while Gallatin's admonishments offended Briggs, the surveyor was too dedicated a public servant to allow these criticisms to interfere with his work schedule.

Still, Gallatin's policy of retrenchment created problems for Briggs. He had difficulty attracting and retaining competent deputies at the authorized rate of four dollars per mile. In setting the compensation at this level, Briggs was sure that Gallatin and Congress had failed to recognize the high cost of living in Mississippi Territory and the difficulty of surveying terrain matted over with thick cane and interspersed with deep gullies, rocky creeks, and steep hills. As early as February 10, 1804, Briggs reported that the surveying was "now completely at a stand[still]."[58]

With claimants reluctant to come forward, Briggs reported that he could not "commence the survey of claims" for at least a year. Therefore he and Commissioner Williams set off for the nation's capital, ostensibly "to correct defects of the land-law of this territory . . . and of those likely to occur in Louisiana." Unaware of the political motive behind the excursion, Gallatin was furious since Congress had already made the suggested changes in the law. Still, Briggs continued to agitate for better wages for his deputies. He kept up his complaints until an exasperated Gallatin bluntly informed him that Congress had no intention of increasing the compensation and that he was not expected "to complete your work in that scientifick manner which was desirable." Instead, Gallatin ordered him to make the surveys "as correct as can be done at that rate."[59]

In response, Briggs made a determined effort to expedite the work by notifying his two deputy surveyors, George Davis and Charles DeFrance, of Gallatin's instructions. Unfortunately, in directing his spleen on them rather than Gallatin, Briggs, always the firm taskmaster, pushed the two deputies too far. Davis, the more volatile of the two, brought charges against Briggs for dereliction of duty, which Gallatin felt obliged to investigate. He commissioned register Thomas Williams and Dunbar to investigate the matter "privately." Briggs grew suspicious, and he seized the first opportunity to return to the nation's capital. He unexpectedly left on November 18, 1806, bearing secret dispatches from Gen. James Wilkinson and never returned.[60]

For several months thereafter, surveying in both districts stopped until Gallatin named a replacement. In March 1807, he replaced an oversensitive Briggs with a methodical Seth Pease, a surveyor of less distinction but more stability. In clarifying his duties, Gallatin left no room for ambiguity. "I will repeat what I had often urged to your predecessor," he wrote. "The speedy completion of the survey of private claims & public lands in the Mississippi Territory is an object of great national importance which has been delayed much beyond our rational expectations."

Pease diligently brought the surveying of public lands to a point where Gallatin was prepared to announce the opening of a land office.[61]

Meanwhile, hundreds of incoming settlers were caught in a vicious cycle. Upon arrival in the territory, the heads of families, expecting the sale of public lands to begin no later than the summer of 1805, were disheartened to discover no land offices and the prospects for future sales discouraging. Short of cash, they, more often than not, lacked the resources to purchase private lands, either from individuals or anxious speculators. In fact, most of them arrived in the territory with more dreams in their heads than dollars in their pockets. A few of the more destitute, attracted by Spanish offers of free lands, moved into adjacent West Florida.[62] While a few chose to rent or lease lands, a majority opted to squat upon unoccupied land free of Indian title. Then, as soon as they had made some improvements upon the land, they petitioned the federal government for preemption rights. Not wishing to give undue encouragement to intruders, Gallatin opposed extending preemption rights to them, but he worried lest a sympathetic Congress acquiesce in the face of strong pressure.[63]

By late 1808, Gallatin had additional reasons for demanding land sales. By then the effects of the Embargo Act, which drastically reduced revenues from imposts, was beginning to be felt by the Treasury Department. Consequently, in early 1809, Gallatin authorized the opening of a land office at Nashville even though the surveying was incomplete. Unfortunately, Gallatin's woes did not end. Most of the customers, including preemptors, brought their lands on credit. Consequently, the economic depression, which subsequently hit the territory, made it difficult if not impossible for a number of them to meet the payments on time. With monotonous regularity, they petitioned the federal government for an extension, and, more often than not, they received it.[64] The unraveling of conflicting claims and the disposal of millions of acres of unsettled lands was a seemingly unending process that kept territorial affairs in turmoil until statehood and beyond.

CHAPTER 6

Ruffians along the Border

As the settlers in Natchez District began to reflect on their first decade under American rule, they had good reason for optimism. The population had grown steadily, if not sensationally, the economy was vibrant enough to encourage the more affluent to import foreign wines and fashionable household furnishings, and their closest neighbors no longer seemed to be the threat they once were. Nonetheless, not everything was so rosy. The competence of their political officials, both elected and appointed, failed to keep pace with the signs of progress. Bitter partisan feuds, intense personal rivalries, and anxiety over land titles continued to undermine an otherwise promising future.

Despite the favorable conditions at the outset of his governorship, Robert Williams's honeymoon was short. He had barely entered office before his enemies were scrutinizing his actions and questioning his judgment, and the reasons were obvious and predictable. Unlike his predecessors, Williams had participated in the territory's factious politics and was a known partisan of the previous governor. In the process, he had acquired a few devoted friends but, more importantly, a host of bitter enemies, several of whom were to make his life miserable.[1]

If Williams's appointment surprised some, it jolted the Greens, who had expected West to be the next governor. Embittered by this unexpected and inexplicable development, they blamed Williams rather than Jefferson for the misfortune. After all, Williams was conveniently accessible and Jefferson was not, and as long as the president held the patronage power, it was unwise to antagonize him unnecessarily.[2]

To no one's surprise, the governor's strongest critics were the Greens of Jefferson County, whose patriarch was Thomas. Like so many early settlers, Thomas was a native of Virginia who had come to Natchez District while it was Spanish territory. After temporarily moving to Georgia, Thomas had himself appointed one of four commissioners of the aborted Bourbon County project. Expelled by the Spaniards for his participation, Thomas remained in exile briefly before returning to Natchez, where he took the requisite oath of allegiance, remaining a disinterested and distraught resident until the United States assumed control in 1798. Regaining his thirst for politics, he became, in quick succession, leader of the anti-Ellicott forces, advocate for local autonomy, and vociferous critic of Governor Sargent.[3]

Through a series of carefully orchestrated marriages, Thomas Green extended his influence, enlarged his political connections, and acquired a reputation for intrigue. While the family was still in Virginia, Thomas's only daughter had married Cato West, and the newlyweds accompanied the family to Natchez District. Abner, another of Thomas's sons, married a daughter of Anthony Hutchins, who, together with the Greens, formed the territory's Republican Party. Thomas continued to act as family patriarch until 1804, when he turned the reins over to his eldest son, Thomas Marston. By then, Cato West had emerged as the family's most visible member, becoming its titular if not official head. Consequently, when the Greens sought someone to realize their dream of winning the governorship, they had turned to West rather than Thomas Marston.[4]

Because the Greens' craving for power was so transparent and tenacious, they attracted more foes than friends, and their opponents were as determined to deprive West of the prize he craved as the family was to obtain it. But their opponents had a better pipeline to Jefferson. Although few suspected it, Jefferson had already decided not to appoint West. In fact, he was more convinced of West's unfitness than he was of Williams's fitness for the position.[5]

While the Greens' dislike of Williams was understandable, they were not alone in distrusting the new governor. The "Ancient Inhabitants," or longtime residents, were another. Having already overcome, at considerable personal sacrifice, a host of vicissitudes in converting a raw wilderness into a respectable community, they resented the influx of immigrants who threatened to monopolize the small number of lucrative public offices and introduce unwise social and political changes. As a newly appointed public official, Williams was the logical target since he was cursed twice, both as neophyte and land jobber. His critics could, and often did, regard him alternately as someone uninterested in their affairs or as a charlatan with friends to reward, prejudices to conceal, and alien principles to espouse.

In comparing West and Williams, the "Ancient Inhabitants" came to view the latter with misgivings. They questioned his loose ties to the territory, and a few even suspected him of harboring Federalist tendencies. Expecting the new governor to come from the ranks of those political veterans who by ousting Sargent had introduced an intoxicating spirit of republicanism, they were disappointed when Jefferson selected an ambitious, inexperienced novice who, in their opinion, had neither earned the right to public office nor possessed the maturity to govern.[6]

Initially, Williams believed the attacks were generic and not personal. As his friends repeatedly assured him, only the appointment of West would have satisfied his critics. Even President Jefferson agreed. He advised Williams to build a strong political base and restore political harmony by healing the schism within Republican ranks and by wooing moderate and "well meaning" Federalists. Unfortunately, Williams, by temperament and inclination, lacked the political finesse to pull it off. Instead, he preferred to accept the comforting conclusions of Isaac Briggs, who assured him that the removal of West, the demise of Judge Ker, and the resignation of John Shaw from the legislature would restore harmony.[7]

Upon assuming the governorship, Williams knew he needed a new secretary, and nearly everyone, except the governor himself, expected West to resign. Indeed, the Greens had threatened "that if he [West] was not appointed the Governor he would not act as Secretary." But to Williams this bold pronouncement was more ruse than promise. If Williams doubted West's intention to leave voluntarily, he was positive of one thing—the two of them could never work together. Williams was convinced that West, by carting off the territorial records and seal to Greenville, had deliberately tried to provoke him. For months, West remained defiant, protecting the records in order, as he explained, to uphold the integrity of the office and fulfill his responsibility. In frustration, Williams was compelled temporarily to hire a private secretary at his own expense and to exert legislative pressure.[8]

Consequently, Williams and the loyal Briggs plotted to oust West and destroy his credibility. In their view, West was "too hostile to the present administration and too unpopular . . . to answer any good purpose as Secretary." Convinced that West's days as secretary were numbered, Briggs and Williams had already picked a successor. As early as June 1805, they were recommending Thomas Hill Williams (no relation), register of the western land district. Both described him as a firm Republican, a diffident and disarming individual, and a thoroughly loyal public servant. In other words, his principal qualification was an absence of those traits that Robert Williams had found so offensive in West.[9]

Unfortunately, Thomas Williams was reluctant to undertake additional duties when those of register completely absorbed his time and energy. To him, the land business was more critical to the territory's future than administrative chores. Land, as he succinctly but clumsily put it, was "a subject in which hang if not all their affection, at least all their anxieties." Worried that "the labors of the commissioners conjunctly and of the Register separately will be daily increasing," he agreed to serve only until the year's end.[10]

If Governor Williams expected to silence his critics by depriving West of office, he was sadly mistaken. West and his friends, without a public platform from which to defend themselves or denounce their opponents, took their cause "out of doors." First, they published, in distorted fashion, the correspondence between the governor and secretary in order to air West's side of the controversy. They also denounced Williams for infringing on the secretary's prerogative and for acting in a dictatorial and high-handed manner.[11]

Williams's normal reaction to personal attacks was to respond in kind, but, on this occasion, he wisely took the high road. In deference to friends, who advised him to disregard the outcries of a desperate man, he refrained from starting a nasty imbroglio with West. Consequently, his cautious but calculated conduct deflated West and left him few options. Using as an excuse his squabble with the secretary of the treasury over reimbursement for services rendered as acting governor, West resigned on July 8, 1805, carefully timing the announcement to coincide with convening of the legislature. As secretary, West was responsible for recording the minutes of each session and publishing the laws. By attending only its opening session, West made his subsequent absences especially conspicuous.[12] Nonetheless, Williams had achieved the first of two objectives.

Next he called the legislature into special session, hoping to cajole it into sending a friendly delegate to Congress. Although the summons entailed both administrative expense and personal inconvenience for legislators, which distressed him and disturbed his critics, Williams justified it on the need to discipline West by compelling him to execute his duties and to offer the General Assembly a chance to correct its past shortcomings.[13]

But Williams was disappointed when sharp divisions reappeared. Again, each of the three factions rallied around a favorite for delegate: Federalists behind John Steele, moderate Republicans behind the prominent planter John Ellis, and the Radicals behind Cato West. Williams felt vindicated when the legislature, rather than deadlocking, renamed Dr. William Lattimore delegate and chastised West, requiring him, on pain of a fine, to return the territorial records and publish laws of the last session.[14]

Pleased with the results, Williams presumed he had bested his critics, restored peace to a turbulent frontier, and disciplined West. In late summer of 1805, he gleefully wrote Secretary of State Madison that "Colo. West has had his political frolic" and "all things are quiet." But Judge Thomas Rodney was more realistic. Finding "the party spirit" still "strong and virulent," he believed Williams had "lost the confidence of the people."[15]

In one respect, Williams's rosy assessment was self-serving. For some time, he had wanted to bring his family from North Carolina to Mississippi, and he was looking for the right moment to do so. Although he had Jefferson's approval, he still waited until he thought territorial affairs wore a placid face. He vividly recalled Gallatin's displeasure with his earlier absence, and he had no desire to raise his ire again. Consequently, he put the best facade he could on affairs there. Although he had initially expected to leave in early fall of 1805, he postponed his departure until he believed war unlikely. Unfortunately he failed to anticipate the renewal of unrest along the border and the approaching crisis with Spain.[16]

The Spanish problem was a legacy of the Louisiana Purchase. In the final terms of that treaty, France had purposely left the boundaries of Louisiana ill-defined and despite repeated efforts by American diplomats, the French refused to clarify them. The ambiguous wording implied that the Spanish boundaries of Louisiana were the same as when France possessed it earlier. While West Florida was unquestion-ably part of French Louisiana, Spain later divided the Floridas into two administrative districts. Realizing that the United States coveted West Florida more than upper Louisiana, French diplomats, by leaving the eastern boundary indefinite, subtly prepared the ground for conflict, which not unexpectedly came in 1804.[17]

Unrest broke out along two of the territory's southern borders. One was Baton Rouge–Feliciana District, which stretched along the east-ern bank of the Mississippi River below the international boundary; the other was Mobile-Tensaw District, located south of Fort Stoddert at the confluence of the Tombigbee and Alabama rivers. Initially Jefferson, on the basis of face-saving reports of American diplomats, insisted that both were part of the French cession, and a number of settlers, mostly Anglo-Americans, applauded Jefferson's interpretation. In an effort to pressure Spain into recognizing his inflated claims, Jefferson prevailed upon Congress, in the Mobile Act of 1804, to set up a custom district within the contested region. In response, Spanish officials adopted a threatening posture, and Governor Vicente Folch warned Orleans gov-ernor Claiborne that Spain would forcibly resist any attempt to seize West Florida.[18]

In truth, Jefferson's strategy with respect to West Florida was simi-lar to the one he had employed in acquiring Louisiana. Once more, he preferred amicable negotiation to armed intervention. Unfortunately, James Monroe's efforts to reach an accord with Spanish officials floun-dered in a sea of misunderstanding and vituperation, forcing Jefferson to look elsewhere for a solution.[19]

For a second time, Jefferson turned to a financially pinched Napo-leon for assistance. Through what Jefferson believed was a reliable source, he learned that the French emperor might, for a price, per-suade Spain to recognize America's claims. In fact, he was prepared, if necessary, to pay dearly for the peaceful acquisition of Mobile and to allow Napoleon to share in the largesse, a stratagem that to some smacked of bribery. Jefferson was eager to transform Tombigbee Dis-trict (Washington County) from its present haunt as a refuge for the destitute and profligate into a haven for the virtuous and industrious. All the necessary ingredients (fertile soil, navigable rivers, and temper-ate climate) were present except an unimpeded commercial outlet. As long as Spain controlled the mouths of the rivers flowing into the Gulf of Mexico, the eastern half of the territory would remain a blight rather than a beacon.[20]

But the settlers were not as patient as diplomats abroad or officials at home, and local firebrands were unwilling to wait for Jefferson's peaceful tactics to work their magic. Instead, they took matters into their own hands. Somewhat surprisingly, the earliest conflagrations occurred not in the Bigbee District, where grievances were particularly pronounced, but in the western part of West Florida at Feliciana, where conditions appeared to be more tranquil and promising. There were reasons for this anomaly.

Of the two districts, Feliciana was both more prosperous and better populated than Tombigbee. Located along the eastern bank of the Mississippi south of the thirty-first parallel, Feliciana offered settlers easier access to foreign markets and was less vulnerable to Indian depredations than its eastern counterpart. Although both sections had their share of restless adventurers, only Feliciana, because of its known advantages, was a hotbed of land speculation. Expecting the United States shortly to secure control, several absentee claimants, such as Senator John Smith of Ohio and Daniel Clark Jr. of New Orleans, employed special agents and sent them scurrying into the district in anticipation of American control. These advance agents, who were frequently as untrustworthy as they were reckless, arrived during a time of disquietude.[21] Between 1801 and 1803, Louisiana had changed rulers three times, creating conditions ripe for intrigue.

A number of settlers, following Jefferson's lead, assumed that Feliciana was now part of the United States, and they acted accordingly. Speculators and conspirators, seeking to take advantage of the transition, rushed into the area. Later reports that West Florida was not part of the purchase and that Spain was intent upon keeping it were both upsetting and inviting.[22]

Most distressed were Feliciana speculators who planned to dispose of their flimsy claims by selling them to the torrent of expected settlers, eager to buy and possessed of ready cash. Conversely eastern settlers, though hopeful that Mobile was included, were more cautious and less exuberant than their neighbors to the west. Having already endured years of discomfort, they were disinclined to entertain wild dreams of fantastic profits, and their disappointment was less pronounced. Moreover, Anglo-American settlers in Feliciana, unlike those in Bigbee, remained under an alien government.[23]

Given these circumstances, it was only a matter time before disturbances erupted. Although the Kemper brothers—Reuben, Samuel, and
Nathan—were the recognized fomenters of the ensuing unrest, they
were actually more pawns than perpetrators. The Kempers had first
moved to Feliciana in early 1802 as agents of Senator John Smith of
Ohio, who three years before the Louisiana Purchase had acquired 750
acres in Feliciana Parish near the village of St. Francisville, located equi-
distant between Baton Rouge and the international border. While in
Cincinnati, he met Reuben Kemper, a strapping Virginian with wanderlust whom he hired to assist in operating a store on his estate at a newly
established town that he named New Valentia.[24]

The partnership was doomed from the start. Neither party trusted
the other, and the objectives of the two parties were clearly incompatible. In early 1804, a frustrated Smith persuaded the Spanish government
to exile not only Reuben Kemper but also his two brothers, Samuel and
Nathan, who earlier had joined him there. But the Kempers were not
ready to leave. Sensing the displeasure of some Anglo residents with
Spanish rule, they prepared to seize whatever opportunity came their
way.[25]

Consequently, the Kempers defied the Spanish eviction order, bar-
ricaded themselves in a log cabin, and scoured the countryside for compatriots, threatening anyone who refused to cooperate. They fended off
the first Spanish effort to expel them, killing a constable and "taking the
skin of another with lashes" before fleeing to Pinckneyville, a small hamlet north of the international border, ahead of a second assault. Despite
repeated Spanish protests, American officials in both Mississippi and
Orleans territories declined to hand over the Kempers. Instead, they
promised only to investigate the incident and take appropriate action,
a response that served to confirm Spanish suspicions that the Kempers
were acting as agents of the Jefferson administration and were intent
upon seizing West Florida.[26]

Fortunately, Spanish officials exercised remarkable restraint. While
American officials winked at the outrages and undertook only perfunc-
tory action, Spanish officials adopted firmer measures for keeping the
peace. When several militiamen from Feliciana, dismayed by American
indifference, threatened to end the incursions by crossing the line and
capturing the Kempers in their lair at Pinckneyville, Spanish officials
stopped them.[27]

Meanwhile, Samuel and Nathan Kemper dispatched brother Reuben to New Orleans, where he contacted Juan Ventura Morales, former intendant of Louisiana, who, in concert with Daniel Clark Jr. and Edward Livingston, was deeply involved in land speculation in Feliciana. In anticipation of the province falling into American hands, Morales, whose official duties included disposal of public lands, had granted several of his associates sizeable tracts of valuable lands in Feliciana. Morales, who saw advantages in cooperating with the Kempers, instructed Edward Randolph, his agent in St. Francisville, to draw up and deliver a declaration of independence to the two Kempers still in Pinckneyville. Meanwhile, during the late summer of 1804, the Kempers had assembled a small band of disciples who supported themselves by robbing and pillaging their Spanish neighbors.[28]

On the morning of August 7, 1804, Samuel and Nathan Kemper, with Randolph's document in hand, crossed into Feliciana, accompanied by some thirty armed ruffians recruited largely in Mississippi Territory. According to one official, they "raised up a Standard bearing Seven Stripes, white and blue [,] and two stars at the upper end." An eyewitness testified to seeing them wearing "strange Cockades," flying a distinctive flag, and blowing "a kind of french horn."[29] Hardly anyone knew what to make of this motley crew. Some were amused, others indifferent, and a few frightened.

Spanish officials were not among the amused. Instead, they concluded that "the District [was] in a state of Insurrection." Unbeknownst to them, the Kempers had a more limited, if no less bizarre, objective in mind. They planned to overwhelm the Spanish fort at Baton Rouge, kidnap its commander, Carlos Grand-Pre, and hold him hostage until Governor Folch consented to grant West Florida its independence in exchange for the commandant's release.

Failing to accomplish this objective, the Kempers offered to negotiate, but Grand-Pre, convinced that he held the upper hand, demurred. The Kempers luckily fled north, barely ahead of a force of 150 volunteers that the governor had rapidly raised in loyal settlements along the Amite and Comite rivers. Meanwhile, Daniel Clark Jr., representing Reuben Kemper, who had remained throughout the disturbances in New Orleans seeking fiscal support for his brothers, intervened on behalf of the Kempers. In exchange for wholesale pardons, he promised that the Kempers would lay down their arms and pledge to keep the peace, but Grand-Pre, aware of Clark's extensive personal interest in West Florida lands, refused to bargain with either the Orleans counselor or his clients.[30]

In contrast to Spanish officials, who believed that Claiborne and other like-minded expansionists were using the Kempers to further their own ends, American officials dismissed the incident as a harmless border skirmish. Both Claiborne and Rodney believed the "Kemper Riot" had created more noise eastward than was warranted. Claiborne accused Spanish minister Chevalier Casa de Yrujo of converting the affair into "a pretext for calumniating our administration." Nevertheless, American officials on the spot could not treat it so cavalierly. With encouragement from Claiborne, who was constantly bombarded with complaints beyond his jurisdiction, Acting Governor West dispatched Thomas Rodney to the tiny border hamlet of Pinckneyville, where he was surprised by the primitive conditions. He saw only "one tolerable house" and a tavern, owned by one of the Kempers, which "was full of ordinary fellows of his party—Drinking and playing Billiards." Rodney took depositions from the Kempers as well as from Arthur and William Cobb, reputed to be the ringleaders of the recent disturbance, and visited with Edward Randolph at his home near Pinckneyville.[31]

In his subsequent report to West, Rodney ridiculed the insinuation that President Jefferson was "underhandedly incouraging that insurrection" on the sensible grounds that if the charge were true, "the Spaniards would have been driven out of that Territory in a few weeks." Instead, he labeled the Kemper affair a "private quarrel" between a few individuals who were "obliged to leave [Feliciana]" and Spanish officials determined to oust them. Nevertheless, a weary Rodney, before leaving the border, admonished the American banditti for their imprudence and warned them against using American soil as a base for further depredations against Spain. Still, he assured authorities that "everything was quiet."[32]

The ensuing truce lasted less than a year. By the late spring of 1805, the Kempers were at it again. This time, it was Robert Williams and not West who responded to Grand-Pre's irate demands to restrain the insurgents. Although Williams denounced the Kempers, criticized their behavior, and promised to take appropriate action, he soon dropped the matter.[33] Williams was too busy answering his own critics and too aware of the public's hatred of Spaniards to pay attention to the escapades of a few border ruffians.

Tired of trying to redress grievances through diplomatic channels, Spanish officials resorted to clandestine measures. Offering $1,500 for the capture of each Kemper, they sparked the interest of the brothers' bitterest enemies. On the night of September 3, 1805, a party of twelve whites and seven slaves, in disguise and "armed with guns, Clubs & knives & Pistols," crossed the demarcation line around midnight and entered Pinckneyville, where two of the three Kempers were known to reside. Stationing sentinels around the hamlet, Samuel Horton and two of his slaves barged into the home of Nathan Kemper. After tying Nathan with a rope, they dragged him to the gallery, where another party appeared with brother Reuben in tow. According to Nathan, Reuben was bound and severely beaten, his face and shirt covered with blood. Under the glare of a full moon, Nathan was able to identify most of the kidnappers, including Samuel and Abraham Horton and four of their slaves. The two families had been feuding for years, and the Kempers were hardly surprised when they spotted the Hortons.[34]

The armed invaders then escorted the two prisoners to a secluded clearing near the border where by design they met a second party from Pinckneyville with a third Kemper in custody. Once across the line, the Kempers were delivered to a small Spanish guard under the command of Capt. Solomon Alston, who hastily marched them to a prearranged rendezvous at Willing's, or Tunica, Bayou, where the brothers were placed aboard a barge for transporting to Baton Rouge. On the journey downstream, the Kempers knew the escort had to pass by Point Coupee, located on the American side of the river. Upon approaching the fort, the prisoners cried out for help, identifying themselves as American citizens abducted by Spanish soldiers. The American commander, Capt. William Wilson, immediately dispatched a detachment to overtake the Spanish vessel and rescue the Americans. Upon learning of this affair, Governor Williams ordered Captain Wilson to send both the Kempers and their abductors, under guard, to Fort Adams for interrogation.[35]

By now, Williams began to discern a pattern. A few weeks before the Kempers' abduction, a small detachment of "12 Spanish Light Horse" crossed into southeastern Wilkinson County near Ticksaw Creek in search of William Flanagan, an alleged murderer. According to Thomas Holden, a local resident, the soldiers came to his house, inquiring into the whereabouts of Flanagan. After Holden insisted that he had not seen Flanagan "for over six months," the soldiers, "at the point of a sword," angrily ordered him to accompany them. Luckily for Holden, some friends suddenly appeared, causing the Spaniards to scatter. Immediately thereafter, Grand-Pre requested Governor Williams to extradite Flanagan for the premeditated murder of Joseph Sharp. Although Williams refused to comply, the Spaniards later caught the elusive Flanagan, took him below the international boundary, and threatened to imprison him indefinitely unless he would agree to surrender his horse, saddle, and bridle on the spot.[36] Not surprisingly, Flanagan gladly returned home on foot.

Now it was Williams's turn to dispatch sharp notes of protest to Grand-Pre. He also placed the territorial militia on alert and ordered Lt. Col. John Ellis of the Fifth Militia Regiment to station two companies along the border, one at Ticksaw and the other at Pinckneyville, and examine "all equivocal characters passing the line from below and especially if at night." Unfortunately, these precautions gave rise to a false rumor, supposedly spread by Col. Henry Hunter, that the governor planned "to take Baton Rouge."[37]

Meanwhile, Williams again dispatched Judge Rodney to the border to uncover the facts. After spending two days at Fort Adams examining key witnesses, Rodney sent the Spanish troops home and placed the Kempers under peace bonds not to disturb either the Spanish or the Americans. But this resolution left the Kempers free to pursue court action against their kidnappers and to resume their escapades along the border. As Rodney discovered, reaction to the Kempers was mixed. Some thought the Kempers had received exactly what they deserved; others considered "this Hostile aggression as a high Indignity to the United States." Rodney thought it a prelude to "more provocative operations."[38]

Rodney had good reason for his conclusion. By the spring of 1805, the notoriety of the Kempers was so commonplace that rumors of their future plans had become both widespread and exaggerated. A resident of Baton Rouge, described only as "a Gentleman of respectability," reported that Reuben Kemper, Arthur Cobb, and another "late Insurgent" had sailed from New Orleans to New Providence where they expected to secure "English Commissions for themselves" and authorization "to raize a body of Brigands." Supposedly, the three plotted to return "in an armed Vessel loaded with every necessary Military Store" and proceed across Lakes Pontchartrain and Maurepas and up the Amite River, where they were to meet a second party. Together, they planned "to enter the

District . . . with a view of plundering all, of massacreing many and if supported by the English of conquering" West Florida. According to the same source, among "those marked particularly for assassination" were Grand-Pre, a Spanish captain, and two abusive magistrates, and "the entire settlement of Bayou Tonica, and several of the Inhabitants high up Thompsons Creek." According to a second informer, another "Band of these Brigands" were "to perpetrate the most diabolical Deeds," but its leaders, restrained by "fear of rousing the United Force of Spain and America and thus cutting off all retreat," abandoned the project.[39]

While American officials publicly deplored the exploits of the Kempers and cautioned others against engaging in rebellious activity, they were not entirely displeased with the disturbances. In fact, Jefferson found them useful in furthering his strategy of annexation. In his eyes, both he and the insurgents had similar grievances and common objectives; they differed only in the methods for redressing the complaints and securing the desired goals. While Jefferson preferred peaceful negotiation to armed intervention, he was not opposed to a spontaneous and popular insurrection if propitious and under proper direction. Since the 1790s, Jefferson had believed that, in the contest for control of the American continent, time was on his side and that the United States was destined by nature to expand westward and eventually dominate the Western Hemisphere.[40]

As interesting as the Kemper affair was to inhabitants on both sides of the boundary, it was part of a broader international conflict between Spain, allied with France in its struggle against England, and the United States. By 1805, tensions along the borders had reached a critical stage, and neither protagonist showed signs of wavering. The Jefferson administration adamantly refused to relinquish its rights to West Florida. Spain, still smarting from Napoleon's perfidy in selling Louisiana, was determined not only to retain West Florida but also to shrink American claims in the Province of Texas. France, stymied in its military operations after the British destroyed the combined French and Spanish fleet at Trafalgar, sought an alternative strategy for defeating the British.[41]

In the American Southwest, the situation was equally complicated as pressure mounted and grounds for compromise diminished. Spain reinforced its garrisons at Pensacola, Mobile, and Baton Rouge and made aggressive moves from its eastern base in Nacogdoches (in the Province of Texas) into western Louisiana. Although the United States claimed the Rio Bravo (Rio Grande) as the western boundary of the Louisiana Purchase, American officials made no attempt to press the point. But they became alarmed in 1805 when Spanish forces penetrated across the Red River where the United States had established Fort Claiborne, garrisoning it with a small detachment under Capt. Edward D. Turner. Initially, American officials were more afraid that Spain might incite the Indians to prey on the exposed settlers and entice their slaves to escape into Texas than they were of Spanish aggression.[42] It was not until 1806, after the Spanish troops from Mexico began to erect forts east of the Sabine River, that inhabitants of Mississippi Territory took serious notice of this situation.

Of more immediate concern in early 1805 was Spanish interference with American commerce along the Gulf coast, especially those streams comprising the Alabama River system. Spain not only imposed "ruinous" duties of 12 percent ad valorem on both exports and imports passing through Mobile, but it also tried to regulate traffic on the rivers, confiscating the ship and cargo of those caught carrying contraband. In a few instances, Spain's officials intercepted vessels conveying supplies for Fort Stoddert and the Indian factory at St. Stephens. But those same officials promised to lift the restrictions if the United States would reciprocate by granting Spanish vessels free access to Baton Rouge. Fearful that Spanish officials would use the river port as a base for smuggling and freebooting, the United States rejected the overtures.[43]

Almost no one believed that Spain was strong enough to possess West Florida indefinitely. In fact, settlers in the Old Southwest had a better appreciation of Spanish vulnerability than officials in the nation's capital or diplomats abroad. Rodney, in October 1805, reported that it was "almost the Unanimous View of our western citizens that [the United States] ought at once to wrest all the Sea Coast." It was only a matter of time, he surmised, before the United States would either seize this strip of territory or secure it through diplomacy.[44] On the other hand, Jefferson still hoped that Spain would recognize it as part of the Louisiana Purchase, but the longer Spain possessed it, the less likely that became.

In this altercation, more was at stake than the nation's honor. Jefferson was aware that if West Florida was part of the Louisiana Purchase, then the United States would not have to honor land grants made subsequent to the French cession. He also despaired of the "wild speculation" occurring in Feliciana and other parts of the Floridas.[45] For these reasons, Jefferson was reluctant to take West Florida by force.

As Spain grew more obstinate, Jefferson, with Madison's concurrence, began to promote a new tactic, one he had favored since the early 1790s. Advocate of a policy similar to what was later called "manifest destiny," Jefferson believed that Providence had singled out the United States for special blessings and predestined it for greatness. It would become, in his opinion, the dominant power in the Western Hemisphere and perhaps in time of the world as well. According to Jefferson, the United States had a duty and responsibility to spread its "empire of liberty" across the whole continent so all North Americans might enjoy the benefits of liberty and pursue the blessings of happiness.[46]

But Jefferson's policy of expansion was as unique as it was innovative. Instead of depending upon military power to secure its objectives, he fostered the migration of peoples.[47] By encouraging American citizens to settle in foreign territories contiguous to the United States, Jefferson hoped to populate these areas with a Republican vanguard that, in time, would overthrow tyrannical governments, oust their rulers, and seek annexation to the United States. Through this process, Jefferson expected to promote expansion without embroiling the nation in a messy and costly war. Since this strategy worked better against a weak than a strong neighbor, he preferred to keep the Floridas in Spanish hands and out of those of England or France. Accordingly, as long as nothing changed, Jefferson confidently expected the two Floridas, sooner or later, to become part of his "empire of liberty."

CHAPTER 7

Security and Settlements

In the aftermath of the transfer of Louisiana in late 1803, relations between the United States and Spain worsened along both sides of the international boundary. Although Spanish officials acquiesced in the transfer, they considered Napoleon's actions duplicitous. Congress's decision in 1804 to authorize a customhouse at Mobile encouraged Spain to restrict the introduction of contraband and to reimpose a duty on foreign goods passing through Mobile, including military supplies for Fort Stoddert and provisions for the trading post at St. Stephens.[1]

The western boundary of the Louisiana Purchase was another pressure point. After the Americans claimed the entire coastal region east of the Rio Grande River, both nations strengthened their positions by dispatching troops into the borderlands between the Trinity River in the Province of Texas and the Arroyo Hondo in Orleans Territory. By late 1804, rumors were rife that Spain intended to reclaim all or part of its former territory west of the Mississippi River. These reports, which Spanish officials purposely planted in order to retain friendly ties with the Indians, unduly frightened Americans.[2] As disagreements between the two nations intensified and war seemed imminent, Jefferson began to reassess western policies, focusing on two critical questions: how to improve communication with New Orleans and Natchez and how best to deploy its limited military forces.

Improved communication with remote areas was hardly a new problem. As early as 1799, Secretary of State Pickering was flabbergasted that dispatches from the Southwest took six weeks longer to arrive than those from abroad. "Passage of letters from Natchez," he lamented, were "as tedious as from Europe." The scarcity of news troubled Winthrop Sargent. He once thanked Spanish governor Gayoso for furnishing him "with foreign intelligence," explaining that "tis so very long since I have heard from the United States by the great river that I am almost induced to believe the Ohio has quite run dry." Additionally, Pickering was dismayed to learn that Congress had not appropriated funds for improving mail service between Nashville and Natchez.[3] Written communiqués traditionally went down the Ohio and Mississippi rivers, a relatively easy journey compared to return upstream. Descending the rivers, while not without peril, was far less arduous than ascending them, and only the hardiest boatmen attempted it. Instead, most returned overland, trudging along whatever "devious & narrow" Indian path they could find, the most famous being the Natchez Trace.[4]

Indeed, officials from Pickering to Claiborne lamented the lack of adequate communication with the far-flung outposts of Natchez and St. Stephens, which, according to General Wilkinson, were in "the most critical & exposed part of our country." They also knew that reliable mail service to the Old Southwest depended primarily on upgrading the Natchez Trace and developing new roads. To convert the primordial Trace into a dependable road, Pickering proposed to remove the thick underbrush and widen the roadbed, bridge the numerous creeks and small streams, build causeways through the swamps, and establish accommodations at twenty- to thirty-mile intervals. Except for a few miles at the end of each terminal, the Trace traversed Indian territory, requiring consent of the Choctaw and Chickasaw if improvements were to be made and stands opened.[5]

In response to pleas for establishing "houses of entertainment" along the Trace, Congress appropriated fifteen thousand dollars "to defray the expense of such treaty or treaties, as the President of the United States shall deem it expedient to hold with the Indians south of the river Ohio." Acting with dispatch, Jefferson instructed Secretary of War Henry Dearborn to arrange separate conferences with the four principal southern Indian nations. After selecting three commissioners (James Wilkinson, Benjamin Hawkins, and Andrew Pickens) to treat with them, Dearborn invited the Cherokees to meet at Southwest Point in southeastern Tennessee on August 1, 1801; the Chickasaws at Chickasaw Bluffs (Memphis) on September 1; and the Choctaws at Fort Adams on October 1.

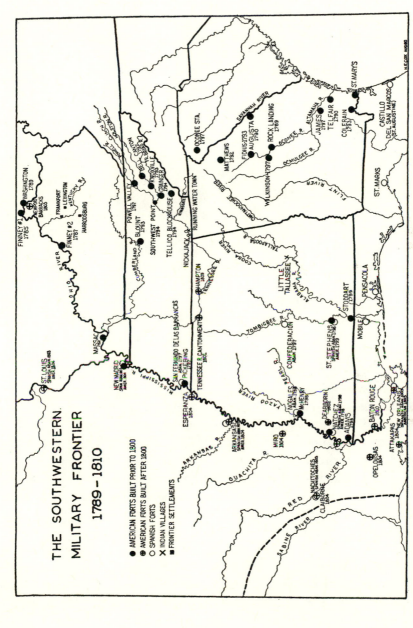

Map by Harold E. Cox (Thomas P. Abernethy, *The South in the New Nation, 1789–1819* [Baton Rouge, La., 1961]).

Since Jefferson wanted some Creek lands, Dearborn postponed conferring with them until he had secured concessions from the other tribes.[6]

Dearborn cautioned the commissioners to proceed gingerly in their talks with the chiefs. They were not to "give the Indians an opportunity to reply with a decided negative" or induce "in them unfriendly and inimical dispositions." From the Cherokees, Chickasaws, and Choctaws, he wanted permission to erect a wagon road through their territories, set up stands at convenient spots, and operate ferries across major rivers.[7]

The Cherokees proved the most obstinate. They rejected all entreaties regardless of how delicately they were expressed. "The roads you propose," declared one chief, "we do not wish to have made through our country." The Chickasaws and Choctaws were more accommodating. They consented to roads through their nations but refused to allow white-owned "establishments of entertainment," opting to operate their own stands and ferries and to pocket the profits. The Chickasaws, thanks to the ingenious George Colbert, were especially adroit negotiators. In agreeing to "a highway for the citizens of the United States" and themselves, they stipulated that "the necessary ferries over the water courses" were "deemed to be the property of the Chickasaw nation," a clause designed to protect Colbert's lucrative ferry across the Tennessee River.[8]

Once Congress designated Natchez Trace a post road, Dearborn was eager to begin improvements. Appalled by the extravagant demands of private contractors, he ordered General Wilkinson to employ an otherwise idle "military in clearing & in making causeways & bridges" and erecting "a Block house near Hoolkey Creek . . . about half way between Nashville & Natchez." Wilkinson put Lt. Edmund P. Gaines in charge of surveying the terrain and selecting the shortest route. Thanks to cooperation of the Choctaw and Chickasaw, work proceeded at a steady pace.[9]

But the administration's excitement waned after the postal department discovered that expenditures exceeded income. According to Postmaster General Gideon Granger, the upkeep of "that road has heretofore cost three thousand dollars yearly," while revenue was only "twelve hundred & six dollars thirty seven cents." Nevertheless, before the government halted the project, Gaines had "explored and laid out [the road] from Nashville to Grindstone ford," reducing the distance between Natchez and Nashville by fifty miles. Still, it took the average post rider at least six days to complete the circuit.[10]

Thereafter, concern about cost ebbed and flowed with each new crisis. For example, after the Spanish intendant in late 1802 withdrew the right of deposit at New Orleans, expenses became less critical. Granger hired a private agent to carry the federal mails weekly "from Nashville through the Wilderness to Natchez" at the "rate of fifty miles" per day for a "price of six thousand dollars a year." "The state of the country," he explained, "appeared to require this measure," boasting that it would "greatly accelerate the progress of mail . . . so that we shall be able to hear from each other in a little more than half the time that was heretofore required."[11]

Dearborn implored Wilkinson to speed up "the road cutting business." He recommended employing "a regular succession of parties of thirty men each," relieving them "once a month," to hew through the forest a gash sixteen feet wide, half "to be cut close to the ground, and smoothed for passengers." Since the object was to develop a "comfortable road for Horse and foot passengers," Dearborn thought it more important "that the swamps and streams be causewayed & bridged" than that the bed be cut a particular width. But after the War Department transferred the military elsewhere, improvements languished again.[12]

The Natchez Trace was not the only postal route envisioned by Granger. After the United States acquired Louisiana, New Orleans, not Natchez, absorbed the government's attention, and officials in Washington sought a more direct pathway than the circuitous Natchez Trace. Since a new road would necessarily pass through Creek country, Dearborn opened negotiations with that tribe. After two abortive attempts, federal commissioners, by bribing friendly chiefs, received permission to build it and operate stands.[13]

Reliable communication also necessitated establishing, at convenient locations, post offices managed by competent postmasters as well as upgrading existing post roads and starting new ones. Although the problems of distance and terrain appeared nearly insurmountable, federal officials were determined to overcome both in order to respond more expeditiously to crises that, on every frontier, were yearly occurrences. Otherwise, distant officials, without adequate knowledge and susceptible to local prejudices, could be compelled to make on-the-spot decisions that might propel the nation into needless conflict.

Convinced that New Orleans, "in the ordinary course of affairs must become the greatest entrepot for merchandize in the world," Granger urged construction of a turnpike suitable "for travelers on horseback at a small expense" and for conveying federal mails "at the rate of 90 miles in a day." But, as late as 1805, the only feasible road between Washington and New Orleans was the elongated one that ran first through Fredericksburg, Maryland, then Knoxville and Nashville in Tennessee, and finally to Natchez, a distance of "nearly 1500 miles." Meanwhile, the federal government, in the interest of better security, extended the road to Fort Adams, located near Loftus Heights just north of the international border.[14]

The most traversed stretch was that between Natchez and Nashville. Built piecemeal and for diverse purposes, it was uneven in quality and without public accommodations. Originating sometime in the mid-eighteenth century as a poorly marked footpath for Kentucky boatmen returning home after floating produce down the Mississippi River, it quickly attracted a wider assortment of patrons ranging from preachers to slave traders. By the late 1790s, however, regular post riders had replaced boatmen as its most frequent travelers.[15]

Thanks to the well-publicized exploits of the notorious Mason and Harpe gangs, who infested the region around the turn of the century, the Trace gained an undeserved reputation for violence. After the fortuitous capture and execution in late 1802 of two men, identified by their abductors as members of the infamous Mason gang, instances of murder and robbery declined. Still, as a precautionary measure, Secretary Dearborn stationed, "at the cantonment on the Tennessee River," a detachment of twenty-five soldiers "to apprehend any persons who have or shall be guilty of murdering, robbing, or in anyway annoying Post Riders or any other persons peaceably traveling the road." Thereafter the Natchez Trace was no more dangerous than other pathways through wild, sparsely settled country inhabited by wary Indians, white traders of questionable character, and an assortment of ambitious half-breeds.[16] Still, most travelers exercised caution by traveling in groups rather than singly or in pairs.

Postmaster General Granger faced constant pressure from territorial officials for better mail service. Hardly a month passed without some complaint from Governor Claiborne. "The irregularities in the Post," he declared, have arisen "from the difficulties of [traveling] the Wilderness road between the Mississippi Territory and Tennessee." Riders were "frequently delayed by indisposition, High Water or the loss of a horse," inconveniences that could not be relieved "until the road can be settled."[17]

In the absence of public accommodations, weary travelers along the Trace were left to fend for themselves. Fortunately, local residents, native and Anglo, proved to be more friendly and generous than the government, and few sojourners went without bed and bread. Contrary to conventional wisdom, the Indians seldom molested travelers; instead, they usually came to the aid of lost or stranded parties.[18]

As traffic along the Trace picked up and Indians grew more acquisitive, a number of privately owned stands or stations, offering lodging and food to tired and hungry travelers, sprang up. Initially, both the Choctaw and Chickasaw had refused to grant the federal government permission to set up stands for fear they would promote settlement. As they recognized, stands consisted of more than inns for travelers; they required adjacent gardens, stables, and housing for the workers, both black and white. To ward off unwanted population growth, enterprising Indians, especially mixed-bloods, opened places of accommodation at convenient locations.[19]

To encourage cooperation and reduce friction, the federal government required whites to operate establishments jointly with Indian chiefs or other important tribesmen. In fact the number of privately operated taverns grew at such a steady pace that the government lost interest in opening public stands. The names of these establishments were interesting and revealing. A few bore such descriptive and colorful names as Pigeon Roost, Buzzard Roost, and Coon Box, but most took the name of owners, the best-known being Doak's and Brashear's Stands.[20] One acquired national notoriety as the scene of a sensational and controversial tragedy. In 1809, the disfigured body of Meriwether Lewis was found at Grinder's Stand in Tennessee, touching off an enduring debate over whether his death resulted from suicide or murder. Fortunately, such tragic occurrences were rare, and sojourners found travel on the Trace more tiresome than threatening.[21]

Nevertheless, traffic was insufficient to keep roads in decent repair, forcing the federal government periodically to clear away the underbrush, fallen limbs, and trees and, once horse and wagon traffic increased, to remove tree stumps left by sloppy contractors. In 1808, for example, the postmaster general contracted Gen. James Robertson of Tennessee to widen the stretch between Pigeon Roost and Grindstone Ford for "six dollars a mile." Later Granger found Robertson's work unsatisfactory and compelled him to redo it, subject to inspection by the local postmaster.[22]

More important than the comfort of travelers was need for faster communication and tighter security. After 1805, as war with Spain, France, or England appeared likely, the federal government devoted more attention to erecting additional highways through the territory. Granger in particular was determined to find a shorter route than the Trace for expediting mail delivery. He decided that the shortest route to New Orleans was through the Carolinas, Georgia, and "the Mobile Settlement and the Post Oak landing," a distance "not much" more than "one thousand & fifty miles." Unfortunately, identifying a feasible route was easier than erecting it, and Granger encountered one problem after another, compelling him to admit that "success has not been great."[23]

In his efforts to improve security, Granger had to contend with more than upgrading existing Indian trails and transforming them into durable wagon roads. He had to extract concessions from uneasy chieftains who questioned if the revenue from stands and annuities was enough to offset likely disadvantages. Improvements led to more settlers and a spurt in economic growth, both of which threatened to undermine, if not to destroy, their traditional way of life.[24]

Surprisingly, Indians failed to develop a strategy for preventing or retarding these developments. Instead, several chiefs, especially the Choctaw and Chickasaw, succumbed easily to the white man's wiles by accepting annuities and individual stipends or, more properly, bribes. As a result, they unintentionally cooperated in the destruction of Indian cultures and the demise of their tribes as independent nations. Although a few, mostly half- or mixed-bloods, stood to profit from the improvements, others benefited little, and not everyone welcomed them. Younger, warm-blooded warriors showed their displeasure by stealing horses and other livestock, robbing and harassing travelers, and extracting "gifts" in exchange for safe passage. Some turned the practice of horse stealing into a profitable enterprise by "finding" the horses they had earlier stolen and collecting rewards from the government. But, as one disgruntled victim recalled, they always returned the sorriest horses and kept the best.[25]

There were other problems as well. One was the cost of establishing an efficient communication system. For Jeffersonian Republicans, frugality and retrenchment were the linchpins of good government, and members of the president's cabinet, especially Gallatin and Granger, kept expenditures to a minimum. Yet the expense of governing an expansive nation was always greater than expected. The administration also faced difficulty in recruiting and retaining reliable post riders, postmasters, and mail carriers, and its reliance on an underpaid and poorly disciplined military was problematic.[26] At one point, Granger became so frustrated with locating trustworthy postmasters that he abdicated the task to Governor Williams.

Likewise, sickness and crippling injuries plagued postal operations. Newcomers to the region were especially vulnerable to fevers and other debilitating diseases that thrived in the hot, humid climate of the lower Mississippi Valley. More than one official found himself incapacitated upon arrival. Granger in 1805 contracted with Francis Abraham to convey the mail between Coweta in western Creek country and New Orleans. Shortly after reaching the Crescent City, he was confined to bed "by a fit of sickness," and when he finally reached Fort Stoddert, presumably on his way to Coweta, he discovered that "all the horses that were placed on the route for the purpose of transporting the mail had either died, or been stolen by the Indians." To Granger's chagrin, Abraham paid eight hundred dollars to procure "a new set" of sturdy horses. Still, a "mortified" Granger had to report, six months later, that "not a single mail has he furnished."

But recurring illness was not the only reason for mails to go undelivered and schedules unmet. Drunkenness was another cause, and, as Granger recognized, diseases were more curable than inebriation. Even the habitually compassionate Granger was forced to order the mail contractor in Nashville "to dismiss his drunken post rider."[27]

Officials continually worried about the number of misplaced or lost letters that might fall into the wrong hands. The situation was especially critical in Tombigbee. For instance, John Caller felt compelled, because "the passage of paper from this [place] to the City of Washington [was] so uncertain," to dispatch "several copies [of a petition], different ways that they should not fail in Reaching the president." In 1804, mismanagement of the post office at Loftus Heights forced Granger to replace the postmaster. According to complainants, he had allowed "letters and newspapers" received there to be "thrown upon the floor . . . left for examination of any person," including "the evil disposed." Anxious about the security of personal letters, Granger ordered that private correspondence and newspapers "be sent in separate portmanteau." He dismissed the Natchez postmaster for allowing some confidential letters, addressed to the commander in chief, "to be broken open." Likewise Granger learned, to his dismay, that one postmaster, after misplacing the key, had cut into a locked mail bag in order to extract "a Package for Port Gibson."[28]

If these directives failed to prevent the pillage of letters from poorly supervised post offices or ensure tighter security, they were certainly prudent measures. For example, Richard Claiborne, postmaster at Washington, happily reported in late 1804 that "every thing is smooth here." Nevertheless, complaints of suspected espionage by postal officials and irresponsible acts of contractors and riders persisted. Mismanagement of accounts and sloppy bookkeeping led to the dismissal of careless postmasters. For instance, Abijah Hunt, sometime postmaster at Natchez, left office owing the government $733.14.[29]

Meanwhile, Granger's efforts to open a shorter route to New Orleans met with little success. On March 3, 1805, Congress appropriated a sum not to exceed six thousand dollars for the establishment of "a post road from Fort Stoddert to New Orleans" to connect with an earlier route between Coweta in Creek territory and Washington, D.C. Granger expected it to reduce the distance from the Crescent City to the nation's capital by more than five hundred miles.[30]

Granger wanted a more expeditious route between New Orleans and Georgia than "the path usually travelled between those places" because it was "devious & so obstructed by water courses and swamps that the mail cannot be carried upon it with regularity." On the other hand, a reliable informant apprised Granger that the government should not "calculate upon a regular mail from Fort Stoddert to New Orleans in any other way than by water communication," which entailed the cooperation of Spanish officials suspicious of American intentions. After nine failed attempts to deliver the mail through Creek country, Granger, finally at wit's end, contemplated seeking Spanish permission to set up a temporary mail service "from Fort Stoddert to New Orleans by water." Meanwhile, he asked Judge Toulmin to arrange for delivery along "the Horse Path from Fort Stoddert to either Pinckneyville or Natchez on a three-day interval" and Lieutenant Gaines "to look out [for] a practicable Road to the Pascagola" River, securing "a light Boat or Canoe . . . to descend that River to its mouth."[31]

Most of these good intentions were for naught, falling victim to one or more obstacles: gross mismanagement, escalating costs, faulty information, volatile international relations, or human foibles. Nonetheless, Granger persisted in his determination to improve mail service, shore up security, and promote increased commerce. In the summer of 1807, he asked Gaines to survey two new pathways, one between Muscle Shoals on the Tennessee River and Southwest Point located along the Hiwassee River in southeastern Tennessee, and the other between the Muscle Shoals and Cotton Gin Port on the upper reaches of the Tombigbee River.[32] The object was to locate a shorter route between Washington and Natchez by redirecting the post road through Southwest Point and Knoxville, thus bypassing Nashville.

The route Gaines recommended ran "from the head waters of the Big Black, at Pigeon Roost" to Cotton Gin Port, and thence to Muscle Shoals and finally to Southwest Point. It would benefit the eastern half of the territory since the Tombigbee River could easily be made navigable, or "boatable," as Granger and Gaines put it, as far north as Cotton Gin Port. Furthermore by redirecting it southward, it would pass through "a much drier" terrain without "water courses" to impede travel and where the road "may at all times be crossed without danger or difficulty, even in times of the highest freshes, by the help of footlogs." Also there were no swamps requiring causeways, and none of the creeks, "even when the rains are not immoderate," would "take a Horse above the Knees."[33]

Granger expected the Tombigbee project, by establishing closer ties with Fort Stoddert, to populate the eastern half of the territory. Unfortunately, these plans initially ran awry of the half-breed Scotsman George Colbert and his protected ferry across the Tennessee River. Fearful that a new wagon road might seriously lower his profits, Colbert was able to block its development temporarily, and it was not until 1810 that George Strother Gaines, Edmund's younger brother, convinced the Chickasaws to open it to general use.[34]

The difficulty of travel through the Creek country was painstakingly documented by Isaac Briggs. On his return journey from Washington, D.C., in late 1804, Briggs and a companion, at Jefferson's urging, went overland in order to take "observations of latitude and longitude" at strategic points along the way. Even before they entered Creek country, Briggs was exhausted. Upon reaching the eastern lower Creek village of Coweta, he reported that the overland trip was "both to body and mind,

the most fatiguing journey" he had ever endured. But worse was to follow. He and his associate, forced to enter Creek country without a guide,
managed somehow to locate, after four days of hard travel and without
spotting a single soul, Benjamin Hawkins's residence on the Flint River.
From there they proceeded to "Point Comfort" (grossly misnamed), just
south of the Tallapoosa River. Covering 120 miles in seven days of laborious travel, they and their horses swam the swift Chattahoochee River
and waded across six creeks. It took them five more days to reach the
Tombigbee River. After hacking their way through thick canebrakes and
dense wilderness, they crossed the Pascagoula and Pearl rivers and the
Rigolets before arriving at New Orleans, a journey that consumed four
months and covered more than a thousand miles. It was no wonder that
a fatigued Briggs, upon reaching New Orleans, succumbed to "a dreadful fever." But he had done his duty, and the course he documented
became the Federal Road.[35]

In building the Federal Road from Milledgeville, Georgia, to New
Orleans, Granger encountered obstacles similar to those he faced in his
earlier efforts to transform the Natchez Trace from an Indian trail into
a post road. After Congress in 1806 appropriated the necessary funds,
Granger initially placed operations in what he thought were the capable
hands of Benjamin Hawkins. He was to widen the existing horse path
from Georgia to Fort Stoddert by "four to six feet" at a cost not to exceed
$6,400. But prolonged illness forced Hawkins to neglect the work and
compelled an exasperated Granger to employ the services of Gen. David
Meriwether, a Georgia speculator and politician.[36]

While the road was under way, Granger contracted with Col. Joseph
Wheaton to establish a regular express service between Georgia and Fort
Stoddert. Shortly afterward, Wheaton also succumbed to illness. He was
felled by "high billious fever" and a fall from his horse, and once more
Granger had to change personnel. As a result, the work proceeded slowly
and costs rose sharply, and Granger began to doubt the project's feasibil-
ity. A true Jeffersonian, he opposed "large expenditures in an unsuccessful attempt to force rapid mail service through an immense wilderness
filled with streams and marshes where no sustenance or aid can be given
to either man or beast."[37]

While Granger was correct in identifying the boggy and uneven terrain as the primary cause of delays and escalating costs, they were not
his only problem. As early as 1807, the Upper Creeks, who resided along

the lower reaches of the Chattahoochee River, raised serious objections to a highway bisecting their nation. As they feared, the road attracted a set of undesirables whose outrageous conduct encouraged the Creeks to retaliate.[38]

In the summer of 1805, Hawkins reported that some Indians had shot a post rider and seized the mail, which happily was recovered. Later, Col. Constant Freeman notified General Wilkinson that "two post riders were killed in Creek Country . . . and the mails robbed." "I suspect," he conjectured, "the Postmaster General must abandon this route." But Creeks were not the only offenders. In 1808, four white travelers seized an Indian lad, grabbed his new knife, and proceeded to strip and beat him. The Creeks also complained about intruders on their lands and travelers who grazed their livestock in fields adjacent to the highway.[39]

In retaliation, embittered Creeks refused to abide by the treaty requiring them to set up places of accommodation and threatened harm to any who tried to do so. An irritated Gaines accused them of contriving "to keep our mails and citizens who travel through their country, exposed to all the dangers and inconveniences of an extensive wilderness, by opposing the erections of stations on the road." Despite numerous setbacks and false starts, Hawkins proudly proclaimed, in December 1811, that the road was finished.[40] Completion fortuitously came before the War of 1812 erupted.

The same roads that carried post riders also brought settlers. Although Indians feared that a flood tide of immigrants would accompany the opening of roads, their apprehensions were not immediately realized. Instead, most immigrants came by traditional ways, either by sea from the east coast or down one or more of the several streams flowing into the Gulf of Mexico. The vast majority floated down the Mississippi River, landing initially at Natchez before proceeding to a final destination. By 1810, clearings in the forest and old Indian trails and cow paths provided crude passages from one settlement to another within Natchez District, where travel by horseback was relatively easy. Unfortunately, the same was not true of Tombigbee District, where travel remained uncertain and difficult, and rivers provided the main arteries of access.

With few exceptions, newly appointed territorial officials ventured to the territory by one of several rivers. The first two governors came via the Ohio and Mississippi rivers, Sargent from Cincinnati and Claiborne from Nashville. John Steele, the territory's first secretary, also traveled mostly by water. After going overland from North Carolina to eastern Tennessee, he took a boat down the Holston, Tennessee, Ohio, and Mississippi rivers to Natchez. Horse B. Trist, a Virginian who expected to be named territorial secretary, came down the Mississippi. On his way downstream, he stopped briefly at Fort Massac, near the confluence of the Ohio and Tennessee rivers, where he added a companion, and the commanding officer supplied him with a tent. He then left by boat for Chickasaw Bluffs. After resting there for two days, he boarded "a large flatboat belonging to [an] Irishman." Before reaching Natchez, he had spent "twenty tedious days" on the river.[41]

Some preferred to take passage first to New Orleans and from there to ascend the Mississippi, usually in a makeshift sailboat or light keelboat, while others resorted to the more arduous method of oaring or warping upstream. Those going to Tombigbee District usually arrived by water, upriver from Mobile or down the Tombigbee or Alabama rivers. Before completion of the Federal Road, only a handful were bold enough to venture overland through the sparsely inhabited Creek country. Like public officials, the few well-to-do usually went by river or sea.[42] Only the less fortunate took alternate routes, and they left no record of their experiences.

Of the numerous officials who traveled some distance to the territory, Thomas Rodney kept the most thorough account of his journey. On August 14, 1803, he set out from Dover, "Dalaware," in his "son's chaise and horse," accompanied by William B. Shields and a few family members. They went north to Pennsylvania and then took the turnpike west to York. There Rodney bade farewell to his family while he and Shields continued to Wheeling, Virginia, where they contracted with two young men to build a "batteau, 30 feet long and 8 feet wide," equipped with four oars, a square sail, and two double berths along each side, "covered with a painted canvas." During a two-week stay at Wheeling, Rodney and Shields conversed with Meriwether Lewis, who was preparing for his famous trek to the far West.

Along the way, Rodney and Shields picked up additional companions. By prior arrangement, Maj. Richard Claiborne, who was to become Rodney's clerk on the western board of land commissioners, met them at Wheeling. At Cincinnati, Thomas Hill Williams, also on his way to Natchez, joined the entourage. The trip downstream was lengthy and tiresome but otherwise uneventful except for a near-fatal mishap north of Natchez. The boat hit a large embedded tree limb—or, as Rodney called it, a "snag"—that tore a wide gash in the vessel's bottom. Able to save the boat and salvage most of its contents, they were stranded for two miserable days on a mud bank awaiting repairs.[43]

Rodney's adventures were similar to those who preceded and followed him, but, in one respect, they were unique. Unlike Sargent, Steele, and Claiborne, he did not fall victim to the region's omnipresent fevers. He arrived in good health and, except for an occasional cold or cough, remained free of illness. In fact, he was bedridden only once from a debilitating fever, despite his advanced years. In April 1805, he wrote his anxious son that "the weather here is very Temperate and pleasant and I continue in perfect health." But most newcomers required a period of adjustment, or "seasoning." While most survived the initial attack and few succumbed, Judge Kirby and Trist were among the unfortunates who died within a year or so of arrival.[44]

From 1798 to 1812, the population of the territory grew at a steady if unspectacular pace. It was not until the years following the War of 1812 years that Mississippi Territory experienced a population explosion or "fever," as the phenomenon was then called. The period from 1800 to 1819 became known as the "Great Migration," when thousands of pioneers crossed the mountains and settled the Old Southwest and Northwest. A succession of favorable treaties, one with England in 1794 and the other with Spain in 1795, opened the western floodgates. The perfection of a practical and inexpensive cotton gin in the 1790s fueled the growth of the Southwest, where the fertile soil and temperate climate were extremely favorable to raising upland or short-staple cotton. Simple and inexpensive gins quickly sprang up everywhere. By 1800, as one observer noted, "almost every farmer of considerable force has a horse gin on his farm."[45]

Indeed, cotton production not only accompanied the increase in population but reinforced it as well. As early as 1797, the white fiber had become the territory's staple crop, replacing the less dependable tobacco and indigo. For instance, William Dunbar, that same year, informed a friend that "cotton has become the universal crop of the country" and boasted that he alone had gathered twenty thousand pounds of clean cotton. Between 1797 and 1808, the district's cotton production soared from fewer than two thousand bales a year to more than five thousand, despite a steady decline in price.[46]

During the first decade of the nineteenth century, population kept pace with economic development. In Natchez District alone, the population rose from 7,667 in 1800 to 30,053 in 1810, while the Tombigbee District grew at a slower rate, increasing only from 1,250 to 2,010. But the most impressive gains occurred in the newly opened Tennessee Valley, most of which took place during the last three years of the decade in the vicinity of modern Huntsville. In 1804, John Hunt moved his family from Tennessee to the springs that soon bore his name. In the next few years, hundreds of squatters, mostly from the same state, poured into the area adjacent to Hunt's springs. Once land sales began in 1809, the floodgates opened, and by late 1810, the area contained 4,699 individuals, a fifth of them slaves. In recognition of this sudden spurt of inhabitants, the territorial legislature in 1808 created Madison County to include the entire Tennessee Bend.[47]

What brought these immigrants rushing into the Old Southwest in unprecedented numbers? Part of the answer was the people's general restlessness. Although hardly the first foreign visitor to note the "strange unrest" of Americans, the perceptive Frenchman Alexis de Tocqueville expressed it as well as anyone. "In the United States," he wrote, "a man builds a house in which to spend his old age, and he sells it before the roof is on; he plants a garden and lets it just as the trees are coming into bearing." To be sure, mobility and wanderlust were important characteristics of early nineteenth-century Americans.[48]

The quest for independence and a better life motivated many to seek new lands, especially those that promised to yield immediate returns and sustained profits. As the South Atlantic states became more crowded and as excessive planting of tobacco and other soil-draining crops exhausted the land, opportunities for economic advancement dwindled, causing the rising generation as well as depressed farmers to look elsewhere. For instance, a recent settler in the Virginia Piedmont in 1800 found, to his amazement, a "scene of desolation that baffles all description—farm after farm . . . worn out, washed and gullied" with "scarcely an acre . . . fit for cultivation." Other regions of the Old South were no more promising. Another saw nothing but "dreary and uncultivated wastes" of "barren and exhausted soil, half naked negroes, lean and hungry stock," unkempt fences, and dilapidated houses.[49]

In contrast to these depressed conditions, Mississippi Territory seemed, as one planter stated, "the land of promise, flowing with milk and honey," or, as another described it, "the garden of all America." Indeed, with few exceptions, newcomers waxed eloquently about the mild climate and clean air, the abundance of succulent fruits, the plethora of flowering trees and bushes, and the boundless supply of fresh vegetables available most of the year. "Indeed the air is always so pure here," Judge Rodney rhapsodized. "We have green peas and strawberries here all the month of April," and "the evergreen Magnolia are now in bloom." Everywhere he went "the atmosphere . . . was perfumed" with their fragrance.[50]

Not everyone was as effusive as Rodney. Horse B. Trist was more ambivalent. He deplored the absence of society, the prevalence of offensive manners, and the predominance of federalism among the wealthy planters and merchants. Among "the well born," he lamented, Republicans were "more scarce than Plums in a Scotch Pudding." Where ignorance was not "the order of the day[,] . . . Drunkenness and discipation take the lead." It was, he concluded, "not a pleasant Picture." Yet he acknowledged that "money in great plenty [was] to be made here by agriculture & with superior Talents, a man must rise."[51]

More critical still was the British sailor who stopped briefly at Bayou Pierre on his way to New Orleans. He found Natchez District depressing. After enduring incessant noises of croaking frogs and bellowing alligators and endless swarms of vexatious mosquitoes, he asked rhetorically, "and this is the country to which so many poor devils remove to make their fortune? Damn my precious eyes," he continued, "if I would not rather be at allowance of a mouldy biscuit a day in any part of Old England . . . [than] live in such a country to own the finest cotton plantation, and the greatest gang of negroes in the territory."[52]

As a rule, commentators were more positive than negative. Certainly, Judge Rodney was not alone in imploring his relatives to join him in Mississippi Territory, and others like Governor Claiborne were especially persuasive. In fact, Claiborne not only convinced his immediate family to move first to Natchez and later to Louisiana, but one brother, a nephew, and a handful of distant relatives also joined him in one or both of these locations. Kinship ties were always a strong inducement for moving west, and in the case of Mississippi Territory, they were especially pronounced.

Long before Horace Greeley uttered his famous adage "Go West, young man," several generations of Americans had anticipated his advice.

Indeed the lure of the West was irresistible. Generally, those seeking new homes and fresh opportunities moved directly west, rarely diverting to the south or north. As a result, most immigrants came from an adjacent or nearby state. Not surprisingly, they mostly came from Georgia and Tennessee, with the Carolinas, Virginia, and Kentucky not far behind. They expected to move into a region similar in climate and soil to the one they had left, and for those from the southern and lower border states, they looked either to the immediate west or the southwest.[53]

While most came voluntarily, if not always enthusiastically, there was one notable exception. Hardly any African Americans moved to the territory by choice. Slavery had come to the region with the first European settlers, and by 1800, it had taken firm root in Natchez District, while in Tombigbee District, its presence, though clearly noticeable, was less pervasive. Indeed, slavery became the preferred system of labor in most tropical and semitropical climates, and Mississippi Territory was no exception. In Natchez District alone, the black population increased from 3,222 to 14,423, while the percentage of blacks in the total population rose from 42 percent to 48 percent. Although a few were native Africans, the vast majority were Creoles, mostly from the West Indies and the older South. Having been raised in the institution, they were less likely than first-generation slaves to engage in rebellious behavior, and consequently the territory was largely free of insurrections. Yet, as whites well knew, black resentment could easily lead to violence at any moment, and fear of insurrection was never far from the minds of white Mississippians.

If most immigrants came in quest of land, it was not the only magnet attracting them. Opportunities for professionals, especially lawyers and medical doctors, were boundless because of confusion over land claims and the unhealthy environment, and there was persistent need for educated persons. For example, Abner Green, desperate for a "female teacher" to instruct his six daughters, offered to provide a suitable candidate with room and board at his plantation home, reportedly "one of the best in the territory," and an annual salary of five hundred dollars. According to Judge Rodney, a "dancing master who understands music well could make a fortune here." Lawyers were in constant demand, and in a society where the propensity to sue was ubiquitous, the supply of talented attorneys never kept pace with an insatiable demand. As Rodney informed his son, "Lawyers make a fortune here."[54] Even those with only a rudimentary knowledge of the law managed to make a good living. Not surprisingly, a number of the successful lawyers used their newly acquired wealth to purchase land upon which to settle or speculate. In Mississippi Territory, as elsewhere in the South, ownership of land was the best measure of aristocracy and respectability, and most immigrants expected to join the landed gentry.

CHAPTER 8

"Some Dark Mysterious Business"

On January 10, 1807, Aaron Burr, the territory's most illustrious visitor, made a third and final visit to Natchez.[1] For the past year his name had been linked to an assortment of schemes ranging from establishing a settlement in Louisiana to heading a conspiracy to dismantle the Union and seize Spanish Mexico. Moreover, he reportedly had the ear of other prominent adventurers whose alleged talents for intrigue and skullduggery matched his own.[2]

The reasons for these rumors were as apparent as the person associated with them was infamous. Early on, Burr was known as a man on the rise. Both charming and disarming, he was an enigma to friend and foe alike. He possessed an uncanny ability to captivate people with his grace and wit. Yet few trusted him, for there was something mystifying and sinister about his character. He was too ambitious for the times, too self-serving in an age of deference, and too foreboding to win the abiding loyalty of even dedicated disciples.

Burr's ascension to political prominence was meteoric.[3] Elected in 1791 to represent New York in the U.S. Senate, he became a founder of the fledgling Republican Party. In recognition of his political acumen and the state's importance in the crucial elections of 1800, Burr wrangled a place on the party's presidential ticket. Although some southerners had serious reservations about the enigmatic Burr, party managers still endorsed him as Jefferson's running mate. In the bitter and hard-fought elections of 1800, the Republicans, anxious to elect the full ticket, neglected to have Jefferson receive more electoral votes than Burr. Instead the two tied, throwing the final choice to the lame-duck House of Representatives, where the Federalists had a comfortable majority.

The Federalists, believing Burr more amenable than Jefferson, rallied behind the New Yorker and stayed with him through thirty-five ballots, while Hamilton warned his congressional friends that they were pursuing a dangerous course. Finally, on the thirty-sixth ballot, enough Federalists abstained to elect Jefferson. In the aftermath, a majority of Republicans, including Jefferson, blamed Burr for prolonging the suspense and tossing the nation into a state of near-anarchy.

Having lost the president's confidence, Burr began to fish in new and troubled waters. Maintaining ties with Federalists, he restored those with Republican allies in the hope of recouping his political fortunes. An opportunity arose in 1804, when distraught Federalists approached him with a scheme as daring as it was diabolical. Unnerved by the Louisiana Purchase, which, in their minds, relegated them to insignificance, a contingent of extremists, the so-called Essex Junto, led by the dour Timothy Pickering, proposed formation of a Northern Confederacy to include not only disaffected New England but also the pivotal state of New York. To accomplish this improbable scheme, they required a congenial cohort in Albany, and Burr was the perfect ploy. Not only was he available, but he was also a political outcast, and he readily consented. While dissident Federalists backed Burr, their support was insufficient to place him in the governor's chair or keep the confederation alive. In a fit of pique, the chagrined candidate, blaming Hamilton for his ignominious defeat, challenged him to the fateful duel that closed Burr's career in the East. After killing Hamilton on the dueling ground at Weehawken, New Jersey, the vice president found himself under indictment for murder. Fleeing to Philadelphia, he stayed with the family of Charles Biddle and renewed his Revolutionary War friendship with Gen. James Wilkinson, whose wife, Ann, was Charles's cousin.

The two wartime compatriots soon discovered a mutual interest in western affairs. At the time, Wilkinson was a recognized authority on the lower Mississippi Valley, and Burr relied upon Wilkinson's knowledge in formulating his own plans. But the two men had more in common than fascination with the frontier. Ambitious and adventurous, both relished the good life but lacked the means to sustain it and constantly sought ways to replenish an empty pocket.

Though alike in many respects, they were different in others. Burr was effusive and indiscreet, while Wilkinson was taciturn and circumspect. Wilkinson was a pragmatist, and Burr a hopeless visionary. Burr was more trusting of people than Wilkinson, who was aloof and diabolical, and eventually they grew wary of each other. It was a collaboration doomed to disaster.

In 1805, Burr undertook a whirlwind tour of the West, stopping briefly at Natchez en route to New Orleans, where he conversed with several disgruntled individuals. These included Daniel Clark Jr., unofficial American consul and outspoken critic of Governor Claiborne; Edward Livingston, an astute lawyer and former New York politician from one of that state's finest families; and Juan Ventura Morales, Spanish intendant of West Florida. According to Claiborne, Morales had "more information but less principle than any Spanish Officer" he knew. Burr also met members of the Mexican Association, a shadowy organization of swashbucklers dedicated to "liberating" Mexico from Spain.[4]

During his travels to and from New Orleans, Burr visited other impetuous westerners, including Andrew Jackson, Senators John Brown of Kentucky and John Smith of Ohio, retiring Senator Jonathan Dayton of New Jersey, Governor William Henry Harrison of Indiana Territory, and, of course, General Wilkinson. Some, including Wilkinson, had been associated with an earlier separatist movement known as the "Spanish Conspiracy," which sought to transform Kentucky into a small republic affiliated with Spain.

In 1787, Wilkinson had floated downstream from Frankfort to New Orleans, where he extracted from Louisiana governor Esteban Miro an annual pension of two thousand dollars and the privilege of selling Kentucky produce in exchange for swearing allegiance to the Spanish crown. His principal intermediary was the conniving Daniel Clark, whose feet, like Wilkinson's, were planted in two camps—Spain's and America's. But ratification of the Constitution and establishment of a new government put a halt to these endeavors, and Wilkinson saw his pension fall into arrears.[5]

Returning east, Burr renewed his conversations with British minister Anthony Merry, whose enmity for Jefferson was enormous, and through the auspices of Dayton, he opened communications with Spanish min-

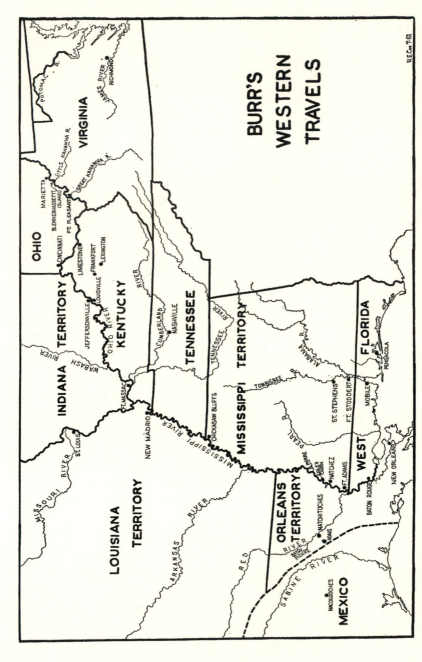

Map by Harold E. Cox (Thomas P. Abernethy, *The South in the New Nation, 1789–1819* [Baton Rouge, La., 1961]).

ister Yrujo, another inveterate foe of the president. Apparently in cooperation with Merry, Burr solicited British assistance for his embryonic
West Florida plans, which, he expected, would delight Smith, Clark,
and other land speculators in Baton Rouge and Feliciana. Yet, according
to Dayton, Burr's interest extended only to Mexico and not to West Florida. Already Burr was telling one story to some and another to others. If
anything, Burr appeared more like an incipient conspirator in search of
a conspiracy than a traitor in quest of men and money.

In the end, Burr's dickering with England and Spain accomplished
little. England refused to take the bait, and Spanish officials dismissed
Burr's overtures since they had Wilkinson to keep them abreast of developments. Nonetheless, Burr's western junket buoyed his spirits. He found
the people restless, the region in turmoil, and war between Spain and the
United States imminent. The times, Burr believed, were propitious.[6]

Meanwhile, Spanish officials in Texas grew more aggressive than
those in West Florida, largely because Spain placed a premium upon
retaining Mexico. They moved additional troops into Texas, and Governor Antonio Cordero transferred his headquarters to Nacogdoches, near
the Sabine frontier, and dispatched a small party of troops to establish an
outpost at Bayou Pierre. In response, Secretary of War Dearborn ordered
Maj. Moses Porter, commanding officer at Natchitoches, an American
settlement on the Red River some fifty miles southeast of Bayou Pierre,
to prevent the Spaniards from crossing the Sabine River. On February
5, 1806, Capt. Edward D. Turner, with a detachment of sixty men, dislodged Spanish soldiers from Adais, a cantonment about fourteen miles
west of Natchitoches.[7]

The administration's uncharacteristic firmness was due more to diplomatic failures abroad than to frontier disturbances. James Monroe was
unsuccessful in persuading Spain to recognize America's claim to West
Florida and Texas, and he departed for Madrid in disgust. Fearing Spanish contentiousness, Dearborn, in late spring of 1806, put Col. Thomas
Cushing in command of Natchitoches and instructed Wilkinson to
transfer his headquarters from St. Louis to New Orleans and consult
Governor Claiborne about defense of the Southwest. While Wilkinson dallied in St. Louis, he cautioned Cushing to avoid hostilities with
Spain, in contravention of Dearborn's instructions. Fortunately, Spain
had no more desire than Wilkinson to provoke war, and, in early April
1806, Governor Cordero recalled his troops to Nacogdoches.[8]

Simultaneously the United States frightened Spain by sending two exploring expeditions into the far Southwest. Jefferson authorized Capt. Richard Sparks and Thomas Freeman, accompanied by forty soldiers, to explore the upper Red River and establish friendly relations with Caddo Indians. The expedition proceeded even though Governor Claiborne failed to secure Spanish approval despite assurances that its purpose was "exclusively scientific" and unconnected with "political views unfriendly to the interests of his Catholic Majesty." The Spaniards later overtook Freeman's party and forced the explorers to return to Natchez.[9]

These forays into Spanish Territory caused officials in Texas to retaliate. Spanish soldiers reoccupied Bayou Pierre, and later Cordero stationed a scouting party within seventeen miles of Natchitoches, remaining nine days before retiring. The situation along the Sabine frontier had reached a critical stage when General Wilkinson assumed command of American troops from Colonel Cushing.[10]

To be sure, Mississippi Territory was alive with rumors, some true but most not, and there was good reason for alarm. Spain closed the port of Mobile to American commerce, Governor Grand-Pre required aliens traversing West Florida to carry a passport specifying their business and destination, and reports of Spanish intrigue with the Indians, especially the Choctaw, were pervasive. In June 1806, Choctaw interpreter John Pitchlynn had reported that Spanish officials had provided "some powder and Lead" to 1,100 Choctaws and invited them to return in three months "to receive great presents and a great talk from the great mingo [Governor Folch] at Pensacola." The parlay, according to Pitchlynn, created "much confusion" among tribesmen and infused "strength and vigor" in those opposed to the "American mingoes."[11] Judge Toulmin "fear[ed] bad times" ahead because Spanish interference with Indians "puts the life of everyman here [Tombigbee] in jeopardy." In retaliation, inhabitants of Washington County called for a boycott of Spanish trade and threatened to censure anyone who had "commercial intercourse" with Mobile or Pensacola.[12]

Earlier, Governor Williams had left for North Carolina, leaving territorial affairs to the newly appointed secretary, Cowles Mead, who arrived four days later. A Virginian by birth, Mead, who spent his late adolescent years in Georgia, was only twenty-nine years old at the time. Flamboyant in appearance, theatrical in demeanor, and bombastic in speech, Mead often acted with more dispatch than discretion. He quickly enmeshed himself in local politics, aligning with the governor's critics and naming William B. Shields and George Poindexter his aides-de-camp. Shortly thereafter, Mead courted and won the hand of Abner Green's daughter Mary, a marriage that further tied him to the growing anti-Williams faction.[13]

Mead immediately faced a series of crises, the first over West Florida. Initially he discounted reports of Spanish tampering with the Indians as "the offspring of false rumors," but within weeks, he changed his tune, now certain that Spanish authorities had invited the Choctaw to Mobile "for some mischievous purposes." By late June, Mead was so sure of Spanish perfidy that he recommended sending "several companies of troops through the Indian nations to keep the peace and to erect a fort near them on the Pascogoula River."[14]

But as events unfolded, Mead's problems were less with Spain than with the notorious Caller brothers. As he soon learned, the Washington County militia, headed by Col. John Caller, "contemplated an attack on Mobile." Fortunately, the level-headed Judge Toulmin persuaded the impetuous Caller "to desist." Shortly thereafter another scheme, involving some "thirty men" who planned "to proceed to Mobille and destroy the Town by fire," was likewise "uncovered and prevented."[15]

The Spaniards, aware of these threats, reinforced Mobile with troops from Pensacola and dispatched "nightly patrols" to intercept marauders. Capt. Thomas Swaine, commanding officer at Fort Stoddert, reassured the Spaniards of his government's peaceful intentions, but they were not mollified, and even he soon grew apprehensive, after receiving repeated "hints that the attack will yet probably be attempted." Mead was equally uneasy. Annoyed that Caller's "conduct had aroused a vigilance in our enemy which may obstruct our future views in that quarter," he urged him to exercise "patience" and to endure gracefully "this partial evil until relief can be given by the United States."[16]

Meanwhile, unrest along the western border flared up again. Spanish troops crossed the Sabine and reoccupied Bayou Pierre. A month later, they advanced "their main body [of men] to within 17 miles of Natchitoches and their patroles as far as Bayou Funda," only seven miles from the nearest American outpost. Claiborne estimated their strength at "one thousand, the great part Cavalry," and warned that "reinforcements are daily expected." He accused the Spaniards of seizing three American citizens, granting asylum to "several fugitive slaves," and ripping down the "American Flag" in the "Caddo Nation of Indians." Hostilities, he believed, were unavoidable.[17]

The War Department implored General Wilkinson to hasten to New Orleans with four hundred troops and dislodge the Spanish. Not wishing to exchange the pleasures of St. Louis for the discomforts of the field, Wilkinson was in no hurry, although he instructed Colonel Cushing to avoid hostilities unless attacked. At the same time, Claiborne and Mead, meeting at Natchez, pledged to expedite organizing the militia. Expecting "rupture with [the Spaniards] ere long," Mead shifted his attention from Mobile to the Sabine after news there began "to bespeak decisive hostility." Both Mead and Claiborne, eager to chastise the dons, chafed at administrative dawdling. "I really wish from the bottom of my heart to give the Spaniards a fight," Claiborne told Mead, "but I cannot go counter to the orders of constituted authority."[18]

But Mississippians preferred to seize West Florida than chase Spaniards out of Bayou Pierre. Mead informed Dearborn of their desire to take the Floridas. "If one drop of blood should be spilt by the Spaniards on the southern borders of Louisiana it shall be immediately expiated at Baton Rouge. I am disposed," he continued, "to act decisively & promptly" in order to "circumscribe our enemy in Mobile and Pensacola [so] as to Cut off all communications with Indians."[19]

Nevertheless, when asked to furnish five companies of militia to counteract "hostile movements" in Texas, a pleased Mead eagerly complied. "The alacrity with which the inhabitants flew to their ranks, joined to the general ardor pervading the whole territory," he crowed, "induces me to believe that every reliance may be placed in this people for personal aid if requisite to their honor as a free & spirited nation." He was confident that enlistees were sufficient to meet any contingency. "Volunteer corps," he reported, "are organizing in every county which I trust will spare a draft."[20]

The only pressing problem was "want of arms," and Mead had an answer. "For them," he declared, "we look with confidence to Baton Rouge, where they can be had by one bold assault." Later he was more specific. "Sir, can't the Floridas be taken and then paid for?" he queried Dearborn. "Can't we be permitted to make use of the insolence of Spain on one side of Louisiana as a just cause of attack on them?" He yearned to lead Mississippians into battle. Because of "the insults of Louisiana I burn to deal back in blows upon the Floridas," he declared.[21]

On September 12, 1806, Wilkinson, while at Fort Adams on his way to Natchitoches, alerted Mead to have the territory's "elite Corps . . . ready to march on the 26th Instant." So long as the Spaniards occupied "the disputed territory," he planned to force them "to recross the Sabine." To do so, he told Mead, he might have "to Speak to them in a tone, which may not be perfectly acceptable."[22] In that event, he needed to augment his troops with militia from Orleans and Mississippi territories.

Anticipating hostilities, Mead mustered four companies, including Poindexter's elite Mississippi Blues, to rendezvous at Washington and instructed Col. John Ellis's regiment in Wilkinson County to assemble at Fort Adams. Spanish aggression on "the western borders of Louisiana," Mead informed Dearborn, was "as much an act of hostility to us as if committed within the Mississippi Territory." The inhabitants, he boasted, were "all alive with the expectation of war with Spain" and "never [before] was more ardor or solicitude manifest[ed]." Shortly before the militia left for the western frontier, Mead placed Ferdinand L. Claiborne, brother of the governor of Orleans, in command.[23]

Not everyone flew to arms with such fervor. Col. John Ellis reported that "a number of leading characters" in Wilkinson County strongly objected to mustering the militia. The loudest "were Doctor [John F.] Carmichal, Captain [Edward] Randolph and Robert Semple."[24] Carmichael's opposition was critical. Not only was he a prominent medical doctor and former army officer, but he also was "aid de camp to His Excellency Governor Williams." Earlier, Williams entrusted to his care the stand of arms loaned the territory by the federal government.

But, when asked to furnish Ellis a portion of the arms in his custody, Carmichael balked. According to Ellis, the cantankerous doctor "refused to deliver the rifles except by his [Williams's] order." Mead summoned Carmichael to explain his insubordination, but the doctor, pleading illness, failed to show. A livid Mead removed him as aide-de-camp and instigated court-martial proceedings. Eventually, Mead prevailed upon the temporary commander at Fort Adams, a nervous Lt. George Washington Sevier, to provide the militiamen with muskets. Still, the horse troopers rode out of Natchez "only half equipped."[25]

Claiborne and the Mississippi militia left the territory on October 6, 1806. Four days later, they reached Alexandria, only a short distance from Natchitoches. According to Claiborne, the march was "made with alecrity," and the men demonstrated "much patriotic zeal." Everyone, he continued, "seemed anxious to excel in displaying their solicitude to meet the enimy and exhibit the character of the Mississippi Territory in its true colors." Just as Claiborne was about to resume the march, a messenger from Wilkinson handed him a bombshell. The general ordered Claiborne to return, except for one company of dragoons, to Natchez. "You can imagine," an astonished Claiborne reported, "the chagrin and mortification which prevailed throughout . . . on the receipt of the communication . . . from General Wilkinson." The apparent reason for this turn of events was Spain's decision to withdraw "beyond the Sabine."[26]

The previous August, General Wilkinson had finally departed St. Louis, proceeding southward at a leisurely pace. On September 7, he had reached Natchez, where he made his usual splendid entrance, accompanied by pomp and ceremony. After conferring with the dashing and mercurial Mead, Wilkinson continued downstream to Fort Adams, before starting his ascent of the Red River to the "Rapides," where, on September 18, he met Governor Claiborne, who was marshaling an auxiliary force to expel the Spaniards. Alarmed by the territorial governors' ardor, Wilkinson feared that one or both might, in their youthful inexperience and exuberance, provoke the enemy unnecessarily. Before acting, he wished to assess the situation himself rather than rely on the word of wrought-up officials.[27]

During the ensuing weeks, Wilkinson outwardly pursued a bold and bellicose posture while quietly hinting at conciliation. Like most generals confronting possible hostilities, Wilkinson exaggerated his opponents' strength. He estimated the enemy's force at "fifteen hundred men," most of whom were mounted and operating in a countryside replete with horses and cows and abundant pasturage. In contrast, he had fewer than five hundred men. Dependent upon militia for reinforcements, he was hesitant to deploy poorly trained men in battle. While demanding withdrawal of all Spanish forces from the disputed territory and fearing Spanish intransigence, he dispatched Colonel Cushing to Nacogdoches with a letter to Cordero explaining the reasons for his actions and alluding to compromise.[28]

Luckily for Wilkinson, the Spaniards were also reevaluating their strategy. On September 27, 1806, they had pulled out of the territory between the Sabine River and Arroyo Hondo. Assuming that withdrawal signified a willingness to acquiesce, Wilkinson advanced his troops to within twenty-five miles of the Sabine River, only to discover that nothing had changed. Spain was as adamant as ever.

Nonetheless, Wilkinson attempted a second reconciliation. He dispatched Walter Burling, a prominent Natchez planter acting as his aide-de-camp, to Nacogdoches with a conciliatory offer. He promised to withdraw to Natchitoches and not recross the Arroyo Hondo if Spain stayed west of the Sabine, converting the disputed territory into a no-man's land, pending further negotiations. Spanish governor Simon de Herrera, apparently on his own authority, accepted Wilkinson's offer on November 5, 1806.[29] Thereafter, both governments realized that it was in their interest to observe a "neutral ground."

Wilkinson had reason for wanting a truce. On October 8, Samuel Swartwout, one of Burr's several New York henchmen, appeared bearing a letter, written in cipher and dated July 29. Wilkinson instantly recognized that it was from Burr. Swartwout also brought a dispatch from Dayton, informing Wilkinson that Jefferson intended to remove him as commanding general of the army. Finding the communications untimely and unnerving, he spent the night deciphering Burr's letter.[30]

Burr reported having sufficient funds to launch an expedition down the Ohio and Mississippi rivers and the assistance of the British navy as well as cooperation of an American naval force. He intended to begin his movements on August 1, 1816, expecting to reach the Falls of the Ohio by the middle of November and Natchez a month later. He planned to descend the rivers with five hundred to a thousand men and meet the general at Natchez and decide whether to seize or bypass Spanish Baton Rouge.[31]

For Wilkinson, it was the moment of decision. By morning, he had settled on a course of action. He would alert Jefferson to the danger at hand, conclude the neutral-ground agreement as soon as possible, and hurry to New Orleans, presumably to confront Burr and abort the conspiracy he was about to reveal. For Wilkinson, this decision was easy. After all, he had made a lucrative career out of warning edgy officials of impending threats in exchange for favors and funds. According to Wilkinson, he worshiped Spain and the United States equally, and he wished no harm to either. Since Burr's plans threatened Wilkinson's favorite countries, he took steps to inform both of the New Yorker's intrigues.[32]

As Wilkinson confronted the Spaniards along the Sabine, Burr was not idle. In early August 1806, he had left Philadelphia and headed west, intending, as he told friends, to settle there. Stopping briefly in Pittsburgh, where he contracted for supplies and enlisted recruits, he proceeded downriver to Marietta and then to Blennerhassett Island. Both Harman Blennerhassett and the island were to play prominent roles in Burr's future endeavors.

A visionary Irishman, Blennerhassett migrated to the United States in 1796. Two years later, he moved to a deserted island in the Ohio, located at the mouth of the Great Kanawha River. There he built a rambling, rustic mansion that he furnished lavishly, dissipating much of his fortune. Yet he and his wife became increasingly bored with a bucolic and lonely life, and they fell easy victim to Burr's intoxicating charm when he first visited the island in May 1805. Although Harman was absent, Burr conversed with his wife, an attractive and talented woman. She convinced her husband to cooperate with Burr, and the two men became fast friends. In fact, Blennerhassett was Burr's primary source of funds, and his island a staging area for Burr's western adventure.[33]

From Blennerhassett's, Burr set off for Kentucky and Tennessee, where he renewed earlier contacts and contracted for additional boats and supplies. Along the way, he stopped briefly in Cincinnati and paid his respects to Senator John Smith. In Kentucky, he conversed with Senator Brown, and in Tennessee he revisited Andrew Jackson at the Hermitage. A master of obfuscation, Burr talked opaquely, encouraging his listeners to interpret his words as they wished, and each came away with wildly differing impressions. For example, Jackson was so eager to assist Burr in attacking Spain that he wrote a thoroughly confused Jefferson, offering to raise a regiment.[34]

Burr's erratic behavior and quixotic schemes frightened more people than his allure attracted. Allegations against him and speculations about his plans followed him like a stray dog. Most were nothing more than wild speculation, based upon Burr's loose talk, vague insinuations, harebrained schemes, and brash bravado. Although Burr expected to elicit from his friends more information than he conveyed, the reverse was often the case. He was rarely circumspect, always loquacious, and bewildering to his conversants.

Meanwhile, Jefferson was aware of Burr's mystifying activities. In the spring of 1806, he had begun receiving warnings, most of which concerned a plot of Burr's to separate the West from the Atlantic states.

Not surprisingly, the first warning came from Kentucky, scene of the earlier Spanish Conspiracy. A number of Kentuckians, remembering Wilkinson's involvement in that affair, surmised that Burr's escapades were a revival of these efforts. Several of those involved in the original Spanish Conspiracy were still active in Kentucky politics, and a handful were suspected of collusion with Burr. In addition to Senators John Brown and John Adair, these included three judges—Harry Innis of the federal court for the District of Kentucky; George Muter, chief justice of the Kentucky Court of Appeals; and Benjamin Sebastian, associate justice of the Kentucky Court of Appeals. But Burr's chief accuser was Joseph Hamilton Davies, U.S. attorney for the District of Kentucky, who had the cooperation of former senator Humphrey Marshall, first cousin of Chief Justice John Marshall. Like Davies, the senator was a staunch Federalist and nephew of the chief justice, and Jefferson chose to ignore the reports on partisan grounds.[35]

Displeased with Jefferson's inertia, Davies took legal action, accusing Burr of assembling an expedition to seize Mexico from Spain. Burr, with his attorney, Henry Clay, appeared before the grand jury, which found "no true bill" against him. An elated Burr not only celebrated his victory but also stepped up preparations for the journey down the Ohio and Mississippi rivers.[36]

But Burr's troubles were hardly over. Jefferson continued to receive reports of his furtive activities and portentous conversations with prominent figures, including Col. George Morgan of western Pennsylvania and John Nicholson of New York. A few of those previously friendly to Burr, like Andrew Jackson, grew more skeptical. Surprisingly, Jefferson's reaction was cautionary. He sent Secretary John Graham of Orleans Territory, who was conveniently in the nation's capital, to shadow Burr and report his movements. Apparently Jefferson preferred to let Burr commit an overt act before showing his hand.

On the other hand, Burr, cognizant of the rumors, realized that the longer he tarried, the more likely it was for the accusations to spread and intensify. In early December, Graham warned Ohio governor Edward Tiffin that Burr planned to capture New Orleans, where he hoped to seize the banks, estimated to have deposits of nearly $2 million, and the military supplies stored there. With the funds and equipment, Burr intended, according to Graham, to erect a revolutionary government, forge an alliance with one or more European powers, and liberate

Mexico. All of these speculations seemed plausible as long as General Wilkinson, rumored to be his confidant, was tied up fighting the Spaniards along the Sabine. In fact, some believed that Burr intended to join Wilkinson there for a march on Mexico.[37]

Alarmed by Graham's warning, Governor Tiffin took prompt action. He sent to Marietta two agents to seize Burr's boats, arrest anyone suspected of collaborating with him, and prevent his adherents from descending the Ohio. They confiscated ten of Burr's boats on the river and an equal number of newly constructed ones as well as four unfinished vessels and a large cache of provisions.[38]

These developments sent Burr's recruits into a frenzy. Around midnight on December 10, 1806, they left Blennerhassett Island, hurrying downstream. Surprisingly, they reached the Falls of the Ohio without interruption. There a second group joined them for descent downriver to a prearranged rendezvous at Natchez. At the mouth of the Cumberland River, Burr caught up with the flotilla, which consisted of only ten vessels, one of which contained supplies and the rest some sixty to one hundred passengers. Although Burr refused to reveal his destination, everyone assumed he was heading for Spanish territory.

When Burr joined the group, he was in a hurry. In Nashville, he learned that Wilkinson had made a truce with Spanish officials and was on his way to New Orleans. After leaving Fort Massac, where the commanding officer received him warmly, Burr made only two brief stops— one at New Madrid and the other at Chickasaw Bluffs. On Saturday morning, January 10, 1807, he touched shore at Bruin's landing and headed straight for Judge Peter Bruin's home, where, to his astonishment, his host showed him a copy of the *Mississippi Messenger* containing the president's proclamation and a doctored version of his cipher letter to Wilkinson. Burr was dumbfounded. In his mind, he had committed no crime nor was he a traitor; he had done nothing to warrant Jefferson's allegations.[39]

Meanwhile, Jefferson's mood had changed. After months of disregarding the plethora of warnings, he now had to act. Wilkinson's decision to alert him to Burr's activities forced his hand. No longer able to wait for Burr to incriminate himself, Jefferson summoned his cabinet. Agreeing with its members that he must warn the nation of impending danger, he ordered all post commanders on the western waters to intercept any expedition against Spanish territory and arrest the participants.

Although Jefferson purposely mentioned no names, he obviously had Burr in mind. For instance, Dearborn immediately informed Wilkinson that "Col Burr is generally considered the head [of the conspiracy], but his real object is doubtful." Also, he cautioned, "your name has been frequently associated with Burr, Dayton, and others."[40]

Similar reports circulated in Mississippi Territory. In late June 1806, Judge Rodney had reported a "Great splash" in the newspapers about Francisco de Miranda, the aging Venezuelan adventurer and revolutionary, and his plans to liberate South America, but he saw no connection between him and Burr or Wilkinson. Apparently, these rumormongers were unaware that Burr had conferred with Wilkinson earlier or that many of his eastern friends were supporters of Miranda, who, with assistance of the British navy, hoped to revolutionize Spanish America. Nevertheless, hatred of Spain was so intense that Rodney thought there "was not a person in this part of the world who does not wish him well."

As these reports multiplied, the *Western World*, the leading newspaper west of the Appalachians, dredged up the old Spanish Conspiracy, or, as Rodney called it, the "Kentucky Conspiracy." This story provoked renewed speculation about Wilkinson's role in both affairs. Rodney initially traced the disclosures to the general's enemies in the army, but his friends correctly named Senator Humphrey Marshall the culprit. Nevertheless, reports of Wilkinson's ties with Spanish officials were widespread. Rodney heard from "a lady of this territory that General Wilkinson [had] sent frequent dispatches to Gayoso [and] that her own brother was bearer of his most important communications."[41]

Indeed, Mississippians were more likely to connect Wilkinson with intrigue than Burr. As early as September 1806, Mead had joined the expanding list of the general's detractors. Ironically, he shared his suspicions with Dearborn, unaware that he was one of Wilkinson's strongest defenders. "The people of the territory are convinced . . . that Genl Wilkinson is a Spanish officer," he wrote. "The Old inhabitants all know some fact which leads to this opinion & seem astonished when ignorance of his extreme intimacy with several Spanish Governors, is acknowledged." While dutifully complying with the general's orders, including sending a force to Natchitoches, Mead's suspicions were deep and unalterable.[42]

Likewise, Andrew Jackson in mid-November warned Governor Claiborne of the dangers he faced. "Put your Town in a state of Defence," he admonished, "and defend your city as well against internal enemies as external." Although Jackson offered no specifics, he implored the governor to "Be alert—keep a watchful eye on our General. . . . I fear there [is] something rotten in the State of Denmark."[43]

Wilkinson's behavior served to confirm these suspicions. After arranging a truce with Spanish officials, Wilkinson in mid-November passed through Natchez on his way to New Orleans. Tarrying there for more than a week, he chose the home of Stephen Minor, the last Spanish commandant of Natchez, as temporary headquarters. According to rumors, Minor was one of Wilkinson's confidential Spanish contacts. During the summer of 1805, on his return from New Orleans, Burr had also visited Minor. If renewal of friendship with Minor was not enough to arouse Mead's suspicion, Wilkinson's decisions to transfer the garrisons of Fort Stoddert and Fort Adams to New Orleans and to dismantle the latter's fortifications, leaving the territory practically defenseless, were sufficient. Therefore, on November 13, when Wilkinson requested Mead "to array five hundred men properly officered, with orders to repair to the City of New Orleans as rapidly as possible, for three months service," he refused on the flimsy excuse that the militia was needed to defend the territory against Indians.[44]

By mid-November, the territory was astir. Rodney notified his son, soon to be Jefferson's attorney general, of "a formidable conspiracy in this Country in which a Number of high and Influential carracters are Implicated" but advised him to "say no more on this subject." Two weeks later, he was more forthright. The "diabolical conspiracy," he reported, involved persons in Mississippi and Orleans territories, and the object was "to seize all public arms and ammunition in this country and then take possession of New Orleans." Still, he could hardly "believe that there were men among the Americans so desperate and foolhardy to undertake it unless in combination with some foreign power," and he suspected Spanish collusion. "The people," he reported, were "much alarmed and agitated."[45]

The territory's favorite parlor game was to speculate about likely participants. While the names of Burr and Wilkinson came up repeatedly, there were also rumors about Governor Williams and a few senior army officers. After Wilkinson left Natchez on November 20, speculation centered on him, Burr, Daniel Clark, and the Spanish governors of the Floridas and Texas. According to Rodney, "the Design of the Conspiracy

[was] to unite Kentucky, Tennessee, Louisiana, The Floridas, and part at least of Mexico into an Independent Empire."[46]

Mead was particularly distraught. He claimed to have in his possession enough "full and decisive information" to prove "beyond a doubt" the existence of an "association." From a "gentleman of respectability, hitherto thought by the conspirators to be friendly to their views," Mead learned that New Orleans was "the first place of attack." He dispatched Ferdinand Claiborne to New Orleans with the news. "It is believed here," he reported, "that General Wilkinson is the soul of the conspiracy. Your City," he continued, "is alive with mischievous spirits & they are trained by the active and restless Daniel Clark—he is their head, father, and promotor."[47]

On November 25, General Wilkinson arrived in New Orleans. Although circumspect at first, he eventually divulged to Governor Claiborne and Capt. John Shaw, commander of the U.S. Navy on the New Orleans Station, the contents of Burr's cipher letter of July 29. After perusing it, both were convinced of a conspiracy to revolutionize Louisiana and Mexico and relied on Wilkinson to protect the city against Burr's forces, now believed to exceed two thousand. According to Wilkinson, Burr and his men planned to reach Natchez by December 15. Claiborne alerted the other western governors of the existence of "an armed association . . . under the direction of Colonel Aaron Burr with designs hostile to the Government" and dispatched Maj. J. William Gurley "to Natchez to appraise [Mead] . . . of the Danger, and to concert measures for the defence of our Common Country."[48]

Claiborne proposed sending a militia force to Natchez to intercept Burr before he reached New Orleans, but Wilkinson quashed it. Instead, he asked the governor to declare martial law. Claiborne was against taking drastic action before Burr's objectives were clear, but he still supported Wilkinson's efforts to shore up the city's defenses, to picket the area, and to clamp a temporary embargo on commerce along the river. Wilkinson charged Swartwout and his traveling companion, Peter V. Ogden, with treason and sent an officer to Fort Adams to arrest the pair. Shortly thereafter, he rounded up a number of other suspects and ordered his subordinates to collect evidence against them. To critics, Wilkinson seemed to be conducting "a reign of terror," and even Claiborne began to question Wilkinson's motives.[49]

While Wilkinson was preparing New Orleans against attack, Mead, acting on intelligence from Claiborne, was busy in Mississippi Territory. On December 15, he sent a confidential message to the territorial legislature, alleging "the existence of a plot designed to destroy the connection which exists between this Territory and the Government of the United States" and requesting "a battalion of minute men," subject to his authority. Three days later, the legislature complied, expressing confidence in Mead and pledging to support whatever measures were necessary, "within the law," to quell the disturbance. On December 23, Mead advised everyone to be on guard "against agents of this diabolical plot" and assist in apprehending "any of its agents." Two days later, he mustered four militia regiments.[50]

Despite Wilkinson's frantic efforts to intercept Burr, Mead still questioned his loyalty. Be "on your guard against the wily General," he warned Claiborne, "he is not much better than Cataline—consider him a traitor and act" accordingly. If he could prevent Burr from reaching New Orleans, Mead reasoned, it might "hold the Genl in his allegiance to the U. States." On the other hand, if Burr "passes this Territory with two thousand men," Mead had "no doubt but the Genl will be your worst enemy."

Yet, when Burr failed to appear as expected, officials like Rodney were more amused than alarmed. "The Story of Burr," he wrote, "grows more feeble. . . . The project that Lumed so large lately begins generally to be received with Contempt in the West." Silas Dinsmoor was even jocular. "We are all in a flurry here," he told a friend, "hourly expecting Col Burr & all Kentucky and half of Tennessee . . . to punish General Wilkinson, set the negroes free, rob the banks & take Mexico. Come and help me to laugh at the fun."[51]

Nevertheless, Mead was ready when Burr arrived on January 10, 1807. The next day, the rest of Burr's party, consisting of nine boats and about one hundred men, landed at Bruinsburg. Burr immediately dispatched Davis Floyd and a companion to Natchez, first to contact his friends there and later to drop downriver and confer with Dr. Carmichael at Fort Adams. According to the unreliable medical doctor, Floyd reconnoitered the area in preparation for an assault on Spanish Baton Rouge. Furthermore, he intimated, a second band of recruits, perhaps as many as ten thousand, was on its way from Kentucky and Tennessee to join Burr below Natchez. Burr's intention, he declared, was not to split the Union but to seize first Spanish West Florida and then Mexico.

After Floyd quietly returned to Natchez, Carmichael hurried to New Orleans to inform Wilkinson.[52]

On January 12, Mead learned that Burr was "at Bruin's" from Col. Thomas Fitzpatrick, who immediately sent a detachment to apprehend him and beseeched Mead to assemble "all force you can get to Natchez" and cut off Burr's escape. Meanwhile, Burr slipped across the river and camped his recruits along Thompson's Creek, leaving behind in an unsealed envelope a note addressed to the governor. Again Burr professed his innocence. His object, he said, was "agriculture and [my] boats the vehicles of emigration." But he threatened to resist "any attempt to coerce him" and abjured Mead not to provoke hostilities. "It is hoped Sir," he pleaded "that you'll not suffer yourself to be made the instrument of arming Citizen Against Citizen and of invoking the Country in the Horrors of Civil War," based on the word of "a man notoriously the pensioner of a foreign Government."[53]

Burr's message placed Mead in a quandary. Though doubting Burr's innocence and distrustful of Wilkinson, he cherished the honor of nabbing the celebrated fugitive. He told Fitzpatrick that if Burr voluntarily submitted he should "shew him the respect due to his standing" and promise that "every security shall be given to private property." If Burr, however, was "as innocent" as he professed and if he "has been vilified or injured by rumors or [by] the Pensioned [Wilkinson]," Fitzpatrick was to guarantee him "the full and complete protection of the laws of the Territory."[54]

Expecting Burr not to surrender peacefully, Mead took precautionary measures. He ordered the arrest of the "Burr Conspirators," mustered the militia, and prorogued the legislature, advising its members to "suspend the elegance of debate for the Clanguor of military array." Later, he instructed Capt. Joshua Baker to station twenty-five men "on the bank of the Mississippi at or near Fort Adams" and Colonel Claiborne, with three hundred men, to set up headquarters at Thomas Calvit's home, near the mouth of Coles Creek midway between Bayou Pierre and Natchez. They were to seize Burr's flotilla if he or his associates attempted to flee. The next day, Mead advised Captain Shaw, Wilkinson, and Maj. John Minor at Concordia of Burr's presence.[55]

Momentarily Burr was out of harm's way, safely ensconced on the Louisiana side. While Burr pondered his future, Mead, seeking to ascertain his intentions, was surprised when Burr welcomed officials to his camp. On January 15, Col. W. H. Wooldridge and two subordinates crossed the Mississippi in a skiff provided by a self-assured Burr and spent time conversing with him. Wooldridge reported seeing no more than sixty unarmed men, four flatboats, and five barges.

The next day, Fitzpatrick, accompanied by sixty dragoons, also visited Burr, who offered to surrender and face trial. Indeed, he was sure that no jury would convict him of treason because of the inhabitants' disdain for Spaniards and Wilkinson. Moreover, he did not relish falling into the clutches of the vengeful general. Burr not only denounced the general's actions as "perfidious," but he also pronounced the published cipher letter a "vile falsification." The reports, he said, were "utterly false . . . and the inventions of wicked men, for evil purposes."[56]

On January 16, Mead's two aides, Poindexter and Shields, offered Burr safe conduct to meet with territorial officials at Calvit's. There Burr agreed to give himself up and to permit his boats to be searched and supplies taken. Escorted to the town of Washington, Burr was to appear before the supreme court on February 2. For some reason, Burr did not sign a recognizance until January 22, when Judge Rodney persuaded Benijah Osmun and Lyman Harding, two resident Federalists, to act as securities, each posting a bond of $2,500. Burr put up the remaining $5,000 and promised "not [to] depart Without leave of Said Court."[57]

Free to enjoy the pleasures of Natchez, Burr quickly became a celebrity. The Federalists embraced him openly, entertaining him royally and throwing elaborate balls in his honor, and he became Colonel Osmun's house guest at Windy Hill Manor. One of the territory's staunchest Federalists and a confirmed bachelor, Osmun had admired Burr since their days together in the Revolution. Osmun's nearest neighbor was Maj. Isaac Guion, who likewise enjoyed Burr's friendship. Another neighbor was the widow Price, whose husband had been robbed and murdered on a journey to Natchez. He left behind a daughter, the graceful Madeline, who, according to older settlers, was "a miracle of beauty," and Burr was instantly smitten by her good looks and captivating charm. Supposedly the two fell madly in love, and according to an enduring legend, Burr planned to take her with him after his anticipated acquittal.[58]

But Burr's friends were not limited to frustrated Federalists or army officers discharged by Jefferson's retrenchment policies. They also included a number of people who hated the Spanish, and Burr convinced them that he wanted to chastise the dons, not to split the Union.

Like Andrew Jackson, they were ready to follow anyone who promised to end the Spanish threat. Others had not forgotten Wilkinson's abrupt discharge of the Mississippi militia in 1806.

On January 20, 1807, the *Mississippi Messenger*, the territory's leading newspaper, joined the rising chorus in praise of Burr and condemnation of Wilkinson. The editor rhetorically asked his "fellow citizens" if it was not time "to pause and reflect." In contrast to Burr, who had always been "submissive to the law," Wilkinson had set up "a military despotism . . . in New Orleans," while Mead, acting with "moderation," had prevented "our citizens from being transported elsewhere for trial." Moreover, "Burr threatens to invade the Spanish colonies, and our citizens arm against him. Our laws, our Constitution, and dearest principles of liberty are invaded, and we are silent and calm spectators."[59]

The legislature also displayed an anti-Spanish bias. On January 17, it unanimously adopted a resolution, introduced by eastern representatives James Caller and Lemuel Henry, protesting Spain's "continued obstruction of commerce on the Alabama, Tombigby, Mobile and Paspagola" rivers. The harassment, warned the legislators, must cease or else "the whole country from Georgia to the Pearl River will be entirely abandoned to Indians and Spaniards." It was no accident that its adoption coincided with Burr's courting of Caller and Henry, who later assured Burr that had he gone to Tombigbee instead of Natchez, he would have found ample support for attacking Mobile.[60]

Several thought Wilkinson had willfully exaggerated the danger. Burr's ragtag forces were never the thousands he claimed nor did they threaten anyone. Despite all of the "weighty alarm," authorities discovered only "nine boats and one hundred men," most of them "boys or young men just from School." They were, Mead acknowledged, "really ignorant and deluded, . . . dupes of stratagem." A search of Burr's "badly loaded" boats uncovered a "large supply of flour, pork, whisky, and corn meal," provisions more suited to settlement than military expeditions. Burr's arsenal consisted of only "three muskets, six fuseus, eleven rifles— two blunder busses, thirteen brace of pistols, five swords, and three or four pounds of powder."

Thereafter, some inhabitants displayed more apprehension of Jefferson's reaction to Burr's alleged plot and more sympathy for Burr's objectives than Wilkinson's abuse of the Constitution. For instance, Rodney threatened "to put on old '76 and march out in Support of Col.

B[urr] and the Constitution" if General Wilkinson "or any other military should attempt to remove his person out of the Mississippi Territory prior to his trial."[61]

Burr's fear of Wilkinson was real. Earlier, Wilkinson offered Dinsmoor five thousand dollars for capture of "the arch traitor." He also dispatched Capt. Moses Hook and three associates, disguised in civilian clothes and armed with pistols and dirks, to Natchez with orders to capture Burr. Governor Claiborne joined the general in soliciting first Mead and later Williams to send the "Arch Conspirator" to New Orleans, requests they ignored. Instead, Mead asked Wilkinson to furnish him with whatever evidence he possessed against Burr. Both Mead and Rodney, despite misgivings about Burr, were determined to bring down Wilkinson and close an affair that was embarrassing everyone.[62]

On the other hand, a number of Mississippians were uneasy as long as Burr's rootless partisans roamed the territory. While Rodney took depositions from a handful of Burr's adherents (Comfort Tyler, Alexander Ralston, Carmichael, and Blennerhassett), Mead received reports of "some restless spirits . . . about Natchez who evince a hostile disposition to the views of the government and favorable to the designs of a man now in custody." He ordered Colonel Claiborne to "apprehend every person of this description and take them before a civil officer" for questioning. "The number of Burr[']s friends require much vigilance," he declared, and "their contumacy must be curbed."[63]

To be sure, Burr's leaderless associates were aimless and disillusioned. Yet, tippling more than treason characterized these poor miscreants, unceremoniously abandoned in a strange and inhospitable environment. Eventually, the government came to the same conclusion and released all of them, even those slated for trial. A majority, including Blennerhassett, became local residents, furnishing the territory with an assortment of young talent ranging from schoolteachers and dancing masters to tavern keepers and medical doctors.[64]

In late January, shortly before Burr's trial, Governor Williams returned from North Carolina to resume his duties. Burr, thinking him more sympathetic than Mead, paid him a visit. After all, they had served together in Congress, but Williams gave Burr no encouragement other than promise of a speedy and fair trial. Two days later, John Graham, the president's peripatetic prosecutor, arrived on the scene. First he called on Burr, who reiterated his innocence. It was absurd, Burr declared, to contemplate separating the Union by force, although he hinted that an attack upon Mexico was feasible.[65]

The next day, Graham furnished Williams what little evidence he had collected while expressing displeasure with Judge Rodney's haughty dismissal of it. But Williams's response was no more encouraging than the judge's. He believed that, since Burr "had committed no indictable offence within the Mississippi Territory," he should be tried in a federal court whose jurisdiction was undeniable.[66]

Nevertheless, Williams's presence had a soothing effect. According to Judge Rodney, if the governor had "not arrived opertunely," the example of "General Wilkinson['s] arbitrary conduct" might have "been soon followed here." Others were less certain, and Rodney continually had to calm those who "ran to him" in panic. The military, he explained, might arrest suspects, but only the courts could convict them. The governor, he assured everyone, was "determined to adhere to the constitution and laws." In fact, the present "danger was so trifling as not to justify any arbitrary measures," and he took comfort in believing that the "mass of the people were in full support of the government."[67]

On February 2, 1807, in the midst of this unsettling atmosphere, Burr and his attorneys, Lyman Harding and William B. Shields, appeared before the Supreme Court of Mississippi Territory, Judges Rodney and Bruin presiding. Also in attendance was a crowd of curious spectators as well as the required number of jurors and likely witnesses.[68] The territory had never witnessed such a dramatic event, and the little hamlet of Washington was hard-pressed to accommodate the throng. They came from far and wide and included such notables as Judge Harry Toulmin, who was there to observe the conduct of his peers.

Confusion plagued the proceedings from the outset. The first controversy involved impaneling the grand jury. As required by law, the county sheriff had summoned seventy-two "freeholders," the first twenty-four to serve as a grand jury and the rest as petit jurors. A question quickly arose over whether to "Impanel the Grand Jury" in the order summoned or "draw them from the general list by lot." Skeptics were sure the sheriff had deliberately placed the names of prominent Federalists at the top of the list to guarantee Burr a favorable hearing. With Attorney General Poindexter absent, the court opted to adjourn.[69]

On February 3, the reconvened court accepted Poindexter's opinion, seconded by Burr's attorneys, that the grand jury should be impaneled as summoned, and the presiding judges swore in the first twenty-four names. Judge Rodney then opened the proceedings with "a comprehensive and impressive charge," after which Burr requested to "say a few words." He asked the jurors to disregard any "Impressions made on their minds by the Vague Reports and Newspaper publications." Since no evidence existed that he had "written or Said anything" treasonable, he was prepared to prove that "he had been accused [to] Cover and Conceal the Crimes of Others." Whereupon, Poindexter objected to allowing Burr to speak, "but the Court Stoped him" since "It was Improper To hear any argument at This Time."[70]

The following day, Poindexter surprised the court by calling for the jury's dismissal since "he had nothing to Lay before it." He had discovered no "testimony which brought the offences charged against Colonel Burr, within the jurisdiction of the Courts of the Mississippi Territory." Furthermore, the territorial supreme court "was not a Court of original jurisdiction," and it could only hear cases on appeal. The judges, in the interest of "public safety," he argued, should "convey the accused to a tribunal competent to try and punish him."

Burr was furious. He vehemently denounced Poindexter's motion, observing "that if the Attorney-General had nothing for the Grand Jury, he had." Sensing that he was among friends, Burr insisted that because he "had been detained To have his conduct Enquired into That the Jury Should proceed" with the inquest. "If he was Guilty They Might Say So, and If Innocent . . . they might say So" too. Poindexter's motion to dismiss failed when the judges disagreed, Bruin for and Rodney against, and the grand jury retired to begin its examination of witnesses.

Presently, the grand jury returned "with sundry presentments," which one observer labeled "purely partisan." The jurors declared that Burr was neither guilty "of any crime or misdemeanor against the laws of the United States or of this Territory" nor had he "given any just cause for alarm or inquietude." They denounced "the late military expedition fitted out against the person and property of said Aaron Burr" and pronounced "the armistice (so-called) concluded between" Mead and the suspect "as highly derogatory to the dignity of this government." Finally, they assailed the "late military arrests, made without warrants" as "destructive of personal liberty." They regretted the measures "adopted in a neighboring Territory," which, in their opinion, "must sap the vitals of political existence, and crumble this glorious fabric in the dust."[71]

Offended by the tone of the presentments, Shields rushed to Mead's defense. As a participant in the Burr negotiations, he possessed firsthand knowledge of Mead's actions. In his opinion, supported by Rodney, the grand jurors had acted outside "the pale of their jurisdiction." Before dismissing them, Shields asked the court not to read the presentments, expecting them to become "the subject of animadversion." The measures "complained of," he stated, were taken "to save the effusion of human blood." Furthermore, he continued, Colonel Burr had "unhesitatingly expressed a temper voluntarily to submit his conduct to judicial inquiry."[72] Even Rodney agreed that Mead had acted on instructions from the federal government and not on his own.

One immediate result was an irreparable estrangement between Mead and Williams. Like Cato West before him, Mead refused to perform his duties as secretary, turning them over to a hired assistant. On the other hand, Williams became increasingly friendly with Mead's critics, including Federalists. Although never Burr's advocate, he took advantage of the public's adverse reaction to Mead's performance.

Another victim was Judge Rodney. Even after the grand jury cleared Burr, Rodney refused to rescind the recognizance. Again Bruin dissented, arguing that the bonds were valid only if he were indicted. Instead, Rodney insisted that Burr remain under the court's supervision, and he ordered the sheriff to demand his appearance at the court's next session. Burr's attorneys were aghast. Rodney's ruling, they protested, was arbitrary and unconstitutional, and they asked the court to dismiss their client. Again the judges divided, killing the motion.[73]

Instantly, Burr went into hiding. He fled to Bayou Pierre, taking refuge at the home of Bruin's son-in-law, Dr. John Cummins. Upon learning of Burr's defection, Governor Williams declared him a fugitive and offered "$2,000 for his delivery here to me." From his place of hiding, a befuddled Burr penned two notes to the governor. "I have seen your proclamation," he wrote; "It was unworthy of you to lend the sanction of your name to a falsehood. The recognizance in which I was bound was on condition that I should appear in case of an indictment . . . and not otherwise." Williams pleaded that he could not interfere with the judicial process. When the supreme court reconvened on February 7, Burr was not present. Poindexter "ordered the Sheriff to call out Aron Burr on his recognizance." Harding objected, questioning its validity as drawn up by Rodney, but the court ruled that since Burr was absent without cause, his bonds were forfeited. On the other hand, Rodney took no action against Burr's accomplices, most of whom roamed freely about the territory. Annoyed by Rodney's inconsistency, Williams consulted Judge Toulmin, who obliged by issuing warrants for the arrest of Burr, Floyd, Ralston, and Blennerhassett.[74]

On February 10, another bizarre incident excited the people. That evening, "a negro boy, the property of Doctor Cummins," came to the home of William Fairbanks and asked for directions. He was riding Burr's horse and wearing "his surtout." Suspicious, Fairbanks searched the youngster and discovered, attached to the boy's cape, an unsigned note allegedly in Burr's handwriting addressed to Comfort Tyler and Davis Floyd. "If you are together," it stated, "keep together and I will join you tomorrow night—in the meantime put all your arms in perfect order. Ask the bearer no questions but tell him all you may think I wish to know."[75]

Although the note was an obvious hoax, people were ready to believe anything. The governor arrested forty of Burr's men, confining them for twenty-four hours. Fearing that Williams might initiate another "reign of terror," Rodney pronounced the arrests unconstitutional. As he informed Colonel Ellis, one of Burr's strongest supporters, he was determined "to uphold the Constitution," and he vowed not to deviate "even if it displeased the President or any of his officers." It was "better [to] be assailed by 10,000," he declared, "than that the officers acting in Support of the Government Should violate the Constitution."[76]

To Rodney this whole matter seemed like an amusing reenactment of the earlier Kemper affair. "And Burr," he stated, "only appears the greatest Don quixote of the two—The Mountain has surely brought forth a Mouse." Later, Rodney observed that "All is Military Bustle, and the Constitution and Laws are forgot[ten] but will no doubt revive again when this Windy Storm blows over." Yet, when Blennerhassett, Floyd, and Ralston presented him with writs of habeas corpus, he freed them on the ground that Toulmin had no jurisdiction in Natchez District; then he inexplicably reversed himself, ordering them held on charges of unlawful combination to commit conspiracy.[77]

Meanwhile, Burr saw no hope but flight. But, before departing, he assembled his followers. In a brief, emotional speech, which brought tears to several eyes, he quieted the mutinous spirit and pleaded patience. He could not pay them, he said, but they were free to sell the boats and provisions and divvy up the proceeds. Bidding them farewell, he rode off on a horse provided by Colonel Osmun and accompanied only by Maj. Robert Ashley, former agent of Philip Nolan and someone familiar with the country.[78]

For the next six days, Burr's whereabouts were unknown, or, as Wilkinson put it, "his designs continue equivocal."[79] Then, about eleven o'clock on the night of February 18, two strange-looking men appeared on the road to Wakefield, seat of government for Washington County. One rode several paces ahead of the other, and both were attempting to conceal their faces. It had been raining heavily, and the rivers and streams were swollen to the edge of their banks and a few were impassable.

The first rider was "on a small tacky of a horse," with a bearskin draped over a well-worn saddle and a tattered woolen blanket covering his grungy garb. Over one shoulder hung a tin cup, and a butcher knife protruded conspicuously from his belt. Deliberately dressed as a river boatman, he wore a soiled white hat that concealed much of his face. The two passed by the land office where register Nicholas Perkins was standing in the doorway. The lead rider went by without looking up, but the second stopped and asked Perkins for directions to the home of Maj. John Hinson. Perkins explained that, because of the swollen streams, it might be difficult to reach his place, and besides, he said, Hinson was not there. Without uttering another word, the two men proceeded in the direction Perkins had indicated.

As Perkins pondered why strangers were wandering around Wakefield late at night, he wondered if one was not the notorious fugitive featured in the governor's proclamation. The likelihood seemed strong enough that he awakened Sheriff Theodore Brightwell to seek his advice. The two then decided to call on the Hinsons, where they found the wayfarers talking with Mrs. Hinson. Perkins became extremely suspicious when one of the strangers appeared reluctant to speak or show his face. Convinced that he had accidentally happened upon Burr, Perkins slipped away and headed for nearby Fort Stoddert, where he informed Lt. Edmund Pendleton Gaines of his suspicions.

Early the next morning, Gaines and Perkins, accompanied by a sergeant and three enlisted men, set off for Hinson's. Along the way, they bumped into Burr and Brightwell on the road to the nearest ferry. Across the river, the road forked, one branch leading to Pensacola and the other into Creek country. Gaines recognized Burr instantly. Protesting that he was not subject to military arrest, Burr offered no further resistance. Gaines then escorted him to Fort Stoddert and placed him in confinement awaiting instructions.[80]

Meanwhile, on the morning of Burr's departure, Ashley also left the Hinsons to visit Col. John Caller. Ashley explained that Burr's original plan was to take Baton Rouge, but General Wilkinson had foiled it. Now, he related, Burr wanted to devote his energies to seizing Mobile, and he inquired if Caller and his friends would assist him. He assured Caller that Burr had no hostile designs upon the United States. As Ashley anticipated, Caller showed interest in the enterprise. But Ashley's pleasure with Caller's response was quickly dampened by news of Burr's arrest and confinement, and he immediately disappeared into the woods.[81]

During his four-week confinement at Fort Stoddert, Burr divided his time between playing chess with Mrs. Gaines, daughter of Judge Toulmin, and contacting Spanish friends. Reportedly, he had several confidants in Mobile and Baton Rouge, including Morales, the notorious land speculator. A Spanish captain of an armed vessel coming upstream asked to speak with Burr, but Gaines forbade it. On another occasion, Burr sought to bribe the guards in assisting his escape.[82]

While Burr was contemplating his next move, Gaines became more and more apprehensive. He knew of the strong support Burr enjoyed in Tombigbee District, and he wished to be rid of his troublesome truant as quickly as possible. In fact, during Burr's confinement, Gaines was under constant pressure from the local officials to release him. They regarded Burr as a savior who had come to release them from Spanish tyranny, and they blamed Wilkinson and federal officials for thwarting his plans. Gaines dismissed these assertions as the work of "restless intriguers," displeased by the arrest of "their disinterested imperial friend Burr." Nevertheless, after Burr tried to contact the Callers, Gaines arranged for his transfer to the nation's capital.[83]

Governor Williams also wanted Burr gone. On March 1, he sent Silas Dinsmoor to Fort Stoddert to return the prisoner to Natchez for trial in a federal court. But before Dinsmoor arrived, Gaines had engaged Perkins to escort Burr to the nation's capital. On March 5, Perkins, assisted by a handpicked guard of eight soldiers, departed with Burr intact. Along the way, he received orders to take Burr to Richmond for trial before the federal district court.[84] To the relief of almost everyone, Burr left Mississippi Territory for the last time.

CHAPTER 9

The Williams Imbroglio

Aaron Burr left a long shadow. What some called "Burrism" came to dominate territorial politics for some time. To be sure, Governor Williams's feelings toward Burr were both protean and puzzling. At times he thought Burr only a misguided patriot; otherwise, he considered him guilty of misprision, or worse. The same ambivalence characterized the attitudes of others, who, like Judge Thomas Rodney and Secretary Mead, vacillated between approving Burr's avowed aims while questioning his character.[1]

Rodney was not the only person to follow Burr's trial closely, and like most stalwart Republicans, he rallied behind Jefferson's efforts to disgrace the "arch traitor." According to him, Jefferson was "highly esteemed and respected" in the territory, and his star had "been rising in Estimation Ever since I came here." But he was hardly unbiased since Jefferson had recently made his son, Caesar A. Rodney, attorney general and put him in charge of prosecuting Burr.[2]

Unfortunately the administration's star witness was Gen. James Wilkinson who, during his cross-examination, proved so unreliable and evasive that he barely escaped indictment. But Wilkinson's loudest detractor, the acerbic John Randolph of Roanoke, was equally controversial. Hardly a defender of Burr, Randolph despised Wilkinson, whom he characterized as "the most finished scoundrel that ever lived." Correctly suspecting that Wilkinson was a Spanish pensioner, Randolph called him "the mammoth of iniquity" and a villain "from the bark to the very core." He was horrified when the administration "embark[ed] its reputation in the same bottom" with the deceitful Wilkinson. "Perhaps," he stated, "you never saw human nature in so degraded a situation as in the person of Wilkinson before the grand jury." Yet, "this man stands on the very summit and pinnacle of executive favor."[3]

Several Mississippians, especially Federalists, concurred with Randolph's assessment of Wilkinson and skepticism of Jefferson. Though wary of Burr, Mead maligned Wilkinson as mercilessly as Randolph did, and he too was amazed that Jefferson should embrace a man so utterly scandalous and duplicitous. Moreover, Mead had his own quarrel with the administration after Madison refused to reimburse him for his travel expenses to Mississippi.[4] "Poverty drove me to this Country," Mead complained, and "my office has robbed me even of the little pittance that I brought with me." Surely, he pleaded, "the general government" would reward him for "the constant vigilance & exertion" he displayed during the Burr threat.

To him, the contrast between his treatment and Wilkinson's was outrageous. As long as "Genl Wilkinson and his mercenary bands [wore] the laurels which should deck the brows of the brave yeomanry of this Territory," he could not "keep down the glow of discontent." While loyal Mississippians were enduring unimaginable hardship, marching "twenty-four hours without food" and sleeping "without blanket or tent, under the deepest snow ever seen in this Territory," Wilkinson was wasting "hundreds of dollars to magnify a bubble." Mead was also incensed that "the officers and people [here] are passed over in silence [and] the whole western world is swallowed up in unexampled virtue and unparalleled patriotism of Genl Wilkinson."[5]

Mead reserved his sharpest barbs for Governor Williams. Interpreting Williams's reply to Burr that "it would be as improper as it would be undignified in me, to enter into any stipulations as to your Surrender" as censure of his own conduct, Mead accused him of favoritism toward Wilkinson. He also resented the governor's depiction of his "acts as improper" and the rebuking he received for continuing "to charge him [Wilkinson] a traitor."[6]

Acrimony between the two officials dated from Williams's return in late January 1807. Under the pretext of greeting the governor, legislator George Poindexter drafted an address designed to acclaim Mead's performance rather than welcome him back. "While you were absent," it read, "the political horizon . . . has worn a dubious and menacing aspect." The

Spaniards reared "the standard of their monarch," and when an association of citizens, under "the artful and enterprising leader," sought to "dismember the western States and territories from the union," the people "repaired to the post of danger with a firmness." It was so blatantly partisan that James Caller, a representative from Washington County, demurred from supporting it.[7]

Unbeknownst to Williams, his unexpected reappearance disrupted Mead's plans for advancement. By then Mead had assembled a corps of trusted friends, who included, besides the Greens and West, Edward Turner, Poindexter, Shields, and Colonel Claiborne. With their support, he expected to become governor, and he came close to succeeding. According to one report, the president was prepared to name him governor in early 1807, "when the arrival of the Capitulation . . . with Col. Burr, at the seat of Government palsied the intention."[8]

Indeed, Mead had acted as if he were already chief executive. He encouraged the legislature to enact some special-interest laws, a few self-serving and all controversial. Unfortunately, Mead delayed signing them, and Williams vetoed several, including bills to remove the name of Wilkinson from one county and create two new ones, abolish the mayor's court in Natchez, empower the county courts to appoint additional officials, and disband the elite "Adams Troop of Horse." Finding these measures deliberately spiteful, Williams denounced them as "Calculated to thwart [his] opinions and course of Administration."[9]

If this rebuff was not enough to arouse Mead's ire, Williams's personal attacks upon him were. Convinced that Mead was a reincarnation of Cato West, Williams accused him of resurrecting "that party spirit which [had] formerly interrupted the individual happiness of the people, the harmony of Society and public tranquility of this country, thereby weakening their confidence in the government." He headed what one editor disparagingly called "the disappointed junto" and what Williams labeled an "unprincipled combination." Mead's chief lieutenants were Poindexter and Shields, both of whom had played prominent roles in the Burr affair. Although the avuncular Judge Rodney insisted that he never "meddled in political affairs," both Poindexter and Shields kept him informed of the governor's misdeeds.[10] Later, they enticed Ferdinand L. Claiborne to join the cause.

This "triumvirate" (Mead, Poindexter, and Claiborne) had personal as well as partisan reasons for hating the governor. Poindexter objected to Williams's protecting Briggs from charges of misappropriation of public funds and gross negligence of duty. Earlier, Briggs had bankrolled his brother's foolhardy operation of a sawmill that went bankrupt, and Poindexter drew a sinister connection between Briggs's fiscal peccadilloes and the brother's failed enterprise. In late 1806, Briggs, conveying a confidential message for Wilkinson, had left unexpectedly for the nation's capital to exonerate himself. Fearful that Briggs might succeed, Poindexter finagled, with Mead's collaboration, to get himself elected to Congress, where he could counteract Briggs's misrepresentations. According to Williams, the legislators, believing Poindexter was "the most proper person to combat his [Briggs's] representations," chose him even though they "thought him among the worst of men as to morals and political integrity."[11]

Shields and Claiborne broke with Williams for other reasons. Shields, more a faithful disciple than a leader, usually followed Poindexter's dictates. Less choleric than his friends, he cautioned Poindexter against losing his temper or recklessly castigating his opponents and admonished him to "be on your guard, behave with prudence and calmness." By acting thus, he said, "you may cover [your seducers] with shame and confusion." Shields joined Poindexter in denouncing Briggs for malfeasance, and he was especially upset when Williams bypassed Poindexter for attorney general. But it was the governor's appointment of Seth Lewis, a "violent" Federalist, that made him livid.[12]

A late convert to the anti-Williams faction, Claiborne soon became its most vocal member. Two factors drove his animosity. First, he felt Williams had dallied too long before giving him command of the militia. Second, he had maneuvered, in the late summer of 1806, to restore his brother, then under attack in New Orleans, as governor of Mississippi Territory. Accordingly, he and his friends drafted a set of resolutions praising his brother and lamenting his transfer to Orleans. Nonetheless, they realized that, to be successful, they must remove Williams to make room for either W. C. C. Claiborne's return or Cowles Mead's promotion. The election of Poindexter as territorial delegate was a first step, for it gave them a voice in Congress, where they hoped to extirpate Williams's reputation.[13]

George Poindexter had resided in the territory fewer than five years. Arriving in Natchez in 1802, he rose rapidly in territorial politics. Between 1803 and 1807, he held a variety of positions, including attorney general, despite rudimentary training in law and a reputation for rowdiness. But he overcame these deficiencies with a sharp intellect, an incredible memory, and a charming personality. Still, Poindexter was unable to curb his explosive temper or his fondness for frolic. According to his older brother, George from childhood "was rather disposed to insubordination." Shortly after joining the Baptist Church in his native Virginia, he was expelled for refusing to cut off his queue, which most members viewed as "a violation of Paul['s] directive about long hair."[14]

On the other hand, Williams was his own worst enemy. Convinced that Mead was a clumsy buffoon who misjudged the people, the governor considered him an easy target. "Although the people of this territory," he told Jefferson, "are generally wealthy and live well, even bordering on a degree of luxury and extravagance, they appreciate plainness in their officers." In fact, he reiterated, they "respect office without adulation— expect dignity . . . not foppery." In his opinion, Mead had egregiously blundered by addressing the General Assembly "with an air disgusting to the people," and he confidently predicted that this latest effort "would terminate as a similar Conduct did two years ago."[15]

Initially, Mead's behavior irritated the governor without riling him. But after Williams disagreed with his assessment of Wilkinson's character and vetoed his legislative measures, Mead curtly announced that he "no longer consider[ed] myself one of the Governor's Cabinet counsel." In imitation of his brother-in-law West, he refused to hand over the official papers and churlishly notified Williams that he had employed William Pope, son of a well-respected, deceased army officer, to handle his clerical duties. Unlike West, Mead had a plausible excuse for his obstructionism. Wounded in a recent duel with Robert Semple, one of Burr's numerous recruits, he took to bed for several weeks. Afterward, Williams jokingly remarked that if Mead settled all his quarrels as he had with Semple, "he will have quite enough to consume the most of his time, if not his life." Happily, Williams's faith in Jefferson was not misplaced. In response to pleas that he could not govern effectively as long as Mead was secretary, the president in the summer of 1807 replaced Mead with Thomas H. Williams.[16]

The anti-Williams faction launched its "torrent of abuse" by smearing the governor with "Burrism." As Williams acknowledged, no one had handled the Burr episode well. "Such are the misterious ramifications of Burr's Conspiracy," he wrote, "as to favour the lighting of Suspicion on the heads of almost every man in office and in power." Throughout Burr's lengthy trial, the Meadites were "the most clamorous ag[ains]t General Wilkinson," denouncing his conduct "as improper" and "him as a traitor." They criticized Williams's ill-advised appointment of Carmichael as aide-de-camp, which even Williams acknowledged as a mistake, informing Jefferson incorrectly that "since his return, I have had nothing to do" with him.[17]

Like Jefferson, Williams often spoke rashly and before thinking, and sometimes his outbursts were harsh and tasteless. For instance, in the presence of Poindexter, Williams criticized Mead for calling out the militia after Burr's initial appearance. The men, he declared, "would have been much better occupied in their cotton fields." More damaging was Williams's characterization of Burr as "an honest unfortunate man." Later, following Burr's acquittal, Williams, according to Claiborne, was jubilant. "I told you," he exclaimed, "that the United States could not graze Colo Burr."[18]

In April 1807, the governor's opponents carried their campaign "out of doors" and into the taverns and coffeehouses of Natchez and Washington that played so prominent a role in the political and social life of Natchez District. They also relied upon a friendly press to persuade an apathetic public and an obstinate administration that Williams was unfit to govern. But none of their accusations resonated more effectively than favoritism toward Federalists. According to Poindexter, Williams filled too many territorial offices with "disbanded" military officers, such as Isaac Guion, whom he named "Brigade inspector and adjutant General of the Militia," and former "adherents of Governor Seargeant" like Seth Lewis and William Dunbar.[19]

Charges of "Burrism" and "Federalism" became their favorite themes. In May, they published in the *Mississippi Messenger* a scurrilous letter, under the signature of Col. Joshua Baker, president of the Legislative Council and one of the governor's critics. Established in 1804 by Timothy and Samuel Terrell, the *Messenger*, one of the territory's two newspapers, had fallen under the control of John Shaw, who used its pages to pour forth his special blend of venom after Samuel Terrell had resigned in disgust. According to Williams, Samuel Terrell, "the principle Editor of this paper would not condescend to p[r]int their abuse," and Timothy had to employ "Shaw, the blackguard" to perform the dirty work. Shaw was hardly a neophyte in the game of newspaper warfare, having previously been a hired scribbler for the West faction. He now employed his poisoned pen on behalf of what Williams called "that political Junto."[20]

Baker's letter was clearly a forgery. Known to be illiterate and slovenly, Baker was considered incapable of penning such a clever piece of writing, and Williams concluded that either Mead or Poindexter had written it. Soon thereafter, Williams learned through a confidential source that Baker had recently paid Poindexter sixty dollars, and he publicly named Poindexter author of the scurrilous letter. The remuneration, Poindexter claimed, was for legal fees and not, as the governor insinuated, a subterfuge. Unmoved by Poindexter's denial, Williams took him and Baker to court, charging them with libel and defamation of character.[21]

Williams simultaneously attempted to answer Baker's criticisms and justify his conduct to Jefferson. He had neither shielded Burr nor, as his critics implied, abetted his escape. Acknowledging that he had appointed some ex-Federalists, he was, he explained, merely following the president's example and advice. "The course which I have pursued," he wrote, "has been in strict conformity with your own ideas of propriety." He only wished to heal "those political distractions" by not "proscribing [from office] honest well meaning men heretofore federalist and now sincerely disposed to concur with the National sentiment and measures." Besides, he contended, Mead had "appointed as many, Nay more[,] of this description to office during his administration than I have done during the whole of Mine."[22]

This controversy ignited a vituperative newspaper battle between Shaw's *Mississippi Messenger* and Marschalk's *Mississippi Herald & Natchez Gazette*. Unfortunately, people remembered Andrew Marschalk's earlier association with Governor Sargent and the Federalists. Still, Williams found his literary talents serviceable and his loyalties sufficient.[23] For Marschalk's part, he hoped to regain the post of public printer that he had lost to the Terrells.

The two editors, like their counterparts elsewhere, made little or no pretense at objectivity, engaging in a "no-holds-barred" style of journalism. Since Mississippians, then and later, enjoyed a good fight, they found the weekly exchange of insults entertaining. While lacking the flair or guile of a Benjamin F. Bache or a William Cobbett, two of the nation's most talented editors, Shaw and Marschalk possessed a remarkable penchant for scurrility.[24]

If Marschalk was a more talented writer, Shaw was a better lampooner, and Williams the perfect target. Furthermore, the governor's opponents, though hardly skillful politicians, had an uncanny knack for picking the right issues at the right time, and eventually they, rather than the better-placed governor, emerged victorious. Sometimes their warfare had its farcical moments. For example, after Poindexter took special offence at the governor's disparaging remarks about the militia, which he interpreted as "expressions derogatory to my character as a man of honor," he issued Williams a challenge.[25]

Dueling was a favorite way for gentlemen to uphold their honor throughout the Old South. Generally, the combatants were more intent upon defending their manhood than mortally wounding their opponents. But there were notable exceptions. For instance, several prominent figures, including Andrew Jackson and Governor Claiborne's private secretary and brother-in-law, Michael G. Lewis, challenged their detractors with intent to kill, Jackson successfully and Claiborne's brother-in-law less so.[26]

But few duels ended as tragically as these. More often than not participants were content merely to graze an opponent. For instance, Mead had suffered a "slight wound in his right thigh" in a duel with Robert Semple. Three months later, Maj. Michael J. Love had a "ball pass through the middle of his left thigh" in a confrontation with Charles F. Shackleford. The *Messenger* reported that Mead was "fast recovering" and that Love's injury was "not dangerous."[27] In a few cases, antagonists, after an exchange of harmless shots, shook hands and retired from the field of honor satisfied that they had preserved their honor without drawing blood.

It was rare for a gentleman to shun an "invitation," but when William T. Voss, a bricklayer and sometime captain of the militia, delivered Poindexter's "invitation," Williams spurned it, pleading that official duties precluded his acceptance. Despite Poindexter's unremitting efforts to embarrass the governor with accusations of cowardice, Williams refused to be drawn into a custom he thought barbarous. He would not "involve either his public or private character with such a man," he said, implying that Poindexter lacked "sufficient standing in society" to qualify as a gentleman. Enraged by this aspersion on his character, Poindexter denounced Williams as "a scoundrel and rascal," and accused "the Mighty Chief" of hiding behind his official station to avoid the consequences of his actions. According to Poindexter, "if such unmerited aspersions" remained "uncontradicted," he could not, as territorial delegate, redress the people's grievances.[28]

Williams wisely ignored Poindexter's ranting but foolishly killed the messenger. He revoked Voss's commissions as justice of the peace and alderman of Natchez on the grounds that he was "guilty of such improprieties and disregard of your oath of office as to Disqualify you as administer of the laws." Specifically, he charged Voss with violating the statute against dueling, but, as everyone knew, the reason was personal. Not surprisingly, Voss's removal touched off a new round of invective between the "Williamsites" and what Marschalk called "the wide-mouthed junto."[29]

An "aggrieved" Captain Voss denied that he had "disregard[ed] the oath of office." Viewing the governor's arbitrary actions "as derogatory of the dignity which ought to characterize the chief magistrate of a respectable community and [as] a flagitious attack on my character," he asked Colonel Claiborne, his superior officer and comrade in calumny, to summon a "court of inquiry on my conduct, in conformity to the rules and articles of war." Williams abruptly objected. He assured the colonel that he meant no "disrespect to you or Voss," while reminding him "that the civil authorities or any of its determiners are not Subject to the Superintendency or Control of the Military." In retaliation, Voss went public. In a letter to the *Messenger,* he sarcastically explained to "the little great man [Williams]" why he was requesting a court of inquiry. "He did not wish," he said, "to involve any of his friends by the personal delivery, knowing Mr. Williams' readiness to construe the most harmless note addressed to him, into an invitation to violate the peace." Williams then angrily revoked Voss's other appointments, including his captaincy in the militia.[30]

Williams himself then resorted to the courts. He asked Attorney General Seth Lewis to issue warrants against Poindexter and Voss for violating the ordinance "against the evil practice of dueling." According to this law, convicted offenders were ineligible to hold a public office and subject to an unspecified fine or imprisonment up to twelve months. Although an obliging Lewis hauled both officials before the city court of Natchez, Mayor Samuel Brooks dismissed the charges for lack of "sufficient probable cause."[31]

Even though this episode ended in impasse, it raised the rancor of partisanship, lessened respect for public officials, and enriched the press. The *Messenger* boasted that it had added a hundred subscribers, despite the nefarious efforts of the governor to prevent its delivery in Wilkinson County, where residents were upset with Mead's earlier efforts to divide the county and erase Wilkinson's name. Meanwhile, Shaw and Terrell stepped up their ridicule of Williams and Marschalk. The *Messenger* particularly delighted in reminding its readers of the *Herald* editor's political apostasy. According to Shaw, Marschalk had become the solicitous court "jester to his royal highness, the Prince of Groom" and spokesman for "the Tory gentry," gleefully labeling the governor's supporters "federalists, alias tories, alias Williamsites."[32]

Nonetheless, they were less successful in persuading the public that the governor had acted arbitrarily or capriciously in his attempt to thwart the will of the legislature. To the populist-minded Meadites, the General Assembly better represented the public than the executive. Williams disagreed. Because his opponents had secured their seats through a combination of fraudulent votes and scandalous behavior, he, not the legislature, spoke for the wishes of the wealthier and better-educated citizenry.[33]

Mead and his supporters also faced an even more agonizing problem. As Judge Rodney appreciated, territorial governors possessed powers denied most state executives, some of which exceeded those of British colonial governors. In defining the duties of territorial officials, the Confederation Congress had followed the British colonial system in clothing territorial executives with sufficient authority to school inhabitants in the virtues of republican government. Despite its many advantages, this model made conflict between an appointed governor and an elected assembly almost unavoidable. In fact, the history of territories was replete with controversy and dissension, and the acrimonious conflict between Williams and his detractors was more typical than exceptional. While the issues varied from one territory to another, the process was the same. Williams was so enamored with exercising these prerogatives that he had difficulty extricating himself from what was becoming an inescapable dilemma, and he continued to lose rather than to gain support from that small group of influential men who wielded political power and hankered for office. If Williams understood the need for constitutional authority in a frontier environment better than his opponents, he was more inclined to abuse it than exercise it judiciously. Surprisingly, none of his opponents drew the obvious analogy between their resistance to tyrannical government and that of the Patriots of 1776.[34] Instead, the contest degenerated into a conflict between two immovable forces rather than a debate over fundamental principles.

As a result, party labels, although applied constantly, were shibboleths rather than guideposts. While both factions professed to be the "real" Republicans and devoted disciples of Jefferson, the pugnacious Poindexter could not refrain from abusing Jefferson. Once he blurted out, in the presence of Williams, that he wished "by god the president had federalists and Scotsmen enough to fill all his appointments with," alluding of course to William Dunbar, for whom he harbored intense jealousy.[35]

In the late summer and early fall of 1807, two additional controversies intensified friction between factions. The first was a series of special elections to fill three legislative vacancies due to the death of Samuel Bridges, Henry Hunter's unexpected resignation, and Poindexter's election to Congress. With the assembly evenly divided between friends and opponents of the governor, the contests were especially heated. Mead and Poindexter realized that by capturing two of the three seats, they would control the next legislature.

Styling themselves the "true Republicans," Mead's friends called two public gatherings, one in Claiborne County and the other in Wilkinson County, to nominate candidates for the upcoming elections. They rallied behind Cowles Mead and the lesser-known Micajah Davis of Wilkinson County, both of whom subsequently won. In the final contest, Samuel Cook, canvassing as a Mead supporter, was also victorious. The results, especially the choice of Mead, delighted the governor's opponents and depressed his friends. The *Messenger* literally chortled. Even though "Prince Robert and his myrmidons [had] . . . left no stone unturned, no trick untried," his candidates suffered ignominious defeat. Jubilantly predicting the demise of "Sir Robert," Shaw rejoiced that the reign of "the little quided official band" was near its end.[36]

Conversely, Williams attributed Mead's triumph to corruption and chicanery. According to him, election officials, particularly in Adams and Wilkinson counties, registered preemptioners who, almost to a man, favored Mead and Davis. While the governor also favored enlarging the franchise, he wanted it done legally and "not in this way." Otherwise, he said, the "better part of the community will not vote unless they are entitled," leaving the choice to dishonest citizens. Even in face of these accusations, Mead still accused Williams of "furnishing documents to injure his Election," and Shaw charged him with sending "a messenger in the night . . . with a trumped up electioneering story, designed to injure the election of Mr. Davis." But Williams's enemies celebrated too soon. Two of the victorious legislators proved more sympathetic to Williams than his opponents, leaving the legislature as hopelessly divided as before.[37]

Meanwhile, a bitter disagreement erupted between Williams and Colonel Claiborne over the October 8 muster of the First Regiment of the Adams County militia. Claiborne resented the governor's derogatory comments about the militia in general and the First Regiment in particular. According to him, Williams "was loud in the censure & ridicule of the Militia who had patriotically turned out to oppose and intercept the expidition of Aaron Burr." Claiborne traced the governor's hostility to a suggestion he made during Burr's confinement when he chided Williams to have a "guard placed over him to prevent [his] escape." Taking umbrage, the governor angrily replied "that Burr was safe enough, that he would not leave Washington in an improper manner." Afterward, Claiborne observed, Williams showed "not only a covert hostility to myself but a disposition to expose to executive vengeance every officer of the Regiment who had been active in the opposition made to the would be Emperor." Consequently, he declared, "I was obliged to enjoin him to desist from taken [sic] such unjustifiable liberties with the character of my friends in my hearing."[38] Obviously, Claiborne expected to embarrass the governor.

Commanded by Capt. Benjamin Farrar, one of the territory's wealthiest planters and largest slaveholders, an avid land speculator, and a "violent federalist," the Adams Troop of Horse was "a great favorite with his Excellency." Farrar, who considered Claiborne an arrogant martinet, informed the governor that his company did not wish to muster with the First Regiment, and Williams agreed to review the Adams Troop of Horse separately. Claiborne was furious. Unfortunately, he had earlier consulted Marschalk, who, as an ex-army officer, was familiar with military protocol. But the fiery editor disagreed with Claiborne's contention that all units of a regiment should be reviewed simultaneously, and he reported the conversation to Williams. According to Marschalk, Claiborne became distraught, asserting that Farrar's cavalry "had no exclusive privilege" and threatening to force it to muster with the entire regiment. If Farrar's troopers "came within the reach of his voice on the day of muster," Claiborne "promised to compel them to obey his orders at the risque of the lives of his Regiment."[39]

Military reviews were important social events in a society devoid of pageantry. A time of much excitement, martial ceremonies afforded occasion for pomp and ceremony, accompanied by festivities where the men ate and drank to excess, and the wives and other ladies, dressed in their best finery, came from near and far to celebrate and mingle together. October 8, 1807, began like all muster days, with the First Regiment assembling around noon. Judge Rodney arrived late in the morning, escorting several prominent ladies, including the spouses of Governor Claiborne and Colonel Claiborne. In fact, the colonel's wife was "to present the Regiment with a Stand of Colors." After the review, the regiment customarily paraded down the main street of Washington, passing in front of the Government House to the cheers of the crowd.

But the festivities did not proceed as expected. At the request of Captain Farrar, Williams reviewed the Adams Troop of Horse at an early-morning ceremony before the full regiment assembled. Unaware that Williams had already met with Farrar's company, Colonel Claiborne informed him, late in the afternoon, that the regiment was ready for review. The governor's response was a total surprise. He instructed Claiborne that since there was insufficient space in the town of Washington for the entire regiment to assemble comfortably, his men were to "be marched into the field back of the Town." The ladies, accompanied by several onlookers, dutifully followed the governor's orders; "they got in their carriages" and headed for the newly designated parade grounds. But Claiborne and his officers, "offended at the governor's conduct," refused to budge. After waiting "an hour or two" for the governor to appear, Claiborne dismissed the regiment and contemptuously declined, along with his officers, the governor's invitation to eat with him that evening. Instead, the colonel and his friends "dined at Towsan's," where hard liquor and harsh words flowed freely throughout the night. The ladies, joined by a joyous Rodney, gathered "at Mr. Chews," not wishing to interfere with their spouses' raucous revelry.[40]

Claiborne's insolence was too much for the governor. While Williams had hoped to patch up his differences with Claiborne, he now realized they were irreconcilable. Infuriated by Claiborne's impertinence, which he took personally, Williams stripped Claiborne of his military commission and removed him as "justices of the peace and of the Quorum for the County of Adams."[41]

In wake of these vengeful measures, a rash of resignations ensued. Williams assured Jefferson that, despite endless pressure from Claiborne, the defectors numbered only two, one of whom was Jesse Carter, "Poindexter[']s father in law," but the truth was different. A majority of the officers of the First Regiment, out of loyalty to Claiborne, resigned over the next few weeks. In a forcefully worded petition, the disgruntled officers wondered "why the governor alone should be blind to the valor" of such a celebrated patriot as Claiborne. Echoing the sentiments of Mead and Poindexter, the officers conjectured that "Governor Williams has changed his Politicks and embraced every opportunity to change his officers." In fact, they opined, he had displayed "a total distaste" for "republicanism."[42]

Not only did the governor have trouble retaining capable officers, but he also had difficulty finding replacements for those who left in a huff. Joseph Sessions petulantly declined the governor's offer to replace Claiborne and vowed "to accept no commission under the Government of the Mississippi Territory." If Williams's arbitrary actions added few recruits to the Mead-Poindexter coalition, they hardened its resolve. Even Judge Rodney felt the governor's wrath. "I do not know," he wrote Poindexter, "but [what] my attention to Mrs. Claiborne & Col Claiborne on the Review Day has induced the Governor to number me among his adversaries. For there is a ball at his house To night, To which most the Town was invited, but I was not." He soon joined the swelling cacophony calling for the governor's ouster. Later, William Shields remembered, he firmly stated "in his laconic way Poin. Must succeed."[43]

Still the massacre had not run its full course. Shortly afterward, Williams sacked Mead's father-in-law, Abner Green, as territorial treasurer, for failing to submit his financial report in a timely fashion. Williams had expected to receive it before the legislature met in November, but Green ignored the governor's inquiries, eventually refusing to provide "any information whatever." Again, Williams smelled conspiracy, especially after Green, in imitation of Mead, would neither surrender the office nor deliver the records to a successor. To the governor, Green's defiance was part of a pattern, started by West and continued by Mead, to discredit his administration. They knew, he insisted, "that the Gover-

nor and not themselves [were] responsible for the peace, quiet and tranquility of the Country." Although Green shortly thereafter "delivered
over the Treasury Office, contrary to the advice of Mr. Mead," he subsequently threatened to challenge in the courts the governor's "power of
removal."[44]

The removals were necessary, Williams insisted, because of his
opponents' intransigence. No longer could he afford "to act only on
the defensive" or with "indifference," and their "well-known hostility
demanded of me a different conduct." As part of this strategy, the governor also confronted the legislature. Before adjourning prematurely upon
Williams's return in late January 1807, the Mead-dominated legislature
had quietly postponed its next session by a month, a change that somehow escaped the governor's notice.[45]

In the interim, as noted, the political climate had changed dra-
matically. Fearing that the upcoming session, with three new members, might prove hostile, even to the point of endorsing a resolution
of censure or resurrecting the effort to reinstate Claiborne, Williams
insisted that the legislature could not reschedule its sessions without his
approval. Whereupon his legislative friends tried to prevent a quorum by
withdrawing, but the remaining legislature seated the three newcomers,
hoping in that way to establish a quorum. For the next nine days, these
members waited patiently while the clerk attempted to round up absent
members. Convinced that nothing positive could result from an unauthorized session, Williams, on November 11, prorogued the legislature
until the first Monday in December.[46]

Mead was outraged. Insisting that "the rights of the people [were]
paramount" to those of the executive, he pleaded with his colleagues to
remain in their seats. According to Williams, he "overleaped all order
and decorum" with his outbursts. "He is the wildest man I ever knew in
public." Even Mead's friends were aghast. His antics "open[ed] the eyes
of those disposed to support him," and he was left standing alone. "The
people of this Territory," Williams triumphantly proclaimed, "cannot be
carried into Anarchy as easy as he expects."[47]

But the governor's jubilation was premature. This meeting was no
better attended than its aborted predecessor. Disgusted by the incessant
bickering and faced with an outbreak of sickness, a number of members
stayed away. Even the few attendees did not wish to be caught in the
crossfire, and one of them, George Humphrey of Claiborne County,

resigned in disgust, insisting that he could no longer serve "without making a sacrafice of more than . . . my family and fortune are able to meet with convenient[ly]."[48]

Sometime in late 1807, Mead's partisans had secretly drafted a memorial imploring the president not to reappoint Williams when his term expired in March. Insisting that he had "lost the confidence of nine tenths or a greater proportion of the Republicans of the territory," they enumerated five charges which "constitute[d] his official criminality." They accused him of cavorting with the "most violent of Federal men," abusing "his [executive] powers by refusing to sign a revenue bill," requiring collectors to be freeholders, "covertly interfering" with local elections by ordering sheriffs to "appoint federal managers," and displaying a "strong attachment to the fortunes of Aaron Burr."[49]

Mead came to the December session armed with the memorial, expecting the legislature to endorse it, but lack of a quorum stalled his efforts. According to Williams, the memorial was such "a laughable thing" that, after polling the members, Mead "found the vessel of faction and party in such shoaly waters as to forbid his moving a single knot or ousting a sail for fear of being stove." Even Shields thought it "too impassioned." Although the legislators lingered for another three weeks, they argued incessantly and enacted nothing of importance "except a small alteration in the revenue law, and a memorial to the Congress; and even these were passed with difficulty." Four of the governor's friends then asked Williams to dismiss the legislators. It was, they stated, unlikely that the General Assembly, "with its bare majority," could conduct "any business of real benefit and advantage to the community." Williams happily complied by proroguing the General Assembly "until the first Monday in February ensuing."[50]

His critics loudly denounced this latest display by the dictatorial "Prince Robert," and William Shields gladly joined the thunderous outcry. "The exercise of another prerogative by Governor Williams," he declared, "has excited more lively sensibility if possible than his recent mutations of officers." He characterized Williams's tortured explanation as "a singular specimen of legal logic and technical quibble." Rodney concurred. Most legislators, he said, "were highly displeased," and he wondered if Williams were not motivated by a desire "to prevent their complaining of his conduct."[51]

Yet, Williams, as his opponents acknowledged, had achieved a pyrrhic victory by preventing the legislature from petitioning Congress or Jefferson. Even if the prorogued legislature, postponed until early February, sent a remonstrance, it could not reach the nation's capital in time to influence the president's decision. In fact, Jefferson had already decided to retain Williams, although the news would not reach Natchez until late March.[52]

The delay had nothing to do with territorial matters. By late 1807, Jefferson's attention, in wake of British refusal to make amends for the dastardly attack upon the *Chesapeake,* had shifted attention from domestic to foreign affairs. As Jefferson explained to Williams, upset because his letters went unacknowledged, he was forced, under "the constant pressures of business," to quit "answering letters which do not necessarily require it." But privately the president was troubled by unrest in the territories. As he informed Williams, he lamented "the violence of the dissensions in your quarter" as well as those in "the territories of Louisiana & Michigan. It seems," he continued, "that the smaller the society the bitterer the dissensions into which it breaks." Sounding like Madison in his famous *Federalist No. 10,* Jefferson optimistically predicted that the United States was "to owe it's permanence to it's great extent." None of his rambling soothed Williams, who wanted proof of Jefferson's confidence.[53]

Meanwhile, the governor's detractors continued to swell. The latest was Walter Leake, who had arrived in Natchez in late May 1807 to take his seat on the territorial supreme court. Leake, put off by the governor's apparent favoritism toward Federalists, immediately joined the so-called real Republicans. More importantly, Leake kept in touch with friends in Virginia and Maryland. In mid-December 1807, outraged by the governor's two prorogations of the legislature, he penned a devastating letter to Wilson Cary Nicholas, one of Jefferson's strongest congressional allies. "Federalism, which . . . a year or two ago, seemed to be drooping," he wrote, "now seems to be rearing its head." In fact, the Federalists "begin to take encouragement, and by their conduct seem to consider their success as allmost certain." Detailing a lengthy litany of the governor's transgressions, largely echoing Poindexter, Leake enjoined Nicholas to put control of territorial government once again in the hands of orthodox Republicans.[54]

Meanwhile, territorial affairs were in disarray. Williams had trouble finding replacements for departing militia officers. After a few attempts to reorganize the Adams County militia, he became so displeased with the poor response that he countermanded the orders. For Claiborne's replacement, Williams chose Col. Walter Burling, another of Wilkinson's notorious friends, and even Burling became "a little angry at [the governor's] bungling." Williams had less success in filling civic offices. "You would be really astonished," Shields informed Poindexter, "to observe the lethargy that pervades every department of our Government, except the judiciary."[55]

Nevertheless, Williams continued to reassure Jefferson and Treasury Secretary Gallatin. "The Territory," he declared, "was never more quiet nor better Reconciled to the local and general administration than at present." Dissatisfaction was limited to "the continued efforts of a few," who, he reiterated, "have Run their Race." In fact, he boasted, "a people can't be more" content, even though "Mead-Claiborne and two or three Others make what they can, together with this rascal Shaw."[56]

By early 1808, Williams's opponents were desperate. Colonel Claiborne, accompanied by Abner Green, rode through the countryside sounding the alarm and cajoling wavering legislators to affix their names to the infamous Mead memorial before it was too late. They insisted that if the General Assembly quickly endorsed it and immediately dispatched it to Jefferson, they could block Williams's reappointment. Apparently Claiborne succeeded in pressuring Representative Davis and councilor William Snodgrass, whom Williams described as a "weak, dependent character," into signing it. When James Caller, one of the governor's staunchest defenders, heard rumors to that effect, he was dumbfounded. Both men, according to him, had earlier promised that they would not go along with Mead. Stephen Bullock, another of Williams's friends, was also astounded. After Bullock and Caller confronted Davis and Snodgrass, they insisted that no memorial had been sent. In this assertion, they were right, for Claiborne and Green failed to obtain their signatures.[57]

When the Fourth General Assembly met for the last time in February 1808, a frustrated Mead still could not muster support for his memorial. Nonetheless, an apprehensive Williams, fearing the worst, sent Gallatin the two affidavits from Caller and Bullock, assuring him "that if a thing of the kind has been forwarded to the President, forgery must have been resorted to."[58]

Since Mead was still determined to force the legislators to endorse his memorial, the session was mostly stillborn, even though Williams had outlined a full and impressive agenda. But legislators could not see beyond the question of Williams's qualifications, and the handful of measures they enacted were, in Williams's opinion, premature, unlawful, or deliberately provocative. For example, Mead cajoled the legislature into passing a reapportionment bill in anticipation of Congress extending the franchise to all taxpayers. While Williams favored both an extension of the franchise and reapportionment of legislature, he saw this bill as a ploy to embarrass him. Believing that the General Assembly could not pass a law in anticipation of congressional approval, he was compelled to veto an act that he actually favored, leaving the impression that he opposed democracy. Shortly thereafter, a nonplussed Williams dismissed the legislators for a third time.[59]

Nevertheless, Williams won the first round in his contest with the Meadites when the president reappointed him. Now he had to prove that, with his reappointment, "tranquility" would return to "this community" and respectable citizens would silence the small band of detractors who were "determined to publish to the world the appearance of discontent with the local administration." Happily, he declared, this sentiment was confined to "a small Portion of the Territory and with but few of the Inhabitants."[60] Unfortunately, Williams was unaware that Jefferson had again acted more out of convenience than conviction. The only question left was whether Williams could change his behavior enough to placate his determined critics. If not, the upcoming year promised to be troublesome.

CHAPTER 10

Changing of the Guard

Governor Williams's second term began as contentiously as his first had ended. In dismissing the legislature for a third time in a span of four months, he opted to dissolve both houses rather than merely prorogue or recess the lower one. His reason for doing so was transparent to everyone, although he justified it by the previous legislature's failure "to provide for the printing of the laws and journals of the session."[1] For his second term to be successful, he needed a compliant General Assembly, and the best way to secure it was to replace the current body and elect another. Few questioned that dissolution required selection of a new lower house, but Williams, seeking a different Legislative Council, insisted that dissolution abrogated both branches, necessitating a newly elected House of Representatives to submit a fresh set of nominees for the upper chamber.

To implement this strategy, Williams initiated special elections during the summer of 1808, expecting the voters to repudiate the hotheads. Earlier Williams had assured Jefferson that if he was reappointed, the opposition, out of frustration, would rapidly disintegrate.[2] Yet he soon realized that his understanding of dissolution had actually solidified previous differences rather than splintering existing factions.[3]

But this time around, Williams was wiser. Instead of relying on his own intuition, he solicited opinions from Secretary of State James Madison and Attorney General Caesar Rodney.[4] And with their subsequent approval, he was comfortable in proceeding with his plans.[5] Anticipating success in the upcoming house elections, he expected a cleansed lower house to choose an acceptable list of nominees for the Legislative Council. At the very least, he hoped to be rid of Daniel Burnet, Joshua Baker, and Joseph Sessions.[6]

Williams wanted the new council selected before the fifth General Assembly met in early December.[7] Yet, he was so confident of victory that he promised a few trusted friends that if the people remained dissatisfied he would resign.[8] Unfortunately, no one could keep a secret.[9] His enemies quickly learned of his flippant promise, which they converted into a pledge. If nothing else, his carelessness stiffened his opponents' resolve and transformed their despair into renewed hope that they could oust the obnoxious executive by capturing the next house election.

Ironically, Williams displayed greater faith in the people's judgment than did his erstwhile democratic opponents. Relying on their good sense, he failed to present a slate of candidates for them to support. On the other hand, Cowles Mead and George Poindexter were not so naive. As seasoned politicians, they knew better than to leave so crucial a choice to chance, and they drafted a slate of trustworthy candidates pledged to continue the assault against the governor's arbitrary behavior.[10]

The gullible governor was stunned by the results. Rather than choosing men with whom he could work, the voters picked six of his "most Violent and distinguished Opponents." Only in Claiborne (formerly Pickering) and Washington counties did they elect friendly representatives. In populous Adams County, they chose Mead, Ferdinand Claiborne, and William Shields, together with the moderate Federalist Philander Smith. In Jefferson County, the outcome was more mixed. William Snodgrass, who had signed the Mead memorial but retracted it later, led a field of five moderates, but Williams's strongest advocate, Thomas Fitzpatrick, ran last.[11]

These elections were also important because the people, not the legislature, were to select the next territorial delegate.[12] After some hesitation, Poindexter, bowing to pressure from his persistent friends, agreed to seek another term. Ironically, his cohort Mead, expecting Poindexter to be named territorial judge, was waiting in the wings to succeed him. Needless to say, Poindexter's announcement caught him by surprise, not realizing that Jefferson was reluctant to put the choleric lawyer on the bench. Nevertheless, Mead, in the interest of factional harmony, withdrew and endorsed Poindexter.[13]

In contrast, those loyal to the governor, though still numerous, had difficulty attracting an acceptable candidate. Eventually, impatient citizens of Natchez, on their own initiative, nominated Secretary Thomas H. Williams, who remained strangely silent until John Shaw publicly assaulted him in the press. He immediately retreated, denying that he was ever a candidate, and despite repeated pleas from friends, refused to canvass the territory.[14] Nevertheless, he carried Claiborne and Washington counties, ran well in Natchez, and won nearly one-fourth of the total vote, an indication of Poindexter's ambivalent popularity. Still, Poindexter prevailed by a comfortable margin.[15]

In fact, the governor, blunder-prone as usual, was partly responsible for Thomas's defeat. Late in the campaign, Governor Williams asked Andrew Marschalk to publish two letters of James W. Bramhan, a recent immigrant and friend of Judge Leake, to a pair of Virginia congressmen, both sons-in-law of President Jefferson. Unduly critical of Williams, Bramhan's letters depicted a territory "bordering on direful consequences especially if the present Executive remains and if the people do not get their [land] claims" sanctioned by Congress.[16] Williams had obtained copies from the postmaster at Washington, Samuel Winston, who happened to be his brother-in-law.[17]

Although he had secured the letters in early January, Williams waited until the summer elections to release them. By printing them in Marschalk's *Natchez Gazette*, he hoped to expose the unsavory character of his detractors. In his opinion, the letters were blasphemous and replete with falsehoods, demonstrating a disregard for truth or integrity. Furthermore, he believed, they revealed in his opponents an unquenchable thirst for office and a propensity to use any tactic, including chicanery, to seize control.[18]

Again Williams let his personal prejudices override his better judgment. In publishing letters pilfered from the post office by a relative, he opened himself to the twin charges of tampering with federal mails and falsifying the truth. His predators, smelling blood, demanded to know where and how he had acquired the letters, which, in their opinion, painted an accurate portrait of the territory's deplorable conditions. Their suspicion fell on Winston, who had previously been accused of intercepting mail.[19]

At first, Williams was evasive, wishing to conceal the identity of his accomplice. Ultimately driven to desperation, he admitted obtaining the letters from "a gentleman of the first respectability and standing in the territory." But he attempted to fend off further criticism by insisting that they contained common information. "Most of these office-seekers and political Jackals," he explained, were of "such a babbling disposition . . . that they [could] keep nothing secret."[20] Meanwhile Bramhan's friend Colonel Claiborne learned of Williams's plans "to resign immediately." Pronouncing the report "POSITIVELY FALSE," Williams explained that although he had, on several occasions, declared his intentions, "from motives of private interest," to leave office, he did not plan to do so until sometime after March 3, 1809.[21]

Nevertheless, Williams, by his carelessness, had put himself in a precarious predicament. If he remained in office for another year, he had severely lessened his political clout. On the other hand, if his opponents, by overzealousness, forced him to change his mind and remain governor, he would lose the confidence of his beleaguered supporters. Either way, Williams was in a winless position.

But instead of extricating himself from the dilemma, he compounded his problems by purging his administration of disloyal officials, employing methods that were unduly clumsy and unnecessarily antagonistic. He chose to defame them publicly rather than discard them quietly. On October 7, 1808, he surprised even his staunchest supporters by revoking the commissions of Beverley R. Grayson as auditor of public accounts, justice of peace for Adams County, and clerk of the supreme court and Theodore Stark as clerk of the Adams County circuit court. Neither was prepared to go quietly, and the two aggrieved officials mustered instant sympathy from those who previously had felt the governor's harsh lash. To them, the dismissals were another example of a demented official prone to act tyrannically or, as Judge Rodney put it, to behave like "a mad man."[22]

As for Grayson, Williams thought he had deliberately insulted him. John Brabston, a local resident, complained that Grayson had "treated [him] unjustly" after he had accused "a man of fortune and high standing in the community" of stealing his horse. In reply to the governor's inquiry, Grayson not only dismissed the "unjustified" charges, but he also made a mockery of the incident.[23] Following a heated exchange, Williams stripped him of his offices while an incensed Grayson adopted what had become the method of choice for dismissed officials; he withheld the public records from his successor, Parke Walton.[24]

Stark also fought back. When his replacement, James Dunlap, one of Burr's former accomplices, attempted to assume his duties, Stark was there with a battery of prominent lawyers, including Mead, Shields, and Fielding Turner. After Dunlap's attorney, Charles B. Green, demanded that his client be sworn in as clerk, Shields objected. Arguing that the clerk of this court was "not answerable To the Governor," he declared that Stark could be removed only upon "Conviction of misbehaviour or misdemeanor in office." The governor's power to appoint or remove court clerks, he stated, "ceased with the first Grade of [territorial] Governm[en]t."[25]

By the time Stark took his case to court, Justices Rodney and Walter Leake, both outspoken critics of the governor, were the only sitting judges, after Peter Bruin had resigned rather than face impeachment charges for negligence of duty and official misconduct.[26] Basing their decision on English common law, Rodney and Leake ruled that since Stark was an agent of the court, the governor could not dismiss him. While Rodney agreed with Shields that only the court could appoint its clerk, Leake restricted his opinion to the question of dismissal.[27]

In rendering their torturous decisions, the two judges appeared partisan. An angry Williams, refusing to treat it as conclusive, instructed Attorney General Seth Lewis to enter a bill of exceptions before Judge Leake. Horrified by the governor's defiance of the law, Judge Rodney likened Williams to "a man whose mind is deranged" and reminded the governor "That Laws and not men, rule in our Country." Meanwhile, Shields introduced a motion to hold the governor in contempt for defying the ruling.[28]

Emboldened by the Stark judgment, Grayson instigated similar action. This time the governor enlisted the aid of the "unbiased" Judge Toulmin, who upheld the right of an executive to dismiss his appointees. Shunning Toulmin's opinion, Rodney and Leake ruled in favor of Grayson's plea. There the matter rested, unresolved and festering.[29]

In September, amid this judicial squabble, Williams called the Assembly into special session to choose a slate of ten nominees for the Legislative Council.[30] Not surprisingly, the session was tempestuous, with tempers raw and edgy. After placing Ferdinand L. Claiborne in the speaker's chair, the representatives, aware of Williams's inquiry to Madison but not of the answer, requested the governor to share with them all communications with the administration. With obvious relish, Williams produced Madison's supportive letter.[31]

Whereupon Henry Bullock, one of the governor's favorites, moved to proceed with the nominations. Instantly Mead, seconded by Shields, objected, insisting that since Madison's letter was not "under the Big Seal," it lacked official sanction and should be disregarded. In response, Bullock sagely suggested that the issue be resolved by sending the president a slate of nominees. If Jefferson thought Williams's actions illegal or ill-advised, he could lay the recommendations aside and retain the current councillors.

Shields then rose from his seat, displaying in his raised right hand a copy of the Declaration of Independence, and demanded recognition. Incredulous that the author of this sacred document had abandoned his revolutionary principles by supporting a governor whose actions were more tyrannical than those of George III, Shields proclaimed that the declaration "would stare him in the face." But Mead was even more contemptuous. Declaring that "President [Jefferson] was affected by a Sun Pain" for protecting "the greatest villain [Wilkinson] that ever disgraced the world," he characterized Madison as a "weak debilitated man, greatly affected by fever."

At this point, Henry D. Downs, a representative from Jefferson County who had earlier opposed Bullock's motion, changed his mind, and Speaker Claiborne, not wishing to antagonize incoming President Madison, followed suit. By an eight-to-four margin, the members agreed to begin the balloting. Acquiescing to the inevitable and sensing that the governor had a trick up his sleeve, Mead altered his strategy. Since his supporters had already caucused and agreed upon a slate in case they lost the initial argument, Mead hoped to catch the opponents napping by calling for an immediate vote and ramrodding his choices through the House. Although Philander Smith objected to the procedures, Speaker Claiborne ignored him and ordered the balloting to begin.

Unlike its opponents, the Smith faction, consisting of James Caller, Lemuel Henry, and Samuel Cook, together with Smith and Bullock, had not taken the precaution of meeting beforehand, and Mead's motion, as anticipated, caught them off guard. After Speaker Claiborne refused to countenance further delay, the Meadites, by enforcing strict discipline, were so successful that Smith did not learn the identity of the final nominees until the tellers announced the results.[32]

It was then discovered that one of the Claiborne County nominees, Francis Johnston, not only lacked the necessary property qualifications but also was a resident of Orleans Territory. At first, Cook "believed it to be a fictitious name." The other nominee was the mercurial Daniel Burnet, who switched allegiances after Williams attempted to abolish the Legislative Council.[33] Clearly the Mead faction had cleverly coupled Burnet with an obscure person in order to ensure his reappointment and deprive Claiborne County, where the governor enjoyed substantial support, of its seat on the Legislative Council.

Nevertheless, Williams, despite the poor quality of nominees, managed to salvage something. As he soon realized, the extreme Meadites, in order to secure the renominations of Baker and Sessions, were also forced to compromise with their wavering allies. Consequently, the final list included three respectable but inexperienced planters (James Lea, Joseph Stampley, and Thomas Calvit) as well as John Hanes and John Flood McGrew, two of the governor's defenders from Washington County, where Mead had few adherents. Hanes, a man of meager talents, was formerly sheriff of Washington County, while the popular and well-respected McGrew had recently married the daughter of John Caller.[34]

Determined to eliminate Baker and Sessions, Williams urged Jefferson to select McGrew, Lea, and Calvit. They were, he pleaded, "not only well qualified but [also] known and respected Republicans, so much so that the tongue of slander — has not dared to assail them on that score." By rejecting Sessions, one of Adams County's two nominees, he had to recommend Montgomery. Despite Montgomery's past record of acting "with the [opposition] party in attempting to embarrass me," Williams was convinced that Montgomery, although "deceived" earlier by his friends, now realized the "error of his ways" and "no longer" planned to "act with those characters [the Meadites] when he finds the public good is not their aim." As for the two Claiborne County nominees, the governor could only lament that "It was certainly a shameful thing to nominate this man, Mr Johnston."[35]

While no one was entirely pleased with this outcome, both sides tried to make the best of a sorry situation. In the end, Williams had to acquiesce in the appointment of Burnet and the less-than-reliable Montgomery. Consequently, he was left with the likelihood of having only one trustworthy ally, McGrew, and two prominent but inexperienced men on the council. In seeking to persuade Jefferson to appoint his choices, he enlisted the aid of William Lattimore, who, without knowing six of the ten nominees, dutifully urged Jefferson to select the three moderates. "But from what I know of Messrs. McGrew, Lea & Calvit," Lattimore declared, it was "fortunate for the territory that the nomination admits of the selection of a majority so free from those sinister views and personal resentments, which have produced our present dissensions."[36]

On the other hand, Mead, Poindexter, and Claiborne were equally displeased with the selections. Nevertheless, upon officially submitting the list to Jefferson, as Speaker of the Legislature, Claiborne characterized them as "esteemed Republicans and attached to the Administration of the General Government," and reminded the president that Baker, Burnet, and Sessions had "composed a part of the late Council." These three, he avowed, "possess in a high degree the confidence of this people . . . [and] their reappointment will be more than gratifying." Likewise, Poindexter implored Jefferson to keep the three incumbents.[37]

Once more President Jefferson, who was in the final stages of his second and less satisfying term, refused to hand over the harassed governor to his chronic critics. Faced with an obstinate enemy abroad and mounting criticism at home over his ill-advised embargo, Jefferson had all but abandoned his responsibilities by late 1808, and he was ready to turn the reins of power over to his handpicked successor—James Madison. In this mood, Jefferson accepted Williams's advice. But, if Williams expected the new councillors to assist him in restoring harmony, he was deluded.

The controversy would not die. During the heated debates over selection of nominees for the council, George Davis, a defamed surveyor turned stenographer, slipped into the meeting hall, unnoticed by either Mead or Shields, and painstakingly recorded the inflammatory speeches. Apparently Bullock and Cook were behind this effort, having instructed Davis to record verbatim the biting utterances of Mead and Shields, whose accusations bordered on the seditious.[38] In the published proceedings, Davis edited Shields's intemperate remarks to make them appear as diatribes against the administration. An incensed Shields accused Davis of having "most mischievously and wickedly garbled and perverted his words," correctly identifying Bullock as the responsible party. Afterward Shields threatened to expel Bullock if he were proven guilty of masterminding the affair or collaborating in it.[39]

Instantly Bullock was on his feet, accusing Shields of plotting to oust the governor and insisting that Davis had neither exaggerated nor misrepresented Shields's retorts. As proof that Davis had not doctored the debates, Bullock submitted a litany of quotations from Shields's previous speeches, most of which were as critical of the president as those recorded by Davis.[40] He also accused Shields of attempting "to bribe or . . . to bully" the editors of the *Weekly Chronicle* into suppressing publication.[41] To counteract Bullock's charges, the Meadites adopted resolutions proclaiming the published minutes as "inaccurately and falsely reported" and censuring those responsible for their distribution. Nevertheless, Davis was satisfied that his publication of the debates had crippled the efforts of Poindexter and Mead to retain Baker and Sessions as councilors.[42]

It was not a good time for Poindexter. Not only was he dissatisfied with the new Legislative Council, but also his achievements as territorial delegate were minimal. For example, he tried to restrict the authority of territorial governors to prorogue or dissolve their legislature by attaching a rider to a bill for broadening the franchise in Indiana Territory. By so doing, he provoked the ire of Georgia congressmen led by William Wyatt Bibb and George M. Troup.[43]

The Georgians were enraged by the federal government's failure to fulfill the 1802 agreement with that state. Furious that Congress had not compensated the Yazoo claimants and the president had not removed the remaining Indians from Georgia as the Agreement of 1802 stipulated, they were determined to block all legislation pertaining to Mississippi Territory until the federal government lived up to its commitments. While their anger was not specifically directed at Poindexter, he nonetheless bore the brunt of their asperity. Bibb insisted that Congress could not alter its government while still a territory without Georgia's consent. Besides, Troup pronounced, the Ordinance of 1787 was one of the finest examples of federal prescience. "It was," he said, "composed by the men of 1787 whose integrity was incorruptible and judgment almost infallible," and to amend it was not "necessary or expedient."

Poindexter countered by insisting that it was unwise to clothe a territorial governor with powers reminiscent of royal government or contrary to the principles of the American Revolution. Since these governors could veto all acts of the legislature, they possessed sufficient power to bridle a recalcitrant assembly. His only wish, Poindexter stated, was to protect his constituents from the claws of a tyrannical governor whose actions were "arbitrary and oppressive in the extreme and incompatible with the Constitution."

Specifically, Troup disagreed with Poindexter's contention that territorial governments were comparable to state governments. In his opinion, the founding fathers had shown remarkable insight into human nature by placing the governments of unstable and turbulent frontiers in the hands of strong executives. "In a new country, composed of heterogeneous mixtures of various tempers, characters, and interest," he argued, "it would be highly ridiculous to expect that love of order and obedience to law would always predominate." Congress had "wisely reserved to itself the right to control them," and tinkering with its provisions was irresponsible. Poindexter, he charged, mistakenly "wishes us to treat them not as children but as equals." If Congress caved in, he predicted, "next they will ask for admission [into the Union] before they have the sufficient numbers." Georgia, he declared, would never consent to changing the existing government of Mississippi Territory. Ultimately, the Georgians prevailed when the House of Representatives, by a decisive vote of 58 to 36, postponed "indefinitely" consideration of Poindexter's motion.[44]

Poindexter's constituents were also upset by delay in land sales and the uncertainty surrounding their claims.[45] Preemptioners were particularly uneasy. Due to the crippling effects of the embargo, it was nearly impossible for them to meet the first installments due in January 1809.[46] If most Mississippians continued to support Jefferson's coercive policies, they still suffered severe hardship from cessation of overseas trade. Unsold cotton piled up in local warehouses, shutting off their principal, and sometimes only, source of income. Under these conditions, a number of preemptioners feared losing the land they had so laboriously cleared and cultivated, and they requested relief in the form of temporary extensions. As one petitioner pleaded, "it will be morrally impossible for but a very few pre-emption claimants to make the first payment for their Lands as stipulated by law."[47]

Settlers on lands previously granted to British claimants were equally disquieted. Under existing laws, they were able to secure clear title to the lands upon which they had made improvements only by going to court, a procedure that was both expensive and time-consuming. A few of the more wealthy claimants, none of whom had cultivated these lands, hired local lawyers to plead their cases in federal courts. Indeed, a sizeable number of settlers had come to oppose statehood for fear that federal judges, due to Jay's Treaty, would be sympathetic to British grantees.

If they succeeded, the present occupants of these lands faced ruin and ejection.[48]

Moreover, those suspected of holding antedated Spanish grants continued to occupy "some of the best lands in the Territory," totaling "many thousands of Acres." Without the sworn "testimony of surveyors, chain bearers, markers and other persons present when these frauds were committed," it was impossible to prove them spurious. Not only were such witnesses difficult to find, but they were also "reluctant to give testimony against those who employed them." As one memorialist declared, "many of these false claimants are wealthy and all are possessed with artifice and cunning and doubtless will resort to any means that will comport with the origin of their claims."[49]

Finally, there was the numerous and ever-growing number of squatters. Unable to purchase lands in the absence of public sales, a number poured into the recently acquired lands along the elbow of the Tennessee River in newly established Madison County. Threatened with forcible removal unless they applied for permission to remain as "tenants at will," they refused to leave, waiting patiently for the federal government to open, as promised, land offices at convenient locations. Either from ignorance or inertia, many of them had failed to comply with these conditions, and thus faced imminent expulsion. Indeed, the few who spilled onto Indian territory were sure to be removed by a government anxious to avoid Indian troubles.[50]

Federal officials, especially Treasury Secretary Gallatin, feared the influx of "some pretended" Yazoo claimants once the newly ceded Chickasaw and Creek lands in the Tennessee Valley were surveyed and ready to auction. Fearful that these "pretenders" might intimidate others from bidding on the lands, Gallatin warned Governor Williams against showing favoritism or lending legitimacy to these efforts by appointing to public office anyone connected with the Yazoo frauds.[51] But his fears proved groundless. Few Yazoo claimants appeared once land sales commenced in the spring of 1809, and only one, Michael Harrison, tried to prevent prospective buyers from bidding.[52]

Poindexter, who understood the settlers' grievances and appreciated the fears of federal officials, asked Congress to intervene on their behalf. Despite a valiant effort to secure additional postponements for preemption claimants, he failed to persuade a moribund Congress rendered callous by a spate of desperate pleas for mercy from the ill-effects of the embargo. Northern and eastern congressmen were especially unresponsive since their constituents, by raising perishable products, suffered more from the embargo than did southern planters and farmers, who mostly grew nonperishable staples.[53]

Nevertheless, a resourceful Poindexter, in an effort to counteract his failures, suggested a plan whereby they could delay the first payment for almost a year. They might, he advised, still save their preemptions by submitting the first installment anytime during 1809. An incensed Gallatin denounced this reading of the law. The secretary not only proclaimed it misleading and "erroneous," but he reminded register Thomas H. Williams that "if the first payment be not completed at the time fixed [January 1, 1809] the lands shall and may, from and after that time be disposed of, . . . that is offered for sale."[54]

But Poindexter's crowning denouement was failure to win the judgeship he so avidly coveted. The refusal of a recalcitrant Congress to provide relief to the debt-ridden constituents unquestionably stimulated an interest in the post recently vacated by the senile Peter Bruin. In fact, the timing was perfect, and Poindexter called in as many favors as possible to secure the seat. With firm backing from Judge Rodney, Poindexter won the endorsement of several congressional colleagues and a handful of prominent friends elsewhere.[55]

The likelihood that Poindexter might succeed threw members of the local bar into paroxysm, and a dozen or so protested the appointment. Having "engaged in the practice of law in the same courts" with Poindexter, they could not "hesitate to declare him unfit for it," lacking as he did "the Qualifications necessary . . . for the office to which they are informed he aspires." Nevertheless, his detractors constituted a strange medley, including not only such stalwart Federalists as Seth Lewis and Lyman Harding as well as Bullock, one of the governor's strongest boosters, but also two of his past collaborators—James W. Bramhan and Edward Turner. This curious assortment once more illustrated the fluid nature of territorial politics.[56]

Despite Poindexter's steady string of setbacks, he still retained a firm base of support in the territory. Several of his most ardent friends, despite his obvious shortcomings, tried to buoy his flagging spirits by persuading the General Assembly to pass a set of resolutions praising his work in Congress. Coupling praise with a plea for passage of a law confirming all claims under Spanish warrants and orders of survey, they inadvertently struck Poindexter where he was most vulnerable. Previously, he had shown no inclination to settle conflicting British grants since his clients included such wealthy speculators as Elihu Hall Bay of South Carolina. Bay alone claimed as many as sixteen thousand acres of rich lands under British grants. Additionally, Poindexter's close friend Judge Rodney pressed the claims of his distant relative, Admiral George B. Rodney, whose grants totaled nearly five thousand acres. Little wonder that both wished to have Poindexter on the federal bench.[57]

Fortunately for the embattled Poindexter, Williams's teetering career was rapidly drawing to a close. As resignations from public offices continued to mount and suitable replacements were harder to find, newspapers kept up the tirades against him. In fact, it seemed as if there was no end to the incessant bickering and recriminations, and the upcoming General Assembly promised to continue rather than constrain the discord.[58]

Furthermore, Williams began to realize that even his support in Natchez was waning. After two of the governor's bitterest enemies, William Voss and Timothy Terrell, led a campaign to wrest control of the city from an entrenched oligarchy headed by Samuel Brooks and including Federalist-leaning merchants, Williams grew increasingly disheartened. Voss and Terrell also organized the Natchez Mechanical Society. Originally created "to alleviate the distress of decayed and unfortunate mechanics," the society evolved into a political front to reform city government and root out all Federalist vestiges. In fact, the voters would soon oust Brooks and turn the city government over to the governor's opponents.[59]

In early November 1808, Williams confided to Andrew Marschalk that he was ready to depart. On November 10, the fiery editor, hinting that something extraordinary was to occur, implored the governor's critics to cease attacking his "private and public character." The public, he pleaded, "should wait the result of a development, which will be made, by which it will be seen, that integrity and candor, are liable to imposition and duplicity."[60]

Two days later, Williams notified Jefferson of his plans of "going out of office with you." He had discovered, he said, that "the vast sacrifice" required of high office was too great a price for "the inadequate salary and non attention to my private affairs." Despite a strained effort to put a sacrificial face on his abdication, the truth was that he could no longer endure the incessant and unbearable "torrent of abuse" to which he was subjected. Also the future was unpredictable since Madison would soon replace his faithful defender Jefferson, and Williams was unsure of his resoluteness.[61]

Still Williams kept his intentions secret so as not to undermine his authority during the waning days of his administration. Nevertheless, Mead suspected that something was astir when he recognized a noticeable change in Williams's demeanor. Williams, he said, "pondered aimlessly," strolling "forlorn and hopeless along [the] streets" of Washington.[62] Shortly thereafter, William Thompson confirmed Mead's suspicions when he divulged Williams's plans to the press, triggering a new round of malicious attacks. Furious over the leakage, Williams changed his mind. Having mentioned to "several persons here . . . my intention to Resign," he wrote Jefferson, "it was seized on & connected with other attempts to have me out of office instantly." Then, he continued, it was "published in a way which induces me to recall my intention of Resigning."[63]

But his recantation came too late. With unprecedented haste, Jefferson searched for a suitable replacement and found him in David Holmes, a long-term congressman from Virginia. A tireless party worker, a dedicated Republican, and a man of integrity and good judgment, Holmes proved to be a perfect choice. After consulting with Madison, Jefferson offered Holmes the post. In fact, Holmes, even before receiving the offer, had decided to seek his future in the West. Consequently, Jefferson politely informed the harried Williams of his decision but advised him to keep his withdrawal confidential in order to leave "the impression that his departure was strictly a voluntary resignation."[64]

Meanwhile Williams, assuming he was still chief executive, called the newly elected General Assembly into special session on the first Monday in February 1809. Defiant to the end, several legislators demonstrated their displeasure by deliberately arriving late, delaying the session for three days.[65] By then, knowledge of the governor's earlier intentions was widespread. Still, Williams was noncommittal, expecting Jefferson to acquiesce in his request, and only after Williams learned otherwise was he willing to verify the rumors.[66] Hoping that his successor would come before he vacated the office, Williams waited anxiously for the new governor to appear.[67]

In early March, with a replacement nowhere in sight, a dejected

Williams submitted his resignation, dissolved the General Assembly, turned the government over to his secretary, and departed for North Carolina. Yet his Mississippi career fittingly ended in irony. By not objecting to his second dissolution of the legislature, Williams's opponents actually vindicated his position that a governor could unilaterally dismiss the entire legislature. But his enemies were too busy celebrating to muse over inconsistencies. With loud cheers of joy, legislators, led by Speaker Claiborne, "determined to have a frolic."[68] Joined by other gleeful residents and accompanied by drum and fife, they merrily paraded with lighted torches through the streets of Washington, pausing at Rodney's dwelling, where they lined up in military array and rendered the old judge three cheers.[69] Once the cheering subsided, they awaited the territory's fourth and last governor.

CHAPTER 11

Transformation of a Territory

During its first decade, Mississippi Territory underwent considerable change, especially in Natchez and its environs, which dominated territorial affairs before 1812. The region quickly outgrew its boorish traits, acquiring the early characteristics of a mature society. The economic and social changes accompanying the transformation from a remote outpost to a bustling river port had repercussions throughout the territory. Beneficiaries of a decade of prosperity from cotton production, the early inhabitants created a flourishing society reminiscent of that enjoyed by their ancestors either in the seaboard South or in Old England and Scotland.[1] No longer concerned primarily about self-sufficiency, they began importing excellent Spanish wines, rare and classical books, exotic spices, pure-bred horses, "fashionable carriages," exquisite silks, and fine linens.[2] In 1808, a visitor to Natchez, gazing at the busy waterfront from atop the bluffs overlooking the river, counted eighty-three vessels tied up along the shore. Later, an embittered traveler, who rarely found anything pleasant, was surprised to see the streets of Natchez "literally crammed with cotton bales for the Liverpool [England] markets." He left "with the impression of its comparative prosperity exceeding any town which I have ever seen."[3]

This robust activity not only brightened the lives of well-to-do families, but it also transformed Natchez into a busy inland depot, turning it into a haven for skilled artisans and small shopkeepers as well as aspiring merchants and semitrained professionals, a haunt for restless roustabouts and adventurous travelers, and paradise for those "respectable" citizens who, with pockets bulging, sought a night of frolic, relaxation, or escape. Natchez was entering its brief fling of glory and glamour, legends that still abound in romantic tales of raucous river boatmen and heinous highwaymen preying on the innocent and unsuspecting. Less romantic but more authentic were the memories of those who recalled the shady, narrow streets of Old Natchez, lined with quaint, brick-front shops, and elegant homes ornamented with wrought-iron balconies and surrounded by elaborate gardens and blooming flowers.

A by-product of Natchez's dual role as commercial and agricultural center was the emergence of two towns, one atop the bluff and another "under-the-hill," to handle its diverse activities. The river trade, with its vice and rowdies, was conveniently relegated to the lower reaches of the town and concealed from view of the "better element."[4] During the day, Kentucky and Ohio boatmen, "who, like an alligator, may be said to have lived in and upon the river," unloaded goods from Europe, the Atlantic ports of the United States, and the western states of Ohio, Kentucky, and Pennsylvania. By 1800, the grubby, uncouth river men described themselves as more than an alligator; they had become the fabled "Alligator Horse." This appellation was first bestowed by world-traveler Christian Schultz, who overheard a sprightly conversation among "some drunken sailors . . . respecting a Choctaw lady." The first boasted, "I am a man; I am a horse; I am a team. I can whip any man in all Kentucky, by G—d." A second braggart countered that he was "an alligator; half man, half horse," and he could "whip any man on the Mississippi by G—d." A third boatman challenged the others. "I am a Mississippi snapping turtle," he yelled, with "bear's claws, alligator's teeth, and the devil's tail; and can whip any man, by G—d." In an amusing finale, Schultz reported, the final grant "was too much for the first, and at it they went like two bulls." The fracas lasted "for half an hour, when the alligator was fairly vanquished by the horse."[5]

At night, the "half-horse, half-alligator" men caroused below the hill, seeking friendship more than physical challenges. They patronized the various dens of iniquity, which came alive with noisy merriment as weary boatmen amused themselves with several rounds of hard liquor, accompanied by the singing of bawdy songs. Sometimes a few fun-loving townspeople joined them for an evening of reverie, and together, they frequented the numerous dance halls and gambling houses or one of several grog shops. Indeed, Natchez soon became one of the more notorious and unregulated places on the Mississippi River.[6]

While the newer community "on-the-bluff" was less rowdy and more refined, some of its respectable citizens, who never caroused around the landing after dusk, drank an occasional overdose of Madeira, cognac, or bourbon whiskey and exchanged hefty sums of money at games of chance such as three-up and loo. Nevertheless, these folks not only gained respectability over the years but also managed to establish a reputation for gentility by demanding better law enforcement above than below the bluff, especially after Natchez's incorporation in 1803.[7]

Although Natchez was small by any standard, its size was hardly a good measure of its wealth or refinement. Overpowering the region, it served both as a political center, even after the capital was relocated, and as "the principal emporium for the commerce of the territory."[8] Almost everyone of importance, politicians and planters alike, transacted business there, and their visits were rarely arduous and often pleasant. They found comfortable lodging in one of the town's six public inns. Oftentimes, preferring to mix business with pleasure, they brought along their wives and even their offspring.

During the day, spouses often strolled to the bustling markethouse, where a colorful and "motley mixture of Americans, French and Spanish Creoles, mullatoes, and negroes" plied their trade amid shrieking barkers, swarming flies and bothersome insects, tantalizing smells, and nauseating odors.[9] Some promenaded along the town's shady streets or riverfront. By night, the family enjoyed a Restoration or eighteenth-century play at the old Spanish hospital or patronized one of several dancing assemblies.[10] Even the elderly, who could no longer waltz merrily across the dance floor but who enjoyed the sight of young people having fun, acted with great pleasure as chaperones to "preserve order and Decorum."[11] On special occasions, residents and visitors alike could, for the price of one dollar, hear a ventriloquist at the city tavern, listen to imitations of birds, or witness feats of "herculean Balancing" at Texhada's tavern. To the delight of children of all ages, the only live elephant in the country passed through Natchez in 1810.[12]

Single planters had, during leisure hours, a choice of several pursuits. They might, if a member, attend a meeting of the Jockey Club, visit one of the prestigious learned societies, or eat their meals at the Masonic Lodge (Harmony No. 7); otherwise they relaxed by reading and drinking at one of the coffeehouses or by greeting friends along the streets or in the Commons, which overlooked the river.[13] In these settings, conversation among gentlemen flowed freely, and they were as likely to transact business or arrange some political deal as they were to exchange pleasantries. The social life of this small, opulent community had begun to blossom, and its gentry, though small in number, had sufficient influence to set the tone for the manners and social etiquette of the district.

But Natchez was not the only place where people congregated. If Natchez reigned supreme in economic transactions, the small village of Washington, located only twelve miles to the north, vied with its neighbor for the honor of hosting the territory's social center. Initially a creation of Republican legislators who wished to escape the suffocating influence of Federalist Natchez, Washington quickly gained a favorable reputation as a quaint and quiet community nestled in a paradisiacal setting. One of the major attractions was a medicinal spring named for Andrew Ellicott, who had taken refuge there from yellow fever in July 1797. Ellicott Springs lured both gentlemen and ladies to this idyllic hamlet. There a person might recline under the refreshing shade of "some spreading forest trees," purchase a hot or cold bath for "three eights of a dollar," or soak in "the cool transparent water, either pure or mixed to their taste." One traveler, eyeing the young ladies about town, was smitten with their "tasty and rich" attire, but he found the buildings that lined the road to Natchez drab. Nearby was Fort Dearborn, where the colorful uniforms of officers and distant drumbeats summoning the soldiers to assembly radiated a pleasing atmosphere.[14]

This normally peaceful village came alive on special occasions. After Washington replaced Natchez as seat of Adams County and home of the territory's Supreme Court, court days were especially lively. Other busy times were militia musters and regular meetings of the General Assembly. During these gatherings, lawyers, politicians, merchants, and planters, as well as ordinary citizens, commingled and rubbed shoulders with one another. Usually they transacted business, but sometimes they preferred to watch feats of physical strength, electioneer for office, or just get drunk. A favored few might be invited to an elegant ball attended by the territory's beautiful belles, among whom Peggy Dunbar was the acknowledged leader, or regale themselves with the pleasures of the festive board, "where patriotic and political toasts" were followed by a rendition of martial music and a hearty meal appropriately washed down with one's favorite liquor.[15]

Although Washington and Natchez were the only towns of importance, spotty settlements surrounded Fort Adams, near the international border, and tiny villages sprang up at Greenville, Uniontown, Selsertown, Bruinsburg, Pinckneyville, Woodville, and Gibson's Port. The decayed state of some revealed the shattered dreams of overextended speculators or failure of others to recognize that the region could support only a limited number of risky ventures or get-rich-quick schemes.

For instance, the Greenville bubble of the Greens burst after failing to attract the county seat or a college, and its unoccupied buildings, which sold for "little more than a quarter of their cost," gave mute testimony that settlers were seeking greener pastures. Even John Shaw, author of political diatribes and "Pindaric odes," left Greenville in search of a better spot, first to Natchez and later to newly created Franklin County.[16] Pinckneyville, a notorious haunt for highwaymen and filibusters, was a different matter. Uncharacteristically placid without the presence of the infamous Kemper brothers, it came to life with their arrival, ordering new rounds of "Drinking and playing Billiards" and turning the tiny settlement into a raucous dive. Quiet or noisy, this border community remained beyond the sway of government and became a kind of no-man's land.[17]

Another community characterized by fondness for frolic was Gibson's Port, where one visitor discovered that every house was "either a store, a tavern, or the workshop of a mechanick." Additionally, he noted the presence of "a very mean gaol and an equally bad courthouse," which were constantly occupied because of the people's love of excitement and litigation. "Gambling is carried to the greatest excess, particularly horse racing, cards and betting," he wrote, and "every difference of opinion" became a wager.[18]

As the prevalence of decaying hamlets suggested, most people, from planters to farmhands, rarely ventured far from home, and when they did they usually spent their spare time within a planter's mansion or friend's cabin. For the average farmer, life was monotonous to an almost unbelievable degree, and for them a political fracas or spirited campaign, an emotional religious camp meeting, an assemblage of inquisitive people, a vociferous public protest, or a summons for jury service added spice to an otherwise humdrum existence.

The farmers' dwellings were as stark and unpretentious as their lives. The interior of their homes were more likely than not dirty, badly ventilated (if at all), and crudely as well as sparsely furnished. Nevertheless, most dirt farmers were still able to grub out of their barren acreage enough to survive and procreate. They raised an adequate yield of corn, potatoes, and garden vegetables to keep body and soul together and produced enough cotton and kept sufficient livestock to satisfy essential needs.[19] To supplement a meager income, farmers often engaged in unauthorized cutting of pine, oak, cypress, or cedar trees from the public domain.[20]

To be sure, most inhabitants, though short of luxuries, lived comfortably, if not lavishly, and contentedly, if unpampered. They believed they could improve their lot, and the hope for a better tomorrow never died. If they arrived too late to claim a plot of land in the fertile sections of the territory, they were quick to petition the federal government for removal of the Indians in hopes of securing their own homestead.[21]

Although differences in wealth were visible to the most casual observer, social distinctions were slow to solidify; and an industrious person who accumulated some wealth might find himself the squire of his county, proud owner of a modest estate, or captain of a militia company. The keys to social prominence were possession of land, black slaves, and a good cotton crop. As early as 1810, a few settlers had already made the transition from rags to riches, and more were to follow. For instance, George Poindexter, who had come to Natchez from Virginia in 1802, started a profitable law practice, obtained through influential friends a few appointive offices to supplement his income, and married into a wealthy and prominent family. By 1815, he had amassed considerable property, including eight hundred acres in Adams County alone, forty slaves, and a handful of lots in Natchez, assessed at three thousand dollars. By 1816, he was proudly dating his letters "Ashwood Place" in Wilkinson County.[22] Poindexter's success was not the rule, but neither was it unique.

Early settlers strove to possess one of the district's proud mansions where social life found its gayest and most ostentatious expression. Spanish governor Gayoso led the way with construction of his fabulous Concord, which later fell into the hands of Stephen Minor.[23] Throughout the territorial period, various other pretentious mansions were constructed, and when foreign visitors expressed amazement at the wealth

of early Natchez, they invariably referred to one or more of these elaborate estates. First territorial governor Winthrop Sargent had begun his
Glouster by 1799; by then, William Dunbar had already built his famous
Forest; the Greens were soon to erect their stately, brick Springfield. The
climax came when Jane Surget White employed a Philadelphia archi-
tect and English gardener to complete her fabulous Arlington, instantly
recognized as the territory's crowning architectural achievement.[24]

Guests and visitors to the few plantation estates were lavishly entertained, especially at the midday meal, where they discovered that the
legendary southern hospitality was no myth. Before each meal, visitors
selected a favorite liquor while the host spread across the table an unbelievable array of fresh vegetables and succulent meats. Between meals,
a gentleman might take a quiet nap on the sofa, participate in some
form of hunt, engage the other guests in polite and genteel conversation, or challenge them to a card or parlor game. Occasionally the host
might arrange a horse race in the afternoon or an elaborate ball in the
evening.[25]

Slight wonder that lawyers and justices sometimes found an otherwise arduous legal circuit extremely enjoyable, or that eligible young
men, with more at stake than a pleasurable visit, avidly made the annual
social circuit of the district's "nabobs." Bachelors came calling throughout the year, and they met with sufficient success to keep the tradition
alive for years. Sometimes, especially holidays and summertime, they
were more likely to find heartbreak than romance. During the Christ-
mas season, planters and their families frequently departed for New
Orleans in search of festive activities, and during the hot and humid
summer months, they sought refuge from the oppressive heat in either
shady Washington or the piney woods.[26] After 1813, most of them went
to the windswept coastal region in or around picturesque Biloxi and Pass
Christian. During August, the threat of yellow fever drove planters and
merchants from the sickly river towns into the healthier countryside,
where they usually stayed with relatives or friends whose unpretentious
homes dotted the backcountry.[27]

The planters' leisure was not limited to social gaiety, and some
engaged in more intellectual and educational pursuits. Foremost was an
interest in scientific activities, especially in those fields related to nature.
The recognized intellectual leader was William Dunbar, who was the
only early Mississippian admitted into the prestigious American Philo-

sophical Society.[28] Dunbar was also the moving force behind creation of the Mississippi Society, an early literary group that quickly shed its original political overtones to become the center of the territory's intellectual activities.[29]

Education was another field of special interest. Planters realized the danger of raising an uneducated progeny in an unsophisticated wilderness. Although they failed to establish a college, as initially planned, they successfully organized academies for young men,[30] a couple of library societies, and a few coffeehouses where gentlemen might read the latest magazines, travel accounts, and almanacs.[31] Moreover, they did not entirely overlook religion. For instance, John Bisland and John Henderson, two staunch Scottish Presbyterians, diligently worked to organize a congregation, gaining a charter for the Salem Presbyterian Church in 1807. Governor David Holmes, a zealous Baptist, would be instrumental in organizing the Mississippi Bible Society and served as its first president.[32]

The best indicator of the district's emergent wealth was not the homes of "aristocrats" or their varied cultural pursuits but the rapidly growing black population. Slavery was nothing new to the territory; early immigrants had either brought slaves with them or purchased imported Africans. The number of slaves grew in direct proportion to success in cotton production. While the white population rose from 7,400 in 1801 to 34,800 in 1816, the same fifteen-year span saw the percentage of slaves jump from 42 to 52 percent of the total population. In other words, during the territorial period, the black population grew faster than the white.[33]

Another measure was the increase in families owning slaves. From 1805 to 1815, the number of slave owners in Adams County increased by 30 percent, while in adjacent Jefferson County the number rose by 18 percent. Between 1805 and 1810, as cotton production soared, the percentage of slave masters owning five blacks or more doubled. In Adams County, it increased by 6 percent and in Jefferson County by 26 percent. On the other hand, those owning more than fifty slaves never exceeded 2 percent of white males, and only a handful were truly affluent. Nevertheless, most masters lived comfortably if not extravagantly.[34]

Although the rich grew richer and the poor poorer, there was no overriding advantage for planters to till large holdings of land, and when they did accumulate sizeable tracts it was more for speculation than cultivation. The uncertainty of land titles, which threatened claimants with expensive litigation, the land's amazing fertility for raising cotton (a crop that encouraged intensification of agriculture), the rapidity of settlement in restricted regions (which led to a sudden density of population), and the dilatory work of the land commissioners (which delayed the opening of public lands to sale) combined to discourage large holdings of land. Even after land sales began in 1809, the Chickasaws remained, for some time, in possession of the rich bottomlands north of Walnut Hills.

Despite the scramble for land, a number of white settlers were landless. In 1805, among poll tax payers in Adams and Jefferson counties, only slightly more than one-half paid taxes on land, and in Washington County only one-third did. The percentage of tax payers not assessed for land was 46 percent in Adams County, 42 percent in Jefferson County, and 60 percent in Washington County. Certainly a number of these actually possessed or claimed lands as preemptioners or were squatters. Yet, in 1815, after preemptioners had obtained full rights and were presumably taxed, the percentage of landless residents was still high, 43 percent for Adams (including Franklin) County and 45 percent for Jefferson County. There was no correlation between land ownership and possession of slaves, and a surprising number of slave owners were landless. To be sure, some were younger sons of planters who possessed extensive holdings or masters who chose to lease slaves until better lands were offered at public auction when they planned to bid high.[35]

As the number of immigrants grew and the amount of decent land diminished, some individuals turned to public office as a source of supplemental income. These offices were sought less by the earliest planters, who devoted more of their attention to moneymaking and less to politics, than by their sons and the steady stream of newcomers. While John Bisland, an early Scottish settler, shunned politics, his sons (Alexander, Peter, and John Jr.) were successful office seekers. On the other hand, George Poindexter, the young lawyer from Virginia, scrambled for political patronage upon arrival in the territory.[36]

Following several prosperous years, the early animosity between Natchez merchants and debtor farmers was forgotten, as both reaped substantial profits. In fact, their interests tended to coincide as merchants turned to agriculture and planters entered the world of commerce and trade. For example, Samuel Postlewaite, son-in-law of William Dunbar, was not only a prosperous Natchez merchant, but he successfully experimented with cotton seed to discover that the otherwise useless seeds were well-suited for cattle feed and fertilizer. On the other hand, Ferdinand L. Claiborne, one of the district's wealthier planters, entered a business partnership.[37]

Where difficulties arose, the cause was more personal than economic. For instance, Poindexter acquired a dislike of Abijah Hunt, who, along with his nephew David, operated a chain of cotton gins and owned the largest mercantile firm in Natchez. In 1811, Poindexter mortally wounded Hunt in the territory's most infamous duel. Hunt, a staunch, outspoken Federalist, had always found Poindexter, one of the more outrageous anti-Natchez politicians, repugnant. While others agreed with him but remained silent, Hunt was unable to refrain from expressing his opinions publicly, and Poindexter, touchy about his reputation, refused to let his invectives go unanswered.

An enraged Poindexter forced Hunt to the duel field, where he was determined to be rid of his persistent pest. Subsequently, Poindexter's critics accused him of firing prematurely on the count of two rather than waiting for the final count of three. Perhaps Ebenezer Bradish, who acted as Hunt's second, was responsible for initiating the charge since Bradish, an unrepentant Federalist like Hunt, had earlier clashed with Poindexter in an undignified and well-publicized Natchez tavern brawl. Nevertheless, the accusation lost much of its credibility when Bradish failed immediately to challenge Poindexter, as the *code duello* prescribed; instead, he preferred to keep the charge alive to discredit Poindexter and to derail his promising political future.[38]

Within this complex social and economic milieu, definite political stereotypes emerged. As is true everywhere, politics in Mississippi Territory mirrored the rest of society, and elections were usually won by candidates who fashioned their stance to fit the prejudices and predilections of constituents. But, unlike the residents of Kentucky or Tennessee, Mississippians never elevated rugged men to political prominence. No Daniel Boone, John Sevier, or Davy Crockett emerged, and even the most vocal egalitarians were men of substance and property, such as Anthony Hutchins, Thomas Green, and Cato West.

If some saw in George Poindexter another Henry Clay, he was only a pale reflection of that charismatic Kentuckian. He was not a celebrated Indian fighter, and, despite his best efforts to become a hero at the Battle of New Orleans, he failed miserably. However Poindexter might wish to employ the rough-and-tumble politics of a rugged individualist like Davy Crockett, his Virginia background always stood in the way. He might drink to excess or gamble through the night, yet he rode like a southern gentleman and dressed like a plantation squire. An admiring public loved his theatrical displays and found his bizarre mixture of Virginia gentility and brawling frontiersman amusing.[39]

Until 1813, the Tombigbee region remained isolated and foreboding. As long as settlers there remained under the jurisdiction of a territorial government with its capital in faraway Natchez or Washington, a primeval and almost impenetrable wilderness separated the settlements, causing communication between them to be difficult and sporadic. In fact, "Bigbee" settlers had easier access to the state of Georgia than to Natchez District. Not only did government rest lightly upon them, but the region's remoteness lured undesirables to settle there, and Tombigbee District acquired a reputation, whether justified or not, of attracting outcasts only one step ahead of the sheriff, absconding debtors, and deadbeat husbands and bigamists fleeing familial responsibilities. At least one fled to avoid recognition by a bastard offspring.[40]

When the United States took control of the Tombigbee region in 1799, the district had been without an organized government for nearly two years. Before Congress in 1804 authorized an additional federal judge, the only court was an ineffective county one. In fact, it was not until the arrival of Judge Harry Toulmin that justice truly came to Tombigbee. While one of the territory's two renowned judges, he still faced constant harassment and personal abuse from an unappreciative populace who resented his candor and adherence to the rule of law. For the most part, he and the military commandant at Fort Stoddert were the only official magistrates, and they brought the district what little law and order existed.[41]

More than those in Natchez District, Tombigbee settlers faced sporadic pressure from Indians. Although the latter had good reasons for their belligerent behavior, whites were short on objectivity. They consistently characterized Indians as uncivilized, vicious savages despite their own dependence upon the crops they raised and skins they trapped. Tombigbee residents, like their counterparts in Natchez, interacted with the usually friendly Choctaw, but they also had to contend with the Creeks, who blocked their expansion on three sides. Moreover, they saw nothing wrong with clearing the forest and erecting cabins on lands that either the Creeks or Choctaws had possessed for centuries. These actions more often than not excited the Indians to plunder or steal, thereby keeping the region in turmoil and white settlers uneasy.

Even more annoying were the Spaniards in West Florida. Too impotent to be a serious threat to American hegemony in the Old Southwest, they were nonetheless a persistent source of perturbation. Mississippians found the duties they extracted exorbitant, distrusted their dickering with Indians, especially the Creek, and chafed at their refusal to return escaped prisoners, fugitive slaves, and stolen livestock.[42]

Besides the small federal cantonment at Fort Stoddert, located near the international boundary at the confluence of the Alabama and Mobile rivers, St. Stephens was the only place with a military presence. Initially it was an appendage to an old Spanish fort, first erected in the late eighteenth century and abandoned after the Spanish left. As late as 1805, portions of the old fort were still standing though in dilapidated condition. According to George Strother Gaines, assistant Indian agent, only one of the remaining "block-houses was in a good state of preservation." In addition, "there was an extensive frame war house, which was used as the land office," and a frame dwelling "occupied by the United States Factor." Nevertheless, the fort housed two companies of soldiers and the Indian factory.[43]

While St. Stephens was the largest settlement in the Tombigbee District, it was little more than an exposed outpost. Despite these hardships, early residents were optimistic, based upon a thriving trade in deerskins, but by 1816, fewer than three hundred people occupied its ninety homes, most of which were shabby and ill-kept. Consequently, St. Stephens never realized its early promise. Local schools were slow to emerge, financial facilities were nonexistent, and it was without a newspaper until 1811. The few planters scattered along the Tombigbee were hardly in league with their ostentatious counterparts in Natchez District, and most remained subsistence farmers and herdsmen.[44]

Nevertheless, there were a few signs of progress. As early as 1802, cotton gins were in operation along the principal streams, and the raising of cotton, together with cattle herding and the proliferation of swine, engaged the labor of most inhabitants. The majority clustered along the banks of the Mobile and Tombigbee rivers, but a sizeable settlement, which at least one observer thought was the region's "most opulent and respectable," sprang up along the Tensaw River. Through the annual overflowing of its banks, the Tombigbee River enriched the soil and facilitated trade.[45]

In 1808, the territory's earlier prosperity ended abruptly. Like the rest of the nation, it suffered from the disruption of trade during the Napoleonic wars and from the later retaliatory measures of the Jefferson administration. Jefferson's decision to clap an embargo upon exports threw the territory into despair, which then grew into a serious depression lasting over five years. The embargo bottled up valuable cotton in bulging warehouses and barns and threatened to throw the commercial and agricultural sections into bitter conflict. Its partial repeal in 1809 failed to alleviate these woes since the low price that cotton commanded canceled out the prospects of a new bumper crop, and most planters and yeomen farmers remained mired in debt.[46]

As if low prices were not enough to discourage Mississippians from undertaking new ventures, 1811 brought additional devastation to the territory. The sudden appearance of rot laid waste to cotton fields, followed by a three-year cycle of devastating floods that drowned livestock, destroyed cotton fields, and damaged commercial buildings and private homes. The outbreak of war between the United States and England in 1812 closed most remaining markets for cotton and invited the British navy to patrol American waters, throttling coastal shipping between New Orleans and the Atlantic coast.[47]

Since Tombigbee settlers never shared in the territory's ephemeral prosperity as did their Natchez neighbors, they were less inclined to fall in debt in order to purchase more slaves and less injured by the volatile cotton market. As a result, the economic depression of 1808–1812 was less severe there than elsewhere, and some were unaware of its existence. Nevertheless, those elsewhere felt the impact of falling prices, surplus inventories, and mounting debts. Under unrelenting pressure from indebted farmers, the territorial legislature and courts more frequently than not displayed sympathy for their plight by enacting "stay laws" or other forms of debtor relief and by postponing judicial decisions involving the seizure of property for nonpayments. For once, Judge Thomas Rodney was pleased with the absence of his colleagues from their benches. If judges had faithfully executed their duties, he feared, the territory might be completely ruined.[48]

"In times like these," queried the more depressed citizens of Adams County, echoing the sentiments of many, "who but the cruel and unrelenting creditor, or the miser with his hoards of dollars lying by him," would raise his voice in opposition to measures "which unless adopted, must be to reduce the husband and parent to the extreme of misery and want."[49] The demand for some form of relief became so pervasive that it threatened to engulf every segment of society. In fact, only the support of Natchez merchants for these measures prevented this controversy from developing into another bitter class struggle similar to that of the early 1790s.

Nonetheless, demands for relief split the territory into rival factions. For instance, Edward Turner, a former member of the Green clan, publicly announced, after surveying the somber situation, that he was opposed to ruinous stay laws. On the other hand, Alexander Covington, a recent immigrant, lashed out against greedy creditors, avaricious speculators, and corrupt placemen, while praising the thrifty farmer as "God's chosen" and the "virtuous backbone of society." Another, calling himself "the Planter," sarcastically blamed the writings of Covington, who wrote under the pen name of "Simplicitas," for splitting his previously pleasant drinking club into two snarling factions.[50]

Likewise, a crisis developed over banking and fiscal policies. In 1809, once the worst effects of the embargo had receded, the territorial legislature, after an abortive effort to secure a branch of the Bank of the United States, established the Bank of Mississippi. With its first stock subscription an immediate success, the bank began on a sound footing. Despite the lean wartime years, the directors, consisting of the leading citizens of Natchez, kept the bank on a specie-paying basis even when others were forced to abandon the practice. In 1814, local merchants, confronted with a devastating drain of specie due to an extensive illicit trade with the British through Pensacola and other Gulf ports, pressured the directors into suspending specie payments. Complaining of its adverse effects, angry citizens, led by backcountry farmers, petitioned the legislature to impose an assessment of fifty cents per one hundred dollars on each suspending bank's capital.[51] Natchez bankers, faced with possible bankruptcy and angered by what they considered a spiteful piece of legislation, persuaded river-county representatives to defeat the measure.

In response, opponents of suspension launched an investigation into what they described as questionable banking practices, but after investigators found no evidence of wrongdoing, the legislature extended the bank a vote of confidence. The only opposition came from three die-hard eastern representatives whose hatred of Natchez exceeded their resentment of creditors. Annoyed by their consistent objections to all stay laws, a gathering of Claiborne County inhabitants pleaded with them to consider "the interest and happiness of the whole" territory rather than just those of their contingency.[52] Although the eastern counties had suffered less from the depression than those along the Mississippi, these three representatives revealed a rising antipathy toward the more opulent western settlers.

As the depression's grip tightened and prices plummeted, some considered abandoning cotton and resorting to raising sheep or cattle, but, with return of prosperity, they dropped the idea. In 1817, as the territorial period neared its end, one of the early planters, who had weathered bad times and good, recalled that year as "the finest season I ever saw— peace, plenty and thy mony plenty," and thanked "the Great God that appointed my habitation in this place."[53]

CHAPTER 12

Natives and Interlopers

Although relations between white settlers and southern Indian tribes were generally peaceful in the first decade of the nineteenth century, they were not always so tranquil. During the American Revolution, the southern colonies were the scene of considerable unrest as Indian nations, with few exceptions, either rallied behind the British or stayed neutral.[1] Whenever possible, southern tribes took advantage of the war by playing one rival against the other in order to extract favors in exchange for their support or noncommitment.[2] As a result, portions of the southern frontier, from Virginia to Georgia, experienced sporadic, and often fierce, fighting between American rebels and British Loyalists supported by Indian allies.

While the Creek and Choctaw remained loyal to Spain, who after 1779 allied with France but not the United States, they were not necessarily hostile toward Americans, with whom they traded extensively. Conversely, the Cherokee and Chickasaw cooperated with the British out of hatred for aggressive frontiersmen. Because England and Spain were more generous than the penurious United States in supplying the Indians, they were usually able to secure their friendship. Yet, little fighting occurred in the lower Mississippi Valley because whites there found Indian warriors unreliable. For example, the Chickasaw had failed to alert British officials to the approach of James Willing in 1778, and Governor Galvez, who seized most of British West Florida between 1779 and 1781, depended for assistance more upon African Americans than Indians.[3]

Not wishing to arouse the fledgling republic, Spanish officials sought to use its North American possessions as a buffer against American population pressure by winning Indian favor through trade and gifts.[4] At first the Indians responded favorably to these overtures, not because they were swayed by Spain's power or duped by her wily agents, but because it was in their best interests to do so. For a while at least, Spanish and Indian interests coalesced around a mutual distrust of American pioneers and a common desire to contain them east of the Appalachians. Although Spanish officials wished to keep the frontier stable and serene, Indian chieftains more often than not expected the Spaniards to assist them in protecting their possessions from intruders and ridding their nations of unscrupulous traders and unsavory whiskey peddlers, even if it meant taking up arms. In other words, each participant hoped to use alliances to promote their own pet projects rather than uphold common interests.[5] Nevertheless, the southwestern frontier, even under these complicated conditions, was more peaceful than it might have been otherwise.

Newly created Mississippi Territory was in a precarious position. Located in the midst of Indian country, it contained only two small pockets of white population, Natchez and Tombigbee, and they were separated by nearly three hundred miles of wilderness, most of which the Creek and Choctaw claimed as hunting grounds. The Tombigbee settlement was hemmed in by the Creek to the east and north, the Choctaw to the west and the Seminole to the south. The Natchez District was slightly less vulnerable, but it too was surrounded by the Choctaw to the east and the Chickasaw to the north. The Chickasaw roamed the extremely fertile lands along the Mississippi River north of modern Vicksburg as well as much of the country traversed by the famous Natchez Trace. They hunted extensively in the region, including parts of western Tennessee and Kentucky, while the less hostile Choctaws occupied the strategically important lands between the two white settlements.[6]

Spanish presence was equally or more troublesome. Spain not only controlled the west bank of the Mississippi River but also the important ports of New Orleans, Mobile, and Pensacola. As a result, the Spaniards regulated commerce entering the Gulf of Mexico, effectively blocking, when they wished, Bigbee settlers from trading with the eastern seaboard and beyond and pressuring Indians not to ally with the United States.[7]

At the close of the eighteenth century, Native Americans constituted the largest single bloc of inhabitants in Mississippi Territory. At that time, some 30,000 Indians resided there in contrast to some 5,000 whites and 3,500 blacks, only about 200 of whom were not slaves.[8] Four of the five southern tribes (Creek, Choctaw, Chickasaw, and Seminole) belonged to the Muskhogean linguistic family, while the Cherokee spoke a language that was distinctly Iroquoian. Despite common cultural features, each developed characteristics that set it apart from the others. The Cherokee acquired a reputation for law and polity. The Creek were dexterous diplomats and artful bargainers. The Choctaw excelled in agriculture and were crafty traders. The Chickasaw were proud warriors and skillful hunters and fishermen. The Seminole, composed mostly of dissident and renegade Creek, were fiercely independent and fearless. In the process of lengthy contacts with Europeans, beginning as early as the 1540s with the arrival of Spanish explorer Hernando de Soto, the resilient Indians were flexible enough to adjust to constantly changing conditions. Some like the Cherokee had become more acculturated to European ideas and values than the others, but all of them had adopted enough of the white man's ways to become later known as the Five Civilized Tribes.[9]

Despite their diverse and distinctive traits, the five southern confederacies were more alike than different. They retained much of their traditional cultures, adapting rather than succumbing to change. Of the five, the Cherokee were the most acculturated and the Creek and Seminole the least, but all retained much of their "Indianness." They continued to observe the same gender distinctions as their forefathers—males were hunters and warriors, and women tended the fields, processed raw skins into peltry or coarse clothing, and managed the homesteads. Once their adjacent hunting grounds were depleted of fur-bearing animals, the men were gone for extended periods of time, sometimes up to six months or longer; consequently females, during the hunters' protracted absence, assumed more and more responsibilities, acquiring in the process increased influence.[10] As a result, Native women enjoyed a more privileged position than their white counterparts.

While females exerted considerable power in tribal societies, Anglo-American settlers—who came from a culture that, except in some frontier societies, relegated women to household chores and regarded Indian males as lazy and slothful—were convinced that Native Americans men treated their mates as slaves and not companions. Conversely, most Europeans regarded hunting not as a livelihood but as a sport, restricted to the wealthy and leisurely classes. Even one as knowledgeable of Native cultures as Benjamin Hawkins was not immune from such thinking, and he naively counted on Indian women to support the federal government's civilizing program as a means of escaping endless drudgery.[11]

Indian women were rarely interested in exchanging their lifestyle for that of white females. In fact, the reverse was more likely. A number of white captives, after experiencing a relaxed Native life, were reluctant to return to their former state. Not surprisingly, several white women, after adoption into Indian families, preferred their newfound freedom to their previous position in a patriarchal family structure. For example, Hannah Hales, a Creek captive, resisted all efforts from her Georgia relatives to have her return home. Later, Superintendent Hawkins, aware of Hannah's talents as seamstress and weaver, employed her to instruct Creek women in the mysteries of the spinning wheel and loom.[12]

Most whites also entertained misconceptions about Indian religious practices, believing the Indians devoid of spiritual beliefs and enslaved by superstition and sorcery. The whites saw it as their God-given mission to bring the light of Christianity to a people enveloped in darkness. They expected to save the souls of Indians and to transform the "savage" societies into civilized ones, but Indians both resented and resisted these efforts.

Over the centuries, the Five Civilized Tribes had developed an elaborate system of beliefs that explained to their satisfaction the otherwise incomprehensible mysteries of life. All had a complex creation story, and each believed in a hereafter where the wicked were punished and the righteous rewarded. Unlike Europeans, Native Americans were not monotheistic; instead they worshiped a plethora of gods, most of whom had association with natural phenomena. The sun, "the Great Holy Fire Above," stood at the apex of a vast hierarchy of deities. For example, the Choctaw believed that the sun, with its blazing eyes, constantly watched over and protected them. The sun's earthly representative was the sacred fire, which burned perpetually in their towns and villages, attended by a local priest. Cherokee families assiduously fed the sacred fire a portion of each meal lest the sun take vengeance on them.

Religion was so integral to Indian culture that even their pastimes, including the ubiquitous ball game, had spiritual significance. Festivals and rituals played a particularly pronounced role in their society. Because their life revolved around raising and consuming maize, the most important of these events took place in late summer at harvest time. Creeks called this festival the Green Corn Celebration, or Busk. The purpose of the multiday fast was to usher in the new year and commemorate the one just completed. The priests built a new sacred fire from which women of the villages, after extinguishing the fires in their homes, took embers to start a fresh one. These annual festivals had political and social significance as well as spiritual. The Green Corn Celebration in particular brought the scattered townspeople together, creating a spirit of unity that was crucial to Creek survival and solidarity.[13]

The family was also an integral part of Indian cultures. While monogamous marriages were the norm, polygamy was not unknown; in fact, it was acceptable under proper social and economic conditions. Divorce was also easier and more prevalent among Indians than Europeans. Most Indian societies were matrilineal, with descent passing through the female line, and it fell upon the mother's brothers, or the children's maternal uncles, to instruct male youngsters in the techniques of survival and the attributes of manhood, including the art of warfare and hunting, and to administer punishments when appropriate. Husbands joined the wife's family and became a member of her clan.[14]

The southern Indians were both blessed and cursed by the luxury of living in a land of plenty. The forests provided game in abundance, the rivers and creeks contained a steady supply of fish, and the fertile soil and warm climate yielded a variety of vegetables and melons.[15] Nevertheless, their crude methods of agriculture and their devotion to hunting and trapping left them at the mercy of nature, resulting in alternate cycles of abundance and famine. Their diet was simple and monotonous by European standards. For the most part, they depended on corn as a staple. The meat of the white-tailed deer was thought a delicacy. Despite this dependency upon the forest and upon common fields, or "barrens," which they cleared by the slash-and-burn method, they resided in towns and villages and not, like rural whites, in scattered cabins. In keeping with this lifestyle, the Indians required vast game reserves and acquired a deep attachment to the earth.[16]

In most respects, the towns, which varied in population from fewer than fifty to more than two thousand, were autonomous political and commercial centers. The villages, on the other hand, were tiny settlements, dependent upon nearby towns for subsistence. Located mostly near creeks or streams, towns were widely dispersed. For instance, as late as 1830, the Creek Nation contained some fifty towns, each of which consisted of two or more matrilineal clan neighborhoods, comprising a single kinship grouping. These small agricultural communities were governed by a local council presided over by clan elders. The town councils, which constituted the basic unit of government, made most of the day-to-day decisions. This form of government was well suited to the needs of a people uncomfortable with centralized authority, viewing it as a serious threat to personal liberty.

Partly to guard against the pitfalls of consolidation, the tribes divided themselves into two principal moieties, one representing peace and the other war, so that conflicting viewpoints were represented at each gathering, compelling tribal leaders to seek a middle ground between militancy and subservience. In the case of grave matters affecting the entire nation, the elders met sometimes in district but more often in national councils. There they deliberated at considerable length and in great depth, speaking freely until they reached consensus. Still the local clans were not compelled to accept decisions of the National Council, although they usually acquiesced. Therefore, Indian government was remarkably democratic and consensual.[17]

Nonetheless, their fear of centralization fostered a crippling spirit of factionalism, which was particularly pervasive during the late eighteenth and early nineteenth centuries. In addition to their traditional separation into competing moieties, tribes split over questions of diplomacy, along geographical divisions, and around kinship ties and bloodlines. Because the progeny of mixed marriages between Europeans and Native women inherited the mother's status, a number of mixed-bloods rose to positions of prominence and leadership, especially during the late eighteenth century. The most notable were Alexander McGillivray among the Creek and George Colbert among the Chickasaw. They wielded enormous influence because of their facility with the English language and skill at bargaining, and because of their understanding of the white man's behavior. Additionally, the more affluent acquired large plantations, cultivated by black slaves, where they lived like nabobs on well-stocked and elegantly furnished estates.[18]

There were other reasons for factionalism. Following the American Revolution, Chickasaws split into pro-Spanish and pro-American parties. Creeks divided along geographical lines into two factions. Lower Creeks resided along the southern reaches of the Chattahoochee River and Upper Creeks in the area between the Coosa and Tallapoosa rivers. In contrast, Choctaws never evolved into a unified nation, remaining a confederation of three districts (the Northwestern, the Northeastern, and the Southern). An elected mingo, or principal chieftain, served as executive head of each district. While it was not unusual for one of the three mingoes to exert sufficient power to influence the others, they refused to place full authority in the hands of a single, all-powerful individual.[19] Nevertheless, these internal divisions, valuable as safeguards against consolidation, left them vulnerable to outside pressures and internal intrigue. In the end, factionalism contributed significantly to the disintegration of Indian society, especially after whites gained ascendancy.

Another source of friction between the two contiguous races, Indian and whites, was administration of justice. Although each sought to create internal harmony and stability through swift and sure punishment of deviant behavior, they started with different assumptions. Anglo-Americans held individuals personally accountable for their actions.[20] Those suspected of committing a crime were brought before a court of law where, once indicted, they were tried by a jury of peers. If found guilty, the court pronounced sentence, and a county sheriff enforced the verdict. In cases of serious crimes, such as murder or arson, the usual punishment was either death by hanging or confinement for an extended period. For lesser crimes, a fine was often sufficient punishment. In such a society, jails were essential, and every county in Mississippi Territory eventually erected one or more for incarcerating criminals. Mostly, these were dirty, poorly ventilated, and in disrepair, making escape easy and common.[21]

On the other hand, Indians neither constructed jails nor established courts of law. Nor did they hold individuals personally accountable for their conduct. Instead each clan shared responsibility for its members' behavior, and it alone, not the agents of the state or council, could "close" the matter, usually by some form of retribution. Even in cases involving the unintentional killing of a tribesman, members of the injured clan might, and often did, resort to the code of retaliation. Under this system, the blood relatives of the victim could secure satisfaction by taking the life of either the perpetrator or another member of the same clan. Indians did not regard killings as murder in the European sense of that term, and they were uninterested in determining the cause of or the reasons for bloodshed. They regarded the act itself as sufficient proof of its occurrence, and they saw no need to inquire further. Unlike Europeans, Indians did not distinguish between various types or different degrees of murder, nor did they entertain any notion of justified homicide. Instead, they considered all unnatural deaths as killings. In other words, the slayer was "guilty" of but not "liable" for the misdeed. Finally they saw retaliation as a commodious way of preventing killings from escalating into a civil war between clans or personal vendettas. If Anglo-Americans depended upon a system of revenge to protect society, Indians preferred the practice of retaliation.[22]

On a few occasions, these differences resulted in vexatious jurisdictional disputes. Whites insisted that anyone, regardless of race or position, accused of murder must be tried in a court of law and in accordance with the rules of evidence under English common law. To most Indians, such a complex system of justice was not only cumbersome and prone to error but also prejudicial, and they preferred to enforce order and guarantee peace among themselves without outside interference. On the other hand, white victims of Indian violence found it repugnant to leave punishment of the guilty to offenders. Furthermore, in the few cases where a territorial court sentenced Indians to capital punishment, their blood relatives, according to Native custom, were free to seek retribution on those responsible for the execution. In a frontier characterized by considerable violence and shortage of officials, such controversies were more likely to occur than elsewhere. While Indians rarely resisted white demands to release a suspected culprit, they occasionally demurred, insisting upon punishing their own in accordance with traditions.[23]

Nevertheless, fear that angry Indians might resort to retaliation was rarely absent from the minds of jittery territorial officials. For instance, on the morning of April 11, 1800, a white resident of Natchez mortally wounded an inebriated Indian in what Governor Sargent, in a classic understatement, described as an "Unfortunate affray." Sargent, "knowing the Savage Disposition to Retaliation," had the culprit arrested and placed "in Irons," but he assured "the Chiefs most interested in this unfortunate Business" that the "man committing this act . . . will Receive a very solemn and formal Trial."[24]

A similar incident occurred in late 1801. A Choctaw "of little note" paid a visit to Natchez, where, "having drank too freely of Spirits," he became insolent and unruly. After "an unknown citizen" had soundly thrashed him, the Indian disappeared. Repeated efforts to locate him were unavailing, and "his friends" and relatives, "supposing him dead, [threatened] to retaliate." Governor Claiborne, "to keep those people in good humour," promised to compensate the victim's family, thereby averting what might otherwise have been a serious altercation.

On another occasion, eight Indians, accused of killing a white settler's "work steers," wounding another, and threatening his family with "further Mischief," refused to meet Claiborne "face to face" and explain their behavior. Annoyed by this rebuke, Claiborne dispatched David Berry, interpreter for the Choctaw, to deliver a stern talk to the tribesmen, warning them to cease their wanton destruction of property. "Now Brothers," he unabashedly wrote, "I must inform you, that I do not allow my people to treat a red man amiss, nor will I suffer a red man, to treat any of my people amiss."[25]

While none of these incidents resulted in further bloodshed, all revealed the uneasiness that characterized day-to-day relationships between the ancient inhabitants and the edgy but haughty newcomers or interlopers. Nonetheless, the federal government was determined to keep friction with Indians to a minimum and friendship with them at a maximum.[26] During its formative years (1787–1815), the United States pursued a surprisingly consistent policy toward Native Americans despite the steady change of administrations. Its principal architects were President George Washington and his corpulent but capable Secretary of War Henry Knox, and they were guided by several fundamental assumptions.

First, in their various entreaties with the tribes, federal officials dealt with them as sovereign foreign nations. Under the Constitution of 1787, the federal government had exclusive rights to negotiate with foreign governments and to obtain additional territory, and neither state governments nor private parties could legally acquire Indian lands through purchase or otherwise. Furthermore, Washington and Knox never questioned the Indians' right to possess the territory they had inhabited for generations and to dispose of it by formal treaties acceptable to both parties. Therefore diplomacy, not war or conquest, was the overriding principle of the Washington administration. Consequently, Knox and Washington sought to maintain a precarious balance between the Indians' "temporary" right to utilize the land and the frontiersmen's insatiable cupidity for more fertile soils upon which to cultivate their cash crops.[27]

Additionally, the United States predicated its Indian policy on four general principles. First, it tried to arrange alliances with each of the southern tribes and to delineate as precisely as possible the boundary lines of the various nations, thereby alleviating a principal source of potential friction. In turn, this objective necessitated that the federal government set up a well-regulated and steady trade, based upon Indian customs, with each of the southern tribes. Second, it sought to encourage peace and order among the southern Indian nations as well as to prevent hostilities between themselves and the five confederated nations. As a result, the federal government found it essential to dispatch special agents to reside among the various tribes. The earliest and most influential of these was Col. Benjamin Hawkins, whom President Washington in 1796 had designated special "agent for the district south of the Ohio river."[28] In 1803, Jefferson expanded the number of agents and confined Hawkins's jurisdiction to the Creek Nation. At the same time, he replaced the conniving Col. John McKee with the witty and fun-loving Silas Dinsmoor as emissary to the Choctaw but left the feckless and unreliable Samuel L. Mitchell to reside among the Chickasaw. With respect to Mitchell, Sargent once characterized him as "either Knave or fool, but I strongly suspect the former."[29]

A third goal was to reform Native societies by introducing "the Arts of husbandry and domestic manufactures" and by encouraging, in the words of Secretary of War Henry Dearborn, "the use of the plough and the growth of Cotton as well as Grain." Last and most important, the United States expected these policies to facilitate the purchase of land from the Indians. One of the principal instruments for securing lands was the trading post or factory placed in the midst of Indian territory. The first was set up at Colerain in southeast Georgia, but the government moved it successively westward, first to Fort Wilkinson on the Oconee and later to Fort Hawkins on the Ocmulgee, for closer access to the Creek Indians.[30]

In 1802, Jefferson increased the number of trading posts. Two of these were in or near Mississippi Territory, one at Fort St. Stephens on the Tombigbee River and the other at Chickasaw Bluffs (modern Memphis) overlooking the Mississippi River. They were to provide the Choctaw and Chickasaw, respectively, with ample supplies of merchandise, agricultural implements, and household wares at fixed and fair prices. The factories later afforded the Indians, much to the distress of Hawkins, generous and easy credit, which the Indians were to repay by bringing in pelts (deerskins), beeswax, and other products of the forest.[31]

The principal article in this exchange system was deerskins. At first they brought a handsome return of twenty cents per pound or more, but between 1810 and 1815, the price dropped first to seventeen and later to fifteen cents due to slackening of demand in Europe and disruption of commerce in the Atlantic before and during the War of 1812.[32] In practice, this trade consistently worked to the disadvantage of Indians, an outcome rarely understood or appreciated by them. In their culture, articles had a set and permanent value, unrelated to market conditions. But in a capitalistic economy, the price of goods fluctuated in accordance with the law of supply and demand. With each fall in market price of deerskins, Indians understandably concluded that the white man was cheating them.

For example, from 1802 to 1815, Choctaw hunters brought large quantities of deerskins to the Fort St. Stephens factory, but by the end of the period, they were still hopelessly mired in a debt of more than $7,500 to the federal government. Indian debtors included both influential mingoes and revered chieftains as well as a handful of intrepid traders, most of whom were of mixed ancestry. Because of chronic indebtedness, Indian chieftains were especially susceptible to subtle forms of bribery and flamboyant flattery, and federal officials were quick to take advantage of this vulnerability by offering them individual annuities and personal gifts. In 1801, for instance, General Wilkinson received permission from Secretary of War Dearborn to purchase a fancy saddle for a Choctaw chief.[33] This combination of generous credit and special favors created a corps of cooperative chieftains. Known as government, or "medal," chiefs, they were often receptive to trading tribal territory for satisfaction of fiscal obligations. In fact, Jefferson partially based his Indian policy on the realization that heavily indebted Indians were more likely to sell their lands than solvent ones.

In a famous letter to Governor William Henry Harrison of Indiana Territory, Jefferson candidly summarized his Indian policy. "Our system," he wrote, "is to live in perpetual peace with the Indians, to cultivate an affectionate attachment for them, by everything just and liberal which we can do for them within the bounds of reason," and to protect them "against wrongs from our own people." He especially wished "to draw them to agriculture, to spinning and weaving," and eventually "to promote this disposition to [an] exchange of lands." Finally, he specified, "we shall push our trading houses, and be glad to see the good and influential individuals among them run in debt, because we observe that when these debts get beyond what the individuals can pay, they become willing to lop them off by a cession of land." Unfortunately, the Indians, increasingly dependent upon manufactured goods, needed little encouragement to run up sizeable debts, and it mattered not whether these were federal factories or private houses such as those owned by the Scottish agency Panton, Leslie and Company, or one of its smaller rivals.[34]

Jefferson's policies were never as calculating or as deceitful as his hyperbolic phraseology might suggest. In fact, his pursuit of land was more often for defensive purposes than for greediness or covetousness, and his primary objective was to promote national security rather than to satisfy the rapacity of frontiersmen. For example, in 1802, he directed federal commissioners to seek Indian lands along the eastern bank of the Mississippi River, but when in 1805 they acquired, contrary to his instructions, the central region between the Pearl and Chattahoochee rivers, Jefferson refused to submit the treaty to the Senate. Then, in early 1808, as relations with Spain worsened, he abruptly changed his mind. In both cases, strategic considerations, not land hunger, dictated Jefferson's decisions. Furthermore, neither Jefferson nor his predecessors wanted the factory system to turn a profit or to drive the Indians into hopeless bankruptcy. Instead it was to be a self-sustaining operation, designed more to civilize the Indians than to grab their lands. If the Indians amassed unmanageable debts, it was due more to their own acquisitiveness than to Jefferson's artfulness.[35]

As early as 1790, the government had begun putting these theories into practice. In a series of acts "to regulate trade and commerce with the Indian Tribes and to preserve peace on the frontiers," Congress set up a rudimentary administrative structure designed to promote friendly relations with Native Americans. Although Congress placed overall responsibility for Indian affairs in the hands of the secretary of war, it left day-to-day operations to a host of subordinates. Foremost among these were territorial governors, who acted as superintendent of Indian affairs within their jurisdictions. Reporting to the governors and theoretically subject to their authority was an assortment of resident agents and subagents, interpreters, factors, clerks, and mechanics.

Among the myriad officials, Benjamin Hawkins emerged as the most knowledgeable about and most influential with southern Indians. A North Carolinian by birth and a graduate of the College of New Jersey (Princeton), Hawkins devoted his entire career to public service. A strong advocate of the Constitution of 1787 and a staunch Federalist in politics, Hawkins served as one of his state's first senators. Failing to win reelection in 1795, Hawkins spent the rest of his life among the Indians. From 1796 to 1803, while serving as "agent of Indian affairs south of the Ohio River," Hawkins exercised wide supervision over southern Indians, while residing in the eastern part of the Creek country.[36]

Unfortunately, in its haste to establish machinery for managing Indian affairs, Congress failed to define precisely the duties of officials charged with administration, preferring to allow them maximum flexibility. Responsibilities of territorial governors as Indian superintendents were especially vague and ambiguous. In most matters, the early governors of Mississippi Territory reported to the secretary of state. Since Governors Sargent and Claiborne were personally acquainted with their secretaries of state, they were comfortable with this arrangement, and they consulted freely with Pickering and Madison, respectively, and only rarely with the secretary of war. Nevertheless, repeated efforts on their part to have their duties as superintendent clarified were fruitless.[37]

Neither Sargent nor Claiborne understood the role of Hawkins, especially since the other southern agents reported to him as well as to the governor. Because of his vast knowledge and wide experience, both governors were cautious and sometimes intimidated when interacting with him. Sargent especially was baffled. "Of what Indians has the Governour Superintendence?" he asked forlornly. No stranger to the well-publicized "merits of Colo Hawkins," Sargent queried, "if it be not possible that with the best disposition to the Public Weal in us both, there may not be such 'clashing of our Powers' as may produce inconvenience and injury." He feared that Indians, accustomed to soliciting Hawkins's counsel, might disregard or reject his advice.[38]

The military's role was equally confusing. Charged with keeping the peace and protecting the frontier, the army was necessarily brought face to face with Native Americans. While recognizing the importance of protection on an exposed frontier, territorial governors nonetheless did not wish to elevate the military above civil authority. They feared that military officers, especially Gen. James Wilkinson, might seek to encroach upon, if not usurp, their prerogatives.[39] In fact, Sargent and Claiborne, together with Wilkinson, zealously guarded their privileges.

Based upon his experiences in the Northwest Territory, Sargent was particularly sensitive to military interference. He did not wish to become "a mere Cypher" to the army. There, he explained, "military subaltern officers not unfrequently exercised all his [the governor's] powers, . . . without paying the smallest regard to him, thereby depriving him of almost all his consequence, though as the legitimate agent, all responsibility was his." Sargent was determined that "such conduct . . . not be practiced on me," and thereafter, he kept a steady eye on the cunning Wilkinson.[40]

Even after Pickering assured Sargent that the secretary of war would "put an end to or restrain the intermeddling of subordinate military officers in Indian affairs," Sargent remained skeptical. Then, in early 1799, his worst fears were confirmed. He learned that Wilkinson, unbeknownst to him, had met with "Indian Chiefs of the Choctaw Nation" and had presented them with "Certificates of Commissions" to replace the Spanish ones they had recently rejected. An aggrieved Sargent, displaying more humor than normal, quipped that it would have been more efficacious if the general had supplied Indians with "implements of Husbandry."[41]

Sargent found no joy in his frequent and tiresome encounters with the Choctaw. Considering them "a troublesome as well as a very expensive people," he complained that they were "often in a State of intoxication." This attitude stemmed from his encounters with vagabond and renegade Choctaw who regularly visited Natchez in order to beg for gifts, peddle horses and other stolen property, or dispose of surplus produce to eager townspeople. Conversely, his contact with prosperous Indians who resided some distance from white settlements was limited.

Sargent both pitied and feared the Choctaw, and he tried, as much as possible, to placate them with flowery words and piddling gifts. Whenever they came to Natchez, as they frequently did, Sargent thought it advisable "to keep them in good humour, by a little Bread, Beef, and liquor, and some trifling presents." Otherwise, he explained, they will become "troublesome to the Inhabitants by killing their cattle &c." Nevertheless, Sargent was hard-pressed to satisfy them. A niggardly federal government provided him with few goods to dispense, forcing him at times to purchase, with funds from his own meager salary, supplies for undernourished Choctaws.[42]

A majority of these "pesky" visitors were under the impression that Andrew Ellicott had promised them annuities in the form of goods and foodstuff in return for not interfering with his efforts to run the southern boundary with Spain. Consequently, they came to Natchez, usually in small groups but sometimes in mass, not to harass white settlers, as Sargent assumed, but to collect what they believed was rightfully theirs. After suffering for nearly a decade from severe drought and overhunted forests, most were hungry and some starving.[43] If federal officers reneged on promises, they felt justified in securing their due in more informal and less friendly ways.

Nevertheless, Sargent wanted the depredations stopped, but the bedeviled governor lacked the resources to satisfy the suffering complainants. "A number of families . . . on the road of the Indians," Sargent reported dejectedly, have been "literally eaten out of house and home by them." But, he was helpless "even to offer a Pipe of Tobacco to the Indians" or to mollify them with a conciliatory talk since he was without an interpreter who spoke their language.[44] Despite the jurisdictional confusion and the ambiguities associated with his superintendence, Sargent left office with no serious blemish on his record but without resolution of a single dispute.

His successor, Governor W. C. C. Claiborne, inherited most of Sargent's unresolved problems. But, at least he had one advantage not enjoyed by his harassed predecessor. He reported to a president whose sympathy for western interests was well known and who possessed a keen interest in and a deep understanding of Native Americans. Few presidents before or after Jefferson spent as much time and energy on Indian affairs as he did.[45]

In sharp contrast to his prejudice toward African Americans, whom he dismissed as inferior creatures, Jefferson admired the aborigines. In large part, this empathy emanated from an Enlightenment philosophy and a sense of moral benevolence, and he was determined to bring the benefits of civilization, or European values, to the Indians. Jefferson's meaning of the verb "to civilize" was to impose upon a society characterized by barbarism and ignorance a degree of civility and decorum. In the case of the Indians, Jefferson expected that by introducing plow agriculture, providing Indian children, especially young males, with publicly funded schools, and bringing them the conveniences of modern technology their society would be transformed from a "savage" to a rational and refined one. Such a transformation was possible, Jefferson affirmed, because Indians, in contrast to Africans, were by nature commensurate in every respect to Europeans. "I believe," he wrote in his famous *Notes on the State of Virginia*, "the Indian then to be in body and mind the equal of the white man."[46] But Enlightenment ideas and benevolence alone did not fully explain Jefferson's reasons for wanting to transform Indians from hunters and warriors to agrarian farmers and domestic homemakers. He also reasoned that if Native Americans became freeholders like Anglo-American settlers, they would require less land, thereby freeing up millions of acres, currently reserved as hunting grounds, for the use of industrious white farmers. In the final analysis, it was the white man's quest for land that caused most of the friction between the two races, and Jefferson, always the consummate politician, was keenly aware of the frontiersmen's unquenchable thirst for fertile soil.[47] As the acknowledged champion of western interests, Jefferson conveniently and cleverly coupled his wish to civilize the Indian and the western pioneer's yearning for more lands into an appealing formula.

Nevertheless, Claiborne, like Sargent, thought the "Indian visits to this District . . . frequent and oppressive," and he found that "these poor, idle & humble people are really great pests to this Territory." They "almost entirely depend upon begging and stealing." They were, he lamented, "encamped by the dozens in every Neighborhood & support themselves principally by depredations upon the Cattle, Hogs &c of our Citizens." Exasperated by the "several offences" of a few "straggling Indians," Claiborne in 1802 gave them a firm lecture. "I well know," he said, "that neither your Chief nor People sent you to our settlements. You have come . . . for nothing else, but to drink Whiskey & to spend your time in idleness." Noting that "Several men in the Country have had their Cattle & Hogs killed," Claiborne admonished them "to quit drinking whiskey, for it will make you fools & Old Women" and "to return to your own Land & make bread for your families" and cultivate "corn & Peas." Apparently his message had a good effect. Shortly thereafter he proudly informed Secretary of State Madison "that the Choctaws continue friendly." Most of "those poor Indians who recently supported themselves by begging & plundering," he reported, had returned to their homes in the backcountry.[48]

In this speech, Claiborne not only outlined his own Indian policy but summarized Jefferson's as well, a policy best described as one of pacification and paternalism. Claiborne diligently tried to pacify the Indians through meager gifts. Like Sargent, he knew the Choctaws were accustomed to receiving presents from the Spaniards on a regular basis, but once the threat of European intervention lessened, the federal government was no longer inclined to spend thousands of dollars on supplies for the Indians.

Furthermore, difficulty of transporting Indian goods plagued western officials. It took Claiborne more than three months and "$164 in freight charges" to complete the delivery from New Orleans to Natchez of "three Hogsheads & three Boxes, containing Hoes & Axes & marked 'U.S. Choctaw Indians.'" These articles, which first left Philadelphia in October 1800, did not reach their destination until late June 1802. It was another five months before the Choctaws actually received these goods, due primarily to the tardy arrival of agent Dinsmoor, who had recently been severely wounded in a duel with an army officer in Tennessee.[49]

Supplies for the newly established factory at St. Stephens had to be sent either by water to Mobile or overland from Natchez. Either way the journey was arduous, expensive, and hazardous. The 1802 Choctaw annuity, consisting of diverse trade goods designed for agricultural pursuits, arrived in New Orleans as the Spanish intendant was rescinding the right of American deposit there. Fortunately, Claiborne had arranged for the goods to be transshipped to Fort Adams, and he engaged Lewis Le Fleur, a French trader married to a Choctaw, to transport them by way of Mobile to Fort Stoddert. Apparently Spanish officials placed no impediments in his way, and the goods consisting of "two bails marked 'Choctaw Annuity'; three hogsheads, marked 'U.S. Choctaw Indians'; and one hogshead marked 'Choctaw Annuity, containing goods,'" reached Fort Stoddert safely and intact. Meanwhile, Joseph L. Chambers, the store's first factor, was also in Natchez, and he immediately pressured Claiborne into selecting a site for the Choctaw trading factory lest he "lose the advantage of the fall hunt."[50]

Once the St. Stephens factory opened in 1803, business was brisk. In fact, it was so lively that Chambers in 1805 employed an assistant, George Strother Gaines, to run the trading house, freeing himself to devote attention to registering land claims. According to Gaines, the factory attracted "hunters from all parts of the nation." Even a few Creek Indians from as far away as "the falls of the Black Warrior came frequently to trade." By treating his customers fairly and kindly, Gaines quickly won their respect and friendship. He was especially "careful not to sell the Indians a damaged article of goods without pointing out the damage and reducing the price" accordingly. Whenever, Gaines explained, the "blankets, shawls or cotton and linen appeared to me to be lighter or more flimsy and less durable than they purported to be," he would point out "the defect and reduce the price also." There, as elsewhere, deerskins were the principal "produce received in exchange from the Indians."[51]

The Chickasaw trading house was just as prosperous, if not more so, as the one at St. Stephens. Its first factor was Thomas Peterkin, a modestly successful trader and businessman. Situated on the bluffs overlooking the Mississippi River adjacent to Fort Pickering, this factory became the busiest of fourteen federal trading stores then in operation. In 1809, the Indians brought in pelts worth more than twelve thousand dollars as well as other valuable products. Even during the War of 1812, when conditions for hunting were unfavorable, trade there continued to thrive, and in 1815, the Indians bartered skins worth nearly twenty-four thousand dollars.[52]

Between 1800 and 1807, the United States, through a series of individual treaties with four of the Civilized Tribes (Choctaw, Chickasaw, Creek, and Cherokee), managed to secure enough lands to satisfy the most pressing needs of incoming white settlers. Fortunately, conditions were favorable for peaceful negotiations, and the parties, for the most part, agreed upon the boundaries separating them. Except for the Cherokee and Chickasaw, southern Indians had few overlapping claims like those that plagued officials in the Ohio Valley. Also the Indians usually agreed to accommodate the federal government's need for better communication between the nation's capital and the lower Mississippi Valley.

Negotiations were generally orderly and without serious incident. The American commissioners, while sometimes tough-minded and tenacious, always treated with established, instead of dissident chiefs, and all participants sat as equals. Most meetings were protracted affairs, with much speech making, ceremonial ritual, and gift giving, all of which tried the patience of more than one American official. Southeastern Indians surrendered their lands hesitantly and sparingly, especially in the early years, but once their spokesmen agreed to a cession, they rarely raised objections. On the other hand, they quickly denounced whites when they failed, as they often did, to abide by their promises.[53]

Building on the orderly process of treaty making begun by his Federalist predecessors, Jefferson, in 1801, instructed Secretary of War Dearborn to set up separate conferences with four of the southern tribes,
and Congress cooperated by appropriating fifteen thousand dollars "to
defray" the expense of holding treaties "with the Indians south of the river
Ohio, two of which were of interest to Mississippians." During the fall of
1801, Dearborn summoned the Choctaws and Chickasaws to meet with
federal commissioners at Natchez and Chickasaw Bluffs, respectively.
The primary purposes of the first round of negotiations were to reaffirm
existing treaty lines, seek permission to open public roads through their
nations, and permit places of public accommodation to be established
at convenient intervals. Of the two, the Chickasaws were more obliging.
In a treaty signed on October 24, 1801, at Chickasaw Bluffs, they agreed
to the building of a road (Natchez Trace) through their country and the
setting up of stands along it.[54]

The Choctaw were only slightly less amenable. Initially, Dearborn called for a conference at Natchez, but Hawkins and the other
two commissioners, fearful that disgruntled whites might intimidate the
Indians, transferred the meeting to the less-populated and more secure
Fort Adams. In fact, Hawkins had sound reasons for taking this step.
The large and sometimes straggling delegations of chiefs and warriors
still encountered numerous "acts of Imprudence" on their way to Fort
Adams, compelling Hawkins to request Governor Claiborne to take
appropriate measures to stop the offences. "It is much to be wished,"
Hawkins pleaded, "that the people of this territory could be prevailed
on to observe a friendly deportment towards the Indians particularly on
occasions like the present."[55]

Claiborne's firm proclamation had the desired effect, for Choctaws
were in an agreeable mood. They consented to honor the boundaries of
their previous cessions with the British in 1765 and to permit the United
States to resurvey and remark the western boundary and erect a road
through their country. The American commissioners were also pleased
when Choctaw delegates agreed to take up agriculture and refused to
accept the whiskey offered them, but they were piqued when the delegation failed to allow "stands" along the Trace.[56]

The following year, Choctaws, with considerably less enthusiasm,
agreed to a similar arrangement with respect to the eastern boundary.
During the summer of 1803, when General Wilkinson, "with much

pain & difficulty made out to perambulate the old British Line, from Bogue to Hatchee Teggebby" in Tombigbee District, he and the accompanying Indian representatives discovered, to their surprise, that there existed "several old Lines" rather than the single one they expected. In order to make sure that "two settlements of our [white] citizens, William Hunt & Jesse Warmack," were included in the ceded area, Wilkinson furnished "Mingo Poos Coos & Ala' la' la' Aoomah," the two "chiefs of distinction," with $179 worth of "Factory Goods" from the trading post at St. Stephens. He also notified Dearborn that, "conformably to the Spirit of Your instructions," he had given Poos Coos "the Articles promised him." Once again, bribery played a crucial role in diplomacy.[57]

In 1803, the Jefferson administration launched a second round of conferences. In contrast to the first series, where the federal government sought to establish better rapport with the Indians, the commissioners requested land. To a large extent, these negotiations resulted from the efforts of Panton, Leslie and Company to recover its massive and overdue debts. Choctaws owed the Scottish trading company more than eleven thousand dollars, and Chickasaws owed slightly less than three thousand dollars. With the endorsement of Colonel McKee, a former Choctaw agent and sometime employee of the firm, company officials proposed to invite both tribes to sell Panton, Leslie a portion of land in lieu of paying off their obligations. But first, they had to secure the federal government's permission. Both Dearborn and Claiborne were exceedingly skeptical of the proposed arrangement. McKee, Claiborne insisted, "ought to have been aware of the extreme impropriety of permitting foreigners to possess a large tract of country among any of our Indian nations."[58]

But Dearborn was not averse to letting the United States play the role of facilitator if the Indians wished to sell. In other words, Dearborn was willing for the government to purchase the land and for the Indians, with funds from this transaction, to pay their debts to Panton, Leslie. Accordingly, Dearborn in 1803 instructed Dinsmoor and Col. James Robertson, the celebrated and former Indian agent to the Chickasaw, to inaugurate discussions with Choctaw chiefs on the assumption that they were willing to sell enough land to satisfy their debts. In preparation, Dinsmoor collected a huge stockpile of lavish goods and exotic delicacies. Upon receiving the bill for these luxuries, Dearborn was astounded. It included entries for a number of "delicate spices, anchovies, raisins, almonds, hyson tea, coffee, mustard, preserves, English cheese, segars, brandy, [and] wine." These articles, in Dearborn's opinion, "could not have been intended for the Indians," and he hardly thought them essential for executing "an Indian Treaty, especially in the wilderness."[59]

But the Choctaws proved to be more headstrong and independent than the American commissioners anticipated. Not only had they promised officials of John Forbes & Company (formerly Panton, Leslie and Company) that they wished to pay their debts by ceding some of their lands, they had also petitioned the federal government to the same effect. Therefore their display of obstinacy shocked and dismayed an incredulous Dinsmoor, who was obviously ready to celebrate even before the deliberations commenced. The main point of contention was the location of the lands to be ceded. Jefferson wanted them along the Mississippi River, but the Upper Choctaw were ill-disposed to part with this territory.[60] Consequently, Dinsmoor's first effort to reach an amicable accord with the Choctaw was abortive in spite of his heroic preparations.

Annoyed by Dinsmoor's unauthorized extravagance, Dearborn instructed him to ascertain from Chief Homastubbee what territory the Lower Choctaw were willing to surrender and for what price. "It may not be improper," he hinted, "to make liberal propositions to Homastubbee, separate from the general stipulations." In other words, Dinsmoor was to curry the support of influential chiefs by offering them special favors because, as Dearborn explained, they were "entitled to attention."[61] Dearborn's strategy of bribing receptive chieftains proved more successful than Dinsmoor's plan of filling their stomachs with European delicacies.

In late 1805 at Mount Dexter, the Choctaw ceded more than 4 million acres of land in south-central Mississippi Territory, for which the United States paid them fifty thousand dollars, but forty-eight thousand dollars of it was "to enable the Mingoes to discharge the debt due to their merchants and traders." In addition the treaty stipulated an annuity of three thousand dollars in merchandise for the nation as a whole. Each of the three "great medal mingoes" (Puckshunubbee, Homastubbee, and Pushmataha) was to receive a stipend of five hundred dollars "in consideration of past services" and an annual annuity of $150 "during their continuation in office." Although Jefferson held up ratification of the treaty for over two years, the Senate eventually approved it in January

1808 because, as Jefferson explained, the rapidly deteriorating relations with Spain dictated "a strong settlement of militia along our southern frontiers" and made "consolidation of the Mississippi Territory" imperative.[62] Accordingly, this treaty not only united the Natchez and Tombigbee districts, but it also opened up a sizeable expanse of territory, much of which proved to be more fertile and productive than federal officials had expected.

Choctaws were not the only Indian nation indebted to the Scottish trading firm. So were the Chickasaw. They too were willing to give up territory in order to satisfy their creditors. In a treaty signed at Chickasaw Bluffs in 1805, they ceded the fertile lands northeast of the Tennessee River for twenty thousand dollars "in specie," twelve thousand dollars of which went for the liquidation of their debts to John Forbes & Company. Again, Dearborn hinted at the value of bribery. "If any particular individual among the Chickasaw, who may be opposed to the proposed Cession of Lands, can be induced to change the direction of his influence, by any reasonable means," he told Robertson, "the Commissioners will please to act in such cases, as circumstances may require." The treaty donated one thousand dollars each to chiefs Colbert and Ockoy and an annuity of one hundred dollars to King Tinebe as a "testimony to his personal worth and friendly disposition." Later, Dearborn arranged for Colbert's son to attend a school in Washington for a few months.[63]

After completion of a second round of treaties with the southern Indians, American officials next looked for ways to take advantage of the bounty their diplomacy had yielded. The years immediately following were consumed with selling the newly acquired lands at public auction, attracting new settlers and establishing new counties, improving communications by constructing additional roads and expanding mail service, and accelerating the program of civilizing the Indians. Paradoxically, the sum of these efforts set the stage for a new and more serious sequence of conflicts between Native Americans and Anglo-Americans, controversies that would later culminate in the territory's only serious conflagration between the two peoples.

CHAPTER 13

Manifest Destiny

With the appointment of David Holmes as the fourth and last governor of Mississippi Territory in the summer of 1809, changes were in the air. Not only did Holmes's placid personality help to suppress the partisan rancor that before had characterized territorial politics, but his arrival also coincided with national and international issues arising from Spanish presence in the Floridas and British and French interference with American trade on the high seas. During the next few years, he would face three major crises: rebellions in Spanish Florida, an uprising of Creek Indians, and a British invasion. In June 1809, when Governor Holmes arrived, the most pressing and volatile of the three involved Spanish control of Baton Rouge and Mobile.

To be sure, Spanish West Florida was a tinderbox. This odd-shaped and ill-conceived province stretched four hundred miles along the northern coast of the Gulf of New Mexico from the Mississippi River on the west to the Chattahoochee and Apalachicola rivers on the east. Conversely, it was as narrow as it was long, extending in some spots to less than a hundred miles. And the landscape was as diverse as the individuals who occupied it. The soil adjacent to and just east of the Mississippi was relatively deep and fertile, but elsewhere it was mostly sandy, suitable only for subsistence farming and tending livestock. The climate was generally hot and humid, almost tropical, although cool breezes off the Gulf of Mexico moderated the temperature in those places nearest the coast. Stands of stately pine trees covered much of the terrain, resources that later heralded the rise of lucrative maritime and lumbering enterprises.[1]

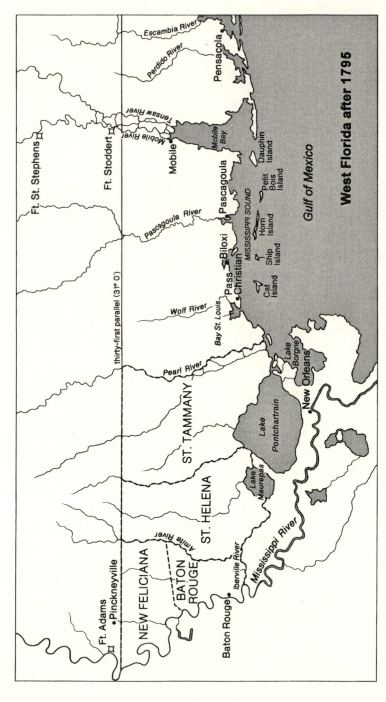

Map of West Florida after 1795 (Thomas D. Clark and John D. W. Guice, *Frontiers in Conflict: The Old Southwest, 1795–1830* [Albuquerque, N.M., 1989]).

The extreme western and most fertile portion of West Florida, known as "Feliciana" or the "Florida parishes," lay north of Lakes Pontchartrain and Maurepas between the Mississippi and Pearl rivers. Containing a heterogeneous population, unusual for that part of the country, Feliciana was characterized by intermittent civil instability and cultural diversity. The population, though modest in numbers, was predominantly young and male and, like most frontier regions, widely scattered. The only settlements of any size were those at St. Francisville and Baton Rouge. Unfortunately, the region soon developed a reputation as an accessible and safe "haven for Tories, deserters and desperadoes."[2]

The early pattern of European settlement in Feliciana was similar to that of Natchez District. First to arrive were the British, usually of English or Scotch-Irish stock accompanied sometimes by black slaves. Later, an influx of Tories, fleeing the ravages of the American Revolution, lent a more sophisticated appearance to the area. They settled along the eastern banks of the Mississippi River, in and around Baton Rouge, where a number of crude but thriving plantations sprang up, and it was there that William Dunbar, the best known of the district's early arrivals, made his initial settlement.[3]

After 1781, when Spain gained control of the parishes, many of the earliest residents left, but a fair percentage, including many Tories, stayed and took the oath of allegiance to "His Catholic Majesty." In an effort to populate the region, Spanish officials tried, with limited success, to lure Canary Islanders, German Catholics, and displaced Arcadians into the Florida parishes. They settled mostly along the Amite River, in and around Manchac on the Iberville River, or along Thompson Creek, a few miles above Baton Rouge. During the first decade of the nineteenth century, French exiles, fleeing slave insurrections in the Caribbean, trickled into parts of West Florida, adding another element to an already polyglot population.[4]

After the Louisiana Purchase of 1803, West Florida was a centerpiece of controversy between Spain and the United States. Jefferson, chagrined by the failure of his diplomats to purchase, as instructed, Mobile as well as New Orleans, insisted that the sale included all territories west of the Perdido River. Nevertheless, the Spaniards, unconvinced by Jefferson's tortured logic, remained in possession of West Florida.[5]

The Florida parishes became a hotbed of speculation after the Spanish intendant, Juan Ventura Morales, began rewarding friends and favorites with extensive grants of dubious legality. Anticipating another change in government, large numbers of aspiring Anglo-Americans settled along the eastern bank of the Mississippi River, just south of the international boundary. Among the immigrants were land speculators and their advance agents, military deserters, and fugitives from justice. The marshes or borderlands to the north attracted an even more adventurous element, who hoped to profit from the unrest they expected or to seize opportunities when they arose.[6]

The Spanish government of West Florida was weak, generally inefficient, and often corrupt, due to the neglect by officials in Madrid. The province was rife with internal dissension as Intendant Morales and Governor Folch vied for the support of prominent residents and competed for favors from superiors in Havana. Although Spain traditionally set up a colonial system of dual authorities, the rivalry between intendant and governor was especially pronounced in West Florida. Each disliked the other, and both appeared more concerned with feathering their nests than promoting the welfare of constituents.[7]

During the first decade of the nineteenth century, Spanish authorities made no sustained effort to disentangle the conflicting land claims, which were as complicated as those in Natchez District, to establish district courts to bridle the restless and criminal elements, or to resolve the numerous civil disputes that plagued every frontier community. According to Orleans governor W. C. C. Claiborne, there was no doubt that "the people of West Florida are at present dissatisfied."[8]

Spanish failure to establish law and order in Feliciana resulted not from willfulness or contumacy on the part of appointed authorities but from their indifference and indolence. Still, the Baton Rouge district became infested with entrepreneurs who found the region an inviting playground for their nefarious schemes and personal vendettas. In turn, misrule invited an odd assortment of outlaws and outcasts, ne'er-do-wells, rascals and roustabouts, budding buccaneers, and clever charlatans. Nonetheless, at no time did the unruly element outnumber the enterprising and trustworthy citizens.[9]

Just to the north, across the international border, resided the infamous and peripatetic Kempers and their filibustering friends who, without additional encouragement, were capable of fomenting considerable distrust and discord. Although the footloose Kempers continued to operate out of Pinckneyville in Wilkinson County (Mississippi Territory), they possessed an uncanny knack for promoting unrest and inciting mischief wherever they went.[10]

They always seemed to show up whenever trouble threatened, stirring up as much hatred of Spanish officials as they could in order to further their own desire for booty and plunder. Indeed, they were quintessential "border ruffians." Until 1810, the Spanish authorities, indecisive and inept as they were, had managed, with the assistance of loyal and law-abiding Felicianians, to keep the Kempers and other combustibles at bay by successfully aborting the Kemper uprisings of 1804 and 1805.[11] Thereafter, the corrupt practices and vacillating policies of the next two commandants failed to sustain the people's confidence, particularly the Anglo-Americans.

East of the "Florida Parishes" lay the less populous but more homogeneous French settlements around Mobile Bay. In fact, French settlements along the Gulf coast had preceded those of the English by more than half a century. Except for a scattering of fishermen and herders along the creeks and streams, they resided for the most part in the struggling seaport of Mobile, located "at the head of the Bay." According to Judge Ephraim Kirby, Mobile in 1804 was "a compact village on a handsome site," consisting of "about sixty families and a greater number of dwellings." Under Spanish control, Mobile became the principal commercial center along the upper Gulf coast even though the provincial capital was Pensacola, a smaller seaport some fifty miles east of Mobile Bay. There the Spanish governor resided, and the council held quarterly sessions. The Spaniards regarded Pensacola as easier to defend and more accessible to the imperial headquarters at Havana than Mobile.[12]

But, as Judge Kirby noted, the port of Mobile had recently fallen on hard times after Spain lost possession of New Orleans. "Once much larger and more flourishing," Mobile, according to him, had taken on the "gloomy appearance of a depressed colonial establishment," and he blamed Spanish officials for the decline. By granting John Forbes & Company (formerly Panton, Leslie) a monopoly of the Indian trade, they had effectively stifled "all commercial enterprize." Still, Kirby believed that "Nature has designated this position for a great city" because of its strategic location "at the mouth of one of the finest navigable waters in the United States, which, at some future time, will accommodate the produce of a fertile interior country."[13]

Between these settlements lay a narrow strip of coastal plain running from Mobile Bay to the Pearl River. As late as 1810, only a small number of Europeans and Native Americans resided there. The soil was barren and sandy, inadequate for extensive agriculture, and its dispersed inhabitants lived off either the sea or the forests. The nearby pine forests were home to a vast assortment of wild and semidomesticated animals, including an abundance of stray cattle and roving hogs. A few farmers planted a little rice, some root and leaf vegetables, and a variety of melons and fruit trees; otherwise, they depended upon trade with local Indians to supply their necessities.

One of the earliest officials to recognize the region's potential was Dr. William Flood, sent by Governor Claiborne to reconnoiter the area. Besides noting its pristine setting and natural beauty, Flood was delighted to find the climate so salubrious. In sharp contrast to the pestilence of the Mississippi delta, the coastal plains between the Pass of Christian and Pascagoula River were surprisingly free of yellow fever outbreaks. In his opinion, this area offered Louisianans "full recompense for the unhealthiness of the Climate of New Orleans" and afforded them "with a delightful summer resort." Two places in particular merited his special praise. "The pass of Christian and mouth of Pascagoula," he reported, "cannot be surpassed nor equalled either in the Mississippi Territory or that of Orleans."

But, in 1810, the population of the coastal strip was barely visible. Only some 430 people, mostly of French ancestry, lived around Biloxi Bay and fewer than 350 along the Pascagoula River. Nevertheless, Flood found the inhabitants pleasant and agreeable. He had never met, he said, "a people more innocent and less offending" or more "universally honest." Unfortunately, they were also illiterate and unchurched. A later official, charged with locating suitable individuals for public office, was unable to uncover a single resident who could read or write. The lifestyle of these fun-loving and carefree people resembled that of Indians more than of Europeans. Having seldom felt the firm hand of government, they hardly cared which nation possessed the region. According to Flood, "they seem to desire only the simple necessaries of life and to be let alone in their tranquility."[14]

Meanwhile, Jefferson continued to covet both Floridas, primarily for strategic reasons, and he realized that Spain's hold on West Florida was too tenuous to last. Agreeing with a recent immigrant that Spanish colonies were like "ripe fruit waiting the hand that dares plunk them," Jefferson was ready to move at the first opportune moment. But he feared that France or England might try to take advantage of Spanish vulnerability and seize one or both of the Floridas before the United States was ready to absorb them. To be sure, the essence of Jeffersonian expansionism was "to conquer without war."[15]

Once his protracted effort to seek Napoleon's aid in persuading Spain to recognize America's claim to West Florida collapsed in the late spring of 1806, Jefferson was more willing than before to undertake assertive steps to secure Baton Rouge and Mobile. Fortunately, Jefferson's aggressiveness was aided by an influx of recent immigrants, largely from nearby southern states, who settled for the most part in the Baton Rouge District. Under the chaotic and inefficient rule of the Spanish, they grew increasingly dissatisfied, not because the government was despotic, but because its policies were lax and unpredictable.[16]

After the lengthy fracas over the *Chesapeake* affair, Jefferson began to rethink his cautious policies toward Spain. The United States, he told Secretary Madison, should avoid hostilities with every European nation except Spain. Fearful that the ruthless and unprincipled Bonaparte might use this occasion to regain heavily French-populated Louisiana, Jefferson opined that "we should declare to the French Government that we will instantly seize on the Floridas as reprisal for the spoliations [that Spain has] denied us." If Spain should agree "by a given date" to compensate the United States, he wrote, "we will restore all [the territory] east of the Perdido. . . . Otherwise, we will hold them forever as compensation for the spoliations."[17]

Fortunately, Jefferson did not have to resort to such forceful and risky measures. Once again, events in Europe, as they had in 1803, dealt Jefferson a favorable hand. In the spring of 1808, Napoleon forced first King Charles IV of Spain and then his son Ferdinand VII to renounce all claims to the Spanish crown and installed his brother, Joseph Bonaparte, on the vacated throne. But not all Spaniards acquiesced in Napoleon's unilateral and arbitrary right to select their ruler. Beginning in the early summer of 1808, popular juntas sprang up throughout the countryside to contest the "intruder king" and pledge perpetual loyalty to Ferdinand VII. The ensuing internal struggle for independence from France left Spanish colonies in the Americas in disarray. These surprising developments both pleased and perplexed Jefferson. "A moment may occur favorable, without compromising us with either France," he hastily wrote Madison, "or for seizing our own from the Rio Bravo [Rio Grande] to Perdido, as of right, and the residue of Florida, as a reprisal for spoliation."[18]

Seeking to take advantage of these encouraging developments abroad, Jefferson instructed Orleans governor Claiborne to convey the administration's support of the Spanish insurgents to influential leaders in Baton Rouge, where unrest with the government of West Florida centered. Claiborne was to assure them that the "patriots of Spain" (supporters of the deposed Ferdinand VII) had no better friend than the United States. But, Jefferson warned, the United States was unwilling to see Spain's North American possessions, especially Cuba and Mexico, fall into the hands of either France or Great Britain. The United States and Spain, he declared, had similar interests. "The object of both must be to exclude all European influence from this hemisphere."[19]

The response in Natchez and New Orleans to these developments was mixed but predictable. The few Spanish citizens were "greatly elated"; British partisans viewed them "as most fortunate"; and the French were "much Chagrine[d]." The initial response of Anglo-Americans was surprisingly subdued. According to Governor Claiborne, who kept close contacts with his friends in Natchez District, "the real Americans . . . seem only to wish, that the ultimate issue may prove favorable to the Interest of the United States." To apprehensive officials, French occupation of Spain confirmed "that Bonaparte had not abandoned the hope of repossessing . . . Louisiana." Others worried that it might injure American commerce. They feared "that England by a monopoly of the Spanish trade may acquire a commercial ascendancy which will dispose her to be still more unjust to the United States."[20]

The immediate reaction was an outbreak of Francophobia that infected Spanish Creoles throughout the Caribbean and Louisiana, forcing a number of French in Cuba and elsewhere "to fly from an enraged populace." While most of them fled to other islands in the Caribbean or West Florida, a handful came to Mississippi Territory. Everywhere they ran into intense hostility from loyal Spaniards, who refused to welcome them, and many were left without a homeland. During early spring of 1810, French exiles in West Florida were forced to leave, most settling in Orleans Territory, but they threatened to return and "take satisfaction for the injury."[21]

Napoleon's deposition of the Spanish Bourbons spawned a host of independence movements throughout the Western Hemisphere. The Creoles of Mexico were among the first to rebel, encouraging similar action by Anglo-Americans in the Florida parishes. From 1808 to 1810, unrest in the Baton Rouge area worsened, due to the inability of the metropolitan government to assist local authorities and encouragement from the Madison administration. Newly arrived Anglo-Americans were especially upset, and they were less inclined than the old-timers to endure passively the rapidly deteriorating conditions. Few favored the inefficient and corrupt government of Carlos de Hault de Lassus, who had only recently replaced the popular but effete Carlos de Grand-Pre.[22]

Confronted with a government fast approaching administrative paralysis, the more dissatisfied, joined by those who were least attached to Spain, took matters into their own hands. Dissatisfied citizens in several districts organized themselves into vigilante groups in a desperate effort to bring peace to the troubled region. "A sense of common danger," Governor Holmes of Mississippi Territory reported, "has induced some of the inhabitants to establish a kind of police, which having no fixed rule for its guide, is consequently in its operation inefficient, and in many instances unjust." As a result, the "respectable inhabitants," were "determined to bring about a change."[23]

The most vociferous was choleric John Hunter Johnson, whose Tory father had migrated to Baton Rouge district as early as 1775. The six-foot, four-inch Johnson and his three brothers called a meeting at his plantation, Troy, to discuss steps to restore order and to end the rampant bribery and pervasive misrule. With little debate, the assembled citizens endorsed his plan of action, and commissioned Fulwar Skipwith, scion of a prominent Virginia family and friend of Jefferson and Madison, to draft articles for a new government. Indeed, Skipwith seemed the perfect choice, having recently returned home after serving as American consul general to France, where he had courted and married a French countess after divorcing his first wife, a daughter of Gen. Nathaniel Greene. By the summer of 1810, he was busily raising cotton on his newly acquired estate of 1,300 acres at the Monterano Bluffs near Baton Rouge and stirring up discontent among his apprehensive neighbors.[24]

Before adjourning, they issued a call for interested citizens of Feliciana to gather at Egypt plantation, only ten miles south of the international border, a location designed to attract sympathizers from north of the border. On June 23, more than five hundred individuals answered the summons, an indication of how widespread dissatisfaction had become. After endorsing the resolutions drawn up at Troy, the large assemblage, with only eleven dissenters, called upon the people to elect delegates to a convention for the purpose of approving the articles drafted earlier by Skipwith.[25]

If several were inclined to favor separation from Spain, others preferred to work with de Lassus in reforming the existing government. In adopting these measures, the mostly Anglo-Americans insurgents were inspired less by the example of popular juntas in Spain, about which they knew very little, than by the extralegal conventions and committees that arose during the early stages of the American Revolution. In other words, they were following American, not Spanish, traditions of protest. Where the collapse of local government was nearly complete, they organized local militias, which operated more like vigilantes than constabularies and in some cases even took over the functions of government.[26]

In reporting these developments to Secretary of State Robert Smith, Governor Holmes concluded that the people, because of "the mixed nature of the population," were divided over "the means best calculated to insure the safety of society." They had split into three "distinctly marked" factions: "An American party, a British party, and a Spanish party." Until lately, Holmes said, there had once "existed a French Party." While the Americans favored annexation to the United States, "the most prudent" were opposed to "taking immediate steps to effect this object, lest by failing of success they might hereafter be punished for the attempt." Nevertheless, Holmes predicted, "they would probably incur the risk rather than be subjected to any foreign power or to encounter the perils of anarchy." On the other hand, members of the British party, he believed, were so eager to see Florida in British hands that they "would readily aid any project to effect that purpose." In the meantime, they would continue to "act in unison with the Spanish party."[27]

On July 25, the "First Convention of West Florida," consisting of fourteen members from four separate districts (later parishes), met at the home of Richard Duvall, some fifteen miles from Baton Rouge. After naming John Rhea of Feliciana District president, the delegates proclaimed loyalty to the Spanish monarch and adopted a lengthy list of grievances. In their eagerness to cooperate with the penniless Spanish administration, they even promised to underwrite the cost of a new government, including de Lassus's salary.[28]

But the Spaniard was no longer in a conciliatory mood. Although de Lassus had previously found the volunteer bodies useful in expelling French exiles, he grew increasingly suspicious of their intent. Yet, by the time he awoke to reality, it was too late. Spanish authority was too impotent to resist the surge toward independence. Caught between a rebellious people and a parsimonious government, de Lassus was reduced to a figurehead.

Before recessing on July 27, the convention agreed to reassemble in mid-August. The ensuing interval was designed to give de Lassus time to reflect on a course of action and the pro-American delegates an opportunity to meet with Governors Claiborne and Holmes. Partisans of the convention movement, sensing that the cause of Ferdinand VII was hopeless and fearing occupation of the province by either France or England, began to view annexation as the most feasible of a dwindling number of alternatives. Agents sent to confer with Secretary Thomas Bolling Robertson of Orleans Territory (Claiborne being in Washington City) and Holmes to warn them that if the United States refused to assist the West Florida revolutionaries, they would be forced to negotiate with Great Britain.[29]

In late August, the convention delegates moved closer to revolution. They approved the ordinances drafted by Skipwith, authorized establishment of armed militia units (later called the "Convention Army"), and chose a set of officials who, together with de Lassus, were to administer the province under a reformed government. Administration of the Florida parishes fell in the joint hands of de Lassus and three associate judges (Skipwith, Robert Percy, and Shephard Brown) assisted by Sheriff John H. Johnson and militia general Philemon Thomas.[30]

At first, the beleaguered Spanish commandant thought it prudent to cooperate with the insurgents. He tentatively agreed to the proposed plans, pending final approval from officials in Pensacola and Havana. But, once the convention adjourned, the mercurial de Lassus proceeded to ignore the insurgent officials and to act as if nothing had changed. Shortly thereafter, General Thomas, "the Ajax of the Revolution," intercepted the commandant's letters to Spanish governor Folch in which he asked for reinforcements, presumably to regain control of the government. Realizing that de Lassus was untrustworthy, the insurgents determined to depose him and seize the undermanned fort at Baton Rouge. On September 26, Rhea wrote Governor Holmes seeking annexation to the United States in case the citizens of West Florida, as he expected, withdrew their allegiance to Spain.[31]

As Rhea had predicted, Thomas, with a small detachment of militia, attacked the fort at Baton Rouge during the pre-dawn hours of September 23. Instructing the attackers not to shoot unless fired upon, Thomas and his men seized the fortification with a minimum of bloodshed and placed de Lassus under house arrest. Hoisting a makeshift Lone Star flag over the "liberated" fort, the jubilant insurrectionists dragged the red and yellow banner of Spain through the streets. Two days later, the West Florida Convention, with only a handful of delegates present, met in the provincial capital of Baton Rouge and drafted a statement justifying their incendiary actions. The following day, September 26, they formally approved a declaration of independence, adopted an official flag consisting of a single white star in a field of blue, and chose Skipwith president of the "State of Florida."[32]

While these developments were taking place in West Florida, American authorities were neither idle nor disinterested. Since the late spring of 1810, administrative officials in Washington were aware of these disturbances, and Secretary Smith had informed Holmes that "the alarming and interesting situation of West Florida has very properly engaged your attention." Meanwhile, by a fortunate happenstance, Governor Claiborne was in the nation's capital, where he had ample time to converse with Madison and Smith about West Florida and what developments there portended for the United States. Claiborne, always the expansionist, insisted that nature had "decreed the union of Florida with the United States, and [that] the welfare of the Inhabitants imperiously demands it."[33]

As a result of these conversations, President Madison authorized Claiborne to write a confidential letter to Judge William Wykoff Jr., who resided at Point Coupee, "opposite Baton Rouge." After reminding Wykoff that the United States had never abandoned its claim to Florida "as far eastwardly as the Perdido," Claiborne reviewed in suffocating detail the critical state of affairs in Spain and throughout the Americas. With collapse of "the Supreme Junta . . . on the Peninsula," he concluded, the Spanish colonies were in a state of flux. "Carraccas has," he noted, "already made a movement towards Independence, & it is not improbable, but [that our] neighboring provinces may be disposed to follow the example."

Consequently, he advised Wykoff to seek out his friends in St. Francisville and Baton Rouge and "assure them . . . of the friendly disposition of the American Government." Also he was "to quiet the apprehensions" of former Tories by promising them that "their past transgressions will not be remembered to their injury" and by assuring them that "the prodigal Son mentioned in holy writ did not meet a more heartfelt welcome than they would experience from the American family." Finally, Claiborne hinted, it would be especially pleasing if our "taking possession of the Country [could] be preceded by a Request from the Inhabitants," preferably "thro' the medium of a Convention of Delegates. . . . Can no means be devised to obtain such Request?"[34]

Six days later, Secretary Smith penned a similar letter to William H. Crawford of Georgia. The president, Smith stated confidentially, wished to seek his assistance in locating "gentlemen of honor & delicacy" for an assignment of critical importance.[35] Quietly and deliberately, the Madison administration was beginning to lay the foundation for a peaceful, if somewhat stealthy, seizure of West Florida and for a long-awaited fulfillment of the Louisiana Cession of 1803.

While Claiborne was returning, at a suspiciously slow pace, to New Orleans, Governor Holmes was the only high-ranking American official on the scene; therefore he became the principal conduit of intelligence about occurrences along and below the border. At the urging of Secretary Smith, Holmes dispatched Col. Joshua G. Baker to confer with the Feliciana insurgents. A former president of the territorial legislative council, Baker was for some time a resident of the border county of Wilkinson, and he was personally acquainted with a number of participants. En route to Baton Rouge, Baker stopped to converse with John H. Johnson, who was convalescing from a recent illness. Johnson told him that Spanish authorities were able to "fatten on the spoils of the land" because so many of the inhabitants were military deserters and fugitives. Such people, he affirmed, ought to be "under the conduct of a wise guardian who will transform them from slaves to men." While Johnson acknowledged that the United States should be that protector, he reported that two-thirds of inhabitants had grown disgusted with an American government that treated them as stepchildren.[36]

On his return to Mississippi Territory, Baker was accompanied by William G. Barrow, an outspoken member of the American party in West Florida. As a messenger of John Rhea, Barrow was to ascertain if the United States was prepared to admit an independent West Florida to immediate statehood or attach it temporarily to one of the adjacent territories. Also he was to tell Holmes that he and Rhea were in favor of Florida's immediate annexation to the United States.

At first, Holmes was circumspect. Unaware of the administration's policies with respect to the Southwest, he did not wish to precipitate a crisis or disrupt the favorable developments. "I am satisfied," he wrote Smith, that the occurrences so far were but "an incipient to the more decisive and important measures of asking for the protection of the United States." While acknowledging that many Floridians were opposed to "this step—some from an attachment to the British government and others from personal reasons," he was convinced that "most of the respectable and wealthy wish to look to no other power for protection than the United States." Nonetheless, Holmes concluded, "they are determined to put everything to hazard rather than to submit again to the absolute authority of Spanish officers."[37]

Before September 1810, Holmes pursued a cautious policy. But later in the month, the situation abruptly assumed an ominous appearance. Once the insurgents had captured the fort at Baton Rouge, the Loyalists, who were especially strong in the eastern districts of Feliciana, organized counterattacks against the American partisans. Rumors began to spread like wildfire. For instance, Holmes heard that adherents of the "Spanish Party" were preparing "to raise the Negroes in their behalf." One of his informants, Col. Hugh Davis, a justice of the peace in Wilkinson County, was particularly alarmed by the prospect of a slave uprising. "I fear," he reported, that "this spirit of revolt may extend its baneful influence in Mississippi Territory," and he worried lest the region "become the scene of a St. Domingo." Furthermore, he concluded, "nothing but obedience to law and respect for government prevents a number of the inhabitants from flocking to the Standard of the party who stile themselves Americans." Later, a disquieted Rhea alerted Holmes to the likelihood that Spanish officials were planning to incite the Indians against the dispersed and defenseless insurgent families.[38]

With rumors so rampant and settlers along the border so fitful, Holmes recognized that he must "take immediate measures for the safety of the people . . . who reside[d] near the line." Consequently, he requested Col. Thomas Cushing, commanding officer of Fort Dearborn, to station two companies of soldiers along the international border "where it crosses the Road near Pinckneyville." He also placed various territorial militia units on alert, and ordered all company commanders to elevate their forces to full strength, but he specifically instructed them "to avoid taking any part in the present contest. My only object," he reiterated, was "the safety and property of our Citizens." His immediate fear was "an insurrection of the slaves," who he knew to be "very numerous in the upper part of the province." Cushing was to intercept all slaves attempting "to cross [the border] from either side," but not "to stop white people passing from one side to the other."[39]

In late October 1810, President Madison, fearful of British intervention in light of Spanish impotency, determined to act decisively. He issued a proclamation, dated October 27, extending American sovereignty over West Florida from the Mississippi to the Perdido River. This territory, he asserted, belonged to the United States by virtue of its treaty with France in 1803. Although the United States had suffered Spain to occupy it from a wish to be conciliatory and from an expectation that it could be obtained through normal diplomatic channels, continued forbearance on the part of the United States might, he insisted, be erroneously "construed into a dereliction of their title or an insensibility to the importance of the stake." By immediately occupying the territory, Madison expected to invalidate all land grants issued by Spanish officials since 1803, thereby thwarting the designs of such grasping speculators as Governor Claiborne's archenemy Daniel Clark Jr.[40]

While leaving the door open to further negotiations with Spanish officials, Madison instructed Claiborne to take possession of the disputed region and to incorporate it, at least temporarily, into Orleans Territory. But in case Claiborne failed to arrive in timely fashion, the administration set up contingency plans. On November 2, and again on November 15, Secretary Smith wrote Governor Holmes and Gen. Wade Hampton, Wilkinson's replacement as commander of the Southern and Western Army, authorizing them to occupy Baton Rouge and its environs if Claiborne was unavailable. Regrettably, Hampton did not arrive in Natchez until January 1, and Holmes was in the midst of an important session of the Mississippi legislature.[41]

Yet, news of the president's proclamation did not reach West Florida or other parts of the Southwest for another three weeks, and events there were proceeding as if nothing had changed. On November 10, Floridians marched to the polls to choose members of their first legislature, which subsequently met at St. Francisville on November 26. After selecting John W. Leonard to preside over the Senate, the two houses, meeting jointly, elected Skipwith governor by a unanimous vote. His inauguration three days later officially launched the Lone Star State of Florida. With the new governor's enthusiastic endorsement, the legislature laid plans to extend its jurisdiction as far east as the Perdido River. It authorized the establishment of a special expeditionary force, under the command of Col. William Kirkland, which was to cooperate with like-minded patriots throughout the region to wrest the remainder of West Florida from the Spaniards and incorporate it into the new state.

Fortunately, Claiborne arrived in Natchez as scheduled. He reached the little river port on December 1 and conferred immediately with Governor Holmes. They agreed that "a great majority of the Inhabitants of the District of Baton Rouge would receive with pleasure the american authorities." Yet, both were apprehensive about "the intrigues of certain individuals, believed to be hostile to the United States, and of a few adventurers from the Territories of Orleans and Mississippi of desperate character and fortunes," several of whom were part of the Convention Army garrisoning the Baton Rouge fort. As a precaution, Claiborne ordered Col. Leonard Covington, from nearby Fort Dearborn, to descend the Mississippi River, with "seven to eight hundred men," to Pointe Coupee and await further directives.[42]

Meanwhile, Claiborne arranged for distribution of the president's proclamation of October 27 throughout the Florida parishes. He sent four hundred copies to Colonel Cushing and dispatched Audley Osborne and another trusted friend with several hundred more to St. Francisville and Baton Rouge, while he and Holmes later distributed twice that number in Feliciana. Of the two executive officers, Holmes was usually first on the scene. As Claiborne acknowledged, he had profited handsomely from "the confidence which [Holmes's] upright course of life had inspired." Because of his calm demeanor, Holmes was able to make "such explanations to influential characters as greatly promoted harmony and good will."[43]

On December 6, Holmes entered St. Francisville just as Florida's first legislative session was adjourning, and he immediately discussed Madison's proclamation with both bewildered legislators and curious citizens. Later he met privately with Governor Skipwith, who expressed displeasure with the president's actions. Skipwith was piqued because

Madison had failed in his proclamation to acknowledge the existence of the free state of Florida or his position as chief executive. Also unhappy with Governor Holmes's strained justification of the federal government's intervention, a distraught Skipwith, accompanied by "three or four members" of the Florida legislature, left immediately for Baton Rouge.[44]

Afterward, Holmes crossed the Mississippi River to Point Coupee, where, by prearrangement, he consulted with Claiborne. Also present were Hunter and Osborne, both of whom assured the two governors that the people of Feliciana were ready to recognize Claiborne as chief executive. Heartened by this news, Claiborne and Holmes departed immediately for St. Francisville, escorted by "Companies of Cavalry and Riflemen." After Madison's proclamation was read aloud, Claiborne assured the assembled crowd that he was there "to protect them in the enjoyment of their liberty, property and religion." Then he ordered the "Florida flag . . . to be taken down," replaced by "the Stars and Bars." As the Lone Star flag was lowered, Claiborne was delighted to hear "the militia and Citizens cheering."[45]

The next day, Holmes left for Baton Rouge, where he expected to encounter "some opposition." There he discovered the Florida legislature had reconvened, and the old fort, under the command of Col. John Ballinger, a seasoned frontier fighter from Kentucky, was manned by "one hundred and twenty men and thirty pieces of Artillery." That evening, Holmes again met with Skipwith, who this time was more conciliatory. He showed a willingness to turn over the fort without insisting, as he had previously, upon a set of prior conditions. Before he had demanded that the United States agree to certain propositions before turning the fort over to Holmes and Claiborne. These included "a formal recognition of the sales of land under Spanish authorities," reimbursement of the debt contracted by the convention, and a full pardon for army deserters as well as an honorable "discharge from the services of the United States." When neither Claiborne nor Holmes showed a willingness to negotiate, Skipwith backed down. He was never one to turn harsh words into rash action.[46]

On the morning of December 10, Holmes, accompanied by a subdued Skipwith, went to the fort and conferred with Colonel Ballinger. Holmes expected, with Skipwith's assistance, to convince Ballinger to surrender the fort peacefully. A few hours later, Governor Claiborne and Colonel Covington, with some four hundred federal troops, made a dramatic appearance. They had come, Claiborne announced, to take formal possession of the Baton Rouge fort. At first, Ballinger seemed hesitant and befuddled, but after some tense moments, he ordered the Convention soldiers to "march out and stack their arms." By prior agreement, Claiborne "readily assented" to show respect for the Lone Star flag when it was struck. He also promised to leave the army deserters, many of whom were among those marching out of the fort, "undisturbed until the president's pleasure respecting them should be known." Precisely "at three oclock, . . . a detachment of United States Troops" took possession of the recently evacuated fort, and the short-lived free state of Florida collapsed as unheralded as it had arisen.[47]

But the peaceful occupation of the Florida parishes brought other complications and unresolved questions. What was to be the status of West Florida? Should it be permanently attached to Orleans Territory, or was a portion to be added to Mississippi Territory? Some Floridians hoped, and a few expected, the United States to grant them immediate statehood. Two additional points of interest to the insurrectionists were the permanent status of deserters and disposal of the debt incurred by the Convention government. Also, what efforts, if any, should be made to assuage Skipwith's wounded feelings? Finally, was Claiborne authorized to seize all of West Florida, including Mobile, or was the extreme eastern part to be left in Spanish hands? In late December, Claiborne was distressed when he learned that Spain still occupied Mobile and that Spanish governor Folch was determined to remain there.[48]

Fortunately, these questions were easily settled, and the federal government proceeded in short order to do so. In the opinion of its officers, West Florida was not ready for statehood. After considerable debate, Congress divided it between the newly admitted state of Louisiana and Mississippi Territory. It left the Florida parishes to Louisiana, but the rest of the coastal region, including Mobile, was incorporated into Mississippi Territory.[49] Eventually Congress also appropriated forty thousand dollars to reimburse the West Florida Convention, and the War Department made no attempt to punish the numerous deserters who had participated in the affray. In fact, the federal government had already extended amnesty to any soldier who returned voluntarily, and many later became valuable citizens of Louisiana or Mississippi.[50]

Understandably, Fulwar Skipwith continued to harbor resentment against the Madison administration. Specifically, he disliked "the hostile means & manner" which Claiborne had employed in assuming control of West Florida, and he thought the timing unfortunate. If the United States had waited a few months longer, he believed, Floridians could have easily seized Mobile and possibly Pensacola. Finally, unlike most participants in the rebellion, he pointedly refused to accept any offices in the new government.[51]

With the incorporation of West Florida, only the "Mobile Question" was left unresolved, but shortly Mobile, too, would be added to Mississippi Territory.

CHAPTER 14

The Mobile Question

Between 1803 and 1811, unrest along the international boundary was just as prevalent above as below the line. To Bigbee settlers, acquisition of the coastal plain between the Pearl and Perdido rivers, especially the port of Mobile, was as important to them as possession of New Orleans was to inhabitants of Natchez District. Without free and unhampered access to the seas, neither district could prosper, and, as Judge Thomas Rodney declared, Tombigbee Settlement faced ruin. Failure to address this question was a source of steady irritation to the residents of Washington County.[1]

Their resentment was widespread and deep-rooted. From the outset, the federal and territorial governments had neglected the Bigbee settlers, but this disparity in treatment of the two districts was especially noticeable after 1803.[2] Although elated by Jefferson's insistence that the French cession included Mobile as well as New Orleans, they were disappointed when the federal government failed to take decisive action.

This sense of isolation and neglect, combined with Jeffersonian inertia, drove Tombigbee settlers to seek separation. Nearly three hundred miles of dense wilderness separated them from the nearest Anglo-American neighbors, and travel between the two settlements was always uncertain and usually hazardous and arduous. According to one disgruntled official, it was "about as easy, to pass by land from hence, to Georgia, as to Natchez." Once the United States obtained free navigation of the Mississippi River, settlers in Washington County demanded the same for the Tombigbee. As General Wilkinson predicted, the anticipated increase of population there "must at an early period, Awaken the dormant claims of the Inhabitants, to the free Navigation of those rivers to the Ocean, which will become indispensable, not only to their accommodation, comfort and happiness, but to their very preservation."[3]

By early 1803, Bigbee settlers were awakened and aroused. Wilkinson pleaded with Spanish officials to open the waterways "on the grounds of natural law" and "the General Usage of Nations in Amity." Although hardly optimistic, he was surprised by Spain's response. He had expected Spain to permit "the free passage of an unarmed vessel into the Mobile, Spring and Autumn, on the Bona fide Certificate of the Secretary of War or the Commanding General" so long as it was "employed solely for the public service of the United States," specifically for supplying Fort Stoddert and the Choctaw factory at St. Stephens.[4]

Instead, Spanish officials consented only to "free passage, via New Orleans, for provisions & public property to our Establishments within the Mobile [that is, Fort Stoddert]." They refused to permit unhampered intercourse with the Choctaw factory even though, as Wilkinson argued, it was in the interest of both nations to pacify the Indians. More distressing was the imposition of ruinous duties on their commerce. "By recent orders," an incensed official reported in early 1804, Spanish authorities have refused to allow any article "whether it be the produce of the country, or of foreign production or manufacture, . . . to go by the Port of Mobile, either to or from this country, without paying twelve per centum, on its value, as estimated by the Spanish officials of revenue."[5] As a result, Tombigbee inhabitants paid taxes to both Spain and Mississippi Territory.

Not only did these obstructions deprive the citizens of a decent living, they also threatened to retard the district's growth despite its bountiful resources. General Wilkinson was not the first or the last to tout Bigbee's roseate future when he proclaimed it "the preferable district of our whole country, and must progress rapidly in Population and Wealth. I hold it," he continued, "to have three fold the superiority of the Banks of the Mississippi."[6]

Others agreed. For instance, Thomas W. Maury, when offered a choice of three offices, opted for the position of receiver for lands east of the Pearl River because of its "superior advantages." Nevertheless, as long as Spain possessed Mobile, Wilkinson recognized that its vast potential could be realized only if Bigbee settlers made their dissatisfaction known. Therefore, by late fall of 1803, the settlers petitioned Congress, specifying their grievances and requesting creation of a separate government for the "district of Washington independent of that of the Mississippi Territory."

With population "estimated at more than three thousand," Tombigbee, according to petitioners, was capable of supporting itself. If "the free navigation of the Mobille[,] Tombecbee and Alabama rivers [were] secured, the amount of revenue arising from impost duties in this District, would exceed the necessary expenses in support of a separate Territorial Government." Presently, they declared, "our inhabitants . . . are subjected to laws enacted at the distance of nearly three hundred miles from us" by legislative bodies "composed of people different in their manners and customs [and] different in their interests." Nature, they argued, never "designed the two countries to be under the same government."[7]

Jefferson, aware of its strategic importance, began to collect information about the district, but he was reluctant to use it as an excuse for precipitous action. At first, he relied upon Ephraim Kirby, but after Kirby's unforeseen death in 1804, the president came to depend heavily on Judge Harry Toulmin. Indeed, Toulmin was a fortuitous if improbable choice for a federal judgeship in a "remote and secluded district" like Tombigbee.[8]

An Englishman by birth and dissenting minister by preference, Toulmin fled his native country in 1793 to escape persecution from a repressive British government frightened by the excesses of the French Revolution. After briefly touring Virginia, where he conferred with Madison, Toulmin, armed with letters of introduction from him and "several other respectable characters," settled in Lexington, Kentucky. With the assistance of Jefferson's friend John Breckinridge, Toulmin became president of Transylvania Seminary in February 1795.

Toulmin's presidential tenure was stormy and short-lived. It ended in 1796, when he hastily resigned, citing as his reasons inadequate pay and insufficient support from the school's board of trustees, composed mostly of conservative ministers. His unorthodox religious beliefs and outspokenness hardly endeared him to a governing body made up of staunch Presbyterians who thought his theology was "tainted with Socinian errors."[9]

Shunning both the ministry and a career in education, Toulmin was, for the remainder of his life, identified with the legal profession despite rudimentary training in law. On the early frontier, knowledge of law was often more a liability than an asset, and Toulmin quickly gained a reputation as a promising scholar and competent counselor. From 1796 to 1804, he served as secretary of state for Kentucky, where, according to an admirer, he officiated "with great propriety . . . and made such proficiency in the Study of Law" that the governor appointed him, together with the state's attorney general, "to make a compilation of the Criminal Common Law." In 1804, after a change of administration, Toulmin realized that his "politics had been too open and decided to suit the taste" of the new executive. He was guilty, he said, "of the never to be repented of, and unpardonable sin of drawing my first breath in a foreign country," and he sought a position in one of the fast-growing western territories—Orleans, Mississippi, or Indiana.[10]

First he notified Secretary of State Madison of his desire to move west. Then he solicited endorsements from Senator Breckinridge and Caleb Wallace, another prominent Kentucky Republican. Wallace described him as "a Gentleman of liberal Education, good Genius, agreeable manners, and remarkable attention to any business he engages in." Despite the efforts of local citizens to have Rodominick Gilmer, friend of the popular Caller brothers, appointed judge for Washington County, Jefferson selected Toulmin, imposing him on people schooled to be suspicious of magistrates with whom they were unfamiliar.[11]

Toulmin settled permanently along the Tombigbee River near "McIntoshes Bluff," naming it Wakefield in honor of Oliver Goldsmith's vicar. There Toulmin revealed himself to be a student of the classics and a stickler for law and order in a frontier region unaccustomed to firm government and unfamiliar with the vagaries of common law, and he soon ran afoul of restless residents intent upon freeing the district from Spanish oppression.[12]

Although Toulmin gained the respect of the law-abiding populace, he incurred the lasting enmity of the unsavory elements, and his arrogant behavior made it difficult for people to be lukewarm toward him. Inhabitants either admired or despised him. Yet he won the confidence of then governor David Holmes, who, like Jefferson and Madison, came to depend upon him for information and succor. The indefatigable judge also promoted the region's economic development by improving mail delivery and opening, with the assistance of James Caller and Lemuel Henry, a road between Fort Stoddert and Natchez.[13]

A valuable press agent for Tombigbee, Toulmin still found time to promote the welfare of his three children, making sure they found suitable spouses. One daughter married Capt. Edmund P. Gaines, sometime commandant of Fort Stoddert, and the second a son of Gen. James Wilkinson, while his only son took Col. James Caller's daughter as bride.

Toulmin's respect for the law was uncompromising. For instance, in the summer of 1808, a Spanish subject allegedly murdered a Frenchman on the Tensaw River just above the international border. After the suspect fled below the line, Toulmin asked the Spanish commandant to arrest the culprit. But, if the Spaniard preferred to try him in a Spanish court, Toulmin promised to produce the evidence against him. "I embrace this opportunity of doing myself the honor," he informed the commandant, "to assure you that I feel exceedingly solicitous that no facility should ever be afforded, by a difference of national jurisdiction between settlements so contiguous, to the vicious and abandoned on either side of the line, to commit depredations with impunity." He was, Toulmin declared, "always ready to cooperate with good men of both governments in the suppression of villainy and licentiousness."[14] But this attitude hardly endeared him to those, like the Callers, who harbored a deep distrust of Spanish justice.

Yet Spanish commercial practices were not the settlers' only complaints. They objected to the federal government's land policies, which, in their opinion, failed to consider local conditions when resolving conflicting claims. Since most of the fertile lands were originally granted to British claimants, the settlers feared lest unfriendly federal courts dispossess them. Even Toulmin dreaded the possibility. "I am persuaded," he wrote, that "it will produce heart-burnings and fix deeply a spirit of litigation which for a long period of time will be fatal to the peace, to the industrious habits and consequently to the prosperity of the country."[15]

The settlers also chafed at Jefferson's decision not to submit the favorable Treaty of Mount Dexter, signed with the Choctaws in 1805, to the Senate for ratification. John McGrew, one of the district's prominent settlers, was especially upset. The treaty conferred upon him a grant of 1,500 acres, "which the Choctaw had given him in recognition of his friendship and assistance." The tribe wished to reward him for having "preserved many of them from famine," and, according to Toulmin, "he had uniformly endeavored to keep them peaceable and . . . firmly attached to the American government."[16]

Others objected when the federal government located the Choctaw factory at St. Stephens. They wanted it placed in a remote spot, preferably in Indian country, to discourage Choctaw and Creek customers from molesting defenseless residents. Other annoyances were cattle rustling by both Natives and Anglos, illicit slave trade through Spanish Florida, and a rash of "negro-stealing" by vengeful Indians and unscrupulous white traders.[17]

Prior to 1809, the history of relations between the Tombigbee settlers and the federal and territorial governments was one of patience on the part of the former and forbearance by the latter. Despite their vulnerability and weakness in numbers, Tombigbee settlers became increasingly annoyed at both Spanish intransigence and American insouciance. Spain refused to loosen its grip upon American commerce and renewed its earlier efforts to win the friendship of Creek and Seminole Indians. Once again, the settlers reacted in customary fashion; they petitioned for division of the territory.[18]

To accomplish this objective, the Tombigbee settlers marshaled an assortment of arguments, one of which, if not convincing, was at least novel. Eschewing the Madisonian formula that a vast and diverse nation was the best antidote against an abusive majority, they revived the theories of the French philosopher Montesquieu. "Where the body politic is too widely extended," they insisted, and "where the constituent principles of power consist of distinct and insulated communities, the Legislative Assembly . . . will partake of the weakness and discordance of the elements out of which it is composed." As a consequence, "the public good will be over looked in a contest for local advantages." In their view, legislators were "in danger of becoming a mere band of partizans, struggling, perhaps, for their personal emolument merely, but labouring at best for nothing more than some paltry advantage to their respective sections."

Furthermore, they insisted, "the additional expence of a new Territorial Government [was] trifling indeed" when compared with its potential. Give us "a Government of our own, and you will give us respectability; you will give us population; you will give us strength." At present, the petitioners asserted, they "were subjected to enormous taxes . . . while enjoying scarcely any advantage from the expenditures of the public money." In fact, they were "mere cyphers in the Territorial Government" due to "the remoteness of our situation, and the total dissimilarity of their channels of Trade," which, they complained, gave "the people of the Mobile and its adjacent waters, no common interest with those of the Mississippi."

A separate government, they argued, was necessary "to prevent our country from becoming the asylum of the abandoned and to cause life to be secure, property to be safe, and the Laws to be respected." Finally, they wanted a government "adapted to our situation," one that would "deliver us from the heavy burthen of foreign oppression." Presently, they argued, "we pay to the Spanish monarchy, Twenty four per centum on our active capital," 12 percent on the "proceeds of our sales" and an additional 12 percent "on our purchases." "Are we Americans or Spaniards?" they wondered. "Shall we support the Republic of the United States, or the Spanish monarchy? Our Principles,—our habits,—our affections,—our hearts, drive us to you,—but you,—shall we say it,— dare we pronounce the dreadful curse drive us back again to the Spaniards! No: you do not:—we will not believe it . . . We do not ask for your relief:—for we know it will be granted."[19]

It was against this backdrop that the "Mobile question" was agitated and eventually resolved. In late June 1810, Spanish governor Maximilian de St. Maxent set off the initial alarm. He complained to Col. Richard Sparks, American commander of Fort Stoddert, that a set of ruffians, "named Expedition of Mobile," planned to seize Mobile and "destroy all the houses of commerce." Intercepting a cache of letters written to Mobile resident Zeno Orso, he identified Joseph Pulaski Kennedy as the leader of what he called a pack of "villains."[20] In turn, Sparks notified Secretary of War William Eustis, reassuring him that he had taken the necessary measures to placate the Spaniards and to prepare the garrison.

Sparks confirmed the existence of a "general and powerful combination" led by Kennedy and supported by malcontents like the Caller brothers and the infamous Kempers. He attributed the renewed resentment to Spanish mistreatment of immigrants from west Tennessee and Kentucky. As they passed through Mobile on the way to upper Tombigbee, custom officials subjected them to protracted delays and ruinous duties on their personal property, including such items as "furniture, wearing apparel, [and] farming utensils." They arrived penniless and thoroughly vexed, and their rude treatment rekindled among old-timers a latent hatred for Spaniards who possessed, in their opinion, "the power to intercept and harass emigrants to this country." Others wondered why "Savages were free to pass on the waters every day to Mobile, reaping every advantage therefrom, trading with a foreign nation and paying the U.S. no duties," while the government permitted Spanish officials to impose ruinous duties upon them. Why, they asked, did federal officials persist in showing favoritism toward a people "ready to turn their tomahawks against" white Americans?

Yet, according to Sparks, the principal reason for the Mobile Society's success was due to a set of "designing demagogues, . . . ready at all times to foment popular discontent and fan the embers of sedition" by seizing upon "every plausible subject of complaint." Like other demagogues, they relied "on moments of turbulence, and public distraction, for the acquisition of popularity" and upon "the result of anarchy, as the only opportunity of acquiring wealth." He described Kennedy as "a young man, educated in the Eastern states, ambitious, and intriguing, and popular." Sparks regarded him as someone "without real talent," but he recognized that, as a "seditious intrigue[r]" and master of "the low arts that secure popularity," Kennedy was without peer and "a man of engaging address, popular manners, and daring." While Sparks "doubt[ed] his capacity to conduct," he knew that Kennedy was "seconded by a character [John Caller] who has been several years a resident of this country" and who was "well calculated to meet any deficiency, of the first."

Despite his optimistic evaluation of conditions, Sparks remained apprehensive. He was unsure if his forces were sufficient to withstand an uprising since he believed the conspirators, before "acting in a hostile manner against the Towns of Mobile and Pensacola," planned to assault Fort Stoddert, seize the ammunition, and disarm the federal troops. His situation, he said, was deplorable and untenable. "Death, Desertions, and Discharge" had left him "almost without men" due to the soldiers' "unaccountable aversion . . . to this place," conditions that discouraged reenlistment and invited desertion. He asked the War Department for reinforcements, requesting "four compleat company's of infantry, and one of Artillery [as] requisite to meet the approaching state of things."[21] Unfortunately, the federal government was unable to assist as long as the army was preoccupied with protecting the frontier north of Baton Rouge.

Judge Toulmin painted an equally dismal picture. "Surrounded by indians, cut off and entirely detached from & unknown to the main body of the territory to which it is a part," Tombigbee District was more "open to unprincipled intrigue & restless ambition," he asserted, " than in any spot of equal extent." Additionally, the fretful settlers felt "totally unrepresented in Congress," since "the Mississippi [territorial] delegate represents us about as much as the Middlesex members represented the American colonies in the British Parliament." But he questioned if the grievances were sufficient to justify an armed uprising, and he dismissed rumors "of a projected expedition against the Spanish settlements [as] idle fear."

After a few discreet inquiries, however, Toulmin concluded "that the expedition had been many months in contemplation." He no longer thought its objective was "a mere predatory incursion" into Spanish territory. Instead, the rebels planned "a conquest of the country," and he feared that, like Burr before them, they favored "a new government under the protection of some foreign government." In conversations with Kennedy, who admitted his own involvement, Toulmin learned that the rebels proposed to query the two Georgia senators, William H. Crawford and Charles Tait, about the likelihood of annexing Florida, once the Mobile Society had dislodged the Spaniards from Mobile and Pensacola. According to Kennedy, Col. James Caller, not himself, was "at the head of the expedition."

Toulmin thought Kennedy overly optimistic. He doubted there was "such unanimity among the people of this country as Kennedy seemed to calculate." The "old tories," he believed, were disposed "to remain submissive subjects of the powers that be." The "other old settlers," in his opinion, possessed too much property "to risque that for the sake of pre-eminence." With respect to newcomers, most of whom hailed from Georgia, Toulmin was less confident. Since many were illegal squatters on public lands, he feared they might join the naysayers rather than the "ancient inhabitants."

Toulmin attributed Kennedy's confidence to the rapport he enjoyed with militia officers, who, he believed, were the soul of conspiracy. "It is probable," he wrote, "that many appointments in the militia have been made with reference to" it. "The militia officers of this country," he reasoned, "have been in the habit of exercising very extraordinary powers," and the Callers had carefully filled the ranks with "friends of the expedition." Toulmin asked himself why the leaders "have been extremely solicitous to prevent a division of our territory" when the "great body of the settlement favored it." Was it because they wished to keep the agitation alive?

Determined to preserve the peace, Toulmin promised to "use all the exertions I can to ward off the meditated blow." Since he had to "rely on argument & persuasion merely," he wished his superiors to understand how formidable the task was. "Every thing here is done by private intrigue," he explained, and with the people so widely scattered, it was impossible "to see many of them at a time."[22]

The rumors also worried Governor Holmes. At first, he was cautious, partly because he was ill-informed due to irregular mails, but mostly because Feliciana dominated his attention. He was nevertheless concerned enough to schedule a visit to the eastern counties during the summer of 1810, but the resignation of Secretary Thomas Williams temporarily aborted his plans.

But Col. James Caller's request to resign his militia commission aroused the governor's suspicion. Imploring Caller to reconsider, Holmes cautioned him against participating in "some lawless aggression upon the adjacent Province of West Florida." It would, he declared, "ruin the individuals who might engage in it—injure the reputation of the country, and be productive of much mischief." His importunings were successful in preventing Caller's resignation but not his later participation in the cabal against Mobile. More importantly, the governor feared lest this unlawful foray of American filibusters upset plans to secure Baton Rouge.[23]

Meanwhile, the Spaniards were not idle. In early September, Holmes learned that the Spanish commandant at Mobile had entertained "a considerable number [estimated at between 250 and 600] of Chaktaw indians belonging to the six-Towns." According to informers, the Spaniards intended to use them to defend the town against an attack by Americans "residing on the waters of the Tombigbee." Holmes was livid. He reminded Governor Folch that the Choctaw were "under the protection of the United States" and that no one had "the right to engage their personal services for the purpose of forming a military force."[24] But, his stern warning failed to deter the beleaguered Spaniard.

In mid-September, however, Holmes concluded "that there might be more cause for apprehension" than he had "first concieved." He asked Toulmin to seek out the principal dissidents and dissuade them from participating in an illegal and fruitless enterprise. He also took it upon himself to admonish the three regimental commanders (James Caller, Joseph Carson, and James Patton). By "resorting to force for the purpose of freeing themselves from the exactions and restrictions to which their commerce" was subjected, they would, he warned, "retard rather than facilitate the object of their wishes." If the attempt was made, he asserted, "I shall rely upon your exertions to aid the civil authority to suppress it." He reassured them that Congress, at its next session, intended to give serious attention to "our relative situation with West Florida."[25]

Governor Holmes also warned his aide-de-camp, Maj. John Hanes, who only recently had resigned from the territorial assembly, that "nothing could be attended with more injurious consequences to the interest of the Citizens of Tombigbee, than an attempt of this nature." Finally, he implored Secretary of State Robert Smith "to strengthen the post at Fort Stoddert" with an additional contingent of "regular Troops," and asked Colonel Sparks, who was in a better position to "give correct information upon the subject than any other gentleman friendly to the Government," to ascertain if an attack was imminent.[26]

Momentarily, in late September, the situation improved. "The enterprize I presume is entirely abandoned," a delighted Holmes concluded. But his optimism was premature. This time it was residents of Mobile instead of the Bigbee settlers who sounded the tocsin. They reported a force of 1,600 men en route from Baton Rouge, intent upon seizing Mobile and Pensacola and incorporating them into the Convention of Florida. In early October, the insurgents in Baton Rouge and Feliciana, after establishing a provisional government, determined to extend their jurisdiction into the eastern districts, justifying their actions on the president's proclamation of October 27, 1810.[27] Although the conventioneers' principal objective was Mobile, they intended to liberate the Biloxi and Pascagoula settlements as well.

A hastily constituted committee of safety solicited support from the eastern districts (Biloxi, Pascagoula, and Mobile) and dispatched Reuben Kemper and Joseph White, who reportedly were to encourage the citizens to choose representatives to the upcoming Florida Convention. Expecting the undermanned and poorly trained Mobile garrison to capitulate, Kemper headed straight for Fort Stoddert, reaching it on October 24.[28]

In conversations with Judge Toulmin, Captain Gaines, and Colonel Sparks, Kemper displayed restraint. He had come, he stated, to bring "offers of good will and friendship" to the people of Tombigbee and not to stir up trouble or disobey the law. Although he refrained from venturing "below the American boundary," Toulmin became apprehensive after he met with the Callers and Kennedy.[29] As Toulmin expected, Kemper found Kennedy and the Callers kindred spirits. His earlier suspicions, Toulmin reported, have now "ripened into certainty."

In meetings with the Callers and Kennedy, Kemper displayed a different face, making it clear that the Convention anticipated annexing the Mobile District, peacefully if possible, forcibly if necessary. Meanwhile, he commissioned Kennedy a major in the Convention Army of West Florida.[30] By accepting the commission, Kennedy reasoned, he could pursue an aggressive agenda without running the risk of violating the Neutrality Act of 1793 or facing interference from federal authorities. On the other hand, the Caller brothers, when approached by Kemper, were noncommittal but hardly disinterested.

Toulmin followed a strategy calculated to prevent bloodshed and to uphold American honor. First, he tried to suppress "the projected expedition" by exposing its folly in an address to the grand jury. To be sure, Toulmin was as eager as the hotspurs to drive the Spaniards out of the Floridas, but he wanted it done legally, either through negotiations with Spanish officials or by invitation of the inhabitants. He acknowledged that a majority of the inhabitants of Mobile "wish[ed] a change [of government]," yet, he also knew that as long as Spanish troops were present, "no man will stand forward as an advocate for it." The French, who made up the bulk of the Mobile District's population, were "generally peaceable, domestic men, who have no idea of encouraging civil commotion." Therefore, he concluded, any effort "to obtain possession of the country by pacific means," without a prior arrangement "with the Spanish officers," was foolhardy.[31]

Convinced that "the people of Mobile" would never voluntarily join the West Florida insurgents, Toulmin calculated that the best way to defuse the situation was to convince the Spanish officers to leave peacefully. Thus he decided to contact Governor Folch personally, correctly sensing that he was friendlier than other Spanish officials toward the United States. Once in Mobile, however, he discovered a people alarmed by incessant rumors of an impending American attack. Several were preparing to flee Mobile and seek refuge in the nearby countryside or across the international border. He then sought out James Innerarity, who, as longtime agent of John Forbes & Company, enjoyed the governor's confidence.[32]

Toulmin found him guarded but receptive. Both wanted to preserve the peace. The judge proposed that "the most infallible method of averting the impending storm" was for a high-ranking Spanish official, preferably the governor, to request the American government to "take possession of the country." At least, he argued, this arrangement "w[oul]d unquestionably be a sufficient reason with the convention at Baton Rouge to suspend all hostile approaches" and "paralize any intrigues which might be going on with any European power."[33]

Toulmin surmised that Spanish officials were fearful that Napoleon might take advantage of the unrest to regain a portion of France's lost empire in North America, and the presence of a large French population in Louisiana and West Florida reinforced his apprehensions. In fact, Governor Folch recently had expressed concern about "the influence which the French Agents in Louisiana [might] exercise in these disturbances."[34]

While Innerarity found Toulmin's suggestions inviting, he cautioned him "that to hint such a thing at Mobile would be construed into treason." Nevertheless, he was aware, like Toulmin, that the residents of Mobile were not averse to a change of government if done honorably and without fanfare. Lamenting the fact that Folch was in Pensacola, Innerarity acknowledged that the Spanish governor "was a man of sense" and likely to "calmly weigh a suggestion without criminating the author," and he agreed to approach him.[35]

Meanwhile, Folch was encountering pressures of his own. He too wished to restore friendly relations with the United States. Earlier, in separate letters to Sparks and Holmes, he had attempted to justify having summoned the Choctaws to Mobile. He invited them, he explained, not to defend Mobile but as scouts to warn him of strangers "with hostile appearances." He, too, was eager to preserve "the good harmony" and prevent "the reported disturbances" from escalating into violence. Likewise, Sparks promised to "exert every legitimate power he possessed to support the good understanding between his catholic majesty & the U.S."[36]

Meanwhile, Toulmin and Gaines, with intermittent encouragement from Sparks, continued to seek out Innerarity in the hope of securing enough concessions from Spanish officials to upset the efforts of Kemper and Kennedy or at least to discourage distraught settlers from joining them. Toulmin believed that if he could cajole Folch into removing the duties on American commerce, which even Kemper acknowledged was the greatest grievance, he might embolden several to desert.[37]

By mid-November, Toulmin's efforts began to bear fruit. Although Governor Folch preferred peaceful relations, he was reluctant to deal directly with unauthorized agents. Consequently, he enlisted the services of Col. John McKee, a former Indian agent whose name, according to Toulmin, had been unfairly linked to Burr, and entrusted him with confidential dispatches for Secretary of State Robert Smith. Unless he received immediate reinforcements and additional funds, the Spaniard hinted, he planned to relinquish Mobile. Folch also intimated to Captain Gaines, who was in Mobile distributing copies of the president's proclamation of October 27, a willingness to cooperate. As proof, he promised to abolish the tariff duties on American goods, but he could leave Mobile only with approval of Havana and Madrid. Meanwhile, he was under orders to defend Mobile against hostile attack.[38]

Unaware of these negotiations, the insurgents grew bolder and more self-confident. Convinced, as even the somber Toulmin acknowledged, that the "judicial arm [was] extremely feeble," Kennedy assured his confederates that they were in no danger from the law. No "jury of their countrymen," he asserted, would punish them for driving the hated dons from Mobile. Furthermore, Kennedy, by attracting a majority of militia officers to his cause, he had effectively co-opted that body. He also expected a contingent of the Convention Army of West Florida to arrive momentarily.[39]

The bizarre drama, which had been building for months, suddenly came to a climax in late November. Colonels Kemper and Kennedy, newly commissioned as officers in the revolutionary Convention Army, summoned "the Expeditionary party" to rendezvous at Fisher's Bluff, which the rebels dubbed "Bunker Hill" after the famous battle in Massachusetts. At first, Toulmin, accompanied by his son-in-law Gaines and "another friend or two," planned to visit the rebel party and remind the assembled men "of the impolicy and rashness of proceeding in the enterprise." But, on further reflection, Toulmin, with Colonel Sparks's endorsement, altered his strategy. Instead, he sent Gaines to Mobile to secure from Folch "an official declaration as to his intentions with regard to duties." If he could persuade the Spanish governor to abolish the detestable duties, even temporarily, Toulmin reasoned, then he might forestall Kemper's zealots from attacking Mobile.

In the hope of buying precious time, Toulmin alerted the settlers of his plans. He distributed circulars informing them of Captain Gaines's "voyage to Mobile, & [of] the prospect of an abolition of duties." At the same time, Toulmin drafted an open letter, addressed to a justice of the peace "residing in the neighborhood of the place of rendezvous," but intended for the partisans. Sparks immediately ordered two soldiers "in a small canoe" to deliver it personally to the magistrate. But the ever-alert Kemper spotted the couriers and arrested them as military deserters, after which he mockingly notified a nonplussed Sparks of his good deed.

Colonel Sparks immediately dispatched a trusted officer to retrieve the two "deserters" and to invite Kemper and Kennedy to accompany him to Fort Stoddert for a conference with Toulmin. The two insurgent leaders not only declined Sparks's offer, but they also informed him that they had assembled "under the protection of the Star (the Convent[io]n Flag)" with the intent "of making war upon Spanish possessions." In their opinion, they were acting legally and not "in violation of American law."

None of these developments surprised Toulmin. Yet he still hoped to frighten the more reasonable participants into deserting, thereby destroying the Kemper party's effectiveness. Consequently, he sent a second letter, addressed jointly "to Col. Callier [sic] and Major [William] Buford," both of whom he "understood were of the party," informing them of Folch's plans for "the abolition of duties" and the "prospect of a cession of the country." Unfortunately, as Toulmin later learned, when Buford shared the letter with the men, he altered its contents to make it appear that the judge actually favored the project rather than admonishing them to disband.[40] Toulmin's actions, instead of disheartening the filibusters, emboldened them. Shortly afterward, Kemper moved his contingent across the bay "to a bluff nearly opposite the town of Mobile." A few days later, Folch, informed "by an old man" of the insurgents' whereabouts, "attempted to cross the bay with a force to disperse them," but a "violent storm forced the Spaniards to withdraw." The weather refused to play favorites. The same rains that forced Folch to call off the attack also altered Kemper's strategy.

Once the Kemper and Kennedy forces relocated their encampment to the east shore of Mobile Bay, they paused to await arrival of supplies earlier stored near Fort Stoddert. To elude officials, the boatmen took a circuitous route to the encampment. Instead of continuing down the Tensaw River to the bay, they veered off through Bear Creek. Even though the supplies were late in coming, the men were ecstatic since the boats contained, in addition to ammunition and food, several casks of whiskey. Tardy or not, the welcome provisions, together with a round of fiery speeches by Kemper and Kennedy, buoyed the men's spirits.

But the men's mood was as volatile as the weather. The anticipated reinforcements from Baton Rouge had still not arrived, and they never would. Unbeknownst to Kemper, the West Florida officials, shortly after the ragtag volunteers left Feliciana for "the neighbourhood of Mobile," countermanded their orders after receiving a copy of President Madison's proclamation of October 27. Now that the United States had annexed the entire coastal region of West Florida, including the Mobile District, they saw no need for further military action.

A feeling of despair gripped the insurgents. Not only was there no news from Baton Rouge, but the residents of Mobile District were unresponsive to Kemper's overtures. Expecting to discover "the people below the line sufficiently numerous to revolutionize themselves," they instead found "them few and under the influence of the [Spanish] garrison," too timid to join a movement for their own freedom. Their disposition ran the spectrum from disappointment to despair, and they fell into quarreling among themselves. One of them, Dr. John Pollard, was so seriously wounded in a drunken brawl that he was taken to Fort Stoddert for medical attention.

Facing, at this juncture, both internal dissension and an intensifying rainstorm, the filibusters resolved to split up. Kemper, with a few of his companions, returned by horseback to the Tensaw settlements, where he hoped to recruit a more dependable force to overpower the feeble Spanish garrison at Mobile, which reportedly consisted of fewer than eighty men, half of whom were unfit for duty. Meanwhile, the rest of the rebel party rowed across Mobile Bay to a clearing on the west side along Saw Mill Creek, only twelve miles north of the town. There they set up camp, expecting to be joined shortly by "two companies [of volunteers] from Pascagola, and a troop of horse" from above the line.

Momentarily tossing caution to the wind, the jaded men fell into frolicking—drinking, dancing, and fiddling the night away. Shortly before midnight, a Spanish force of two hundred men surprised the unsuspecting and groggy merrymakers. The thirty or so insurgents scurried in all directions, leaving behind four dead and ten captives, one of them William H. Hargraves, a Washington County justice of the peace.[41] Folch quickly dispatched his prisoners in chains to Pensacola, from where he transferred them to Havana for trial. Despite Governor Claiborne's repeated and anguished pleas for mercy, the poor devils were destined to spend the next five years in the wretched dungeons of Castle Moro.[42]

Meanwhile, Kemper's associates faced a different set of problems. Upon returning to American soil in quest of fresh recruits, they soon found themselves under arrest. For weeks, Toulmin had been taking depositions from the local residents in preparation for the insurgents' return. While a few of the deponents were suspected collaborators, most were Toulmin's friends and confidants who recently had conversed with one or more of the firebrands. Those arrested included Reuben Kemper, Chief Justice John Caller, and William Buford, but Kennedy escaped the dragnet by entering a plea of habeas corpus.[43] Capt. John McFarland, whom Toulmin later described as "a saltmaker on the public lands," also eluded his pursuers. After defiantly notifying the sheriff that "he would have [Toulmin's] blood, McFarland fled into Spanish territory."

On the other hand, Caller and Kemper were surprisingly candid. John Caller admitted engaging a "Kentucky boat" to transport supplies to the insurgents and being "present with the party below the line." But, he insisted, he was "merely as a spectator." Like John Caller, Kemper denied aiding or abetting the military expedition; instead, he was acting as "a citizen of Florida," and all of the "people who joined him" below the line had formally subscribed to "an oath of fidelity to the Convention." Furthermore, he insisted, "the enterprise" in which they were engaged "was a laudable and an honourable one." Neither he nor his followers ever "intended to injure the United States or the citizens of Florida." A thirst for "rapine," he swore, was not an objective. They had come to free the inhabitants, not to plunder them, and they took only "what was necessary," careful to pay for what they procured. According to one participant, "Nothing but eatables was taken."[44]

Before he released the three prisoners on bail, pending court appearance in September, Toulmin offered them the opportunity "to rebut the charges, or . . . cross examine the witnesses." Unfortunately, "for want of any place," Toulmin conducted the hearings, which consumed nearly four days, in "Cap[tai]n Gaines' quarters." They accused Toulmin of attempting to intimidate them by strategically placing armed guards, with fixed bayonets, around the room in an effort "more to ridicule the Prisoners and their acts than to enter into a fair and candid investigation." Later, Toulmin's detractors "industriously circulated" reports that the judge, by informing Folch of the location of the insurgents' camp, was responsible for the massacre at Saw Mill Creek.[45]

The controversy over Toulmin's methods exacerbated public feelings for several months. Kemper's hatred for Toulmin was boundless and unbending; he once described Toulmin as a "base Devil filled with deceptive and Bloody Rascality." Largely out of empathy for the insurgents and resentment of Toulmin's tactics, the grand jury refused to indict Kemper and his confederates. Three months later, John Caller took out a writ against Judge Toulmin, entering "a plea of trespass" against him, charging him with "false imprisonment," and asking for damages of "ten thousand dollars."[46]

If the motives of Kemper and Kennedy were not booty, as they proclaimed, those of Sterling Dupree were. A notorious freebooter who resided two miles below the international border, Dupree took advantage of the confusion to satisfy his lust for power and appetite for pillage. After accepting a major's commission in the Convention Army, Dupree, with "a party of forty men," raised havoc among French settlements along the Pascagoula River. After compelling the residents either to swear allegiance to the Florida Convention or remain neutral, he plundered the estate of John B. Nicholet, lately deceased, and commandeered three schooners to transport the loot, consisting of five or six "Negroes, dry goods and household furniture." Dupree and his compatriots, according to one informant, seized "about 10 or 12 Thousand Dollars" worth of personal property, including "a number of cattle and several slaves," and would have taken "all the negroes on the bay had they not been hide out" by their "inoffending" masters.

Following instructions from James Caller and Kennedy, Dupree carried the stolen goods across the international boundary and unloaded them "in a canebrake." Later, in an attempt to conceal his role, he conveyed the "plundered property" to his brother in Washington County. Meanwhile, angry French inhabitants sent thirteen vigilantes to recover their purloined "Vessels and property." Although they exchanged shots with the Dupree party, they were no match for the better-armed raiders, who "beat off" the pursuers, killing one and wounding two.[47]

While Dupree was rampaging through the country, Kemper and Kennedy were also active. Out on bail, they collected "a second party of men" in lower Tombigbee, where animosity toward the Spaniards was especially pronounced. An incredulous Colonel Sparks "could not believe" that Kemper "mediated a second attack on the Town of Mobile, or that he would take steps calculated to disturb its tranquility after he knew of the President's decree." Kemper, he said, wished to repay the Spaniards for their attack at Saw Mill Creek by "commit[ting] depredations on the Inhabitants" of Mobile. "Probably," he observed, Kemper's purpose was to "deluge it in blood."

Assuming that the citizens of Mobile, "secure in the declarations of the President of protection," were "determined to take no part in the affair," Sparks dispatched Captain Gaines with three officers and "fifty men" to take up a position "in the vicinity of the Town" and prevent Kemper's party from engaging in any further "effusion of blood with its horrid attendant consequences." Sparks also "sent a Gentleman to induce [Kemper] to return or otherwise take no active part" in the proceedings. Since Sparks and Claiborne expected the Spaniards to evacuate the fort shortly, they were determined to suppress "Kemper's project" before it was too late. Although Claiborne regretted that "the force under Captn Gaines [was] . . . so limited," he dutifully instructed Sparks that if the fort were "not tendered on the demand," he should inform the Spanish commander that he was "restricted from using force against him" and that the American troops were there only to deter the Kemper party.[48]

Upon arriving in Mobile, Gaines induced Kemper and his men to return to Fort Stoddert on promise that they would be reinstated in the militia and allowed to participate in Mobile's capitulation. On December 22, Gaines sent a courier to Capt. Layento Perez, commandant of Fort Charlotte, demanding the surrender of Mobile under the terms specified in the president's proclamation of October 27. Predictably, Perez pleaded that he could not act without instructions from Governor Folch.[49] Nevertheless, Kemper's party quietly retired, lending support to Reuben's claim that neither he nor his recruits were interested in plunder and wished only to wrest Mobile from Spanish hands.

Still, Sparks planned to dislodge the Spaniards, and he became more aggressive, believing he was authorized by Claiborne and Madison to occupy the territory west of the Perdido River. Accordingly, he "called out five or six companies of militia" and ordered them, together with "a Company of mounted riflemen," to reinforce Gaines at Mobile. Difficulties in supplying the soldiers on short notice delayed their departure until early January, and by then the situation had changed drastically.[50]

Gaines was no longer in charge of operations. On January 3, 1811, Cushing, pursuant to orders from Secretary of War Eustis, arrived off Mobile Bay with five gunboats and two companies of regular soldiers to occupy all garrisons abandoned by the Spaniards. Cushing too had come not to seize Mobile but to prevent the Kemper firebrands from disrupting the peace. According to a relieved Toulmin, the timely arrival of Cushing "really saved this country from becoming a scene of plunder and desolation."[51]

Nevertheless, Governor Claiborne was disgusted; he expected to occupy the territory west of the Perdido River, and he privately poured out his bitterness to Gen. Wade Hampton, who had recently replaced Wilkinson as commander of the southern army. "The state of things at Mobile," he wrote, was "really unpleasant. I wish to God the Government would give orders to take the fort." Later he expressed similar feelings to Paul Hamilton, Madison's secretary of the navy. In "my opinion," he declared, "the Bayonet alone will put us in possession of Mobile and of East Florida and the sooner it is resorted to, the better." It was, he declared, time to discard diplomacy in favor of a call to arms.[52]

In fact, Claiborne was so disturbed that he contemplated using underhanded methods. According to two reliable officials, he had quietly authorized his brother, Ferdinand Claiborne, to approach James Caller when he visited Natchez in late November 1810. Ferdinand was to encourage Caller "to hurry on to the Tombigbee, raise the militia immediately and take possession of the Town of Mobile before Smith[']s instructions were made publick."[53]

To be sure, Claiborne was a rampant expansionist, if not a full-fledged jingo. Pleased with Madison's forthright speech to Congress in December, which he described as "firm & dignified," Claiborne anticipated hostilities with Great Britain. Then, he said, the federal government should "banish all European influence from the Continent of America — Mexico should without delay be rendered free & independent as well as "the Island of Cuba." "It is the real mouth of the Mississippi," he declared, and once it was in America's hands, "western Commerce would be safe."[54]

Meanwhile, in late January, Secretary of State Smith authorized John McKee and former Georgia governor Mathews to open negotiations with Spanish officials in Pensacola for the peaceful transfer of Mobile District. Under the impression that Spain was ready to negotiate, McKee drafted a letter to Governor Folch, outlining the terms of a proposed evacuation, and entrusted it to Ralph Isaac for delivery.[55] Arriving in Pensacola on February 25, 1811, Isaac had three amicable but inconclusive conversations with Folch, who explained that when American officials first approached him, "he was covered with difficulties—threatened by Kemper & his party at Tensaw—by Dupree at pascagola . . . & lately destitute of funds & other succours." Under these conditions, he had hoped that "he could with honor present his sword to the U. States." Now, he declared, the situation had changed. "The insurgents were not formidable . . . & he had received from his government the relief he had so long expected." Besides, he continued, "the capture of Baton Rouge has produced a new order of things." When, on March 22, Mathews and McKee still had not heard from Isaac, they decided to contact Folch directly, requesting a personal interview. Again Folch refused, but Mathews was persistent. In April, he went to Pensacola, where he demanded a private conference, but Folch was as obdurate as before.[56]

Although Madison was disappointed that Spain continued to occupy Mobile and Pensacola, he was not distraught. Throughout the controversy, he feared the motives of England and France more than those of Spain, and he hoped to dislodge the dons before the British, or possibly the French, seized the Floridas. In early January 1811, Madison had prevailed upon Congress, in a secret session, to endorse the so-called No Transfer Resolution. The resolution declared that "the United States, under the peculiar circumstances of the existing crisis, cannot, without serious inquietude, see any part of the said [Spanish] territory pass into the hands of any foreign power."[57] His purpose was to send England a stern warning—stay out of Florida or else.

Nevertheless, Madison was cautious. He did not wish to invite British intervention by seizing Mobile. But once the United States had declared war against Great Britain in June 1812, he was more comfortable with unleashing the military although he failed to move with sufficient dispatch to please Claiborne. It was not until early spring of 1813 that newly appointed Secretary of War John Armstrong ordered General Wilkinson, only recently acquitted of treason by a military court-martial, to dispossess the Spaniards from Mobile. Two weeks later, Wilkinson left New Orleans with seven companies of infantry and one of artillery for the Pass of Christian, where he expected to find Commodore John Shaw with three gunboats. Not only were no boats in sight, but a mishap, during a severe gale, almost brought the general to "the unprofessional end of death by drowning instead of shooting."[58]

While waiting for Shaw, Wilkinson grew impatient. He sent some twenty men aboard a small vessel armed with a three-pounder to blockade the port of Mobile. At the same time, he ordered a detachment of four hundred troops from Fort Stoddert to take up position on the eastern bank of Mobile Bay, preventing the Spaniards from reinforcing Fort Charlotte and putting them in a hopeless predicament.

On April 13, 1813, the beleaguered Perez called a council of his officers. With only sixty dispirited and starving soldiers trapped in a dilapidated fort with only sixty pieces of artillery, several of which were painted logs, Perez had no choice except to surrender. On April 15, the Spaniards marched out of the fort and boarded American vessels for Pensacola. Later that same afternoon, the jubilant Americans celebrated with booming cannons as they watched the Stars and Bars hoisted over Fort Charlotte.[59]

Acting under an earlier law that had incorporated the coastal strip between the Pearl and the Perdido into Mississippi Territory, Holmes had already organized the region into Mobile County. Now the exuberant governor proceeded to Mobile, where he joined in the celebrations and appointed officials to govern the town. Heralding Mobile as another New Orleans, he hoped to prevent an outbreak of smuggling by setting up the appropriate judicial tribunals and appointing revenue officials. For the moment, he put Toulmin in charge of the federal courts. Apparently, the harassed judge had his sights on the governorship of the rumored "Territory of West Florida" or a judgeship in a newly created Federal Court for the District of Mobile.[60]

Meanwhile, Holmes had other problems to consider, but the one that caused the greatest anxiety was fear of an Indian uprising.

CHAPTER 15

The Creek War

While Spain continued to attract the territory's attention, its officials also began to take note of restlessness among the Indians, especially the Creek and Seminole.[1] Although relations between Natives and white intruders still appeared peaceful, there was reason to believe that the traditional conflict between a hunting culture and an agricultural society was about to escalate.

As the territory's population increased with the steady flux of immigrants, the Anglo population grew at a faster rate than that of the Natives. Because the federal government, as late as early 1808, had not begun selling public lands, a sizeable number of Anglos spilled into Chickasaw or Choctaw lands before new treaties were ratified or boundaries drawn. In response to Indian complaints, the federal government occasionally attempted halfheartedly to remove them.[2] Yet these efforts were rarely sufficient to satisfy aggrieved Indians, whose hunting grounds were being depleted of game, forcing them to hunt across the Mississippi River and be away for extended periods.[3]

The tensions manifested themselves in numerous ways. One was an increase in interruption of mail service between the nation's capital and Fort Stoddert or Natchez. In early 1811, Benjamin Hawkins reported that "the post rider from the west has arrived without the mail." It was, he lamented, "the third failure in succession." Young warriors in particular viewed post riders as harbingers of dreaded change, and they frequently displayed their apprehensions by harassing or killing mail carriers, touching off cycles of complaint and retaliation. In response, federal officials invariably instructed the resident Indian agent to investigate the circumstances and where appropriate to insist upon retribution, usually in the form of reduced tribal annuities. For more serious crimes, they demanded delivery of the accused or proof that chiefs had carried out appropriate tribal punishments.[4]

More serious were the conflagrations between frontier families and roving bands of Indians, which invariably led to cries for revenge. One occurred in the spring of 1808 along the Duck River, just north of the Tennessee River, where a band of angry Creeks, numbering several hundred, ambushed an isolated settlement, killing "three white families." Like other frontiersmen, Andrew Jackson blamed the British, conveniently overlooking the fact that the victims were squatters. "It appears," Jackson wrote, "that the Creeks who perpetuated this horrid massacree has been excited to this hellish act, by the instigation of white men agents under foreign influence, who have stimulated those barbarians to lift the scalping knife and Tomahawk against our defenceless women and Children."[5]

Later a party of Choctaws attacked white inhabitants in Wilkinson County. According to the complainants, the Choctaws committed "considerable mischief by burning houses and killing livestock." Upon examination, however, Choctaw agent Dinsmoor concluded that "the fault on both sides is so glaring that I am in hopes to hear no more of it," and General Wilkinson dismissed it as "a mere drunken frolic."[6]

Sale of illegal whiskey was a perennial problem. Occasionally, inebriated Indians, after purchasing spirits from unlicensed white traders, engaged in wanton destruction of property or inflicted bodily harm on innocent persons. This traffic was particularly prevalent along the rivers, especially at Chickasaw Bluffs, where Chickasaw agent James Neelly made repeated complaints to federal authorities. Choctaw chieftains were so incensed that they asked Dinsmoor to pay future annuities in goods instead of cash as a way of restricting the purchase of distilled spirits by their countrymen.[7] Apart from a poorly enforced licensing system designed to root out illegitimate traders, the federal government did little to stop the nefarious traffic.

Indians feared that Jefferson's belated decisions in late 1807 to ratify the Treaty of Mount Dexter and to renew negotiations with the Chickasaws were designed to populate the region with whites. They opened thousands of new acres, luring settlers and calling for improved communications with the nation's capital. The threat of war with England caused the War Department to join the postmaster general in clamoring for new roadways to connect the army's scattered posts throughout the South.[8]

Predictably, the Indians' reactions were mixed. They both appreciated and feared the military's presence. They applauded the army's efforts to remove intruders, but they recognized that soldiers were as likely to overawe as to protect them. The forts invariably attracted an ancillary population whose livestock scattered Native game, whose plows scarred the landscape, and whose merchants specialized in distilled spirits.[9]

The persistent presence of Spain in the Floridas and of Great Britain in Canada was another source of anxiety for white settlers. While federal officials regarded Spain a nuisance, they considered the British a formidable threat. Since the close of the American Revolution, Spanish officials had relied upon Indian friendship to preserve peace and prevent their North American possessions from falling into hostile hands. Spain's objective, despite the fears of American frontiersmen, was not to encourage the Indians to take the warpath but to retain their allegiance in case of trouble with England or the United States.[10]

Nevertheless, Spain understood that southern Indians acted in their own interest, taking advantage of animosities among neighboring European nations by playing one antagonist against another. Still, one important, if unintended, result of this strategy was a growing reliance upon the products and services of foreigners, which threatened to undercut Indian independence and undermine traditional values. Moreover, Jefferson's civilization program was beginning to show signs of success. "It is a pleasure," gloated Choctaw agent Dinsmoor, "to see with what success the fields are enlarged, the fences good, & the crops abundant." Hawkins also praised the progress of the Lower Creeks in embracing "civilization" even if he despaired of converting the more resistant Upper Creeks.[11] Unfortunately, this process was never fast enough to please impatient western settlers who coveted immediate possession of their lands. Intermarriage between Indian women and European men, mostly trappers, traders, and government agents, reinforced this trend, especially after a number of their progeny rose to positions of power and prestige among southern tribes. This transformation was especially prevalent among Lower Creeks and Cherokees, both of whom had a history of continuous contact with Europeans.[12]

Spanish borderland diplomacy depended upon regular exchanges of trade goods and generous gifts, articles that Spain was ill-prepared to furnish, and her officials had to rely upon Scottish and English traders for most of these provisions. Therefore, British involvement with the southern tribes did not cease in 1763 but persisted during the early 1800s as Spanish power waned in the Americas while that of Great Britain expanded.[13]

The lingering British presence in the region disturbed both federal officials and local settlers. Andrew Jackson was not the only southwesterner who saw their devious hand behind every Indian disturbance. He viewed with horror the likelihood that Great Britain might regain a foothold along the Gulf coast or entice Indians to raise their tomahawks against defenseless settlers. By late 1811, war between the United States and Great Britain seemed imminent, not so much because of conditions in the Southwest as because of England's disregard of America's neutral rights on the high seas and impressments of her sailors.[14]

By mid-November, when President Madison summoned Congress to an early session, the patience of some members, especially those from exposed frontier areas, appeared exhausted, and Mississippians applauded the emerging martial spirit. It was time, they believed, for America either to defend its honor or submit to foreign dictation. As one Mississippian declared, the British have left "us only to decide between base submission & manly resistance." Like other western congressmen, George Poindexter was fed up with Madison's reliance upon economic coercion as the best tactic for forcing the British to recognize America's right to trade freely with belligerents. He feared that "we shall have non intercourse until the nation will be overrun with old maids and witches." Later the fiery delegate declared that "we really do intend to pull John Bull by the nose . . . if [he] had rather be pulled by the nose than to open his ears and grant us our humble petition" for justice.[15]

Once Congress declared war in June 1812, Mississippians received the news "with great satisfaction from a thorough belief that no other course could have rescued the government from degradation." Throughout the territory, people gathered at public rallies to proclaim their approval. Nearly five hundred citizens of Wilkinson County "unanimously adopted with three cheers" a set of resolutions in support of Congress and Madison. "On this subject at least," they resolved, "we are all Federalists, all Republicans, all Americans." A few were willing to "disclaim" their exemption as a territory from "a direct tax" and to demand their "right to participate in the general burthens when our independence is effected."[16]

Similarly, citizens of the town of Washington voiced their approval. "Having exhausted the peaceful course of dignified remonstrance and having done all that justice could require," Madison and Congress had acted properly. They were "ultimately compelled to vindicate the rights essential to the sovereignty and Independence of our Country against the unjust pretenses and aggression of the British Government" by an appeal to arms. The townspeople promised "to act in unison with our worthy and sensible Executive Governor Holmes," and even praised the "patriotism of General James Wilkinson."[17]

No one was more eager to confront the British and their Spanish sycophants than Andrew Jackson. In fact, he was ready as early as the spring of 1812 to lead Tennesseans into battle against the Creeks. Once war was declared, Jackson volunteered to fight the British either in Canada or the Old Southwest. But federal officials, still remembering his connection with Burr, disregarded his overtures. Then, in October 1812, Secretary of War James Monroe instructed Governor Willie Blount of Tennessee to raise 1,500 volunteers and dispatch them to New Orleans to assist in the "defence of the lower country." Ignoring the administration's suspicion, Blount chose Jackson to command one of the state's two regiments.[18]

In late December, Jackson ordered his trusted friend Col. John Coffee to take a troop of four hundred cavalrymen down the Natchez Trace, while Jackson loaded the infantry on flatboats for descent to Natchez, where he planned to rendezvous with Coffee for a march to New Orleans. Unfortunately, the winter of 1812–1813 was one of the coldest on record, and the armada had difficulty navigating the ice-filled Cumberland and Ohio rivers. Nevertheless, on February 15, 1813, Jackson's troopers arrived safely but shivering at Natchez. There, to his surprise, he received three communiqués from General Wilkinson. Needless to say, Jackson and Wilkinson were not on the best of terms after the Tennessean testified against the general in the Burr trial. Neither was eager to cooperate with the other, and Jackson was suspicious when Wilkinson ordered him to remain in Natchez pending instructions.[19]

His final orders arrived on March 15, in a curt dispatch from incoming Secretary of War John Armstrong notifying Jackson that his troops

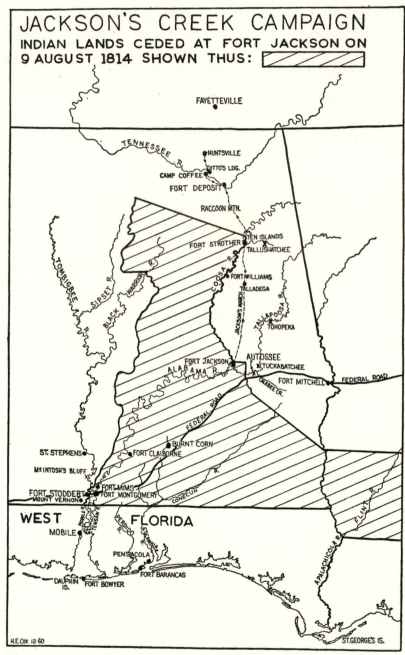

Map by Harold E. Cox (Thomas P. Abernethy, *The South in the New Nation, 1789–1819* [Baton Rouge, La., 1961]).

were not needed and instructing him to dismiss them. Jackson was livid. While Armstrong offered only vague reasons for his precipitous orders, Jackson had a ready answer. The culprits were that archtraitor Wilkinson and his spineless toady Armstrong. Left stranded in the midst of hostile Indian country and four hundred miles from home with insufficient clothing, food, and other supplies, and bereft of adequate arms, Jackson could not contain his rage.[20]

Yet he refused to abandon his soldiers in Mississippi Territory, where they might fall prey to Wilkinson's recruiters; instead he led them back to Tennessee. Both decisive in his demeanor and protective of the men's welfare, Jackson seemed as tough as hickory wood, and the troops affectionately bestowed upon him the lasting sobriquet of "Old Hickory." Despite the adversities, his men were home by mid-April, grateful to be there but bitter over their treatment.[21]

During the war's early stages, the Old Southwest was the scene of little military action. The federal government concentrated its forces along the northern frontier in a vain hope of dislodging the British from the Great Lakes and seizing Canada in order to ransom it in exchange for recognition of American maritime rights. Another reason was to prevent the British from enticing the Indians northwest of the Ohio River into a defensive alliance or from encouraging them to forge a formidable Indian confederation under the leadership of the Shawnee Prophet (Tenskwatawa) and his charismatic brother Tecumseh. These two Indian leaders, one spiritual and the other political, were convinced that the Indians could preserve their heritage only by unifying and resisting further white encroachments on their ancestral lands and the attempt to "civilize" them. They drew upon a long tradition of nativism, dating to Pontiac and Neolin.[22]

By 1811, Tecumseh had solidified most of the northwestern tribes into a confederation dedicated to a policy of white containment and restoration of a traditional lifestyle. He challenged them to give up whiskey, return to worshiping their ancient gods and spirits, and reject the white man's civilization of plow agriculture and household manufacture. By late summer, Tecumseh was ready to carry his crusade into the South, where he expected to find a receptive audience.

On August 4, after an inconclusive meeting with Governor William Henry Harrison of Indiana Territory, Tecumseh left Vincennes, accompanied by Seekaboo, a Shawnee prophet, and some twenty warriors. After passing through Kentucky and Tennessee, the party reached Chickasaw country, where Tecumseh expected to spread his message of distrust for the white man's plan of civilization and of his land-grabbing practices. "The white race is a wicked race," he declared, in one of his favorite orations. "Since the day when the white race had first come in contact with the red men, there had been a continual series of aggressions." The Shawnees have already been driven "farther and farther to the west," and the same fate, he predicted, would befall the southern tribes unless "the power of the whites was forever crushed."[23]

Tecumseh and his party first met with a delegation of prominent Chickasaw chieftains led by George Colbert. Although they treated the Shawnee party with respect, they were not swayed by Tecumseh's eloquence or imposing presence. Following the lead of Colbert and other mixed-blood chiefs, the Chickasaws rejected Tecumseh's invitation to join his coalition. Historically, they had regarded the northern tribes as enemies, and they were hardly prepared to cooperate with them in a movement fraught with danger and likely to divide them. Since Colbert had personally profited from his association with neighboring whites, he did not wish to jeopardize the advantages he had forged.[24]

Next, Tecumseh journeyed to Choctaw country, where he spent several weeks going from town to town promoting his pan-Indian crusade. There too he encountered an entrenched set of powerful mingoes (Pushmataha, Puckshenubbee, and Mushulatubbee) who were both pro-American and highly acculturated. Pushmataha and Mushulatubbee were fearful of losing their influence if the Choctaws joined the pan-Indian movement. By this time, Pushmataha and the other medal mingoes had secured control of the allocation of annuities granted the Choctaw for their land cessions, and they wanted no outside interference to threaten their hegemony.

The three medal chiefs employed their considerable influence to persuade the Choctaws to reject Tecumseh's overtures, although they were unable to prevent a few dissidents from later joining the Creek war party. Of the Five Civilized Tribes, Choctaws were the most pro-American and anti-British. Pushmataha proudly boasted that they "had never shed the blood of white men in battle," and he saw no reason to anger them now. War, he prophesied, "would end in the ruin of their nation." Weary of the Shawnee's prolonged presence, the three mingoes warned Tecumseh that "if he did not leave the country they would put him to death." To ensure a safe and expeditious departure, they instructed David Folsom, a mixed-blood and district chieftain, to escort the visitors across the Tombigbee River.[25]

Tecumseh had more success with the Creeks. There he discovered a people undergoing change and divided over how to react to threats from within the nation as well as without. For years, Creeks had faced relentless pressure from Georgians to cede their remaining lands within that state. Little by little, the Creeks had given in to these demands. In 1805, they agreed to the Ocmulgee River as the boundary between themselves and Georgia, leaving them with only the southwest corner of that state. They also permitted the United States to mark a horse path through their territory and to set up places of accommodations. Although a few prominent Creeks benefitted financially from operating stands and ferries along the route, younger Creeks resented the concessions. Roads invariably brought in new settlers, many of whom squatted on Indian lands and grazed their cattle on Indian soil, destroying vegetation and chasing out game. Newly opened roads also attracted drifters and marauders, who stole Native property, and whiskey dealers, whose intoxicating products debauched the young.[26]

By late 1810, some of these predicted developments were beginning to occur, much to the distress of young Creek warriors. The road to Fort Stoddert introduced a host of settlers trudging through the Indians' homelands, bringing whiskey to corrupt the Natives and livestock to trample down their cornfields. Then, in the summer of 1811, as relations with Great Britain deteriorated, the federal government planned to erect additional roads and clear the Coosa and Alabama rivers of all impediments in an effort to facilitate communications and to bypass Spanish interference with trade through Mobile. Horse paths, suitable only for post riders and travelers, would no longer suffice; the government needed military highways.[27]

One of the projects, "a waggon road" from Tennessee to Tombigbee, was particularly troublesome to Upper Creeks since it would bisect their territory. Afraid the new pathways would lead to altercations similar to those that had occurred along the Federal Road, several chiefs, led by the indomitable Tallassee King (Hopohielthle Micco), raised strong objections. They were especially worried about reactions of "young people," who, they feared, would proclaim that "the old people are crazy" and afraid to "protect our rights." These improvements, the Tallassee

King predicted, "would bring trouble on our country." But, according to Hawkins, the reason for Creek resistance was that the chiefs could not "restrain their young men from committing depredations on the property" or stop them from buying whiskey. Nevertheless, by the fall of 1811, the War Department had determined, with or without Creek approval, to construct the new roads and to improve navigation on the Coosa, and it fell to Hawkins either to secure their approval or to inform them of the government's decision.[28]

Long before 1810, Benjamin Hawkins had become a dominant force among the Creek Indians. Appointed special agent to the southern Indians in 1796, he had devoted his public career to defending the Creeks and promoting their cause, setting up his agency along the Flint River in order to reside among them. In an effort to enhance his influence, he encouraged them to consolidate authority in the hands of the National Council, which met twice a year, once each at Tuckabatchee and Coweta. Hawkins hoped to enlarge his own authority by decreasing that of the local towns and to promote the federal government's agenda of keeping the peace, acquiring additional Indian lands, and civilizing the Creeks. By 1810, Hawkins believed he was on the way to achieving these objectives.

Hawkins spent most of his time promoting the government's "plan of Civilization," a policy that he embraced wholeheartedly and soon became "his hobby horse."[29] He converted the Creek Agency into a model farm to demonstrate the advantages of scientific horticulture and herding over hunting and gathering and to extol the benefits of a sedentary over a migratory lifestyle. To accomplish these objectives, Hawkins thought it necessary to reform Creek government by modeling it after that of the United States. Favoring a government that was both centralized and representative, he persuaded the chiefs to establish an executive committee with authority to take action between meetings of the National Council.

At the opening of each council, Hawkins delivered a "state of the Nation" address in which he promoted his plan for civilizing the Creeks by distributing farm implements and household manufactures. He also prevailed upon the council to adopt a legal system that transferred law enforcement from the local clans to a group of trusted "law menders," specifically charged with promoting justice and punishing the guilty. This new system, designed as a convenient means of preventing clan vengeance, constituted a radical departure from traditional ways of enforcing order by introducing the concept of individual guilt for crimes and by depriving clan kinships of the right to defend relatives.[30]

Nevertheless, Hawkins's reforms failed to win universal approval. While Lower Creeks generally supported them, Upper Creeks were more resistant. In fact, Hawkins's efforts exacerbated existing division between the Upper and Lower Creeks and created new schisms in the Upper Creek towns. The latter split was more along generational lines than blood ties since mixed-bloods were in both factions, even though they were more likely to oppose than applaud Hawkins's efforts.

Furthermore, personalities and tribal affiliations played key roles. Hawkins enjoyed the firm allegiance of William McIntosh, Bird-Tail King, and Little Prince, all Lower Creeks, but attracted only intermittent and grudging support from Big Warrior, who recently had replaced Mad Dog as leader of the Upper Creeks. Hawkins found Big Warrior excessively avaricious, thirsty for power, and untrustworthy. Although discontent with Hawkins's policies was widespread, it was strongest among the two least-acculturated Creek tribes (Alabama and Kossatis), who considered his civilizing plans disastrous.[31]

Upper Creeks also questioned Hawkins's motives. Few believed he acted in their best interests, and they especially distrusted the mixed-bloods who seemingly followed his advice blindly. In exaggerating his influence among the Creeks, Hawkins relied too heavily upon the goodwill of the "so-called medal chiefs," who personally benefited from his friendship. Several Creeks resented the fact that the federal government showed favoritism by singling out certain chiefs for special favor. By 1811, these divisions, especially those among Upper Creeks, were rapidly solidifying, setting the stage for an outbreak of civil strife between those friendly to the United States and those who resented the white man's interference in their affairs.[32]

It was in this unsettling atmosphere that Tecumseh made his dramatic appearance at the Creek National Council at Tuckabatchee in late September of 1811. News of his coming attracted a large throng of nearly five thousand participants including a few Choctaw and Cherokee. Hawkins was also in attendance, prepared to deliver his customary address to the nation.

The Shawnee visitor was an imposing figure. According to the legendary Indian fighter Sam Dale, Tecumseh was "about six feet high, well put together, not as stout as some of his followers, but of an austere coun-tenance and imperial mien." Dressed in buckskin shorts and leggings adorned with silver ornaments, Tecumseh had painted his face with red and black markings below the eyes. A retinue of similarly dressed north-ern disciples and a handful of converts from the southern tribes accom-panied him into the town square.[33]

Although Tecumseh, who supposedly came south at the invita-tion of Big Warrior, had promised to address the assembled crowd, he waited until Hawkins left. Satisfied that the Creeks intended to remain peaceful and loyal, Hawkins quietly slipped out, but not before instruct-ing his Creek allies to keep a close eye on the enigmatic guest. But Hawkins dismissed Dale's dire warning that "the Shawnee intended mis-chief," assuring his friend that "the Creeks were entirely under his con-trol." Tecumseh's visit, he pronounced, was simply "one of show and ceremony."[34]

After Hawkins's departure, Tecumseh delivered his long-anticipated address. First he sought to shame his listeners into altering their behav-ior. They had, he proclaimed, deserted the ways of their ancestors and had unwittingly become like the white man. "Your tomahawks have no edge; your bows and arrow were buried with your fathers." He called them to repent and forsake the white man's culture. "Let the white race perish!" he shouted. "They seize your land; they corrupt your women; they trample on the bones of your dead!" Drive them back, he thun-dered, "into the great water whose accursed waves brought them to our shores!" Nonetheless, he advised them to be patient and await the proper time to avenge these injustices.[35]

Tecumseh's message was simple and straightforward. Only by return-ing to the ways of their fathers could the Indian nations successfully preserve their culture and stop the steady encroachment of whites on ancestral lands. Southern and northern tribes must band together or per-ish separately. Tecumseh realized that warfare between the United States and England was probable, if not inevitable, and that Indian successes were more likely to occur during times of trouble than periods of peace. By uniting against the "Long Knives," the Indians, he assured his listen-ers, could rely upon Great Britain and possibly Spain to supply them with those essentials for survival. Finally, he advised the Creeks to resist further land cessions and ostracize those chiefs seduced by Americans.

While Tecumseh emphasized political unity and tribal solidarity, others in his entourage preached repentance and regeneration. Foremost among them was Seekaboo, who, because of his keen knowledge of Indian dialects, had accompanied Tecumseh as interpreter. The mysterious Seekaboo was a holy man who had fallen under the intoxicating spell of Tecumseh's brother, Tenskwatawa (the Prophet). Seekaboo successfully proselytized a number of mixed-bloods whose fathers had been Tory sympathizers and who continued to harbor resentment against the Americans for their treatment during the Revolution.

One of Seekaboo's disciples was Josiah Francis of Autauga. A trader like his father, Peter, Josiah was deeply in debt to John Forbes & Company, and he, together with a number of other debtors, blamed the Scottish company for manipulating the Indians into selling their lands. Francis found Seekaboo's message so compelling that he in turn prevailed upon other Upper Creeks to become "subordinate prophets." His converts included such influential persons as High-Head Jim (Jim Boy), Paddy Welch, and Peter McQueen, all of whom were soon to replace the older, pro-American headmen. They directed most of their hostility at Big Warrior, who had profited from monopolizing the public stands along the new Federal Road, and they blamed him for letting the white man corrupt Indian society. They also denounced Hawkins's civilization program and accused Big Warrior of cooperating with him. Shortly afterward, most of the prophets transferred their allegiance from Big Warrior to the aged Tallassee King.[36]

Nevertheless, Tecumseh's influence, even among the young warriors, was never decisive. Only the Upper Creeks showed much interest. He and Seekaboo had merely intensified an already smoldering resentment of Hawkins's faltering program of civilizing the Indians. When Tecumseh, accompanied by some thirty warriors, including a handful of Creek converts, finally departed in December 1811, he left Seekaboo behind to complete the business of conversion. Except for Upper Creeks, the southern tribes had rejected his schemes for Indian unity, and even some Creeks remained aloof. Big Warrior and Samuel Moniac were unreceptive, and William Weatherford (Red Eagle) characterized Tecumseh's message as ill-advised. The Creeks, Weatherford declared, must not become involved in the white man's wars; the best course was to remain neutral. On the other hand, Big Warrior was more bewildered by than opposed to Tecumseh's proposals, and several thought Tecumseh either crazy or a clever trickster. In the final analysis, internal dissensions, not Tecumseh or the exhortations of Seekaboo, would be responsible for the Creek Civil War.[37]

To be sure, the causes were numerous and elusive. Disagreement over Hawkins's plans for civilizing the nation, repeated white encroachments upon Creek lands, opposition to the building of roads and the clearing of streams through their nation, the rise of the prophets to positions of prominence, especially among the young warriors, as well as the traditional divisions between Upper and Lower Creeks were all important factors. Most humiliating of all was the National Council's decision to punish those tribesmen responsible for killing innocent whites.

The use of Creek "law menders" to track down individual offenders of the white man's law especially infuriated a rising faction of Creek militants, dubbed "Red Sticks" by the Americans. In contrast, white violations of Indians went largely unpunished. Nevertheless a wishful-thinking Hawkins boasted that his civilizing policies were making steady progress. In early February 1812, he reported that many of "our Indians are . . . occupied in spinning, weaving, making new settlements or improving those heretofore made." He estimated that "nine-tenths of the lower Creeks have left their old towns and . . . are forming settlements on the creeks and rivers where the lands are good and the range for stock good."[38]

During the spring of 1812, a series of routine and unrelated incidents took place in the Old Southwest. Unfortunately, in the suspicious atmosphere of that time, whites viewed them as ghastly affairs requiring immediate retribution. In March, several drunken Autossees shot and killed Thomas Meredith, whom Hawkins characterized as "a respectable old man," on the post road near Sam Moniac's place of entertainment, some 150 miles from the Creek Agency. The half-breed Moniac called it "an accident," but Meredith's son, an eyewitness, and Hawkins labeled it murder. Hawkins called upon Big Warrior to uncover the culprits and exact justice for the "outrage." The obliging and pro-American chiefs dutifully complied, and a pleased Hawkins, in late June, informed the war department "that the Indian who murdered Meredith was put to death on the 19th."[39]

Two months later, Alexander Cornells, interpreter for the Creeks, informed Hawkins that four Indians, "without the least provocation," had murdered Arthur Lott. This time the jittery chiefs acted promptly, since Lott was a friend. They executed the four men responsible, an obsequious gesture that angered the Creek militants.[40] The executions stimulated Josiah Francis and the Creek prophets, or medicine men, to seek additional converts. They promised to call upon the Great Spirit to shield the Creeks from further harm. In particular, they insisted, the Spirit would protect them from white bullets and render their enemies harmless. They began to perform the "Dance of the Lakes," which Tecumseh had taught them, and to threaten the unconverted with death and destruction from angry spirits. They climaxed these ceremonies with convulsions. On one occasion, Sam Moniac encountered some Indians camped near his home on the Federal Road. A member of the party, whom he recognized as "High-Headed Jim," or Jim Boy, came up to him and shook hands. Then suddenly, Moniac reported, he "began to tremble and jerk in every part of his frame, and the very calves of his legs would be convulsed, and he would get entirely out of breath with the agitation."[41]

The prophets' warning of impending doom seemed confirmed when a series of earthquakes, beginning in December 1811, rocked the region. Although the epicenter was miles away, people felt the tremors in distant Charleston, South Carolina. During the quakes, several Creeks recalled Tecumseh's forewarning to Big Warrior. Upon returning to Detroit, he promised, he would stamp his foot so hard that "the very earth shall shake." As one Creek supposedly declared, Tecumseh must have reached home.[42]

On May 12, another inflammatory incident occurred along the Duck River in Tennessee. A band of eleven Creeks from the village of Hillaubee, acting upon a false rumor that some whites had killed an Indian woman, fell upon the unsuspecting Crawley family. The vengeful Indians first attacked the children while they were playing in the yard. Martha Crawley hid herself and two of her four children "in a potato cellar under the floor." Before the Indians spotted them, they had slaughtered two of Martha's children and three of a visiting neighbor woman's, together with a male boarder. They then took Martha, wife of John Crawley, a river boatman who was away on business, hostage and forced her to march long distances on foot through thick brush and prickly briars and to cook for them on their return home. According to Mrs. Crawley, her captors "offered no further violence."[43]

Shortly thereafter, George S. Gaines, Choctaw factor and Indian trader, learned from Tandy Walker, a former government blacksmith living among the Creeks, of Mrs. Crawley's capture. At the urging of Mrs. Gaines, Walker visited the Hillaubees and secured her release. Although she was "in bad health, and her mind a good deal impaired" and her "limbs and feet . . . still in a wounded condition," she soon recovered. Several months later, the Gaineses arranged for her return to Tennessee, where "she was delighted to find her husband and the two children she had hid in the potato cellar, alive."[44]

This unusually brutal incident aroused the anger of white citizens in Tennessee and Mississippi Territory. Andrew Jackson was one of those whose anger boiled over into vengeance. Always ready to defend the helpless (women and children) and to denounce bloodthirsty Indians and brutal British, Jackson bristled at the atrocities. "My heart bleeds," he proclaimed, at "the news of the horrid cruelty and murders committed by a party of Creeks, on our innocent wives and little babes." The perpetrators, he roared, "must be punished — and our frontier protected." He chastised George Colbert for allowing the Creeks to pass through the Chickasaw Nation "carrying along with them stolen horses, scalps, and a white woman prisoner," and sent a stern warning to the Creeks. If they refused to punish the murderers, Jackson threatened, "the whole creek nation shall be covered with blood, fire shall consume their Towns and villages, and their lands shall be divided among the whites." He challenged Colbert to prove his friendship by sending him "the names of the creeks who have killed our women and children."[45] Despite Jackson's call to arms, the War Department, still suspicious of Jackson's motives, failed to take action.

White settlers in Tombigbee District were equally alarmed. As early as March 1812, rumors circulated of a proposed attack by hostile Creeks against white settlers on the forks of the Tombigbee and Alabama rivers. Col. James Caller, who detested Indians as much as Jackson, instantly sent spies to ascertain the truth of these reports. Then, without waiting for a response, he asked Capt. Edmund P. Gaines to supply him with "all the ammunition and arms [stored] at the Choctaw factory." He also alerted Maj. John Bowyer, commander of Fort Stoddert, "of the dangers of the country" and placed the militia on alert. Judge Harry Toulmin, whose suspicions of Caller were boundless, insisted that the militia colonel had "greatly magnified" the danger. Yet, even Toulmin refused to discount the possibility "that a troublesome chief called cap[tai]n Isaac may be brewing mischief."[46]

Upon ascertaining that the rumors were grossly exaggerated, Toul-min accused Caller and his fellow firebrands of deliberately inciting peaceful Creeks. "At least," he concluded, they have "acted as if they were anxious to bring on an indian war." He feared lest they "thwart the efforts of Col. Hawkins" to civilize the Creeks and "render success-ful the attempts of the Spaniards to enlist the Creek nation in their ser-vices." He also berated Caller for mustering two militia companies "on a groundless, idle rumour" and for dispatching "a party of rangers" with the "avowed design" of killing innocent Indians. They, he asserted, "had wantonly & without provocation fired upon" a party of Indians, and "some peaceable Choctaws were almost beaten to death in Washington County." While acknowledging that a "vigorous system of preparation" was essential, Toulmin wanted it "under the guidance not of fanatics but of men of intelligence, moderation, and courage."

Hawkins also urged caution. He blamed the British for deliber-ately provoking the Lower Creeks, who, he insisted, had promised to remain neutral. But when civil strife broke out, Hawkins stepped up efforts to bring the guilty to justice. By August, he reported that the loyal chiefs had executed six of the supposed murderers and had cropped and whipped seven others for stealing, all of whom were members of the faction opposing Hawkins's civilizing program. The chiefs also agreed, under pressure, to reduce their annuities by nine hundred dollars as compensation for damages inflicted on innocent white settlers.[47]

Despite this display of good faith by loyal Creeks, Caller and Col. Joseph Carson were not impressed. They considered Hawkins too indul-gent toward his "Creek children" and too dependent on transforming Indian society. In their minds, he himself was a victim of Creek duplic-ity. Tennessee governor Blount was also skeptical of what he incoher-ently described as Hawkins's "round about ways of giving satisfaction."[48]

The long-postponed civil war between Creek factions finally erupted in the spring of 1813. Several Creek, led by Little Warrior, were returning home from an extended visit with the northern Shawnee. While passing through Chickasaw country, they mistakenly heard that war had erupted with the United States, and they promptly slaughtered seven white fami-lies near the mouth of Ohio River. Based upon a "garbled report" from James Robertson, the recently appointed Chickasaw agent, Hawkins was outraged. Robertson described the victims' bodies as "most cruelly man-gled, showing all the savage barbarity that could be invented." Sensing that his reputation was at stake, Hawkins acted with uncharacteristic haste. He instructed Big Warrior to punish those responsible and to prevent any further depredations against defenseless white settlers. These atrocities, he insisted, were not "done by thoughtless, wild young people," but were deliberately committed "by a party under the command of two chiefs."[49]

Hawkins was both pleased and disturbed by the Indians' response. "The chiefs are more alarmed than I have ever known them to be before," he informed the secretary of war. Recognizing the need to regain control of Creek affairs and to retain Hawkins's confidence, the complaisant chiefs sent a party, led by William McIntosh, to carry out the death penalty imposed upon Little Warrior and his seven companions. Armed and defiant, the war party refused to surrender; instead the culprits took refuge at Hickory Ground, a holy place, where the Creek law menders, finding them holed up in a house, executed their bloody assignment. Shortly thereafter, a satisfied Hawkins reassured the War Department. "I think," he reported, "it will put an end to all cause of alarm in the agency."[50]

Instead of restoring stability, as Hawkins predicted, these developments provoked Josiah Francis and a number of other Creek prophets into open defiance of the obsequious chiefs. By this time, the headmen of the Upper Creeks had lost touch with their constituents and were totally responsive to the dictates of Hawkins. The prophets, sensing a growing spirit of alienation, persuaded the Upper Creeks to transfer their allegiance from Big Warrior and "his court-house gang" to them.

They also instigated a program of revenge against those responsible for the executions, calling for eradication of every vestige of the hated white civilization, including the slaughtering of livestock, the burning of agricultural fields, and the destruction of those villages loyal to Hawkins. They declared personal vendettas against Hawkins, McIntosh, Alexander Cornells, and Big Warrior and ordered Tuckabatchee, the seat of government and stronghold of the peace party, destroyed. By this time, more than half the Upper Creeks had joined the reform faction. Big Warrior, surrounded by enemies and short of allies and ammunition, sent Cornells to seek reinforcements from the Lower Creeks. Although Hawkins dispatched enough warriors to lift the siege of Tuckabatchee and to rescue the beleaguered loyalists, he conceded that the Creek Nation was hopelessly fractured. Still he tried to scold the medal chiefs into remaining loyal, warning them of the dangers that would befall the nation if they joined the prophets.[51]

Just as the peace party turned to Hawkins for assistance, the war party, the Red Sticks, sought the aid of Spanish officials in Pensacola. Without adequate arms and ammunition, two of the white man's articles they refused to scorn, the militant prophets sent a sizeable force, variously estimated at one hundred and three hundred warriors, to Pensacola. They came armed with a letter from a British official in Canada, which Little Warrior, before his assassination, had given to High-Head Jim. It supposedly included a promise that Spanish officials would supply them with ammunition.[52]

En route to Pensacola, this party, led by Peter McQueen and High-Head Jim, plundered the property of James Cornells, a half-blood who opposed the prophets, severely beat a black servant, abducted a male boarder, and seized Cornells's wife, whom they later sold into slavery in exchange "for a blanket." After burning the houses of Sam Moniac and Leonard McGee, they carried off a "large quantity" of cattle and several slaves.[53]

Upon reaching Pensacola, they encountered unexpected difficulty. Governor Mateo Gonzalez Manrique refused to supply the Creeks with shot and powder, insisting that the British dispatch was a letter of introduction, not a pledge of support. McQueen was furious. He accused the governor of having two tongues and behaving like Americans. The enraged tribesmen then approached John Innerarity, brother of James and a merchant of John Forbes & Company whom High-Head Jim earlier had tried to intimidate by lapsing into one of his infamous convulsions. To get rid of the pesky guests, Innerarity offered them some trifling gifts, which the infuriated Indians either tossed in the air or trampled underfoot.

Eventually, the harassed governor sent them away with a thousand pounds of powder and an equal amount of shot. Far from satisfied, the Indians left in a huff. On the return journey, the convoy of some hundred packhorses, loaded down with ammunition and other supplies, reached Burnt Corn Creek, a few miles north of Mobile, on July 27, 1813. There, McQueen's warriors stopped to prepare their noon meal.[54]

News of McQueen's visit to Pensacola had traveled rapidly. James Cornells, upon returning home to find his property destroyed and his wife missing, assembled a force of mixed-bloods and whites, who went in search of his spouse and her abductors. Although preoccupied at the time with the acquisition and governance of Mobile, Governor David Holmes, based upon a plethora of reports and depositions, also believed that "the Creek Indians are now engaged in active hostilities against the United States." Persuaded that the war party had "gain[ed] the ascendency," he ordered "into service six companies of infantry and two troops of cavalry to aid the regular forces to protect the inhabitants of the Eastern frontier of our Territory." If, as he believed, the British government was ready "to assist the indians through Pensacola with arms, ammunition, and men, we shall have to receive aid from the State of Tennessee."[55]

Even Judge Toulmin, who earlier had discounted reports of imminent danger as "greatly magnified," joined the outcry. By midsummer of 1813, he was imploring Governor Blount to send the Tennessee militia to their rescue. "Much consternation prevails here," he reported; "the people are building forts in every direction." He estimated that there were only "10,000 inhabitants of all ages and colors" scattered over some "150 square miles" east of Pearl River. "Our population cannot defend itself," he declared. Like Holmes, he blamed the British for stirring up the Indians and the Spaniards for arming them. "I regard it," he concluded, "as a ramification of the war with England."[56]

Later, Toulmin also denounced the Spaniards. "What shall we say about the Spaniards? Is it safe to have such a Neighbor?" he queried, answering the question as he posed it. "It is true," he concluded, "that the possession of the country [Florida] should be in the hands of a nation capable of maintaining its own rights and exercising its own will." On the other hand, he reminded his countrymen "to draw a line of discrimination between the hostile and friendly parts of the [Creek] nation." Agent Gaines painted an equally dismal picture. "The settlements on the Mobile and Tombigbee," he informed Governor Blount, "have lately been thrown into the greatest alarm and confusion. . . . Our whole settlement," he continued, "will be broken up without timely aid from your state."[57]

At the moment that Holmes and others were venting their anger, hostilities had already erupted, and the aggressors were not Indians but whites. To be sure, white settlers were in an uproar; families in exposed settlements were abandoning their homes and taking refuge in one of several hastily built stockades or hiding in nearby swamps and canebrakes. "The people," Toulmin reported on July 23, "have been fleeing all night." Based on the report of two spies (David Tate and William Pierce) sent to Pensacola, James Caller collected a force of volunteers sufficient to intercept the Indians on their return.[58] Consisting of some 180 men, well mounted, colorfully clad, and diversely armed, but ill-disciplined and led by inexperienced officers, Caller's vigilantes resembled a crazed mob rather than a disciplined corps. Early on the morning of July 27, a scouting party spotted McQueen and his warriors encamped along Burnt Corn Creek.

Caller opted for immediate assault. Leaving their horses behind, the militiamen began to discharge their weapons wildly and to run headlong toward the startled Indians, who hastily grabbed their rifles and returned the fire for several minutes before disappearing into a nearby "thick bushy swamp," leaving behind several packhorses laden with powder and other provisions. While a few whites pursued the scampering Indians across a narrow stream, the rest began to either collect the booty or flee the scene. According to Toulmin, "more than two-thirds of them retreated almost at the first fire" and never "discharged a gun." Others, he reported, held their ground and fought bravely.[59]

Once the Red Sticks realized that the enemy was more interested in plunder than fighting, they circled back and charged their assailants, who scattered in all directions, mostly on foot since, in the ensuing confusion, only a handful could locate their mounts. It took days for some to find their way home. In the aftermath, the countryside was left deserted and defenseless. Frightened officials removed the public records from St. Stephens for fear that "a party of disaffected Choctaw, east of the Tombigbee," might join the "hostile Creeks" in ravaging the region. Toulmin was not alone in feeling the bitter pangs of disgrace. "I fear," he lamented, "that the indians will be elated by the character of this conflict and exasperated by its issue." Still, he reasoned, "they will regret the loss of their powder," estimated at "about 300 pounds." A few participants had to endure public censure for their behavior. For example, Caller, who belatedly returned alone, wearing "nothing but his shirt and drawers," became the object of ridicule by his neighbors while citizens of Washington County censured him for acting hastily and foolishly.[60]

Nevertheless, this skirmish changed the nature of the conflict. It redirected public attention from an intratribal conflict to a war of retaliation against whites and disloyal mixed-bloods.[61] Thrown on the defensive, the white settlers braced for the next assault, and they did not have to wait long. On August 30, 1813, the Red Sticks attacked Fort Mims in retaliation for Burnt Corn.

Located on the east side of the Alabama River, two miles below the "Cut Off," Fort Mims was one of twenty or so stockades erected in anticipation of a full-scale Indian uprising, and there an assortment of white settlers sought refuge. Situated in the heart of the Tensaw District, Fort Mims was a square-shaped structure, encompassing an acre of land adjacent to the residence of Samuel Mims, a mixed-blood and respected settler. It also contained a blockhouse, tents for the soldiers, and a number of small cabins erected to accommodate fleeing settlers. Because Fort Mims was the territory's most formidable fortification, some 250 to 300 whites and a few loyal Creek, took refuge there.[62]

Meanwhile, Governor Holmes, putting aside fears of a Choctaw uprising, had dispatched six companies of infantry and two troops of cavalry under Brigadier General Claiborne to protect the threatened settlements. By late July, they had reached Mount Vernon, some forty miles northwest of Mobile, where Claiborne scattered his men among the hastily erected forts. He sent the largest contingent, under Maj. Daniel Beasley, to Fort Mims. Unfortunately, Beasley, an attorney from Jefferson County, was without military experience, addicted to strong drink, extremely bullheaded, and a lax disciplinarian. On August 7, Claiborne had visited the fort and urged Beasley to shore up its defenses and to exercise caution. Although Beasley later assured Claiborne that he had taken the necessary precautions, he misspoke.[63]

Even worse, he repeatedly ignored warnings that hostile Indians were in the vicinity, poised to strike the overcrowded fortification. Sure that the reports were either figments of imagination on the part of scared settlers or the work of mischievous slaves, Beasley not only ignored them, but he also whipped one of two black informants for frightening the refugees. Early on the morning of the attack, when James Cornells reported seeing a large number of Indians in war paint lurking around the fort, Beasley ordered him arrested. Immediately, an incredulous Cornells galloped off, urging others to accompany him, but none did. Instead, Beasley reassured them that the Creeks never attacked a well-fortified stockade.[64]

Cornells's information was accurate. On Monday morning, August 30, 1813, some seven hundred to one thousand well-armed warriors converged on Fort Mims. They were led by Peter McQueen, Josiah Francis, and a frightened and reluctant William Weatherford, or Red Eagle. Apparently, several militant Creeks had threatened harm to Weatherford's family unless he led the assault. Once committed, even if under duress, he drafted an effective battle plan. From intelligence furnished him by a handful of slaves, Weatherford learned that Beasley had left the east gate ajar to provide easy entry and exit. Ironically, Weatherford launched the attack at noon, while the soldiers were consuming their midday meal, a maneuver that pleased those who had been ambushed at Burnt Corn Creek.

The Red Sticks executed Weatherford's plan to perfection. Waiting patiently for the appointed hour, they leaped from hiding places behind brush and concealed ravines, sounding the war whoop as they rushed the east gate. Beasley, who, according to Cornells was intoxicated, grabbed his sword and hurried to the gate, but he could not dislodge the mass of sand that had accumulated around it. Instantly, the enemy was upon him, and he was the first to die. The attackers came in huge numbers, indiscriminately killing everyone, including women and children, much to the anguish of Weatherford, who begged them to spare the noncombatants. The whites fought valiantly as long as possible, yet all but a handful suffered a horrendous death—several were burned, others tomahawked, and a few scalped. The slaughtering continued until late afternoon. By then, few defenders were alive, and they soon perished with the others.[65]

The death toll was staggering. On September 9, General Claiborne sent a small detail under Maj. Joseph P. Kennedy to bury the dead, but most of the corpses had been mangled beyond recognition by preying buzzards and ferocious dogs. Kennedy counted the bodies of 247 of the fort's inmates and more than 100 Red Sticks. In the confusion of battle, between twenty to forty of the fort's residents managed to escape, most of whom made their way to Mount Vernon. Among the survivors were all members of the Mims family, except Samuel, and a few soldiers.[66]

News of the "massacre" spread like wildfire. Governor Holmes was especially distraught. Since the outbreak of war with England, he had tried, with meager success, to organize the territorial militia. The first call for troops came in late summer of 1812 in response to an anticipated attack on Mobile and Pensacola that never materialized due to congressional restraint. Instead, General Wilkinson quietly occupied Mobile without bloodshed, and, to the distress of General Claiborne, the enlistments of the Mississippi militia expired. Most of the men, together with Claiborne, signed up with the volunteer corps assembling at Baton Rouge.[67]

Shortly thereafter, the War Department dispatched the controversial Wilkinson to the Canadian frontier, and named Maj. Gen. Thomas Flournoy, an attorney from Georgia with little military experience, to replace him as commander of the Seventh Military District. Cautious and indecisive, Flournoy was a poor choice. Based upon Hawkins's optimistic reports, he allowed the Creek Civil War to continue unabated. "They must finish their civil war," he wrote, "before they can go to war with us." According to him, his orders were to defend Mobile against attack by Spain or Great Britain, and he focused his energy there.[68]

Nevertheless, in late June, Flournoy permitted General Claiborne to march toward Fort Stoddert with six hundred militia. Heavy rains and swollen rivers delayed his arrival until July 30, when he set up camp at Mount Vernon, some forty miles above Mobile. Ordered "to repel any attack that may be made on any part of the frontier of the Mississippi Territory," he was not to undertake offensive operations. "The defence of the Town of Mobile will be our principal care," Flournoy explained. Upon arrival at Mount Vernon, Claiborne was dismayed to find the citizens in an uproar and the countryside nearly abandoned.

In response, Governor Holmes asked Flournoy for immediate assistance. "Our militia," he explained, "are not well armed" and depleted by so many of the discharged men having enlisted in "the volunteer corps." With the territory's population decline "since the declaration of war," Holmes pleaded, "we shall have to receive aid from the State of Tennessee."[69]

Three weeks later, General Flournoy informed Holmes that he was not authorized "to call for detachments of militia . . . without an order to that effect from the President." The news panicked Holmes. The territory, he declared, lacked the necessary funds to undertake a campaign "in a distant part of the Country," and he vowed to muster no more troops without assurances that the federal government would assume the cost. Flournoy advised Holmes to contact the governor of Tennessee. "His militia will turn out with alacrity." Yet, Flournoy promised, if the Indians were "determined on a serious war," he would "march the 7th Regiment now at Pass Christian to the frontiers." He continued to believe that a Spanish attack on Mobile was more likely than an Indian uprising. "I can scarcely think," he condescendingly notified Holmes, that "the Creek Indians will hazard a war against the United States, upon the extended scale your information from the pioneers, holds out."[70]

Nevertheless, Holmes, without waiting to learn if Flournoy had the authority "to accept a force from the Executive of the Territory in aid of the regular forces under your command," took unilateral action to counteract "the disastrous events that have happened upon the eastern frontier of our Territory." Acting upon the adage that it was better to ask forgiveness than to seek permission, Holmes sent the militia from the western counties, consisting of five companies of infantry and four of horse, to join Claiborne at Mount Vernon. He also prorogued the legislature, freeing its members to serve in the military or engage "in the defense of their Counties." Finally he accompanied the militia as far as Mount Vernon in order to view firsthand the situation there and to confront the timid Flournoy.[71]

Still Flournoy refused to incorporate the Mississippi militia into the federal army. The controversy intensified after the horse troops, under the command of vainglorious Maj. Thomas Hinds, chafed under the "demeaning" duties assigned them, such as guarding deserted cornfields and abandoned log cabins. When the major routed through General Claiborne a sharp note of protest, demanding a chance to engage the enemy, Flournoy was furious. "The injudicious and unmilitary conduct of the dragoon officers under the command of Major Hinds compels me to believe that they are not disposed to cooperate with us in defence of their country." First he turned them over to Governor Holmes "to be disposed of as he may think proper," and a week later, he reprimanded Claiborne for acting "against orders."[72]

Hinds's dragoons, composed largely of aristocrats from Adams County, departed for home in disgust and bitterness. Claiborne also saw his forces depleted by expiration of their enlistments and by the desire of others, given the treatment of Major Hinds, to return to their families. Happily, several hundred Choctaw warriors joined the American cause, reinforcing Claiborne's dwindling forces. At first, Holmes and other officials had feared that the young warriors might cooperate with the disaffected Creeks. But the combined efforts of the medal chiefs, especially Mushulatubbee and Pushmataha, who despised the Red Sticks, and the persuasive powers of agent George S. Gaines, interpreter John Pitchlynn, and Col. George H. Nixon assured Choctaw cooperation. Indeed, more Choctaws were willing to volunteer than the Americans were able to arm.[73]

From the outset, Holmes and Toulmin knew they were incapable of suppressing the Creek uprising without assistance from neighboring states as well as from the regular army. Then, as the field of combat expanded, fighting spilled into two military districts (Seventh and Sixth), creating jurisdictional problems. Secretary of War Armstrong, thinking it best to have a single commanding officer, put Gen. Thomas Pinckney in charge, assigning Flournoy to a subordinate role even though the early fighting had occurred entirely in his Seventh Military District. In a fit of pique, Flournoy withdrew the Third Regiment to New Orleans. Eventually, Armstrong, realizing his mistake, tried to appease Flournoy by dividing responsibilities between him and Pinckney, advising the two generals to cooperate. Flournoy was not pleased, and he resigned in a huff, paving the way for Gen. Andrew Jackson to obtain command of the southern army.[74]

The American strategy for subduing the Creeks was set early, and despite bickering among the generals, it remained unchanged throughout the conflict. Four separate armies were to converge on the Creek country between the Tallapoosa and Coosa rivers. Two Tennessee units, one from the western part led by Jackson and the other from the east under John Cocke, were to move south toward the elbow of the Tennessee River. Another force commanded by Gen. John Floyd was to march westward from Fort Mitchell until it met Claiborne's Mississippians. Along the way, all four units were to erect forts, separated from each other by a day's march, and to build roads for conveying reinforcements and supplies. The plan was to surround the hostile Creeks, preventing other tribes from aiding them or the Red Sticks from escaping.[75]

Despite the soundness of this strategy, several problems plagued the American forces. The most serious was logistics. As Jackson admitted, he feared famine more than the enemy. The invading armies were to destroy villages and torch fields of corn, hoping to starve the Red Sticks into submission. As a result, invaders, unable to live off the land, were forced to store supplies in hastily erected depots, a strategy that proved laborious and unpopular with the soldiers. Furthermore, short-term enlistments and a steady stream of deserters hampered all four units, none more than Claiborne's Mississippi volunteers.[76]

In contrast, the Red Sticks' strategy was less obvious. Torn between wishing to continue punishing disloyal Creeks and defending their homeland from invading armies, the Indian rebels pursued hit-and-run tactics, hoping to avoid a showdown with superior American forces. The Red Sticks proved to be both resourceful and resilient as well as elusive. After the successful attack on Fort Mims, Weatherford and the prophets retreated to Encunchate, or the "Holy Ground," a remote spot located on a small peninsular along the east side of the Alabama River and protected by marshes and thick woods. As sacred soil, the prophets proclaimed it secure from the white man's approach.[77]

In mid-November 1813, Claiborne, reinforced by the Third U.S. Regiment under Col. Gilbert Russell, proceeded with some 1,200 soldiers, including 51 Choctaw warriors, toward the Alabama River, where they erected Fort Claiborne, located about twenty miles south of the Holy Ground. The Mississippi volunteers, although "half-naked, evinced the greatest satisfaction in learning of their destiny." Every man, Claiborne proudly wrote, "repaired promptly to his post." Many, whose terms of service had expired and who "had not received a dollar of their acreage, volunteered for the expedition." Samuel Dale, commander of one company, remembered seeing General Claiborne "shed tears at the demonstrations of patriotism."[78]

On December 23, Claiborne, eager to attack before a majority of his soldiers' enlistments were up, marched toward the Holy Ground. The Indian defenders, believing that "the Holy Spirit" would protect them, fired a few harmless rounds at the enemy, expecting them to disappear or die. Visibly shaken when the attackers penetrated the supposed invisible barrier set up by the Great Spirit, most Red Sticks, including Josiah Francis, hastily fled, leaving the fighting to Weatherford and about forty warriors. Still, Holy Ground was well fortified, and with sufficient defenders, Weatherford might have inflicted heavy losses on the enemy. But he decided that his situation was hopeless. Supposedly he escaped by leaping off a high bluff and landing safely in the swift-flowing Tombigbee River, which carried him to safety.[79]

Afterward, Claiborne destroyed the village, with its two hundred dwellings, and either burned or seized the large quantity of supplies left behind. His men also discovered several letters signed by the Spanish governor, congratulating Weatherford on his victory at Fort Mims, dispatches that confirmed the American suspicion that Spain had assisted the hostile Creeks. Nevertheless, by placing his forces between Jackson's army and Pensacola, Claiborne effectively prevented the enemy from receiving additional supplies from the Spaniards. With the enlistments either expired or about to be, Claiborne disbanded the Mississippi volunteers, leaving the regular soldiers to garrison Fort Claiborne and the other outposts.[80]

Meanwhile, Gen. John Floyd led some 1,500 Georgians and friendly Indians, mostly Cherokee, from Fort Mitchell on the Chattahoochee River into Red Stick country. In late November, they drove the enemy out of the town of Autosse, killing two hundred and scattering the rest. After burning the nearby countryside, Floyd pulled his soldiers back. During what was an otherwise disappointing campaign, Floyd's men killed two important Red Stick chiefs, the Old Tallassee King and the Autosse King, and forced Peter McQueen to flee. Two months later, the Georgians were back in the field. After erecting Fort Hill, some forty miles west of the site of Fort Mims, Floyd's army suffered defeat at the hands of a superbly led band of Creeks, forcing the Georgia militia to recross the Chattahoochee, this time for good.[81]

Nevertheless, most of the fighting fell to the Tennesseans. Jackson, still recovering from a brawl in Nashville, had begun his march southward in early September 1813. Crossing the Tennessee River in late October, he built Fort Deposit, where he planned to store supplies for his fall campaigns. He also expected the East Tennessee forces, supported by a number of loyal Cherokee, to join him somewhere near the Ten Islands on the Coosa River. Short of supplies and plagued by desertions, Jackson solicited the people of Madison County to furnish him "with regular supplies of meal & meat." The "irregularity" of provisions, he explained, had "retarded my progress very much, and I am anxious to reach the center of the creek country, and give them the final blow" before striking "at the root of the disseas pensacola."[82]

Jackson did not have to wait long. On November 2, he sent Coffee to destroy the Creek town of Tallahatchee. According to a gleeful Jackson, he "executed this order in elegant stile," leaving 176 "dead [Indians] on the field" and taking 80 prisoners, mostly women and children, while his losses were minimal, 5 killed and 41 wounded. After the battle, Jackson wrote Governor Blount that "we have retaliated for the destruction of Fort Mims." Meanwhile, Jackson constructed Fort Strother as an advance base while he waited impatiently but futilely for the East Tennesseans.[83]

Five days later, Jackson learned from a friendly Creek that a large number of Red Sticks had surrounded the town of Talladega, intent upon punishing loyal Creeks. Sensing an opportunity to deliver a knockout blow, Jackson set out with 1,200 infantry and eight hundred horsemen. Although his men inflicted heavy losses upon the enemy, Jackson was displeased with the outcome. Three companies left the battlefield prematurely, allowing the enemy to escape. Still, the Creeks left some three hundred bodies on the bloody battlefield. Even so, Jackson refused to celebrate. "Had there been no departure from the original order of battle," he dejectedly reported, "not an Indian would have escaped."[84]

After the inconclusive engagement at Talladega, Jackson faced an even more formidable enemy—starvation and desertion. He had repeatedly tried to stop the men from returning home, but he was never completely successful. Consequently, in the late fall of 1813, he reluctantly decided to suspend operations, awaiting enlistments who finally arrived in late December. Resuming his campaigning, Jackson then engaged the Red Sticks in two inconclusive battles—one at Emuckfaw Creek and the other at Enotachopco Creek. In the second engagement, Jackson barely avoided defeat when his raw recruits fled in "a disastrous retreat." In a display of individual courage, Jackson, with musket balls flying around him, stood his ground and steeled the faltering troops with his courage, leading them in a counterattack that eventually dispersed the enemy. Again, the Red Sticks suffered more casualties than the Americans, forcing the Indians into a defensive stance.[85]

In early spring, a large body of Creek warriors, together with several thousand women and children, took refuge at Horseshoe Bend on the Tallapoosa River. There the river curved sharply, forming a well-protected peninsula with only a narrow neck connecting it to the mainland. The Red Sticks had fortified the tiny neck of this horseshoelike formation with an eight-foot breastwork of logs laid in zigzag fashion. Scattered throughout the wooden walls were small, carefully arranged portholes from which the defenders could lay a deadly crossfire at their attackers. Taking false comfort behind these elaborate fortifications, the defenders felt secure while they confidently awaited the attack that was certain to come.

Although impressed by the Indians' sophisticated preparations, Jackson immediately perceived that their position was a deathtrap. They have "penned themselves for the slaughter," he announced. Realizing that he could bring the war to a decisive conclusion, Jackson designed a clever battle plan. While some of his troops were bombarding the breastworks, Jackson ordered Coffee's cavalry to dislodge a fleet of canoes moored along one side of the peninsula, cutting off all possibility of escape for the entrapped Creeks.

Meanwhile, as a diversionary tactic, another group, consisting mostly of friendly Creeks and Cherokees, crossed the river in canoes and set fire to a number of structures. As his Indian confederates rushed the enemy from one end of the peninsula, Jackson ordered his troops to attack the breastworks. Initially the fighting was intensive, but it lasted only five hours. Having trapped the Creeks, Jackson's troops showed no mercy. According to Jackson, no more than twenty escaped. Among the nine hundred dead Creeks were the prophet Monahel, whose face had been completely shot off, and two other holy men. Jackson lost forty-seven soldiers and twenty-three friendly Indians. "The carnage was dreadful," Jackson wrote his wife, Rachael.[86] Not only were the Red Sticks destroyed, but the Creek Nation was in a shambles.

The United States, largely at Jackson's insistence, extracted a heavy price from the Creek Nation for its transgressions. In the negotiations that followed, Jackson refused to distinguish between friendly and hostile Creeks, blaming the entire nation for the sins of the war party and disregarding the loyalty of others. In his opinion, all of the Creeks were culpable for not restraining the militants and allowing them to murder innocent whites. The federal government insisted upon retribution in the form of land cessions, but Jackson demanded complete recompense for damage inflicted upon the white settlers. He also spoke for most Mississippians, who wanted an end to the Indian menace.[87]

At the Treaty of Fort Jackson, signed in August 1814, the Creeks were forced to cede 20 million acres of choice farmland. Ironically, Upper Creeks, because of their location, were permitted to retain most of the area between the Coosa and Tallapoosa rivers, while the friendly Lower Creeks lost most of their tribal lands. The reasons were strategic, not spiteful. Jackson wished to establish a buffer between the Creeks and the Florida Seminoles by securing a large swath of land between the lower Chattahoochee and Tombigbee rivers. Unfortunately, this territory was home to Lower Creeks, but to Jackson, security outweighed loyalty. A number of Red Sticks fled into Florida, where they joined the Seminoles, setting the stage for continuation of hostilities between whites and Indians in what became the Second Seminole War.[88]

The treaty of 1814 concluded the Creek phrase of the War of 1812. To Mississippians the war brought a harvest of benefits. It spelled the demise of the Creek Nation, opened some of the territory's richest land to white settlement, and set the stage for the eventual removal of the Civilized Tribes west of the Mississippi. In retrospect, the Creek threat was never as serious as the apprehensive settlers thought, though the war's legacy was even greater than anyone had imagined. Jackson had subdued the Creek menace, but Mississippians could not relax while the threat of a British landing at Mobile or New Orleans existed.

CHAPTER 16

Holmes Sweet Holmes

The territory badly needed a respite from a decade or more of incessant wrangling, and residents hoped its newly appointed governor, David Holmes, was the person to provide it. There was good reason for this optimism. Although "confined with a fever" that lasted for "about thirty days" upon his arrival in "the last days of June," Holmes immediately addressed the General Assembly, and he was pleased by what he saw. "The business," he reported, "was conducted with great harmony." Determined "to avoid taking a part in those little collisions" that had led to his predecessor's downfall, Holmes pledged "to cherish peace and good will among the people and to secure a respect for the Authority of the laws."[1]

In contrast to Williams, Holmes was congenial, cooperative but not lackadaisical, attentive to business, and hesitant to act arbitrarily. To be sure, Holmes had entered office at an opportune time, when everyone sought relief from the endless bickering and petty conflicts of earlier times.[2] Moreover, Holmes was refreshingly mild-tempered, non-judgmental, and not overly ambitious. Competent but never brilliant or showy, Holmes displayed a political style perfectly suited to govern a frontier community where politics was rooted in personalities rather than principles. As an outsider, he was not identified with one of the family clans or political factions, and he entered office without personal attachments or a fixed agenda.[3]

Holmes purposely treated the legislature with dignity and respect, pursuing a policy of accommodation rather than confrontation. Although Thomas Freeman was upset by "the Governor[']s delicacy to touch any subject not fully supported in," most people appreciated this trait.[4] No one questioned his commitment to the Republican Party or his strong attachment to Jefferson and Madison, the twin anchors of traditional republicanism. Where Williams was constantly vulnerable to the charge of "political heresy," Holmes compiled an impeccable record of party loyalty.[5]

The sole holdover from the previous administration was Secretary Thomas H. Williams, but unlike his predecessors, Williams had no interest in politics. In personality, he resembled Holmes more than Robert Williams or George Poindexter, and he grabbed the first opportunity to vacate the office, accepting the collectorship of the Port of New Orleans in early January 1810.[6] Holmes's other secretaries were equally competent and cooperative. Henry Daingerfield, a Virginian, replaced Thomas H. Williams until his death in 1815, when Nathaniel Ware, a local resident loyal to Holmes, succeeded him.[7]

Holmes would also later benefit from a shattered Federalist Party, whose opposition to the War of 1812 eventually led to its disappearance.[8] By pursuing a policy of accommodation, not unlike that of President James Monroe, Holmes also ushered in locally what was called the "era of good feelings" nationally.[9] But Mississippi's version was more the result of wartime conditions than the governor's personality. Even before 1812, a number of Mississippians wondered if the incessant bickering and festering factionalism had not discouraged Congress from considering their supplications, and most saw the futility of internecine warfare, especially while the territory was dependent upon federal assistance.[10]

Wartime threats to territorial security served to promote harmony and lessen animosity. Everyone favored ousting the Spaniards from Baton Rouge and Mobile, suppressing the Creek uprising, and teaching the British a lesson on neutral rights. Mississippians rejoiced in Jackson's subjugation of the hostile Creeks in August 1814 and rallied behind his efforts to prevent the British from gaining a foothold along the Gulf coast. Indeed, Jackson's defeat of the Red Sticks at Horseshoe Bend came none too soon since the British were on the verge of opening a southern campaign in which they planned to employ both Indians and blacks. By then, however, the Creek Nation was incapable of lending the British much support. Either the British had waited too long to launch an invasion, or the Creeks had acted prematurely.[11]

Ironically, Jackson was saved from possible humiliation as much by the failure of his opponents to coordinate their efforts as by the prowess of his leadership or the courage of his soldiers. As Tecumseh understood, Indian success came not from unilateral action but in concert with foreign nations. In the case of the Creek War, the conflict was the result of internal divisions and, at least in its early stages, was unconnected with the broader international conflict.[12]

In mid-1814, shortly after he had replaced Thomas Pinckney as commanding general of the southern army, Jackson learned from scouts and spies that the British planned to deposit arms and ammunition along the Apalachicola River in hopes of attracting local allies. Instantly, he marched his troops to Mobile and refortified Fort Bowyer in time to ward off a British assault in September. Meanwhile, a detachment of one hundred British marines under the command of Maj. Edward Nicholls, with initial blessings of Spanish officials, landed at Pensacola and began recruiting Indians and black slaves. Contemptuous of Spaniards, Nicholls, after summoning the "Natives of Louisiana" together, called upon them "to assist in liberating from a faithless and imbecile government, your paternal soil."[13]

Nicholls's odd behavior confirmed Jackson's belief that Great Britain was behind all Indian mischief. "There can be no doubt," he wrote Tennessee's Governor Blount, "but the Creeks and lower Choctaws are excited to hostilities by the influence of the British. If so," he continued, "we will have to fight the combined powers of both." For Jackson, the conflict that began in Tennessee "must end in Pensacola."[14]

Convinced that possession of Pensacola was crucial to British coastal operations, Jackson laid plans to occupy it with or without administrative approval. Taking advantage of Nicholls's insensitivity to Spanish pride, Jackson met only token resistance upon entering Pensacola. Instead, Florida governor Gonzalez Manrique, by welcoming Jackson's army into the city, was able to deprive Britain of a strategic base. Yet, according to Judge Harry Toulmin, the Spanish governor remained ambivalent toward Jackson, who, he believed, "feareth not God nor regardeth man."[15]

Still convinced that Great Britain intended to land its forces along the upper Gulf coast, Jackson returned immediately to Mobile and shored up its defenses. Almost too late, James Innerarity, among others, finally persuaded Jackson that the British planned to attack New

Orleans and not Mobile. Racing his troops across Mississippi Territory, he arrived in New Orleans on December 1, 1814, barely ahead of the British.[16]

In a brilliant campaign, aided immensely by dawdling British officers who were unfamiliar with a terrain better suited for defensive than offensive operations, Jackson won a smashing victory. In the aftermath of their humiliating defeat of January 8, 1815, almost two weeks after signing a peace treaty at Ghent in Belgium, the British abandoned their efforts to possess the Crescent City and the lower Mississippi Valley.[17]

Although this victory saved Mississippi Territory from likely devastation, few of its sons had participated in the glorious campaign. Its contribution was limited to a few rifle companies and Thomas Hinds's celebrated dragoons, who distinguished themselves, winning the accolades of Jackson and Coffee. If few Mississippians were actively engaged in defending New Orleans, all rejoiced in its marvelous outcome, which catapulted Jackson into national prominence and unleashed a wave of patriotic feelings throughout the nation. It undeservedly elevated the image of western frontiersmen from crude woodsmen into the cult of the invincible "Hunters of Kentucky" despite the fact that Jackson's victory depended more on its artillery than riflemen. Legend trumped reality. The Kentucky militia, the "volunteers" of Tennessee, and the sturdy yeomen of Mississippi Territory had routed the same "invincible" British army that had crushed the mighty Napoleon. "It evinces to the world," Cowles Mead declared, "that the United States, by proper exercise of her energy, can contend alone and with success, against the Power that gives the impulse to all Europe."[18]

For Mississippians, the British defeat had special ramifications, and Governor Holmes was one of its first beneficiaries. His popularity rose as the territory recovered and prosperity returned, and so did the people's confidence in their new governor. Territorial governments were administrative nightmares, and Mississippi's was no different. If anything, its experiences were more complex and confused than most others.[19] Fortunately, the phlegmatic David Holmes was well suited by temperament and inclination for the task of administering such an untidy government.

As chief executive, a majority of his time was devoted to mundane matters that were trivial or repetitious. These included filling county offices with competent individuals, commissioning militia officers customarily elected by the enlisted men, creating new counties and designating their seats of government, adjudicating disputes between local officials and distressed citizens, and pardoning or reducing the sentences of convicted criminals whose punishments failed to fit the crime or were unduly harsh.[20] For instance, Robert Harrison, a nobody from Adams County, was convicted of maim and ordered to pay a fine of five hundred dollars and "to stand in the pillory two hours each day for three days in succession." After Harrison stood on display for two days, Holmes remitted the rest of his sentence as well as those of two others who suffered similar punishments. For reasons obvious in a plantation society, most of those granted clemency were convicted slaves. For example, Holmes pardoned "a negro slave named Peter," property of Manuel Madden, who had been sentenced to die for "plotting the death of a fellow slave."[21]

Resignations, frequently the result of petty insults or perceived slights, flooded the governor's desk, requiring him to locate qualified replacements where few existed. Since Holmes's knowledge of remote counties and their residents was limited, he had to rely upon the recommendations of friends or local officials, and even they had difficulty in uncovering individuals both willing and competent to fill the growing list of vacancies.[22] At times new counties were so thinly populated that suitable candidates were not to be found. On occasion, he sent blank commissions to trusted friends, authorizing them to finish the process. Later, he was compelled, especially in newly created counties populated almost entirely with newcomers, to allow local citizens to elect their own officials.[23]

At best, this manner of governing a sprawling frontier was chaotic and inefficient, one that might easily lead to nepotism or sycophancy, both of which were breeding grounds for discontent and corruption. Yet by deferring to the people's wishes and acting fairly, Holmes overcame most of these pitfalls and emerged virtually unscathed. Only rarely did he face the slanderous barbs of outraged citizens upset by his decisions or failure to act in their behalf.

For instance, Anthony Campbell was furious when the governor revoked his commission as lieutenant in the militia. Holmes, he said, was a despot, committing "an act even the tyrant of Britain does not attempt." Likewise, Samuel Montgomery was upset when Holmes failed to make him a field officer. In a "very noisy manner" and a fit of "violent passion," he called the governor "a rascal" for having "treated him rascally." In an ensuing court-martial, Montgomery was found guilty of "ungentlemanly and unofficerlike conduct and for Speaking disrespectfully of the Commander in chief." In defense, Montgomery claimed that since he was not in uniform at the time, he was speaking "as a private citizen" and not as an officer. The "epithets of a more private abuse, left unexplained," he insisted, "should not amount to a military crime."[24]

But because of their local importance, sheriffs and justices of the peace were more often the targets of distressed citizens than militia officers. Justices were responsible for overseeing the counties and providing services to the citizenry and sheriffs for enforcing the peace. For instance, Sheriff Joseph Briggs of Claiborne County was accused of negligence of duty and favoritism toward friends. It took him eight months to respond to the inquiries of an impatient Holmes. Then, in a twenty-five-page defense, Briggs denounced the charges as "wicked and malicious" and the outgrowth of "base motives and prejudices," but Holmes refused to act precipitously. Instead he investigated before taking action, and in Briggs's case, he exonerated the sheriff. Likewise, he dismissed charges brought by Joseph P. Kennedy against Thomas Malone, clerk of the superior court of Washington County. He assured Malone that his inquiry had produced nothing "that could in the smallest degree injure your reputation," and, he declared, "you have my entire approbation."[25]

Yet Holmes did not always side with territorial officials, even those he had appointed. In the case of Sheriff Montfort Calvit of Adams County, the governor permitted him to resign rather than face charges of "malconduct in office," although he did so with remorse. "Notwithstanding the alligations to which you allude," he assured Calvit, "my opinion of the rectitude of your intentions and the goodness of your heart remains unaltered."[26] Later he revoked the commission of Peter P. Pollard, a justice of the peace in Adams County, for conduct that "tends to pervert the ends of justice, and render the office he holds odious and contemptible." According to one pious citizen, Pollard was known to cavort with gamblers and "the worst and most vicious company under the hill" and was "frequently intoxicated."[27]

Because of the governor's forbearance and the deft manner with which he handled the numerous complaints sent him, outbursts like those of Anthony Campbell were rare. More typical was the response of an unhappy militia officer. "My opinion of your goodness is such," he wrote, "that I do not believe you would do any officer intentionally wrong but for want of knowing better." Another maligned official appreciated "the delicacy" with which the governor responded to the accusations "exhibited against him for malfeasance in office."[28]

During the Creek conflict, Holmes devoted most of his energies to organizing and provisioning the territorial militia, a Herculean and thankless task. Aspiring politicians as well as the proud sons of Adams County nabobs envisioned military service as a pathway to fame and glory, and they opted to join only those units destined for action and commanded by neighbors or kinsmen and manned by sturdy yeomen. Invariably, they preferred the cavalry over the infantry, donned, at their own expense, elaborate and ornate uniforms, and thirsted to win lasting laurels by chastising Creeks. As one officer put it, "their old animosity against the Indian has renewed with redoubled force."[29]

Others, however, were unprepared for the drudgery of winter campaigning or privations caused by torrential rains, biting cold and frozen creeks, short rations, and inadequate clothing and bedding. For example, General Claiborne complained that, with cold weather approaching, 250 of his men were "without blankets." During the winter campaigns of 1813–1814, some of the territorial troopers had to survive for eight days "on horse flesh."[30] Proud dragoons chafed at the degrading duties assigned them by General Flournoy, who treated them as undisciplined auxiliaries and refused to provision or pay them. After they complained bitterly, Flournoy sent them home to what he thought was public disgrace; instead Mississippians hailed them as innocent victims of callous officials.[31]

The rank-and-file militiamen had their own grievances. Less eager than their social betters to join the fight, they were more likely to be distressed draftees than rabid volunteers, and a few even failed to report for duty. For those living at the margin of subsistence, the low pay was especially burdensome. Disturbed by the disparity in compensation between militiamen and regulars, Holmes kept insisting upon equal pay for all soldiers until he succeeded.[32] Others, especially those residing on exposed frontiers, worried lest their families fall victim to Indian attack or the dreaded influenza. In response to complaints of militiamen from Claiborne and Jefferson counties, Governor Holmes set up an emergency patrol, manned by "a company of exempts," under the command of Capt. Daniel Burnet, and authorized the residents to erect a few blockhouses as safe havens for refugees.[33]

If the residents feared Indian attacks, Holmes worried about slave insurrections. "Nearly one half of the entire population are slaves," he explained, "and the frontier counties are thinly established. . . . In Slave Countries the Danger of insurrection always exists." Yet the governor showed no comfort in Col. Samuel Stockett's report that the blacks were "generally found orderly and in their usual humbleness."[34]

But he found more solace in the small number of deserters. Mississippians were less inclined to shirk their martial duties than Jackson's Tennesseans primarily because they were defending their homeland and their enlistments were mostly for six months or less. While the vast majority of militiamen answered the call to arms willingly, and some enthusiastically, a fraction was resistant, and desertions, when they occurred, were never welcome. John Ford, a prominent Pearl River planter whose home was on the road to Mount Vernon, was one of the few to complain of deserters in his neighborhood and to ask Holmes to "put a stop" to the "shameful" practice. The reluctance of some militiamen to rendezvous in a timely fashion was enough of a problem that the legislature increased the fine for delinquency from five to ten dollars.[35]

Sickness constantly hampered the governor's efforts to muster the militia and wreaked havoc on soldiers in the field. In fact, more Mississippians died from disease than combat. To be sure, Mississippi Territory was never a healthy place, and the harsh winter of 1813–1814 took its toll. General Claiborne, upon reaching Liberty in the eastern "piney woods" en route to Fort Stoddert, was dismayed to find one-fourth of his two hundred troops sick and unfit for duty. Sometime later an epidemic of measles broke out in the camp at Mount Vernon, causing more suffering. In fact, Claiborne himself returned home in broken health, nursing a lingering wound that refused to heal. He died in the spring of 1815 at the age of forty-four.[36]

As in every war, some militiamen sought special favors. One minister of the gospel requested a discharge for religious reasons, and another poor private asked to be relieved of his duties because his wife "was in a state of insanity" or "confirmed mania." An ensign, who had joined the militia expecting to "perform marches on horseback," received a discharge on account of "rheumatic pains" that prevented him from "performing duties on foot."[37] A handful of junior officers resigned because they disliked their company commander or because the enlisted men had bypassed them for command. Holmes also had to dismiss a few officers upon learning that they were not citizens of the United States. One of those discharged was understandably dumbfounded since, having voted in the last election, he assumed that he was naturalized.[38]

Militia officers were not the only military personnel to resign in disgust or in haste. Col. Joseph Constant, commander of Cantonment Washington, was so incensed when the War Department passed him over for promotion to brigadier general in favor of three of his juniors that he left the army. "As I cannot consider their elevation as complimentary to myself and, as I have no intention of serving in a grade subordinate to them," he informed his superiors, "I take the earliest opportunity of begging you to accept my resignation."[39]

But the governor's principal problems of mobilization were not men but weapons, provisions, and ammunition. Every militia unit called to duty was short of supplies and arms, and a depleted territorial treasury was unable to assume the cost of fighting the hostile Creeks. Even in those cases where the War Department had loaned the militiamen arms, they were frequently "entirely unfit for use." At first, Holmes was unconcerned, since he expected the federal government to absorb the expense by incorporating the militia into the recently authorized provisional army. Unfortunately, General Flournoy thought otherwise, and he refused to call the militia up without specific instructions from the War Department, which, as Holmes knew, would take months to secure.[40]

An annoyed Holmes quickly rescinded his orders for mobilizing the militia, awaiting authorization from the secretary of war. Meanwhile, the beleaguered Tombigbee residents were outraged. Although Harry Toulmin held the overcautious Hawkins primarily responsible for the governor's failure to respond expeditiously, he still accused Holmes of callousness, compelling the governor, on his own authority, to call up four infantry units and two troops of horses, in expectation that federal officials would overrule Flournoy. Fortunately, his faith was well placed, and Holmes narrowly escaped a serious fiscal crisis.[41]

Even though wartime distresses forged an uncommon unity, internal disputes did not disappear completely. But, with interest in statehood growing, Mississippians began to refocus their interest. They were especially eager to settle the controversial Yazoo and British land disputes, which they wished resolved before and not after admission. During the heated elections of 1813, William Lattimore had warned voters that only "the want of . . . Federal jurisdiction, which is necessarily attached to

State Government," had shielded them from becoming "a scene of litigation, as perhaps, has never been exhibited to the world." Additionally, British claimants were growing impatient. Seth Hunt, one of the territory's leading speculators, demanded that Congress either provide suitable financial settlements or authorize appeals to the federal Supreme Court.[42]

Finally, in March 1814, Congress, encouraged by territorial delegate Lattimore and the departure of John Randolph of Roanoke, who for years had been the chief obstacle to settlement, compromised the Yazoo question by setting aside $5 million from proceeds of land sales in Mississippi Territory to compensate claimants. They were to receive stock options, which were legal tender for the purchase of any federal lands, whether in Mississippi Territory or elsewhere. Although this measure removed, as a congressional committee stated, "what was perhaps the most general objection to admission," the British grants remained unresolved.[43]

Despite the dire predictions of several Cassandras, these controversies did not appreciably curtail postwar immigration. On the contrary, settlements in the territory acquired at Fort Jackson occurred faster than the federal government could prepare the lands for sale or territorial officials could set up county governments. Brazen intruders rushed into these concessions, hoping to co-opt choice acreage or harvest virgin timber. In June 1815, Governor Holmes unwittingly encouraged them by incorporating the region into Madison County. Later that year, President Madison ordered all trespassers on public lands removed, but Toulmin persuaded federal officials to postpone the evictions until late 1816 to allow intruders to dispose of the crops they had planted.[44]

Moreover, political controversies continued to plague the territory. Largely a legacy of factional disputes during the Williams administration, these differences were a continuation of the personal feuds between Andrew Marschalk and George Poindexter as well as the sectional rivalry between Natchez and Tombigbee districts. Finally, population explosions in the lower Tennessee Valley added another complication.

The Poindexter-Marschalk imbroglio was an amusing if inconsequential contest between two demonstrative and egotistical personalities. Born in Louisa County, Virginia, in 1779, Poindexter migrated in 1802 to Mississippi Territory, where he opened a law office and set about searching for influential friends and patrons. Arriving in Natchez, as he said, "without friends or introduction and with no resources other than the cash in his pockets and a shining faith in his own ability," he rose rapidly in the labyrinth of frontier politics. It was a climate ready-made for a person of his character and charm, and he rapidly ascended the political ladder, becoming attorney general in 1803, legislator in 1805, and territorial delegate in 1807.[45]

From the outset, Poindexter attracted both devoted disciples and determined foes. Largely because of his erratic behavior and exuberant nature, he was a regular feature in local newspapers. In 1805, he engaged Abner Duncan, a leading Natchez attorney, in a bitter quarrel that aroused considerable interest and elevated him to public prominence. Then, in 1811, he killed Abijah Hunt in perhaps Mississippi's most notorious duel, one in which he was unable to live down the charge of firing prematurely.[46]

Like Poindexter, Andrew Marschalk was well versed in territorial politics. The eccentric printer came to the territory in the late 1790s as a lieutenant in the U.S. Army after serving under General Wayne in the Indian conflicts of the Old Northwest. During his tour of duty at Fort McHenry near the Walnut Hills (later Vicksburg), Marschalk's talents as a printer attracted Governor Sargent's attention, and Sargent employed him to publish the territory's first laws.[47]

After Marschalk had completed the assignment, the two strong-willed men came to a parting of ways, and Sargent looked elsewhere for a reliable printer. Dismissed in 1802 from the military as part of President Jefferson's economy drive, Marschalk, like many discharged officers, settled in Mississippi Territory, where he edited several short-lived and highly partisan newspapers. In 1802, he started the *Herald*, the territory's first newspaper, in which he supported the Federalists. By 1807, however, Marschalk had a change of heart, and he became a professed Republican and defender of Governor Williams, one of Poindexter's bitterest foes. In 1813, Marschalk launched his most successful venture, the *Washington Republican*, where he reserved his most biting barbs for Poindexter and his two allies, Cowles Mead and William B. Shields. Although Marschalk delighted in making their lives miserable, he directed his choicest missives at Poindexter. During the hotly contested campaign for territorial delegate in 1811, he charged Poindexter with mishandling public funds and cheating an elderly woman out of six hundred dollars. While the barbs provoked the thin-skinned Poindexter into chasing a heckler down the streets of Washington with a black horsewhip, he deprived Marschalk of the pleasure of defeating him in the next election by a timely withdrawal.[48]

Poindexter based his decision to resign upon a number of factors. After a disappointing third term in Congress, he was reluctant to face more of the printer's sarcastic jibes. Also, he had failed to add Baton Rouge to Mississippi Territory following the rebellion of 1810 or to secure a satisfactory settlement of British claims. Finally, his position on admission of the territory was equivocal and confusing to friends and foes alike.

But the principal reason was the prospect of facing stiff competition from either the popular William Lattimore, who previously had served two terms as delegate, or Col. Joseph Carson, a prominent planter of the Tombigbee District where Poindexter's name was anathema. Fortunately, the sudden death of Judge David Campbell provided Poindexter with a convenient escape. By calling upon the assistance of his congressional colleagues, Poindexter finally won appointment to the territorial supreme court. In March 1813, Poindexter pleased his enemies and surprised his friends by refusing to seek reelection.[49]

No one was more taken aback by the announcement than Cowles Mead, his close friend and protégé. Expecting to replace Poindexter once he stepped aside, Mead now found himself in an awkward position. In early 1813, Mead, like other Natchez gentry, had volunteered his services to General Claiborne, whose regiment was encamped at Baton Rouge awaiting orders to assault Mobile. Caught off guard by Poindexter's announcement, Mead resigned his military commission, hastened to Natchez, and belatedly announced his candidacy for delegate. By his precipitous action, Mead opened himself to charges of cowardice and unsavory ambition, and his persistent denials did not impress the voters, who returned Lattimore to Congress.[50]

Nevertheless, the judicial bench failed to provide Poindexter with sanctuary from Marschalk's incessant invective. With the offices of his newspaper conveniently located across from the courthouse, Marschalk gleefully printed every innuendo or amusing anecdote he could uncover to discredit the new judge. For instance, he swore that Poindexter, while he was territorial delegate, had deliberately suppressed two memorials from the General Assembly, both of which had urged Congress to compromise British claims. One detractor, calling himself "A Bystander," quoted Poindexter as having uttered, upon receipt of the second of these petitions, that only "damned rascals had signed it."[51]

Enraged by these charges, Poindexter asked the governor to remove Marschalk as adjutant of the militia, but Holmes quietly demurred. He had no desire to become a target of the editor's satirical sarcasm. Thereafter, the enraged judge hauled Marschalk before his court on a contempt charge, and Marschalk spent an unpleasant night in jail. After the editor "refused to answer interrogatories," Poindexter fined Marschalk twenty dollars and required him to "enter into a recognizance of good behavior." Marschalk gladly paid the fine because he had "meant the contempt," but he balked at giving assurance of "good behavior." Not wishing to provide the artful editor additional ammunition to castigate him, Judge Poindexter, after a lecture upon proper decorum, released him on his own recognizance.[52]

But Poindexter's efforts at reconciliation failed to stop the abuse. The following week, a detractor, calling himself "Castigator," took up the cudgels in the *Washington Republican* against the harassed judge. Poindexter summoned Marschalk to reappear in court, and after the editor again refused either to discontinue publishing the scurrilous letters or to disclose the author's identity, the judge clapped him back in jail. But Judge Josiah Simpson surprisingly came to the printer's rescue, freeing him on a writ of habeas corpus, and Marschalk followed with a series of articles on freedom of the press. He likened Poindexter to the despised English judge George "Bloody" Jeffries, while "Castigator" resurrected the story that Poindexter had murdered Abijah Hunt in the infamous duel of 1811. For the next several weeks, the public was both entertained and repulsed by a heated newspaper and pamphlet contest as the *Washington Republican* printed articles and letters from Poindexter's friends, and Marschalk offered the public a collection of the "Castigator" letters for fifty cents.[53]

Unable to silence his critics and wishing a respite from the endless attacks, Poindexter secured a military commission as aide-de-camp to Gen. William Carroll, who was then in Natchez on his way south, where he expected to join Jackson's army in defending New Orleans. Poindexter and Carroll arrived in the Crescent City shortly before the decisive battles of early January. On January 18, 1815, the *Mississippi Republican* proudly printed Poindexter's thrilling account of the magnificent victory at New Orleans. But Poindexter's moment of glory was short-lived.[54]

On February 1, an ecstatic Marschalk published a letter from a "New Orleans gentleman," who reported that Poindexter's behavior was not as heroic as it was claimed. Instead, Poindexter "had disgraced himself at New Orleans." According to the "gentleman," Poindexter "fled to New Orleans from the lines, three or four minutes after the battle commenced." The report of another supposed eyewitness was equally devastating. According to this writer, Poindexter, who was at regimental headquarters when the shelling commenced, became so terrified after one of the enemy's balls demolished a portion of the building where he and other members of the general's staff had gathered that he hid "behind a black chimney in the lap of the negro servant of General Carroll." While Carroll was rushing to the front lines, the "heroic" Poindexter was nursing a flesh wound caused when a falling brick landed on his arm.[55]

Poindexter spent the next month or so refuting the damaging recriminations. He collected and published affidavits and testimonials from General Carroll and others attesting to his courage under fire. But the controversy would not die.[56] Shortly afterward, he traveled to Kentucky to confront those individuals he believed were responsible for spreading the abuse.

First he accosted Dr. Samuel Brown, a former Natchez resident practicing medicine in Lexington. Surmising that Brown was the furtive source of the aspersions, he tried without success to entice him to an "interview." Forced to defend himself in print rather than on the field of honor, Poindexter published his own account of the shadowy events. Brown responded in a fifty-page pamphlet in which he not only reiterated his earlier accusations but also accused Poindexter of attempting to rape "a young lady in the family of General [William] Cocke, Chickasaw Agent." Poindexter's other target was Col. Thomas Percy, whom he blamed for wrecking his first marriage. According to the judge, Percy had seduced his wife, Lydia Carter, before fleeing to Kentucky.[57] Although Poindexter's foray there generated more heat than light, his absence brought a respite at home in the vituperative war.

The situation hardly improved with Poindexter's return. The *Washington Republican* continued to trumpet charges of cowardice against him. Losing his composure, Poindexter, brandishing a brickbat in his right hand, foolishly chased Marschalk off the streets of Washington. Marschalk brought indictment against his assailant, forcing Poindexter to appear before a local justice of the peace and give bond for good behavior. After a bullheaded refusal resulted in his arrest, Poindexter issued a writ of habeas corpus in his own behalf, and his close friend and fellow judge Walter Leake released him from custody. Presently Marschalk replaced Poindexter in the town jail after a jury found him guilty of libel. Judge Leake sentenced him to three months in prison, but the dogged printer refused to be silenced. The slanderous exchange continued throughout the summer of 1815 before the public finally grew weary, and a disheartened Poindexter in late 1816 resigned his judgeship to resume his "station at the bar."[58]

Meanwhile, the Tombigbee District was hardly free of personal acrimony. There the principal object of abuse was Judge Harry Toulmin. Since his appointment as the territory's fourth judge, with responsibility for Washington District, Toulmin had acted as surrogate executive, filling the vacuum left by the territorial governors' failure to give it much attention. To be sure, the governors never deliberately ignored the district, as most Bigbee settlers thought, but pressing problems elsewhere never failed to distract them. In fact, every governor had at one time or another planned to visit the Tombigbee District, but none had done so until Holmes went there twice in 1813.[59] His first visit was to set up a county government for newly acquired Mobile; his second was to protect the western settlements from possible attack.

All of the territorial governors from Claiborne to Holmes had grown accustomed to relying upon Toulmin for advice. Even General Wilkinson, whose son had married Toulmin's daughter, depended at times upon the savvy but often cantankerous judge for counsel.[60] Unlike Holmes, Toulmin was obstinate, inclined at times to be mulish and uncompromising, traits destined to embroil him in needless acrimony.

But Toulmin's greatest problems resulted from the federal government's refusal to appoint a judge for the Mobile District or to designate which of the local courts, if any, could exercise federal jurisdiction. The oversight was hardly the fault of Holmes or Toulmin, both of whom had repeatedly petitioned Congress to correct the deficiencies. The problem became especially acute after the incorporation of Mobile, which immediately led to complications only federal courts could resolve. In the meantime, where were federal cases to be heard?[61]

With encouragement but without formal authorization from Holmes, Toulmin decided to set up special courts to handle admiralty cases.

In the process of exercising his authority in this manner, which to him was the most plausible solution, Toulmin raised a series of thorny questions that had no easy answers and that embroiled him in endless controversy with local officials, several of whom were actively engaged in shady or questionable activities such as smuggling coffee, bribing officials, and evading federal duties.[62]

His principal adversary was William Crawford, one of the land commissioners for the Mobile District. Through support from friends outside as well as within the territory, including the Callers and Kennedy, Crawford became U.S. attorney for the Mobile District. Once in office, Crawford not only refused to cooperate with Toulmin's efforts to prevent smuggling and enforce the federal revenue measures, but he also criticized Toulmin's judicial decisions, some of which admittedly were contradictory or convoluted. According to Toulmin, Crawford fell victim to his "most inveterate enemy," James Caller. "It would seem a little strange," he declared, "that a public officer, would so soon upon coming to this country, imbibe such strong prejudices against a brother officer."[63]

In setting up special courts for federal cases, Toulmin relied upon the clerk of the superior court of Mobile, even though the "suits were brought in the superior court of Washington County." As Toulmin later explained, "in admiralty cases, indeed, I did not conceive that any regard to county limits was necessary." As a result, several of his decisions were overturned on what the tormented judge termed mere "technicalities."[64]

In addition to seeking a fifth judge for the Mobile District, Toulmin maneuvered to get the position himself. To ward off charges that he was not a resident of the district, Toulmin tried to purchase a piece of property in Mobile. Unfortunately, he sought the assistance of that notorious land speculator John Smith of Feliciana fame, who offered him property with a questionable Spanish title. Once more, by his own carelessness, Toulmin immersed himself in unnecessary controversy. He allowed Crawford, who insisted that Toulmin knew the title was "a forgery," to accuse him of fraud.[65]

While Toulmin emerged from these scrapes scared but unrepentant, he sought approval from the people whose interests he had tried so valiantly to protect. In 1813, he offered himself as a candidate for Mobile's first representative in the General Assembly. In a somewhat listless campaign, he handily defeated Sheriff Theodore Brightwell, winning all of Jackson County's fifty-two votes and a slight majority of those in Mobile County. Ironically, Brightwell, who owed his political success to Toulmin's influence, fell victim to the wiles of Crawford and contested Toulmin's election on two counts. He insisted that Toulmin was not a legal resident of the district, and that a territorial judge was ineligible to hold a second office. In response, Toulmin argued that, in a democratic society, voters had the right to select whomever they wished. Moreover, he contended, there was no law preventing an appointed official from serving in that body. Nevertheless, the territorial House of Representatives, by a vote of 14 to 9, disqualified him, but it refused to seat Brightwell and authorized a new election in which, ironically, Crawford emerged victorious.[66]

Even then, according to Toulmin, Crawford continued to utter innuendoes damaging to his character. For instance, before the judge's friends, Crawford "insinuated that the Judge must have been bribed by the old Spaniard!" Later, he accused Toulmin of being a "Tory and a traitor." "If this man practiced on the Mississippi," Toulmin chortled, "he would soon get Marschalked." It seemed, he lamented, "that I might devote all my time to the development & refutation of the various calumnies which are daily fabricated by the sons of envy and malice."[67]

From his new position, Crawford sought to strip Toulmin of his influence. He was instrumental in dismissing the sheriff of Jackson County, whom Toulmin considered "one of the most capable" officials in the territory. Yet Toulmin was careful not to criticize Crawford's recommendations publicly, sarcastically informing the governor that he was sure that Crawford must have "made a case which was plain enough." Still he warned Holmes of the potential danger of relying on Crawford's prejudiced judgment. "These things," he admonished, "give to representatives a factitious power and influence which they ought not to have."[68]

In addition to personal feuds, an earlier conflict between Natchez and the town of Washington reemerged during the elections of 1815. The Mead-Poindexter faction wanted the seat of Adams County returned to Natchez, where it had originally resided until the Republicans removed it to Washington during the "Revolution of 1800." In this bitter contest, a scribbler, calling himself "Washingtonian," accused the pro-Natchez ticket of attempting "to ruin the city of Washington." "Are you willing to support a group," he asked, which was preparing to "take our bread and cheese to surfeit the pampered nabobs of Natchez?" At least one skeptic saw the humor in, if not the absurdity of, the situation. "Two Places, six miles apart, allied by a unity of interests, are at this moment preparing for destruction and hostility." Nevertheless, in 1815, the opposition faction sponsored a "city ticket" that soundly defeated the "country ticket" supported by the *Washington Republican*. Yet Marschalk was not completely dissatisfied with these election results. In the territorywide canvass for delegate, Marschalk had the satisfaction of rejoicing in Cowles Mead's second humiliating defeat at the hands of William Lattimore.[69]

By early 1815, the quest for statehood began to overshadow all other considerations. As Lattimore succinctly summarized in his circular letter of March 1815, the situation has "now materially changed." "The Yazoo claims threaten us no more," he proclaimed; the prospect of "an early extinguishment of the British claims" was bright; and "the return of peace" would likely "remove the necessity of a federal direct tax." Moreover, the revival of local trade would doubtless restore "the current of emigration to our territory," enabling Mississippians "ere long to sustain the burden of a state government without being oppressed by its weight." Therefore, Lattimore concluded, the time had arrived "when, with the permission of Congress, we should prepare for admission into the union of the states."[70]

CHAPTER 17

Statehood

By the time Mississippians sought statehood, the process for adding new states was well established. Between 1789 and 1815, five states had joined the original thirteen, and of these only Vermont and Kentucky had not followed the process laid out in the Northwest Ordinance of 1787. The others (Tennessee in 1796, Ohio in 1803, and Louisiana in 1812) had learned the rudiments of self-government by serving an apprenticeship under a territorial government.[1]

To be sure, the Northwest Ordinance became a model for westward expansion. Unlike the British Empire, where colonies rarely advanced beyond their original status, this ordinance provided a mechanism by which newly settled regions were guaranteed the right to progress from a subservient relationship to one of full equality.

Under its terms, territories were eligible to enter the Union as soon as they attained a population equal to that of the least-populated state or sixty thousand free inhabitants. At that point, the residents could seek an enabling act authorizing them to call a convention, draft a constitution, and request admission. Once this process was completed, a territory then joined the Union on equal footing with other states, the only restrictions being that the government must be republican in form and not in conflict with the Constitution of 1787.[2] By 1815, Mississippi Territory had already set a record for territorial longevity, surpassing Ohio's thirteen-year apprenticeship. Unfortunately, Mississippi's territorial period had coincided with a series of international crises that retarded its development and postponed its entrance into the Union.[3]

Most territories were admitted with their current boundaries intact. When Tennessee became a state in 1796, its boundaries were the same as those of the Southwest Territory, as were Louisiana's when it gained statehood in 1812. On the other hand, there was precedence for large territories to be fragmented before admission. For instance, the Northwest Ordinance specified that at least three but no more than five states were to be formed from the original territory.

This issue—whether to seek admission as one or two states—was to divide the people of Mississippi Territory and delay their entry into the Union. Even though, by late 1816, its population was approaching the required sixty thousand, an intense factionalism, which had plagued the territory from the outset, made consensus on admission problematic. For nearly two decades, the Mississippi River counties had dominated territorial politics and dictated policy, while its officials treated Tombigbeans as stepchildren or worse.[4]

Between 1803 and 1812, Tombigbee settlers thrice petitioned Congress to divide the territory and grant them a separate government. "At present," they pleaded in 1803, "we have only the name of one. We know nothing of our Executive officers . . . [or] our Delegates in Congress, [and] they know nothing of us." In the opinion of eastern settlers, their grievances had been consistently ignored by a government located "nearly three hundred miles away" and separated "by a howling wilderness with its usual inhabitants of savages and beasts of prey." Again, in 1809, they requested a separate government. Insisting that they were treated as "mere cyphers," they objected to paying taxes to a government in which they were not properly represented, and they informed the Congress that they did not "covet the honor of being a part of a state on the Mississippi." On both occasions, a distant and distracted Congress turned a deaf ear to these supplications.[5]

Conversely, a vast majority of western settlers vehemently opposed division largely because it delayed statehood by making it more difficult to obtain the required number of inhabitants. During the territory's first decade, population grew at a steady but uneven pace. The census of 1810, which admittedly was done haphazardly, showed a population of slightly more than forty thousand, more than one-third of whom were slaves.[6] Consequently, most Mississippians came to view the requirement of sixty thousand free inhabitants as almost insurmountable.

Several factors were responsible for discouraging immigration to the

Old Southwest. Delays in opening land sales, an economic depression caused by the Embargo Act and the Napoleonic wars in Europe, and the presence of potentially hostile Indians, especially the Creek, were the most important. Then, in 1812, the outbreak of war slowed migration to a trickle.

But before that, a quicker method of adding population appeared. After the West Florida rebellion of 1810, the United States annexed the Baton Rouge and Pascagoula regions, touching off a heated debate about their disposition. Mississippians wanted both incorporated into Mississippi Territory, elevating its population closer to sixty thousand and improving chances for admission.

But Congress, principally for political reasons, divided these acquisitions between neighboring Mississippi and Orleans territories, adding only the sparsely settled Biloxi and Pascagoula regions to Mississippi Territory and incorporating the rest into Orleans Territory, smoothing the path for its admission in 1812 as the state of Louisiana. At least Mississippi Territory secured access to the Gulf of Mexico, or as unhappy territorial delegate George Poindexter quipped, it "gave us several hundred miles of Sea Coast."[7]

This outcome hardly pleased Mississippians, thwarting Poindexter's attempt to secure early statehood for the Old Natchez District, along with the coastal plains between the Pearl and Perdido rivers. It was especially distressing to Poindexter, who envisioned statehood as the climax of his protracted struggle with Governor Williams. But it also meant that the people could expect no immediate relief from a government that many regarded as tyrannical. Finally, successful in removing the despised executive, Poindexter came to realize that the territory's problems were more structural than personal, and only statehood could satisfy the factious inhabitants.

Consequently, in late fall of 1812, Poindexter introduced "an enabling bill," authorizing "the inhabitants of the Mississippi Territory . . . to form for themselves a constitution and state government." While its initial boundaries conformed to those of the territory, the measure included a "forever irrevocable" clause, which provided that as soon as "the population east of the river Tombigbee" reached sixty thousand "free inhabitants," the state might be "divided into two separate and independent states." Although the House endorsed the bill, the Senate refused to concur due to "the embarrassed situation of the land titles . . . , the want of numbers in its population, and the great division that exists amongst the inhabitants."[8]

Not all Mississippians favored immediate statehood. In fact, ten members of the General Assembly voiced their objections in what was known as the "Beasley Petition." They feared that the expenses associated with statehood would require a significant increase in taxes, which, in their opinion, were already unbearable. "Your Memorialists," they declared, "are compelled to consider as a very prominent objection to the contemplated change for this Territory, the single article of expence."[9]

Also, a group of concerned citizens petitioned Congress, echoing many of the same sentiments. "Suffice it to say," these petitioners related, "the excessive augmentation of taxes consequent upon our admission would be Severely felt by us at this unfortunate time." Without all of West Florida, they argued, the people were incapable of absorbing increased taxes as long as the population fell short of sixty thousand free inhabitants and the territory was vulnerable to foreign invasion. In their opinion, the territory was too dependent upon federal subsidies, particularly during wartime, to risk going it alone. Still Poindexter's abortive attempt to secure admission had one positive result: it encouraged the Georgia legislature to consent to the formation of one or more states out of its ceded territory, depriving those who favored "indestructible admission" of their strongest argument.[10]

Indeed, the Georgia Cession of 1802 was a formidable obstacle to statehood. According to its terms, "the territory thus ceded shall form a state . . . as soon as it shall contain sixty thousand free inhabitants," or earlier "if Congress shall think it expedient." While nothing in this language precluded the admission of more than one state, opponents of statehood insisted upon interpreting the provision literally, especially when it reinforced their predilections. Even after Georgia gave its consent to dividing the territory, a few diehards still insisted that the original agreement required the people's approval before separation was legal, an argument that Congress chose to disregard.[11]

The Creek conflict and war with England dampened any hope of Mississippi's joining the Union during the next few years. Nevertheless, impediments other than wartime conditions and apprehensions over cost and increased taxes brought the statehood movement to a temporary standstill. The most serious impediment was the territory's tremendous size. Of the fifteen states, only Virginia was larger in size, but its population was considerably greater and its settlements more compact. Several senators objected to admitting a territory as large as Mississippi. "We could not avoid," they stated, "being struck by the immense size of the territory, . . . a size disproportionate to the size of any of the largest states." It was, marveled another, "an area twice the surface of the state of Pennsylvania."[12]

To be sure, the postwar controversy over "indestructible" or "divisible" admission followed a decade of sectional conflict. Between 1803 and 1815, Tombigbee settlers had bombarded Congress with petitions outlining their special grievances. These included demands for accelerating the sale of public lands, reducing the minimum purchasable plot to an affordable amount, providing relief to those who had suffered property losses or personal injury during the Creek War, and permitting intruders to remain on lands they currently occupied until offered for public auction.[13]

In 1809, another complication arose with creation of Madison County in the fertile elbow of the Tennessee River. The rapid settlement of this region not only altered the territory's sectional balance by adding a third component to the mixture, but it also created another complication for statehood. For the most part, settlers in this region were generally small farmers and herdsmen, whose interests and aspirations were more akin to the people of Tombigbee than to those in Natchez District, and a close affinity between the two eastern settlements emerged. When offered a choice of joining either the Tombigbee or Natchez districts, inhabitants of Madison County invariably opted for the former. A few even favored combining with the state of Tennessee, where they had long enjoyed social and economic connections, instead of remaining part of Mississippi Territory or joining a new territory.[14]

Nevertheless, despite numerous setbacks and congressional inertia, most territorial legislators remained optimistic, and by late 1814, they were again petitioning Congress. Even as the British were preparing to land a formidable force along the Gulf coast, the General Assembly pleaded with Congress to give Mississippians "the rank of a Sister State of the Union." Acknowledging that the territory was short of population, the petitioners confidently predicted that the recent acquisition of Creek lands "will invite . . . emigration more than sufficient to Justify the measure, before the necessary proceedings can be had to carry it into operation." Cognizant of "the pecuniary burdens which will incur," they promised to overcome them with the same dispatch as they had the Indian menace. In fact, they relished the opportunity of assuming state responsibilities as long as it coincided with freeing them from the shackles of a government "despotic in nature," where the governor appointed "all officers, civil and military" and possessed "absolute veto of all laws" and the legislature was "but a cypher." Indeed, they declared, the present territorial "Government can scarcely be distinguished from that which prevailed in the British North American Colonies."[15]

By the time this memorial reached the nation's capital, however, George Poindexter was no longer the territorial delegate; instead Dr. William Lattimore was the territory's voice in Congress. Although Lattimore dutifully presented the petition to Congress, he opposed admission until resolution of the conflicting British land claims. Fearful that the Supreme Court would validate them, as it recently had the more scandalous Yazoo grants, Lattimore predicted that, once the territory was admitted and subject to the jurisdiction of federal courts, those holding Spanish titles would face a relentless barrage of expensive lawsuits that they were unlikely to win.[16]

Eager therefore to postpone admission while he sought an adjudication of the British claims similar to the Yazoo compromise, Lattimore realized that he had to placate his constituents with some concession. He hoped "to lessen" the most serious "privations of territorial government" by broadening the franchise to include taxpayers, not just freeholders. While successful in this effort, he was unable to wean from Congress an acceptable settlement of the British grants as the clamor for statehood intensified. Realizing that a majority of inhabitants would wait no longer, Lattimore, against his better judgment, succumbed to his constituents' wishes and pushed for statehood.[17]

Initially he favored "entire admission" on the grounds that the territory could not be divided without popular approval. Aware that Congress intended unilaterally to establish the conditions for admission, with or without the territory's concurrence, and that it would never agree to admit a territory with such extensive boundaries, he realized that his constituents must accept division. Taking advantage of the territory's inability to agree, Congress in early 1817 seized the initiative, and a compliant Lattimore readily acquiesced in what he believed was inevitable.[18]

The fact that Mississippians disagreed about immediate admission was to be expected, but the dispatch with which the two sections reversed their positions was surprising. Before 1815, Tombigbee District had been the chief champion for dividing the territory, but as residents there watched their population increase at a faster rate than that of the western half, due largely to the opening of new lands as a result of the recent Indian cessions, they became the loudest advocates for "indivisible" admission.

On the other hand, the residents of the Mississippi River counties also underwent a miraculous transformation. They switched from favoring "indivisible" admission to becoming the strongest proponents of immediate admission of the Natchez District, including all or part of the Florida parishes, and of converting the eastern half into Mobile or Alabama Territory. Nonetheless, while both altered their stances, there was no letup in the rancor between them.

And the old impediments to immediate admission persisted. Foremost among these was the territory's inadequate population. Despite a recent influx of settlers, no one was certain of the exact number of residents in early 1816. Some insisted that if the population was not yet adequate for admission, it would be by the time the cumbersome admission process was completed. Others were less sure. Under these chaotic conditions, territorial officials authorized, with greater optimism than sound judgment, a quick counting of the people, only to discover that the territory's population, including slaves, was about seventy-five thousand, only forty-seven thousand of whom lived west of the Pearl River and no more than 60 percent were free inhabitants. As a result of this disappointing tally, Mississippians altered their strategy; instead of demanding statehood as a right, they now requested it "as an act of courtesy."[19]

Furthermore, a number of prominent individuals, including Judge Harry Toulmin, doubted if the western half of the territory could attract a sufficient population until the Choctaw and Chickasaw Indians were removed from the region northwest of the Yazoo River. Toulmin based this pessimistic prognosis on the fact that the best lands in the Old Natchez District were either presently occupied or already sold, making it impossible for the western counties to accommodate additional immigrants. In contrast, he insisted, excellent lands were still available along the Tombigbee River and in Madison County. Why, he asked, should the sparsely settled counties along the Mississippi River be admitted before the rapidly growing eastern settlements?[20]

Indeed, the record of land sales since 1812 seemed to confirm Toulmin's disquieting contentions. During the previous three years, purchases of land west of the Pearl River had totaled only twenty thousand acres compared with more than fifty-eight thousand in Madison County alone. Furthermore, this figure did not include the numerous intruders who had squatted upon much of the still-unsurveyed lands recently ceded by the Creeks and Chickasaws. Judging from the frantic complaints of Chickasaw agent James Neely, the number of these intruders was considerable. Under these unsettling conditions, Poindexter and Mead began to push hard for early admission of the Mississippi River counties before the Natchez District was completely overwhelmed by an influx of settlers to the eastern half of the territory.[21]

While the territory's immense size and meager population troubled a number of influential congressmen, some Mississippians showed more interest in resolving land conflicts than in obtaining statehood. In fact, several favored postponing statehood until all land controversies were either fully resolved or reasonably compromised. William Lattimore emerged as the chief spokesman for this group. Although he was gratified when, in 1814, Congress removed one of the two obstacles by compromising with the Yazoo claimants, he was displeased that Congress had not also resolved the British grants.[22]

On the other hand, the Yazoo settlement encouraged British claimants to renew their efforts to seek some form of compensation. For instance, attorney Seth Hunt, representing a syndicate of British grantees, petitioned the federal government, demanding that it either arrange a suitable settlement with his clients or grant them access to the federal courts.[23] Lattimore and his friends feared that unless Congress reached an agreement with British petitioners, those holding Spanish titles that conflicted with prior British grants would face "grievous litigation" once the territory was admitted and subject to the jurisdiction of federal courts. Until these matters were resolved, the *Washington Republican* warned, "the right of every land-holder to a seat by his fire-side, must come to a test of a lawsuit if a compromise does not take place."[24]

Meanwhile, the Senate Committee on Public Lands, to whom these petitions were referred, issued a report that added more fuel to the fire. After reviewing the various treaties of 1783 and the Jay Treaty of 1794, its members questioned whether Spain had legally possessed the territory north of the thirty-first parallel. In fact, they concluded, the United States had not officially recognized Spain's right to these lands, an interpretation that threatened to invalidate all Spanish grants.[25] Since a majority of settlers, particularly those in the Natchez District, based their holdings upon Spanish titles, this unexpected pronouncement created considerable alarm.

As in other issues, politics and sectionalism played a prominent role in this controversy. Since most of the British grants were located in the Old Natchez District, western residents were more eager than their eastern counterparts to find an immediate remedy. In fact, Tombigbee settlers actually welcomed the introduction of federal courts as a way of resolving the many maritime and admiralty cases left unattended by the territorial courts. Conversely, Poindexter and Mead were not especially interested in resolving this issue. As lawyers, they had from time to time represented prominent British speculators. Indeed, Poindexter had been accused in 1811 of suppressing a legislative memorial to Congress on this subject, although the actual culprit proved to be Speaker Mead.[26]

Nonetheless, in early 1815, Lattimore launched another campaign for statehood. To be sure, by this time, prospects for admission had improved considerably. Congress had successfully resolved the Yazoo controversy, sales of the newly surveyed lands in the Tombigbee region were brisk, new settlers were arriving in unprecedented numbers, and the approaching peace brought an end to the threat of federal taxes. Indeed, the future of Mississippi Territory seemed bright when, in February 1815, Lattimore introduced an enabling act that would authorize the territory to proceed with the drafting of a state constitution. But debate on this measure had hardly begun before Congress was inundated with personal petitions and legislative memorials. Fearful that Congress might indiscriminately disregard all of these pleas, Lattimore urged his constituents to be more selective in the future.[27]

At least these communications convinced Lattimore that western residents no longer favored admission of the entire territory. Confused and bewildered by their changing attitudes, Lattimore asked the citizens for clarity, but the advice he received was conflicting and confusing. Suddenly, in late October 1816, the most fervent opponents of division took matters into their own hands. They met in a specially called convention at John Ford's plantation on the Pearl River.[28]

Although the representatives to the "Pearl River Convention" came from every section of the territory and fifteen of its twenty counties, the dominance of the eastern half was quickly apparent. The convention dispatched Judge Toulmin to the nation's capital with instructions to lay before Congress its petition for "indestructible" admission. While the delegates specifically instructed Toulmin to "confer and co-operate" with the territorial delegate, cooperation between the two officials was impossible. Lattimore resented Toulmin's attempt to meddle in his affairs, while the judge grew progressively more suspicious of Lattimore's intentions. Therefore, to assist in passing the desired legislation, Toulmin turned to Representative Israel Pickens of North Carolina, shunning his own territory's delegate.[29]

In late 1816, the territorial House of Representatives, by a margin of two votes, endorsed the actions of the Pearl River Convention, but thirteen members signed a proposal urging separation because "Nature never intended the present limits of this Territory to be embraced in one state." Left to decide the question on his own, Lattimore opted for division, partly because he himself was a resident of the western part of the territory but largely because he was convinced that a majority of the U.S. Senate, controlled by men from the western and southern states who were determined to preserve their hold on the upper chamber, favored division. The reason was obvious: division would give the southwestern states two additional senators. Accordingly, he introduced a resolution authorizing the western half of the territory to call a constitutional convention.[30]

While Toulmin's maneuvers were crippling Lattimore's efforts, his bill ran into stiff opposition from eastern congressmen who feared a loss of power to western states. But his perseverance finally paid dividends when Congress enacted two measures more in keeping with his wishes than with those of Toulmin and Pickens. On March 1, 1817, President Madison signed the enabling act that provided for admission of the western half of the territory as the state of Mississippi and reorganization of the rest as the territory of Alabama. A second act compromised the north-south divisional line, running from the Gulf of Mexico to the southern boundary of the state of Tennessee, between easterners who favored the Pearl River and westerners who pushed for the Tombigbee River.[31]

Rather than delay admission further, Lattimore consented to a dividing line that more or less split the difference. As finally drawn, the boundary ran from the Gulf of Mexico, slightly west of Mobile Bay, to the northwestern corner of Washington County and from there directly to the point where Bear Creek emptied into the Tennessee River. The compromise placed Mobile, the entire Tombigbee District, and Madison County in Alabama Territory and left the Pascagoula country (Hancock and Jackson counties), the Pearl River settlements, and the Old Natchez District in the new state of Mississippi.[32] Admittedly, it was not a perfect solution or satisfactory to everyone, but it was acceptable to enough people to smooth the way for statehood.

Nevertheless a few prominent easterners in Washington and Madison counties were extremely displeased with the line Congress drew and with the decision to admit the less-populated western section before the more populous eastern part. On the other hand, Poindexter and Mead, both western residents, were also upset. They lambasted Lattimore for excluding Mobile from the new state and urged Mississippians to reopen in the next Congress the question of where to draw the final boundary line. Both Poindexter and Mead announced their intention to run for the lame-duck seat of territorial delegate in the upcoming elections of May 1817.[33]

Settlers along the Pascagoula River, who rarely supported Poindexter or Mead, now joined them in seeking reconsideration of the boundary line. Indeed, they were so distressed with exclusion of Mobile that they were not "disposed to form a constitution." Meanwhile, Lattimore, who was becoming more defensive, politely reminded his critics that he had been chosen to represent the interests of all sections, not just Natchez, and that Mobile was as close to Savannah, Georgia, as it was to Natchez.[34]

The Enabling Act of 1817 specified that those citizens eligible to vote in territorial elections were to select delegates on the first Monday and Tuesday of June to a constitutional convention. That convention subsequently met in the Methodist meeting house at Jefferson College in the town of Washington for six weeks during the hot and humid months of July and August. The fourteen counties of the newly designated state selected forty-eight delegates, half of whom represented the five counties along the Mississippi River that contained only 47 percent of the population.[35] As long as the river counties could count on the support of Franklin and Amite counties, and occasionally that of Pike County, they would be able to write a constitution that reflected their political views and protected their economic interests. Likewise, representatives from the eastern "piney woods" (Lawrence, Marion, Wayne, Green, and Jackson counties) also championed the interests of their constituents. Not surprisingly, the few conflicts that emerged were largely a reflection of sectional and economic differences.

With the delegates in general agreement, they comprised an unusually homogeneous group. None was an avowed Federalist or anti-Republican, and all professed to worship at the shrine of Jefferson. The vast majority were landowners, a handful of whom possessed extensive holdings. Only three were men of modest means. Additionally, almost all of the delegates had some political experience, and a few had considerable. While David Holmes was the only territorial governor in attendance, three former territorial secretaries (John Steele, Cato West and Cowles Mead), two former territorial delegates (Poindexter and Lattimore), and three sitting judges (Walter Leake, Henry Simpson, and George Poindexter) were there. Among these, Lattimore and Poindexter were especially outspoken and combative.

After selecting Holmes president, the delegates debated the expediency of forming a state government as specified in the Enabling Act. Mead, who had finally been elected territorial delegate in 1817, and Poindexter, with the support of delegates from Jefferson and Wilkinson counties, made one final but futile push to postpone the writing of a constitution in hopes of reopening the boundary question so as to include Mobile in the new state. But these last-ditch efforts failed when the convention rejected, by a 32 to 14 margin, a motion to adjourn the convention until March 15, 1818. Apparently representatives from the river counties dissuaded the "piney woods" delegates from joining Poindexter by promising to locate the state capital on the Pearl River, a pledge they were not to keep until much later.[36]

With removal of this obstacle, the delegates proceeded to adopt a constitution. First, they appointed a select committee of twenty (later enlarged to twenty-one) to draft a proposed constitution. Chaired by Poindexter, it consisted of at least one member from each of the fourteen counties and two from the larger ones. After deliberating for over a week, it submitted its report on July 17. Following a brief adjournment for the delegates to study the committee's work, the convention, operating as a committee of the whole, debated and amended the committee's recommendations between July 21 and August 4. After endorsing most of the alterations suggested by the committee of the whole, the convention, on August 17, 1817, adopted the state's first constitution. Only Cato West refused to sign it. Eventually, forty-five delegates affixed their signatures to the finished product.[37]

The work of the convention reflected both the personal views of the delegates and the political experiences of the territory. Even the eight peaceful years of Governor Holmes had not erased the memory of the bitter feuds during the administrations of Governors Sargent and Williams, and the delegates favored a weak and restrained chief executive. Still they resisted the temptation to reduce the governor to a mere figurehead by requiring two-thirds rather than, as some wanted, a simple majority of the legislature to override the governor's veto.[38] The constitution provided for the popular election of sheriffs and coroners rather than giving the governor this power, thereby preventing future executives from employing patronage to build a personal following as the territorial governors had done.

The judiciary system had also been a source of considerable controversy during territorial times. On three occasions, efforts had been undertaken to impeach territorial judges. Consequently, the delegates were eager to assure and protect an independent judiciary. The constitution provided for "one supreme court, and such superior and inferior courts of law and equity as the legislature may . . . establish" and for legislative appointment of judges who were to serve "during good behavior" or until they reached the age of sixty-five. The last provision stemmed from the unfortunate experiences with a few incompetent and elderly judges, notably Peter Bryan Bruin.[39]

Since the legislature was to be the dominant branch of the new government, it was not surprising that the one issue that threatened to disrupt an otherwise peaceful convention was apportionment of representatives in the General Assembly. The conflict was largely one of sectional advantage. Delegates from the eastern counties, or backcountry, wanted the Senate apportioned equally among the counties and representation in the lower house to be based upon free white population.

On the other hand, delegates from the river counties, with their heavy concentration of slaves, insisted upon counting all forms of property in determining representation of both bodies. After the convention had rejected five proposals to resolve this thorny issue, David Dickson of Pike County moved to reconsider the question of whether it was expedient to form a constitution. Instantly, disgruntled easterners joined the fourteen delegates who had previously opposed immediate statehood in support of Dickson's motion, and Lattimore and his clique were barely able to muster enough support to secure a tie vote, thereby aborting the movement to postpone the drafting of a constitution.[40]

This explosive issue was finally resolved "outdoors." Caucusing together on August 5, during a weekend recess, the members unanimously agreed to apportion representation in the house on the basis of free white population and to guarantee each county at least one seat. Later, the same members decided to base senatorial representation "on the free white taxable inhabitants," a provision that constituted a face-saving victory for the river counties.[41]

Compared with the constitutions of other western states during this same period, Mississippi's was slightly more conservative. Although the franchise was restricted to taxpayers or to those who had served in the militia, most adult white males were able to meet these requirements rather easily. Several other provisions, however, were less democratic. Officeholders were required to possess some property and to pass a religious test. Only two state officials—the governor and the lieutenant-governor—were to be popularly elected; the rest were to be chosen by the legislature. The constitution could be amended only by the laborious process of summoning another convention, an unwieldy procedure in a dynamic and dispersed frontier society. Finally, the convention did not submit its finished product to the voters for their approval; instead, it sent the document directly to President James Monroe for his approval.[42]

Except for a few minor provisions, the Mississippi Constitution of 1817 was hardly innovative. The drafters borrowed most of its provisions from the constitutions of Tennessee, Kentucky, and Louisiana. Indeed, the editor of the faraway *Worcester Spy* succinctly and appropriately summarized Mississippi's constitution. "It is," he wrote, "so similar to the constitutions of many of the other states that its perusal does not excite much interest."[43]

In September 1817, in what was one of Mississippi's few tranquil elections, the voters honored David Holmes by making him the state's first chief executive. They also chose the obscure David Stewart over the better-known and controversial Cowles Mead as lieutenant governor, while Poindexter ran unopposed in the race for the state's only congressional seat. In October, the General Assembly selected Judge Walter Leake and Thomas H. Williams as Mississippi's first senators. In early December, Congress approved the state constitution, passed the resolution of admission, and seated its first congressmen. On December 10, 1817, President Monroe officially signed the act admitting Mississippi into the Union as the nation's twentieth state.[44]

Notes

Abbreviations

The following abbreviations are used in the notes to designate frequently cited publications, libraries, and individuals.

AC	*Annals of Congress*
AE	Andrew Ellicott
AEJ	Andrew Ellicott, *The Journals of Andrew Ellicott* (Philadelphia, 1803)
AEP	Andrew Ellicott Papers (LC)
AGI, PC	Papeles procedantes de la Isla de Cuba, Archivo General de Indias, Seville, Spain
AHR	*American Historical Review*
AJ	Andrew Jackson
AJ, *Papers*	Harold D. Moser and Sharon MacPherson, eds., *The Papers of Andrew Jackson* (Knoxville, Tenn., 1980–)
APW, *MQ*	Arthur Preston Whitaker, *The Mississippi Question, 1795–1803* (New York, 1934)
APW, *Sp-Am*	Arthur Preston Whitaker, *The Spanish-American Frontier, 1783–1795* (Boston, 1927)
AR	*Alabama Review*
ASP	Walter Lowrie et al., eds., *American State Papers* (Washington, 1832–1861)
	FR, Foreign Relations
	IA, Indian Affairs
	MS, Misc.
	PL, Public Lands
BH	Benjamin Hawkins
C&G, *FC*	Thomas D. Clark and John D. W. Guice, *Frontiers*

	in Conflict: The Old Southwest, 1795–1830 (Albuquerque, N.M., 1989)
CC	JFH Claiborne Collection (MDAH)
CM	Cowles Mead
CSS, *Wailes*	Charles S. Sydnor, *A Gentleman of the Old Natchez District: Benjamin L. C. Wailes* (Durham, N.C., 1938)
CW	Cato West
DH	David Holmes
EJ	Governor's Executive Journal (MDAH)
FH, *SIBH*	Florette Henri, *The Southern Indians and Benjamin Hawkins, 1796–1816* (Norman, Okla., 1986)
GC	Governor's Correspondence and Papers (RG 2, MDAH)
GP	George Poindexter
GPP	George Poindexter Papers (MDAH)
H&B, *CW*	H. S. Halbert and T. H. Ball, *Creek War of 1813 and 1814* (1895; repr., Tuscaloosa, Ala., 1995)
Hamilton, "Beginnings"	William Baskerville Hamilton, "American Beginnings in the Old Southwest: The Mississippi Phase" (Ph. D. diss., Duke University, 1938)
Hamilton, *Law*	William Baskerville Hamilton, *Anglo-American Law on the Frontier: Thomas Rodney and His Territorial Cases* (Durham, N.C., 1953)
HT	Harry Toulmin
HT, *Stat.*	Harry Toulmin, *The Statutes of the Mississippi Territory* (Natchez, 1807)
IB	Isaac Briggs
IBP	Isaac Briggs Papers (LC)
James, *Natchez*	D. Clayton James, *Antebellum Natchez* (Baton Rouge, 1968)
JFHC, *Miss.*	J. F. H. Claiborne, *Mississippi as a Province, Territory, and State* (Jackson, Miss., 1880)
JHR	Journal of the House of Representatives (MDAH)
JLC	Journal of the Legislative Council (MDAH)
JM	James Madison
JMH	*Journal of Mississippi History*
JSH	*Journal of Southern History*
JW	James Wilkinson

L&B	Andrew A. Lipscomb and Albert E. Bergh, eds., *The Writings of Thomas Jefferson*, 20 vols. (Washington, 1903)
LBC	Dunbar Rowland, ed., *Official Letter Books of W. C. C. Claiborne, 1801–1816*, 6 vols. (Jackson, Miss., 1917)
LC	Library of Congress
LH	*Louisiana History*
LHQ	*Louisiana Historical Quarterly*
LK, *Spain*	Lawrence Kinnaird, ed., *Spain in the Mississippi Valley* (Washington, 1946–1949)
LSU	Louisiana State University
MDAH	Mississippi Department of Archives and History
MDG, *Politics*	Michael D. Green, *The Politics of Indian Removal: Creek Government and Society in Crisis* (Lincoln, Neb., 1982)
MH&NG	*Mississippi Herald and Natchez Gazette*
MHSP	Mississippi Historical Society, *Publications*
MS, *Poindexter*	Mack Swearingen, *The Early Life of George Poindexter* (New Orleans, 1934)
Ms M	Miscellaneous Manuscripts (MDAH)
MTA	Dunbar Rowland, ed., *Mississippi Territorial Archives, 1795–1803* (Nashville, 1905)
MTP	Mississippi Territory Papers (RG 59, NA)
M6	Letters Sent to the President by the Secretary of War, 1800–1889, Records of the Office of Secretary of War (RG 107, NA)
M15	Letters Sent by the Secretary of War Relating to Indian Affairs, 1800–1823
M40	Domestic Letters of the Department of State, 1784–1906 (RG 59, NA)
M179	Miscellaneous Letters of the Department of State, 1789–1906 (RG 59, NA)
M221	Letters Received by the Secretary of War, Registered Series, 1801–1870 (RG 107, NA)
M222	Letters Received by the Secretary of War, Unregistered Series, 1789–1861 (RG 107, NA)
M271	Letters Received by the Office of the Secretary of War Relating to Indian Affairs, 1800–1824, Records of the Bureau of Indian Affairs (RG 75, NA)

M370	Miscellaneous Letters Sent by the Secretary of War, 1800–1809 (RG 107, NA)
NA	National Archives
PMHB	*Pennsylvania Magazine of History and Biography*
RW	Robert Williams
SBP	Southern Boundary Papers (NA)
SS	Secretary of State
TJ	Thomas Jefferson
TJP	Thomas Jefferson Papers (LC)
TLR	Territorial Legislative Records (RG5, MDAH)
TP	Clarence E. Carter, ed., *The Territorial Papers of the United States* (Washington, 1937–)
TPA, *BC*	Thomas Perkins Abernethy, *The Burr Conspiracy* (New York, 1954)
TPA, *South*	Thomas Perkins Abernethy, *The South in the New Nation, 1789–1819* (Baton Rouge, 1961)
TR	Thomas Rodney
TRP	Thomas Rodney Papers
T225	Dispatches from United States Consuls in New Orleans, Louisiana, 1798–1807 (RG 59, NA)
WC	William Charles Cole Claiborne
WFP	West Florida Papers (LC)
WS	Winthrop Sargent
WSP (MHS)	Winthrop Sargent Papers, Massachusetts Historical Society, Boston
WSP (OHS)	Winthrop Sargent Papers, Ohio Historical Society, Columbus
WSP (LC)	Winthrop Sargent Papers (Personal Miscellaneous File, LC)

Prologue

1. Stanley Elkins and Eric McKitrick, *The Age of Federalism* (New York, 1993).

2. Joel Achenbach, *The Grand Idea* (New York, 2004), 29–46.

3. John Ferling, *A Leap in the Dark* (New York, 2003).

4. William H. Masterson, *William Blount* (Baton Rouge, 1954).

5. TPA, *South*, 74–101, 136–68.

6. *TP*, 5:6.

7. Daniel H. Usner, *American Indians in the Lower Mississippi Valley* (Lincoln, Neb., 1998), 73–86.

8. Cecil Johnson, *British West Florida, 1762–1783* (New Haven, 1942).

1. From Province to Territory

1. AEJ, 176; AE to SS, March 21, 1798, SBP; AE to SS, March 25, 1798, AEP.

2. John W. Caughey, *Bernardo de Galvez in Louisiana, 1775–1783* (Berkeley, 1934), 149–70.

3. J. Barton Starr, *Tories, Dons, and Rebels: The American Revolution in British West Florida* (Gainesville, Fla., 1976), 78–88; Robert V. Haynes, "James Willing and the Planters of Natchez: The American Revolution Comes to the Southwest," *JMH* 35:1–40; John W. Caughey, "Willing's Expedition down the Mississippi: 1778," *LHQ* 15:5–36.

4. Robert V. Haynes, *The Natchez District and the American Revolution* (Jackson, Miss., 1976), 66–87; Eron Rowland, ed., *Life, Letters and Papers of William Dunbar* (Jackson, Miss., 1930), 60–63; Anthony Hutchins to George Germain, May 21, 1778, English Provincial Records, VII, 399–400 (MDAH).

5. John W. Caughey, "The Natchez Rebellion of 1781 and Its Aftermath," *LHQ* 16:57–83.

6. Jack D. L. Holmes, *Gayoso: The Life of a Spanish Governor in the Mississippi Valley, 1798–1799* (Baton Rouge, 1965), 33–135; James, *Natchez*, 31–53. On Spanish policy, see LK, *Spain*, 2:268–69.

7. James, *Natchez*, 33; Holmes, *Gayoso*, 36–37, 38, 49–51, 52; Rowland, *Dunbar*, 76, 77–78. On Dunbar's early life, see Arthur H. DeRosier Jr., "William Dunbar: A Product of the Eighteenth-Century Scottish Renaissance," *JMH* 28:185–227; William Dunbar to his wife, April 4, 1790, William Dunbar Papers (MDAH). See also Arthur H. DeRosier Jr., *William Dunbar: Scientific Pioneer of the Old Southwest* (Lexington, Ky., 2007).

8. Holmes, *Gayoso*, 51, 147n, 199, 233; AE to SS, March 14, 1798, SBP; Minor to AE, March 19, 1798, AEP; Gayoso to AE, April 14, 1798, ibid.; Jack D. L. Holmes, "Stephen Minor: Natchez Planter," *JMH* 42:17–21; Dunbar to his wife, June 6, 1798, Dunbar Papers (MDAH).

9. William S. Coker and Jack D. L. Holmes, eds., "Daniel Clark's Letter on the Mississippi Territory," *JMH* 32:154–55, 166n; Daniel Clark to Hutchins, June 12, 1795, CC; Gayoso to Clark, July 27, 1794, M222; Gayoso to Clark, October 18 and November 14, 1796, ibid.; Beatrice Marion Stokes, "John Bisland, Mississippi Planter, 1776–1821" (master's thesis, Louisiana State University, 1941); James, *Natchez*, 33, 45–46, 51.

10. Gayoso to Clark, March 2, 1796, M222; Clark to JW, March 28, 1798, ibid.

11. William S. Coker, "The Bruins and the Formulation of Spanish Immigration Policy in the Old Southwest, 1787–1788," in John Francis McDermott, ed., *The Spanish in the Mississippi Valley, 1762–1804* (Urbana, Ill., 1974),

61–71; William S. Coker, "Peter Bryan Bruin of Bath: Soldier, Judge and Frontiersman," *West Virginia History* 30: 579–85; LK, *Spain*, 2:257, 338–41, 354–55, 357–64, 379, 395–98, 401–4; Holmes, *Gayoso*, 49; John Carl Parish, "The Intrigues of Doctor James O'Fallon," *Mississippi Valley Historical Review* 16:230–63; APW, *Span-Am*, 129–33.

12. AEJ, 137–40; JW to Gayoso, February 6, 1797, M222.

13. Edmund C. Burnett, ed., "Papers Relating to Bourbon County, Georgia," *AHR* 15:67–79, 297–99, 334–35; Duron and Roberto Corbett, eds., "Papers from the Spanish Archives Relating to Tennessee and the Old Southwest, 1783–1800," *Publications of the East Tennessee Historical Society* 9:125–28; James, *Natchez*, 54–56.

14. LK, *Spain*, 2:135–36, 143–45, 145–50; Burnett, "Bourbon County Papers," 96–97, 335–37, 350–52, 352–53; James, *Natchez*, 56–57.

15. Gayoso to Carondelet, July 20, 1792, AGI, PC, leg. 41.

16. JFHC, *Miss.*, 126–34; Caughey, *Galvez*, 220–28; Holmes, *Gayoso*, 86–94; LK, *Spain*, 2:305–11.

17. Philip Nolan to JW, April 6, 1791, M222, reel 1; James A. Robertson, ed., *Louisiana under the Rule of Spain, France and the United States, 1785–1807*, 2 vols. (Cleveland, 1911), 1:286; James, *Natchez*, 48–50.

18. JFHC, *Miss.*, 139–40.

19. Hamilton, "Beginnings," 189–95; Claiborne, *Miss.*, 140n; Holmes, *Gayoso*, 96–97.

20. Holmes, *Gayoso*, 92–98; Gayoso to Clark, October 18, 1796, M222.

21. JFHC, *Miss.*, 143; Gayoso to Clark, November 14, 1796, M222.

22. JFHC, *Miss.*, 142; AE to SS, January 10, 1799, SBP; Dunbar to John Ross, May 23, 1799, Dunbar Papers (MDAH).

23. Robert V. Haynes, "The Disposal of Lands in the Mississippi Territory," *JMH* 24:226–29; AE to SS, September 24, 1797, SBP.

24. AEJ, 38–40; Daniel Clark, *Proofs of the Corruption of Gen. James Wilkinson and of His Connexion with Aaron Burr* (Philadelphia, 1809): 70. Ellicott's original instructions for "running and marking the southern boundary line" are in Pickering to Commissioners Ellicott and Thomas Freeman, September 14, 1796, M40; and AE to Gayoso, February 24, 1797, AEP: *ASP, FR*, 2:22.

25. AEJ, 41–49; Gayoso to AE, March 12, 1797, AEP; SS to Yrujo, August 8, 1797, M40.

26. APW, *MQ*, 52–56. On Gayoso's doubts, see Gayoso to Clark, Sr., June 17, 1796, Parson Collection, Harry Ransom Center, University of Texas at Austin; Louis Houck, ed., *The Spanish Regime in Missouri*, 2 vols. (Chicago, 1909), 2:133–38; *ASP, FR*, 2:68.

27. APW, *MQ*, 56–60; Gayoso to AE, March 23, 1797, AEP; AE to Gayoso, March 23, 1797, ibid.; *ASP, FR*, 2:73–74.

28. APW, *MQ*, 57; Gayoso to AE, April 1 and May 1, 1797, AEP; Nolan to JW, April 24, 1797, M222; AEJ, 101–3.

29. AE to Pope, March 25, 1797, AEP; Inhabitants in Natchez Country to AE, March 29, 1797, SBP; N. Hunter to AE, March 19, 1797, AEP.

30. *ASP, FR*, 2:75–76.

31. AEJ, 67, 96; AE to SS, April 14 and May 10, 1797, SBP; AE to Pope, April 1797, AEP; *ASP, FR*, 2:73.

32. Proclamation of Baron de Carondelet, May 24, 1797, SBP; AEJ, 91–96; *ASP, FR*, 2:83–84.

33. AEJ, 97–100; Jack D. L. Holmes, ed., *Documentos ineditos para la historia de la Louisiana, 1792–1810* (Madrid, 1963), 318–55; Holmes, *Gayoso*, 190–91; AE to SS, June 27, 1797, AEP.

34. *Papers in Relation to the Official Conduct of Governor Sargent* (Boston, 1801), 20–22; Holmes, *Gayoso*, 191; *ASP, FR*, 2:84, Holmes, *Documentos de la Louisiana*, 319–26; Gayoso to Carondelet, June 12, 1797, AGI, PC, leg. 43.

35. AEJ, 101, 104–5; Gayoso to AE, June 13, 1797, AEP; Hutchins to John Adams, September 7, 1797, M179; James, *Natchez*, 70; Holmes, *Gayoso*, 192–94.

36. AEJ, 111–17; AE to SS, June 27, 1797, SBP; *TP*, 5:11–12, 13–14.

37. AE to CW, July 3, 1797, AEP; AE to SS, July 4, 1797, SBP.

38. Philip Nolan to JW, July 26, 1797, AEP; AE to SS, July 4, 1797, SBP.

39. Holmes, *Gayoso*, 198–99; Gayoso to AE, July 27 and 28, 1797, SBP.

40. Proclamation of Governor Gayoso, July 10, 1797, M179; *TP*, 5:10–11; AE to Joseph Bernard, n.d., AEP.

41. Minutes of Committee of Natchez Country, September 12, 1797, M179; Deposition of Citizens of Buffalo District before Daniel Clark, September 2, 1797, ibid.; AE to SS, September 12, 1797, SBP.

42. Hutchins to Stephen Minor, August 9, 1797, CC; Hutchins to Planters of Natchez, August 18, 1797, ibid.; Proclamation of Stephen Minor, August 16, 1797, M179; JFHC, *Miss.*, 173–74.

43. Gayoso to AE, August 16, 1797, AEP; Dunbar to AE, August 27, 1797, ibid.; Bruin to AE, August 27, 1797, ibid.; Hutchins to "Gentlemen," August 28, 1797, M179.

44. Petition of Inhabitants to Minor, August 25, 1797, SBP; George Cochran to Bruin, August 23, 1797, M179; Deposition of Citizens of Buffalo District before Daniel Clark, September 2, 1797, ibid.; Dunbar to AE, August 27, 1797, AEP.

45. AEJ, 141–43; JFHC, *Miss.*, 175; Minutes of Committee of Natchez County, September 12, 1797, M179; *TP*, 5:4–6; Inhabitants of Natchez to House of Representatives, September 27, 1797, SBP.

46. MS Journal of the Proceedings of Permanent Committee, September

1797, M179; *ASP, FR,* 2:86; Proclamation of Gov. Minor September 20, 1797, SBP. The council consisted of Minor, Dunbar, Joseph Vidal, and Cochran.

47. AEJ, 127–33; Testimony of Christopher Bingaman, October 17, 1797, SBP; AE to James Ross, September 24, 1797, AEP; Gentleman at New Orleans to his Correspondent at Philadelphia, December 8, 1797, M179, reel 15; Starr, *Tories, Dons, and Rebels,* 110–12; Haynes, *Natchez District,* 84–87, 133–42.

48. AE to SS, September 24 and October 7, 1797, SBP; Gayoso to AE, October 18, 1797, ibid.; circular letter of AE, October 13, 1797, AEP; AE to TJ, September 25, 1797, ibid.; circular letter to Congress, September 25, 1797, ibid.

49. APW, MQ, 64; James Wilkinson, *Memoirs of My Own Times,* 3 vols. (Philadelphia, 1816), 1: appendix 32; JFHC, *Miss.,* 197–98n; Merritt B. Pound, "Colonel Benjamin Hawkins: North Carolinian and Benefactor of the Southern Indians, Part 1," *North Carolina Historical Review* 19 (1942): 12.

50. Pickering to AE, June 10, 1797, M40, reel 10; Mathews and Miller to Chairman of Permanent Committee, October 19, 1797, CC; A. Hutchins to Pickering, November 10, 1797, ibid.; AE to SS, October 27, 1797, SBP; T. Hutchins to A. Hutchins, December 21, 1797, ibid.; Minor to Gayoso, October 14, 1797, AGI, PC, leg. 2371.

51. AE to "Old Toney Hutchins," October 7, 1797, AEP; Memorial of Permanent Committee to AE, October 21, 1797, ibid.; Resolution of James Truly et al., October 24, 1797, ibid.; Hutchins to "Those whom it may concern," October 12, 1797, CC; Hutchins to Pickering, November 10, 1797, ibid.; AE to SS, November 14, 1797, SBP.

52. Deposition of Daniel Burnet, November 22, 1797, M179; Hutchins to AE, November 22, 1797, ibid.; AE to SS, November 26, 1797, AEP.

53. Hutchins to Planters, Mechanics & Laborers of the Government of the Natchez, n.d., CC; Report of Hutchins to Committee of Safety and Correspondence, n.d., ibid.; Hutchins to Pickering, November 25, 1797, M179; AE to SS November 26, 1797, SBP.

54. Report of Hutchins to Committee of Safety, n.d., CC; AE to SS, November 26, 1797, SBP.

55. Vousdan to Minor, November 8, 1797, Stephen Minor Papers, Hill Memorial Library, Louisiana State University; Minor to Gayoso, November 26, 1797, AGI, PC, leg. 1500.

56. Bruin to AE, November 3, 1797, AEP; EJ, 161–62; James, *Natchez,* 74.

57. JW to Guion, November 4, 1797, CC; Guion to Capt. E. Beauregard, December 1, 1797; Dunbar Rowland, ed., "Military Journal of Captain Isaac Guion, 1797–1799," *Seventh Annual Report,* Mississippi Department of Archives and History of the State of Mississippi (Jackson, 1909), 59; Guion to Secretary of War, February 25, 1798, ibid., 68–69; AEJ, 162; Dunbar to AE, December 15, 1797, AEP; Gabriel Benoist to Guion, December, 1797, CC.

58. Rowland, "Journal of Guion," 63; EJ, 162; JFHC, *Miss.*, 179.

59. Gayoso to AE, January 10, 1798, AEP; Daniel Clark to AE, January 15, 1797, AEP; Minutes of Meeting of Committee of Safety, February 5, 1798, CC.

60. Permanent Committee to Inhabitants of Natchez, February 1, 1798, CC; Benoist to Guion, February 2, 1798, ibid.; AE to Pickering, February 10, 1798, SBP.

61. AE to Gayoso, February 1, 1798, AEP; AE to SS, February 10, 1798, ibid.; AE to SS, February 10, 1798, ibid.

62. Vousdan to Guion, May 9, 1798, CC; Guion to Lewis Evans and David Ferguson, May 3, 1798, ibid.; Hutchins to Pickering, May 3, 1798, ibid.; AE to Samuel Mitchell, April 9, 1798, AEP; Cochran to AE, April 27, 1798, ibid.; Lewis Evans to AE, April 29, 1798, ibid.

63. David Ferguson et al. to Guion, May 5, 1798, CC; Minor to AE, May 11, 1798, AEP; Cochran to AE, May 19, 1798, ibid.; AE to SS, June 19, 1798, ibid.; Rich Diddep to Guion, May 13, 1798, CC.

64. AEJ, 177–80, 186; Dunbar to AE, May 24, 1797, AEP; James, *Natchez*, 75.

65. Arthur Miller to AE, February 9, 1798, AEP; Pickering to Hutchins, February 12, 1798, ibid., Bruin to AE, April 27, 1798, ibid., Lewis Evans to AE, April 29, 1798, ibid.; Cochran to AE, May 19, 1798, ibid.; Pickering to Mathews, February 18, 1798, M40, reel 10; Hutchins to Pickering, May 5, 1798, CC; AE to SS June 19, 1798, SBP.

66. Guion to AE, June 28, 1798, AEP; Dunbar to AE, July 1 and 6, 1798, ibid.; TP, 5:31. Pickering also expected President Adams to appoint Mathews governor of Mississippi Territory (ibid., 17). Mathews first inquired about the governorship in the fall of 1796 (Pickering to Mathews, October 18, 1796, M40; AE to Guion, June 27, 1798, CC; Lewis Evans to AE, May 29 and July 16, 1798, AEP; AE to SS, July 12, 1798, SBP).

67. Dunbar to AE, July 1, 1798, AEP.

2. "His Yankeeship"

1. *TP*, 5:37. Lewis Evans reported that Sargent "Had the goute accompanied by a slite Fever." He also learned from Bruin that the governor had "not had a Stool" for eight days. "I have often heard it in the mouths of the Vulgar (I do not care a turd for you)," Evans wrote; "His Excellency I suppose would gladly give his government for one for indeed all the World is but trifling to a man who cannot s—t" (Evans to AE, August 13, 1798, AEP).

2. EJ, 182; Evans to AE, August 13, 1798, AEP; James White to AE, August 13, 1798, ibid. Located twenty miles north of Natchez, Concord was then in the

possession of Peter Walker (Gayoso to Walker, February 14, 1799, CC). Mary Joan Elliot, "Winthrop Sargent and the Administration of the Mississippi Territory" (Ph. D. diss., University of Southern California, 1971), 33; James Ripley Jacobs, *Tarnished Warrior: Major-General James Wilkinson* (New York, 1938).

3. Elliott, "Sargent," 4–11.

4. *TP,* 5:27.

5. *MTA,* 282, 243, 268.

6. JFHC, *Miss.,* 208; Ebenezer Dayton to WS, August 7, 1798, WSP (OHS).

7. Lucius M. Sargent to Winthrop Sargent (grandson of the governor), November 3, 1858, WSP (MHS).

8. SS to WS, May 11, 1798, WSP (LC); JFHC, *Miss.,* 205.

9. *TP,* 5:18–22.

10. Evans to AE, August 16, 1798, AEP; *MTA,* 25–29.

11. Evans to AE, August 16, 1798, AEP; Clark to AE, August 24, 1798, ibid.; *MTA,* 21–24, 30–33; AE to WS, n.d. [September 1798], WSP (MHS); AE to Clark, September 16, 1798, AEP.

12. Evans to AE, September 9, 1798, AEP.

13. *MTA,* 35–40; Clark to AE, September 17, 1798, AEP; Minor to AE, September 22, 1798, ibid.

14. Joseph Calvit to WS, October 1, 1798, WSP (MHS); JW to AE, October 19, 1798, AEP.

15. *MTA,* 42–44; Evans to AE, August 13, 1798, September 9, and 10, 1798, AEP.

16. *MTA,* 78; Dunbar to WS, November 8, 1798, WSP (MHS); JFHC, *Miss.,* 208; John Remley Wunder, "The Mississippi Territory's First Experience with American Legal Institutions: Sargent's Code, Its Adoption and Abolition, 1798–1803," *JMH* 38:131–55.

17. *MTA,* 52, 89; TPA, *South,* 153–54.

18. *ASP, MS,* 1:359; JW to WS, August 2, 1798, WSP (MHS); Evans to AE, August 13, 1798, AEP.

19. Isaac Joslin Cox, ed., "Documents Relating to Zacheriah Cox," *Quarterly Publications of the Historical and Philosophical Society of Ohio,* 8:65–66; *ASP, MS,* 1:360, White to AE, August 15, 1798, AEP; *MTA,* 31, 35.

20. Cox to WS, September 3, and 20, 1798, WSP (MHS); Daniel Clark Jr. to D. W. Cox, October 4, 1798, T225; Cox, ed., "Documents," 67–71, 81; *MTA,* 58–59; Evans to AE, October 2, 1798, AEP.

21. *MTA,* 51–52; Gayoso to WS, October 8, 1798, WSP (OHS); Cox, "Documents," 71–72; JW to WS, November 4 and 7, 1798, WSP (MHS); Daniel Clark Jr. to JW, November 30, 1798, M222, reel 2.

22. *MTA,* 76–77, 79–80, 81–82; JW to WS, October 15 and 28, Novem-

ber 4, December 19 and 31, 1798, WSP (MHS). The depositions collected by Wilkinson are in Cox, "Documents," 103–11.

23. *MTA*, 93. Later Sargent testified that only five families left the territory, and all of them returned except for one person who had "migrated to avoid prosecution for malpractice" (*MTA*, 250).

24. *TP*, 5:100–101, 158–59; *MTA*, 59–60, 66, 89.

25. *TP*, 5:63; *MTA*, 54–56, 69–72, 90–91.

26. *MTA*, 33–35, 48, 55.

27. Holmes, *Gayoso*, 235–37; *MTA*, 47; AE to SS, January 13, 1799, SBP.

28. Evans to AE, October 31, 1798, AEP; *MTA*, 48–49; Evans to AE, October 31, 1798, AEP; Judith S. Murray to Esp Sargent, February 1, 1799, WSP (MHS).

29. *MTA*, 110; John D. W. Guice, "The Cement of Society: Law in the Mississippi Territory," *Gulf Coast Historical Review* 1:76–99.

30. These and subsequent laws are in William D. McCain, ed., *Sargent's Code: Collection of the Original Laws of the Mississippi Territory Enacted 1799–1800 by Governor Winthrop Sargent and the Territorial Judges* (Jackson, Miss., 1959). See also Elliott, "Sargent," 105–12; and Wunder, "Sargent's Code," 35–39.

31. *MTA*, 126–27; Lewis Evans to AE, February 23, 1799, AEP.

32. *Laws of the Missisippi [sic] Territory 22nd Day of January . . . 1799 . . . and Continued . . . to the 25th Day of May* (Natchez, 1799), pamphlet in the New York Public Library. See also *TP*, 5:66; and JFHC, *Miss.*, 209.

33. *MTA*, 126–27, 131–36, 145–46; Henry Green to WS, May 15, 1799, WSP (MHS); William Vousdan to WS, April 13, 1799, ibid.; Thomas Calvit to WS, April 19, 1799, ibid.; Thomas Burling to WS, June 3, 1799, GC.

34. Petition of Inhabitants to WS, October 21, 1800, WSP (OHS); Girault to WS, November 2, 1800, ibid.; John Foster to AE, August 18, 1798, AEP; *MTA*, 83–84, 86.

35. Secretary of War to JW, January 31, 1799, James Wilkinson Papers, Chicago Historical Society; Capt. John N. Heth to WS, February 23, 1799, WSP (MHS); *MTA*, 111, 136–37; Corpora Archibald Diddup to Guion, April 8, 9, 21, and 30, 1798, CC.

36. *MTA*, 128–30, 138–39, 141–42, 144–45, 166–67; JW to WS, April 1799, WSP (MHS).

37. *MTA*, 157–58, 168.

38. Ibid., 95–96, 106; JW to WS, January 8, 1799, WSP (MHS); Evans to AE, February 13, 1799, AEP; JW to AE, April 8, 1799, AEP; AE to WS, February 12, 1799, WSP (MHS); Deposition of Hutchins, January 2, 1799, CC; AE to SS, February 21, 1799, SBP.

39. Petition of John Hutchins to Territorial Legislature, n.d. [1800], GC. A manuscript copy of the divorce can be found ibid.

40. *MTA*, 80; William B. Hamilton, "Politics in the Mississippi Territory," *Huntington Library Quarterly* 11:284–85.

41. All of these individuals were signers of the petitions protesting Sargent's policies (*TP*, 5:68, 72, 76, 82, 85; see also James, *Natchez*, 101–2; and William S. Coker and Jack D. L. Holmes, eds., "Daniel Clark's Letter on the Mississippi Territory, *JMH* 32:165–66).

42. The Ellicott Papers contain numerous references to payments due Cochran for supplying Ellicott's party. See also Robert V. Haynes, "The Formation of the Territory, in Richard Aubrey McLemore, ed., *History of Mississippi*, 2 vols. (Hattiesburg, Miss., 1973), 1:187.

43. *TP*, 5:63–66, 78–85, Evans to AE, July 3, 1799, AEP.

44. *TP*, 5:83–85.

45. Ibid., 5:67.

46. Ibid., 5:74, 77–78; *MTA*, 181–82.

47. *MTA*, 201–2; Clark to WS, January 23 and March 9, 1800, WSP (MHS); Girault to WS, July [?] 1800, ibid.

48. Clark to WS, March 9, 1800, WSP (MHS); "A Law in Addition to and Amendment of the Law for the Permanent Establishment of the Militia," May 27, 1800. MS copy in MDAH.

49. *MTA*, 207–8; Depositions of Girault and William Ferguson, May 1, 1800, WSP (OHS).

50. Girault to Pickering, March 3, 1800, WSP (MHS); Roger Dixon to WS, March 4, 1800, WSP (OHS); Harding to WS, March 6, 1800, ibid.

51. Girault to WS, August 19, 1800, WSP (OHS); Dunbar to WS, September 22, 1800, ibid. For a list of appointments, see *MTA*, 318–19, 330–31; JFHC, *Miss.*, 212.

52. Madel J. Morgan, ed., "Andrew Marschalk's Account of Mississippi's First Press," *JMH* 7:146–48; William B. Hamilton, ed., "The Printing of the 1799 Laws of the Mississippi Territory," *JMH* 2:92; Charles S. Sydnor, "The Beginning of Printing in Mississippi," *JSH* 1:49–55.

53. Hamilton, ed., "Printing of 1799 Laws," 88–89; JW to WS, February 9, 1799, WSP (MHS); Marschalk to WS, December 13, 1800, ibid. After completing the laws of 1799, Marschalk was terribly disappointed by the lack of public interest and poor sales (Marschalk to WS, December 15, 1799, ibid.).

54. Green to WS, May 1 and 16, 1800, WSP (MHS). For a brief summary of early territorial newspapers, see Clarence S. Brigham, *History and Bibliography of American Newspapers, 1690–1820*, 2 vols. (Worchester, Mass., 1947), 1:424–25.

55. MTA, 171–72, 184–85; TP, 5:78–82.

56. *Petition of Cato West . . . Published by Order of the House of Representatives* (Philadelphia, 1800), copy in MDAH; *TP*, 5:78–82.

57. *TP*, 5:92–94; *ASP, MS*, 1:214; *AC*, 6th Cong., 2nd sess., 838–54; JFHC, *Miss.*, 216–18.

58. *MTA*, 185.

59. The election returns are in GC.

60. The election returns are in GC; *MTA*, 284–87, 290–91; Ebenezer Dayton to Henry Hunter et al., September 22, 1800, GC; Deposition of Hutchins, July 10, 1800, ibid.; Hutchins to the Speaker of the Assembly, September 29, 1800, ibid.; Hunter to Territorial Judges, October 1, 1800, ibid.; Petition of William Connor, October 2, 1800, TLR.

61. Hunter to WS, October 4, 1800, WSP (OHS); Hunter to WS, October 9, 1800, WSP (MHS); *MTA*, 294–95, 301, 307–8; *TP*, 5:107–8.

62. Presentment to Grand Jury, Inferior Courts of Adams County, November 5, 1800, WSP (OHS).

63. *MTA*, 305–10; "To the Public," November 8, 1800, Mississippi Imprints (MDAH); WS to James Ross, December 1, 1800, WSP (OHS); *TP*, 5:109–17, 113–14.

64. Robert V. Haynes, "The Revolution of 1800 in Mississippi," *JMH* 19:248–50.

65. *TP*, 5:139.

66. *MTA*, 332; Steele to WS, May 23, 1801, WSP (MHS); Peter Walker to WS, June 6, 1801, WSP (MHS).

67. *TP*, 5:126–27; *MTA*, 345–46; Ja[me]s White to [Hutchins ?], n.d., WSP (MHS).

68. Petition of Thomas Green to Legislature, August 28, 1801, TLR.

69. *MTA*, 342–43; Haynes, "Formation of Territory," 196.

3. Frontier Democracy, Republican Style

1. *MTA*, 346.

2. For Sargent's career in the Northwest Territory, see Benjamin H. Pershing, "Winthrop Sargent: A Builder of the Old Northwest" (Ph. D. dissertation, University of Chicago, 1934); and Andrew R. L. Cayton, *The Frontier Republic: Ideology and Politics in the Ohio Country, 1780–1825* (Kent and London, 1986).

3. Daniel Clark to WS, March 14, 1801, WSP (MHS); Dunbar to WS, March 29, 1801, ibid., JM to WS, June 16, 1801, ibid.; John Green to WS, October 21, 1801, ibid.

4. In August 1801, Sargent arranged for publication of a sixty-four-page pamphlet entitled *Papers in Relation to the Official Conduct of Governor Sargent. Published by Particular Desire of His Friends* (Boston, 1801). See also *MTA*, 348.

5. On Claiborne's early career, see Vivian V. Volstorff, "William Charles Cole Claiborne: A Study in Frontier Administration" (Ph.D. diss., Northwestern University, 1932); Wiley Woodrow Jenkins, "William C. C. Claiborne, Governor of the Creoles" (Ph.D. diss., University of Texas, 1951); and Joseph T. Hatfield, *William Claiborne: Jeffersonian Centurion in the American Southwest* (Lafayette, La., 1976).

6. *TP*, 5:100–103; *ASP, MS*, 1:234–37; *AC*, 6th Cong. 1st sess., 625–26; ibid., 2nd sess., 827–54, 1074–75, 1376–81; Hatfield, *Claiborne*, 44; Hamilton, "Beginnings," 553–55.

7. *MTA*, 348.

8. Ibid., 365–66.

9. Ibid., 375–76, 377–79, 385–88, 411–13.

10. Ibid., 428, 435–36.

11. Ibid., 441–43, 477–79, 480–81.

12. Ibid., 480–82, 582–83, 596; *TP*, 5:215–18.

13. HT, *Stat.*, 57–70; *MTA*, 353–54, 383–84, 434.

14. *MTA*, 422–25, 462–63, 479, 509, 575.

15. *MTA*, 535.

16. Hamilton, *Law*, 129–30; *MTA*, 364–65; Phoebe Calvit to Legislature, August 4, 1801, TLR; Presentment of Grand Jury, Pickering County, November 1801 term, GC.

17. The act granting equity jurisdiction was passed January 30, 1802, MS Laws of Mississippi Territory (MDAH); LBC, 1:8–30, 32; Seth Lewis, "Autobiographical memoir," entry of August 28, 1847, Seth Lewis Papers (MDAH).

18. Hamilton, *Law*, 130–31, 178, 184; LBC, 1:42, 161; *TP*, 5:159–74, 215; Lewis, "memoir."

19. *TP*, 5:129–31, 178, 184; LBC, 1:61; David Ker to John Steele, September 19, 1801, in Mary L. Thornton, ed., "Letter from David Ker to John Steele [1801]," *JMH* 25:6–38.

20. Hamilton, *Law*, 3–61; *TP*, 5:218–19.

21. *MTA*, 344–45, 388.

22. Ibid., 351–53, 349, General Assembly to Claiborne, December 4, 1801, GC.

23. MS copies of the laws changing the name of Pickering County to Jefferson County, dated January 11, 1802, and authorizing the legislature to meet in Washington, dated February 1, 1802, are in Pamphlet Laws, 1801–1802, 20–21, 257–58 (MDAH). See also, HT, *Stat.*, 4, 14. The law requiring the "next and all future sessions" to be held in Washington, dated May 10, 1802, is in Mississippi Acts of the Third General Assembly, Mississippi Imprints (MDAH). See also legislative resolution, December 18, 1801, GC; and *MTA*, 324.

24. *MTA*, 376–77; WC to AJ, AJ, *Papers*.

25. JW to Dearborn, March 30, 1802, M222; *MTA*, 388.

26. *MTA*, 432–33, 438–39.

27. Ibid., 381–82, 388, 474–76; Robert V. Haynes, "A Political History of the Mississippi Territory" (Ph.D. diss., Rice University, 1958), 92–93; Hamilton, *Law*, 136, 163, 169–70, 237.

28. TPA, *South*, 74–101, 136–53; APW, *Sp-Am*, 123–29.

29. *MTA*, 541–42; *TP*, 5:154; *ASP, PL*, 1:10.

30. *MTA*, 541.

31. *TP*, 5:192–205.

32. Ibid., 5:205–6, 207–10, 218–19, 223–24, 238–39, 264–78, 303; *PMHB* 43:213–14; IB to Gallatin, September 8, 1803, Office of the Surveyor General, Letters Sent, 1803–1827, RG 7 (MDAH).

33. *TP*, 5:288–89, 302–3.

34. Ibid., 5:279–81; *PMHB* 43:214–15, 219.

35. JW to Dearborn, March 30 and May 30, 1803, M222; *MTA*, 375, 474–76, 433–34, 368, 494, 506.

36. LBC, 1:143, 206, 242–43; *TP*, 5:315.

37. Edward Turner to John C. Breckinridge, February 28 and November 2, 1803, Breckinridge Family Papers (LC); *MTA*, 397–98, 469; *TP*, 5:53.

38. *TP*, 5:266; Turner to Wailes, April 6, 1859, Benjamin L. C. Wailes Papers (MDAH).

39. WC to General Assembly, October 3, 1803, JLC, 2nd GA, 2nd sess., in Mississippi Imprints; HT, *Stat.*, 409–10; *MH&NG*, October 19, 1804; Dunbar to TJ, December 17, 1805, Dunbar Papers (MDAH); William B. Hamilton, "The Southwestern Frontier, 1795–1817," *JSH* 10:396–97.

40. Hodgen and Harris to WS, April 21, 1802 WSP (MHS); Hodgen to WS, May 5, 1802, ibid.; Brigham, *American Newspapers*, 1:425; *TP*, 5:256; LBC, 1:48–49, 96, 156–57, 268; Beaumont to Hutchins and other Gentlemen of the Mississippi Territory, March 24, 1802, GC; WC to TJ, May 30, 1803, TJP (LC). In 1803, the trustees of Jefferson College employed Andrew Marschalk to print up two thousand lottery tickets and paid him sixty dollars (undated invoice, in Andrew Marschalk Papers [MDAH]).

41. *TP*, 5:159–60, 274; *MTA*, 374; *NH&NG*, September 28, 1802, and May 28, 1803; RW to TJ, June 21, 1805, TJP (LC); James, *Natchez*, 104.

42. WC to Legislature, May 4, 1802, GC.

43. HT, *Stat.*, 411–14; *MTA*, 438; *TP*, 5:181–82, 203; Trustees of Jefferson College to People, [January 3, 1803], GC; Throckmorton to Board of Trustees of Jefferson College, March 12, 1803, GC; David Ker to Board of Trustees, March 14, 1803, ibid. There are various subscription lists ibid.

44. Report of the Committee to Select a Site for Jefferson College, March 14, 1803, GC; David Ker to WC, May 31, 1803, ibid.; WC to Ker, June 2, 1803,

ibid.; MS Minutes of Board of Trustees of Jefferson College, March 14, 1803, Jefferson College Papers (MDAH).

45. John Girault to Board of Trustees of Jefferson College, July 25, 1803, GC; WC to Legislative Council, October 17, 1803, ibid.; Board of Trustees of Jefferson College to Legislative Council, July 25, 1803, ibid.; MS Minutes of Board of Trustees of Jefferson College, July 25, 1803, Jefferson College Papers (MDAH). HT, *Stat.*, 414, incorrectly dates the act November 11, 1803.

46. WC to IB, December 2, 1803, GC; *ASP, PL,* 1:148–49; *TP,* 5:333–39; MS Journal of Commissioners for deciding claims to lands in the District West of Pearl River, November 20, 1805, Office of Surveyor General.

47. CW to IB, December 22, 1803, GC; Rowland, ed., *Dunbar,* 76–78, 126–27; *ASP, PL,* 1:70–71; *TP,* 5:46–49. See also James, *Natchez,* 105; and William B. Hamilton, "Jefferson College and Education in Mississippi," *JMH* 37:259–76.

48. The marriage of Magdalene and Ferdinand Claiborne took place on August 19, 1802. Hamilton, "Beginnings," 586; Jack D. L. Holmes, "Anne White Hutchins—Anthony's Better Half," *JMH* 37:207; WC to Ker, June 2, 1803, GC.

49. *TP,* 5:264–72; WC to TJ, May 30 and August 19, 1803, TJP (LC); LBC, 1:280.

50. LBC, 1:207–8; Proclamation of Juan Ventura Morales, October 16, 1802, GC; Hulings to WC, October 23, 1802, ibid.

51. LBC, 1:209–10, 221–22, 233–36, 250–51, 255–56; *ASP, FR,* 2:70; Hulings to JM, October 18, and November 25, 1802, T225; Sam Tenney to WS, January 29, and April 1, 1802, WSP (OHS); *MTA,* 402, 439–40.

52. APW, *MQ,* 176–99; TPA, *South,* 249.

53. APW, *MQ,* 200–209; LBC, 1:140, 230, 256–57; Rowland, ed., *Dunbar,* 120–21.

54. LBC, 1:240, 2 53; *AHR* 22:823 and 21:1–333, 351–55; Daniel Clark to JM, March 24, 1803, T225; Clark to JW, April 13, 1803, M222.

55. APW, *MQ,* 209–17; *AC,* 7th Cong., 2nd sess., 83–85; *The Papers of Alexander Hamilton,* ed. Harold E. Syrett (New York, 1969–), 26:71–71, 82–85; LBC, 1:253; Tenney to WS, January 28, 1803 [misdated 1802], February 27, 1803, WSP (OHS).

56. JM to Irujo, November 25, 1802, M222; JM to WC, November 29, 1802, and January 17, February 14, and March 11, 1803, ibid.; JM to Pichon, February 8, 1803, ibid.; Dunbar to TJ, June 10, 1803, TJP (LC).

57. APW, *MQ,* 204–9, 218–30; LBC, 1:283, 273–74; Harry Ammon, *James Monroe: The Quest for National Identity* (New York, 1971), 203–7.

58. APW, *MQ,* 189–90, 195–96; LBC, 1:267, 277.

59. APW, *MQ,* 224–27, 230–32; WC to TJ, May 30, 1803, TJP (LC).

60. Dumas Malone, *Jefferson the President: The First Term, 1801–1805* (Boston, 1970), 284–96; APW, MQ, 234–36; *TP*, 5:222; JM to WC, July 20, 1803, M40, reel 12; WC to TJ, August 12, 1803, TJP; Memorial of Legislative Council to President Jefferson, November 12, 1803, TLR.

61. WC to TJ, June 23, 1803, TJP; *TP*, 9:3–5, 11–12, 91–94; Gallatin to WC, October 31, 1803, *The Writings of Albert Gallatin*, ed. Henry Adams, 3 vols. (Philadelphia, 1876), 1:167–68; LBC, 1:167–68, 302–3; Abraham Ellery to Hamilton, October 5, 1803, *Papers of Alexander Hamilton*, 26:163–67; TJ to James Monroe, March 21, 1807, L&B, 9:170; Hatfield, *Claiborne*, 102–10.

4. An "Insidious Junto"

1. For instance, see CW to WC, December 26, 1803, CC; *PMHB* 43:225–26.

2. *TP*, 5:70; Malone, *Jefferson: First Term*, 302–10.

3. James, *Natchez*, 3–135; *TP*, 5:437–38; RW to JM, November 6, 1805, GC.

4. *TP*, 5:481–82. On the other hand, General Wilkinson informed the War Department that the transfer occurred on February 4, 1799 (Wilkinson to James McHenry, April 10, 1795, Alexander Hamilton Papers [LC]).

5. Proclamation of Governor Sargent, June 4, 1800, *MTA*, 1:238–40; Haynes, "Political History," 51, 72.

6. Isaac Guion to Wilkinson, June 23, 1798, MS Journal of Isaac Guion (MDAH); Ellicott to Wilkinson, November 24, 1798, AEP.

7. Ephraim Kirby to the President, April 20, and May 1, 1804, *TP*, 5:317–18, 322–26; Wilson Carman to Sargent, May 90, 1800, WSP (MHS).

8. Kirby to the President, April 20, 1804, *TP*, 5:317; Memorial by Citizens of Territory to Congress [referred November 25, 1803], ibid., 279–81; Toulmin to William Lattimore, December 6, 1805, ibid., 437; Hatch Dent to James H. McCulloch, July 14, 1804, ibid., 9:266–67.

9. Richard Lee to Sargent, March 9, 1799, WSP (MHS); Robert V. Haynes, "Early Washington County, Alabama," AR 18 (1965):183–200; Thomas Perkins Abernethy, *The Formative Period in Alabama, 1815–1828* (1922; repr., Tuscaloosa, 1965), 17–18.

10. Ephraim Kirby to the President, May 1, 1804, *TP*, 5:322–26.

11. Schaumburgh to WS January 1, 1800, WSP (OHS); Schaumburgh to WS, October 20, 1800, WSP (MHS); Wilson Carman to WS, May 9, 1799, and January 13, 1800, ibid.

12. *MTA*, 238–40, 285, 295–97, 301, 303–10; election returns from Washington County, August 16, 1800, WSP(OHS); *TP*, 5:107–9; Hunter to WS, October 4, 1800, WSP (OHS).

13. *MTA*, 242–43; *TP*, 5:129, 178, 184; WC to General Assembly, October 3, 1803, JLC, 2nd G.A., 2nd sess.; Dunbar Rowland, *Courts, Judges, and Lawyers of Mississippi* (Jackson, Miss., 1935), 11–12. Like Sargent, Claiborne intended to visit Washington County, but the pressure of "public business" interfered (LBC, 1:170).

14. Petition by Inhabitants of Washington District to the President, n.d., enclosure in John Caller and Ransom Harwell to the President, November 27, 1804, *TP*, 5:353–55. In fact, Kirby's untimely death prevented Jefferson from submitting his name to the Senate (see ibid., 354n; and Rodney to the Secretary of the Treasury, December 1, 1804, ibid., 357).

15. *TP*, 5:367–68; Guice, "The Cement of Society," 84–86.

16. *TP*, 5:226–35, 279–81. See also Haynes, "Disposal of Lands," 226–52; *ASP, PL*, 1:132–58.

17. *TP*, 5:361–66.

18. Ibid., 5:292–95.

19. Ibid., 5:152–53, 236–37, 294, 329–31. See also act of March 27, 1804, in 2 *Statutes* 305. The Treaty of Fort Adams is in *ASP, IA*, 1:658.

20. *TP*, 5:290.

21. Journal of the House of Representative, 2nd G. A., 2nd sess., November 16, 1803; *TP*, 5:290–91.

22. Clifford L. Eagan, *Neither Peace nor War: Franco-American Relations, 1803–1812* (Baton Rouge and London, 1983).

23. *PMHB* 44:58–59, 61, 65–67.

24. Rodney to [C. A. Rodney], January 29, 1804, TRP (LC); *PMHB* 43:225–26, 333.

25. Minor to Peter Walker, February 11, 1804, Stephen Minor Papers, Hill Memorial Library, LSU; West to Claiborne, February 16, 1804, GC; Haynes, "Political History," 115.

26. *PMHB* 43:341–43, 345; 44:299; W. B. Hamilton, "Politics in Mississippi Territory," *Huntington Library Quarterly* 11:285; Hamilton, *Law*, 2:62–63, 76, 216–17; *TP*, 5:129, 130–31, 184; TR to C. A. Rodney, February 15, 1805, TRP (LC); Kemp P. Battle, *History of the University of North Carolina*, 2 vols. (Raleigh, N.C., 1907–1912), 1:104.

27. *TP*, 5:401–2, 266, 270–71, 273; Petition, Timothy and Samuel Terrell, December 5, 1805, copy in GC; Turner to B. L. C. Wailes, April 6, 1859, Wailes Papers (MDAH); Haynes, "Political History," 121. The act of incorporation of the society is in HT, *Stat.*, 409–10.

28. West to Claiborne, December 26, 1803, GC.

29. John Weir to Wm Thompson, February 24, 1803, copy in W. B. Hamilton Collection, Duke University; *TP*, 5:154–55, 307; *PMHB* 44:71; Perrin de Lac, *Voyage dans les deux Louisianes* (Paris, 1805), 83.

30. *PMHB* 43:209–10; Nathan Schachner, *Aaron Burr* (New York, 1937), 301.

31. JLC, 3rd. G.A., 1st sess.; President of the Bank of the United States to West, June 25, 1805, GC. See also Charles H. Brough, "History of Banking in Mississippi," MHSP 7 (1903): 325–47; Robert C. Weems Jr., "The Makers of the Bank of Mississippi," *JMH* 15 (1953): 137–54.

32. L&B, 12:170; *TP*, 9:265; Ammon, *James Monroe*, 245. For Andrew Jackson's interest in the position, see John Spencer Basset, ed., *The Correspondence of Andrew Jackson*, 6 vols. (Washington, D.C., 1926–1933), 1:90–91; APW, MQ, 239–40.

33. *PMHB* 43:365; *TP*, 9:281–84; Malone, *Jefferson: First Term*, 357–59.

34. Sam Cook to CW, February 11, 1804, GC; *TP*, 5:307; Stephen Minor to Peter Walker, February 11, 1804, Minor Papers (LSU).

35. *PMHB* 43:342–43, 345; Minor to Walker, February 11, 1804, Minor Papers (LSU). For Daniel Clark's assessment of Claiborne, see Clark to Wilkinson, May 28, 1803, and October 10, 1804, M222. See also William Plumer, *Memorandum of Proceedings in the United States Senate, 1803–1807*, ed. Everett Somerville Brown (New York, 1923), 220–21.

36. *PMHB* 43:341–42; LBC, 2:111–12; James Brown to John Breckinridge, June 28, 1804, Breckinridge Family Papers (LC).

37. *TP*, 9:163, 146–47, 197–98; ibid., 5:304–7.

38. Ibid., 9:281–82; LBC, 2:345.

39. Jefferson to Dickinson, January 13, 1807, Thomas Jefferson, *The Writings of Thomas Jefferson*, ed. Paul Leicester Ford, 10 vols. (New York, 1892–1899), 9:8–10.

40. Hamilton, "Politics in Mississippi Territory," 277–91; Haynes, "Political History," passim; Haynes, "Revolution of 1800 in Mississippi," 234–51.

41. *TP*, 5:264–76, 350, 371–72, 375; ibid., 9:190–91.

42. Ibid., 5:373–74, 376–79, 402; Joseph Nouye to JM, August 24, 1805, M179. See also Hamilton, *Law*, 73, 216–17.

43. TR to C. A. Rodney, February 15 and 18, April 6, and July 25, 1805, TRP (LC); *TP*, 5:378–79, 381–83.

44. *TP*, 5:405, 413, 420–21; ibid., 9:573–74; *PMHB* 44:290; TR to C. A. Rodney, TRP (LC); *Mississippi Messenger*, September 2, and October 8, 1805; Williams to Shaw, July 22, 1805, EJ.

45. *PMHB* 43:345.

46. Ibid., 43:333, 44:57–58; *TP*, 5:355, 357, 381; Haynes, "Political History," 139–40.

47. *TP*, 5:381, 387–88; TR to C. A. Rodney, December 3, 1804, TRP (LC); JW to Dearborn, December 31, 1805, M222.

5. A Territory in Transition

1. TR to [C. A. Rodney], April 6 and May 10, 1805, TRP (LC); WC to IB, May 21, 1805, IBP; *TP*, 5:380, 385, 400.

2. SS to RW, March 15, 1805, M40; TR to C. A. Rodney, April 29, 1805, TRP, Historical Society of Delaware, copy in Hamilton Collection, Duke University Library; IB to TJ, *TP*, 5:404. There are numerous references in the correspondence of officials to the miscarriage of the mail (see *TP*, 5:350; and WC to IB, May 21, 1805, IBP).

3. Governor Williams to the President, May 17, 1805, *TP*, 5:401, 412.

4. Hamilton, *Law*, 62; *TP*, 5:303–4, 342, 405. On the high cost of living, see ibid., 308; and *PMHB* 43:362–63.

5. *TP*, 5:399, 415.

6. Briggs and Robert Williams became close friends during their journey in 1804 to the nation's capital, where they expected to plead for changes in the land laws (Haynes, "Political History," 117). Rodney recommended Williams as a suitable replacement for the deceased Kirby as territorial judge of the Washington District (*PMHB* 44:177).

7. *PMHB* 43:212–13; *TP*, 5:307, 372.

8. TR to TJ, May 27 and 28, 1805, TJP; Hamilton, *Law*, 83–84.

9. *PMHB* 44:58. The election returns are in GC. See also *TP*, 5:368–69. The composition of the legislature that convened in December 1804 can be found in JLC, 3rd. G.A., 1st sess.

10. *TP*, 5:381.

11. Ibid., 5:361–66, 382–83.

12. TR to [SS], March 7, 1805, TRP (LC).

13. *TP*, 5:380–81, 400; TR to [SS], March 7, 1805, TRP (LC).

14. Petition to West, n.d. [1804?], GC; Dunbar Rowland, *History of Mississippi: Heart of Dixie*, 2 vols. (Chicago, 1925) 1:402.

15. For a listing of delegates taking the oath, see JLC, 3rd G.A., 1st sess.; and CW to General Assembly, December 4, 1804, GC; *TP*, 5:361–62; Haynes, "Formation of Territory," 206–7. Although during the first decade of the nineteenth century the city of Natchez grew at a slower rate than the outlying counties, Adams County still contained nearly half of the district's population in the census of 1810 (Schedule of Whole Number of Persons in Mississippi Territory, 1801 and 1811, Census Records, RG 2 (MDAH); see also William B. Hamilton, "Mississippi 1817: A Sociological and Economic Analysis," *JMH* 29 [1967]: 276–78).

16. *TP*, 5:400.

17. TR to [SS], March 7, 1805, TRP (LC); Haynes, "Political History," 129–30.

18. JLC, January 2, 1805, 3rd G.A., 1st sess.; *TP*, 5:380–81.

19. JLC, January 3, 1805, 3rd. G.A., 1st sess.; *TP*, 5:371–72.

20. TR to C. A. Rodney, January 3, 1805, TRP (LC); *TP*, 5:401–2.

21. JLC, February 26 and 27, 1805, 3rd. G.A., 1st sess.; RW to Legislature, July 1, 1805, EJ.

22. RW to CW, May 14 and July 30, 1805, EJ; RW to Legislature, July 25, 1805, ibid.; RW to JM, May 16, August 5 and 9, 1805, ibid.; *TP*, 5:401–2, 409. See the notation of Parke Walton on RW to CW, May 10, 1805, GC; and W. H. Hargraves to RW, July 10, 1805, ibid.

23. RW to CW, July 17, 1805, EJ; RW to JM, August 9, 1805, ibid.; *TP*, 5:409. See also "An Act Establishing Place where Officers . . . shall Keep their Offices," December 28, 1805, HT, *Stat.*, 201–2. For a brief summary of West's public career, see Hamilton, *Law*, 367n. Later, Williams stated, "I had to receive and bring [the records] from Col West's in baggs" (RW to Albert Gallatin, April 14, 1806, EJ).

24. RW to JM, August 9, 1805, EJ; *TP*, 5:404.

25. Hamilton, "Beginnings," 179–252; TR to C. A. Rodney, July 10, 1805, TRP (LC).

26. *PMHB* 43:346; TR to TJ, April 23, 1804, Gratz Collection (Historical Society of Pennsylvania).

27. *TP*, 5:154. See also Adam Rothman, *Slave Country: American Expansion and the Origins of the Deep South* (Cambridge, Mass., 2005).

28. *TP*, 5:307; *PMHB* 44:71–72, 306–7; Rodney to John Fisher, May 17, 1807, ibid., 306–7; TR to C. A. Rodney, November 24, 1805, TRP (LC).

29. Charles D. Lowery, "The Great Migration to the Mississippi Territory," *JMH* 30:173–92; *PMHB* 44:55; C&G, FC, 161–63.

30. Schedule of the Whole Number of Persons in the Mississippi Territory, Censuses of 1800 and 1810, Census Records (MDAH); Hamilton, "Mississippi 1817," 271–76.

31. The Secretary of War to Claiborne, November 22, 1805, M370; Norman K. Risjord, *Jefferson's America, 1760–1815* (Madison, Wisc., 1991), 264–68.

32. George Poindexter to Thomas Rodney, October 31, 1807, Ms M, Pennsylvania Historical Society, Philadelphia; *Mississippi Messenger*, June 2 and 30, 1807; *TP*, 5:631. See also Bradford Perkins, *Prologue to War: England and United States, 1805–1812* (Berkeley, Calif., 1961).

33. *Mississippi Messenger*, August 13 and 25, 1807; *PMHB* 45:41–42; Declaration of Public Meeting held at Wakefield (Washington County), September 8, 1807, GC.

34. Philander Smith to Jedidiah Smith, August 17, 1809, Philander Smith Papers (MDAH); *TP*, 5:637–39; John R. Grayson to his brother, June 12, 1808, GC. Governor Williams reported that news of the embargo "created a considerable bustle with the plantering as well as the mercantile interest" (*TP*, 5:603).

See also WC to Secretary of War, April 21, 1808, M222; and Dearborn to Colonel Thomas P. Cushing, December 22, 1808, ibid.

35. WS to Pickering, November 15, 1808, Timothy Pickering Papers (MHS); *PMHB* 45:60; *TP*, 5:651–52.

36. Haynes, "Disposal of Lands," 226–34; Malcolm J. Rohrbough, *The Land Office Business: The Settlement and Administration of American Public Lands, 1789–1837* (Oxford and London, 1968), 35–39.

37. *TP*, 5:365; *PMHB* 43:332–33; C&G, *FC*, 161–82; Rohrbough, *Land Office Business*, 44–47.

38. There are numerous references to these incidents in the GC. See also LBC, 1:59–60, 94; *MTA*, 167, 202–3; Secretary of War to RW, September 3, 1805, M370; and Usner, *American Indians*, 75–89.

39. LBC, 1:87–88, 108–9; Merritt B. Pound, *Benjamin Hawkins: Indian Agent* (Athens, Ga., 1951), 139–210; FH, *SIBH*. There are no modern biographies of these agents (*TP*, 5:58–59, 154; C&G, *FC*, 30, 43). Wilkinson was a friend and defender of Dinsmoor, whose behavior at times was bizarre and provoked considerable controversy (Wilkinson to Dearborn, November 14, 1807, M222). For Dinsmoor's heated controversy with Andrew Jackson, see Robert V. Remini, *Andrew Jackson and the Course of American Empire, 1767–1821* (New York, 1977), 162–64. For Wilkinson's favorable opinion of McKee, whom he described as a "man of talent and intelligence," see Wilkinson to Dearborn, May 13, 1805, M221.

40. Anthony F. C. Wallace, *Jefferson and the Indians: The Tragic Fate of the First Americans* (Cambridge Mass., 1999), 188–91; Arthur H. DeRosier Jr., *The Removal of the Choctaw Indians* (Knoxville, Tenn., 1970); Angie Debo, *The Rise and Fall of the Choctaw Republic* (Norman, Okla., 1934). See also John D. W. Guice, "Face to Face in Mississippi Territory, 1798–1817," in *The Choctaw before Removal*, ed. Carolyn Keller Reeves (Jackson, Miss., 1985), 157–80; and Richard White, *The Roots of Dependency: Subsistence, Environment, and Social Change among the Choctaws, Pawnees, and Navajos* (Lincoln, Neb., 1983).

41. *TP*, 5:213–14, 342, 434; "Hints on the Subject of Indian Boundaries," December 29, 1802, L&B, 17:373–77; *ASP, IA*, 1:748–49. See also DeRosier, *Removal of Choctaw*, 28–32; Francis Paul Prucha, *American Indian Treaties: The History of a Political Anomaly* (Berkeley, 1994), 105–10.

42. *PMHB* 43:185; TR to [C. A. Rodney], March 14, 1805, TRP (LC); *TP*, 5:470, 525; Secretary of War to John Forbes, May 2, 1804, and November 12, 1806, M370.

43. *TP*, 5:218, 295, 297, 303, 316, 389, 421; ibid., 9:163.

44. For an in-depth discussion of these difficulties, see Hamilton, "Beginnings," chap. 1; and Haynes, "Disposal of Lands," 236–50.

45. *TP*, 5:192–205; WC to TJ, May 30, 1803, TJP (LC).

46. *TP*, 5:316.

47. *PMHB* 43:350.

48. *TP*, 5:295, 299–300; *PMHB* 43:212, 218–19, 226–27.

49. *PMHB* 43:213; Hamilton, *Law*, 66–68.

50. *TP*, 5:305, 310–11, 331–32, 350, 356–57, 368–69, 375–76, 380, 385, 412; WC to IB, February 14, 1804, IBP; TR to C. A. Rodney, April 6, 1805, TRP (LC).

51. *TP*, 5:412, 446, 490. See also Journal of Commissioners "for Deciding Claims to Land in the District West of Pearl River . . . ," December 1, 1803–July 3, 1807, Records of the Office of Surveyor General, RG 7 (MDAH).

52. *TP*, 5:288–89, 303; Circular Letter, William Lattimore to Constituents, Broadsides, 1799–1830, in Jumbo File (MDAH).

53. *PMHB* 43:349–50, 352, 44:56; Elihu H. Bay to Poindexter, June 19, 1805, GPP.

54. RW to IB, June 1, 1804, IBP; *PMHB* 44:57, 183–84; *TP*, 5:302–3, 312–13, 374–75.

55. *TP*, 5:312–13, 368.

56. Jefferson to Claiborne, May 24, 1803, quoted in Ella Kent Bayard, "Isaac Briggs, A. M., F. A. P. S." *Maryland Historical Magazine* 7:411. See also Rohrbough, *Land Office Business*, 35–36.

57. *TP*, 5:311, 398–99; The Secretary of the Treasury to the President, March 8, 1804, ibid., 5:311.

58. *TP*, 5:304; *PMHB* 43:333; Hamilton, *Law*, 68.

59. *TP*, 5:305, 310–11, 392, 398–99, 410; ibid., 9:190, 197.

60. Ibid., 5:419, 483–84, 488–89, 517; Rowland, ed., *Dunbar*, 352.

61. *TP*, 5:534–37, 724–25.

62. Ibid., 5:422–23, 442, 456.

63. Ibid., 5:280, 364–65, 430, 587–89.

64. Ibid., 5:650, 657. Gallatin became so disgruntled with the credit system that he wanted it abolished (Haynes, "Disposal of Lands," 13–16).

6. Ruffians along the Border

1. *TP*, 5:238–39; Haynes, "Political History," 139. By late July, Judge Rodney was reporting that "they are already abusing him" (TR to C. A. Rodney, July 25, 1805, TRP [LC]).

2. *TP*, 5:401–2, 404; notation of Parke Walton on letter of CW, May 10, 1805, EJ; Williams to West, July 30, 1805, ibid.; Williams to Madison, August 17, 1805, ibid.

3. JFHC, *Miss.*, passim; AEJ, 70–71, 73; Hamilton, *Law*, 427, 447. See also WC to JM, May 14, 1802, EJ.

4. Edward Turner to John C. Breckinridge, February 28, 1802, and November 2, 1803, Breckinridge Family Papers (LC); Hamilton, "Politics in Mississippi Territory," 277–91.

5. *PMHB* 43:342, 345; W. H. Hargraves to RW, July 10, 1805, GC; W. Claiborne to IB, May 21, 1805, IBP.

6. *TP*, 5:270–71; HT to RW, September 11, 1807, GC; Haynes, "Political History," 139.

7. *TP*, 5:404, 412–13; John Shaw to Williams, September 24, 1805, GC.

8. *TP*, 5:402, 404, 414–15; RW to JM, August 17, 1805, EJ. Governor Williams employed John Henderson to assist him (RW to JM, April 7, 1806, EJ; JM to RW, May 7, 1806, GC).

9. *TP*, 5:400, 402–4.

10. Ibid., 5:417–18; TR to C. A. Rodney, April 6, 1805, TRP (LC).

11. RW to TJ, June 8, 1805, EJ; *TP*, 5:415.

12. *TP*, 5:414; RW to Legislature, July 25, 1805, EJ.

13. *TP*, 5:415; TR to C. A. Rodney, July 10, 1805, TRP (LC).

14. TR to C. A. Rodney, July 13 and December 3, 1805, TRP (LC); Williams to Madison, August 9, 1805, EJ. See also Journal of House of Representatives, 3rd G.A., 2nd sess.

15. RW to JM, August 9 and 17, 1805, EJ; *PMHB* 45:51.

16. *TP*, 5:401, 413, 417, 448; RW to JM, November 4, 1805, EJ.

17. The classic study of the Jefferson administration is still Henry Adams, *History of the United States during the Administrations of Jefferson and Madison*, 9 vols. (New York, 1889–1891), chaps. 17 and 24. See also Alexander DeConde, *This Affair of Louisiana* (New York, 1976); Lawrence S. Kaplan, *Entangling Alliances with None: American Foreign Policy in the Age of Jefferson* (Kent, Ohio, 1987); and Robert W. Tucker and David C. Hendrickson, *Empire of Liberty: The Statecraft of Thomas Jefferson* (New York, 1990). For contemporary assessments, see Claiborne to Madison, May 30, 1804, EJ; and *PMHB* 44:172–73.

18. DeConde, *This Affair*, 216–19; 2 *Stat.* 254; LBC, 2:182–85, 221; *TP*, 9:291.

19. *TP*, 9:291; TJ to Monroe, January 8, 1805, Jefferson, *Writings*, ed. Ford, 8:286–92; Dumas Malone, *Jefferson the President: Second Term, 1805–1809* (Boston, 1974), 45–52; Isaac J. Cox, *The West Florida Controversy, 1798–1813: A Study in American Diplomacy* (Baltimore, 1918), 102–38.

20. WC to JM, May 30, 1804, EJ; *PMHB* 44:58–9, 61, 65–67, 172; Malone, *Jefferson: Second Term*, 65–94; Haynes, "Early Washington County," 183–200.

21. Samuel C. Hyde Jr., *Pistols and Politics: The Dilemma of Democracy in Louisiana's Florida Parishes* (Baton Rouge, 1996); Andrew McMichael, "The Kemper Rebellion: Filibustering and Resident Anglo-Saxon Loyalty in Spanish

West Florida," *LH* 43:133–65; TPA, *South*, 333; Andrew McMichael, *Atlantic Loyalties: Americans in Spanish West Florida, 1785–1810* (Athens, Ga., 2007); *PMHB* 44:55; *TP*, 9:898; JW to Dearborn, January 3, 1803, M222.

22. *PMHB* 44:59–60; *TP*, 9: 266–67, 287; LBC, 2:348; Daniel Clark to JW, October 10, 1804, M222.

23. *TP*, 9:191.

24. TPA, *South*, 333–34; Stanley C. Arthur, *The Story of the West Florida Rebellion* (St. Francisville, La., 1935), 20–21. For information on Smith, see Robert W. Wilhelmy, "Senator John Smith and the Aaron Burr Conspiracy," *Cincinnati Historical Society Bulletin* 28:38–60.

25. Cox, *West Florida Controversy*, 152; C&G, *FC*, 46; *TP*, 9:191.

26. LBC, 2:227, 308, 311–13, 330–31. See also Armand Duplantier and Samuel Fulton to Magistrate of Pinckneyville, August 21, 1804, GC; Thomas Dawson to CW, August 26, 1804, ibid.; and WC to Casa Calvo, August 27, 1804, ibid.

27. Testimony of Dr. Thomas Sheppard, August 21, 1804, GC.

28. TPA, *South*, 334–35; Daniel Clark to Wilkinson, October 10, 1804, Records of the Secretary of War, Unentered Letters Sent, Records of the War Department, RG 107, NA.

29. LBC, 2:308–9; Testimony of Champness Terry, August 24, 1804, GC; Governor Carlos de Grand-Pre to Governor Williams, May 29, 1805, ibid.

30. TPA, *South*, 334–46; Cox, *West Florida Controversy*, 157–59.

31. Claiborne referred to it as "Kemper's Riot" (*TP*, 9:315). See also PMHB, 44:59–60; and Rodney Diary, entry of September 12, 1804, in TRP (MDAH). A "List of the Rebels in Feliciana," August 1804, is in Spanish Transcripts, vol. 8 (MDAH).

32. *PMHB* 44:59; Hamilton, *Law*, 76–77.

33. RW to Carlos de Grand-Pre, April 5, 1805, GC; Governor Vicente Folch to CW, June 6, 1805, ibid.; RW to WC, May 22, 1805, EJ. Folch was unaware that Robert Williams had replaced West as governor of Mississippi Territory. In a subsequent letter to Williams, Grand-Pre listed by name those charged with "committing Robberies and Depredations" in Spanish territory and those who were later guilty of "taking refuge" in Pinckneyville (RW to JM, June 14, 1805, ibid.).

34. The most complete account of this episode is in "R. Kemper v A & J Horton," December 14, 1806, Hamilton, *Law*, 245–49. See also TR to C. A. Rodney, September 30, 1805, TRP (LC); "Details of Late Outrages committed in our Territory," September 7, 1805, ibid.; JFHC, *Miss.*, 260–63. There are various sworn statements by the alleged victims, all dated early September, in GC.

35. RW to Captain Wm Wilson, September 9, 1805, EJ; R. Williams to JM,

September 14, 1805, ibid.; RW to Secretary of War, September 14, 1805, ibid.; RW to Grand-Pre, September 30, 1805, ibid.; *Mississippi Messenger*, September 13, 1805.

36. RW to Grand-Pre, September 30 and December 19, 1805, EJ; RW to JM, September 14, 1805, ibid.; Testimony of T. Holden before TR, September 1805, GC; Maj. Joseph Johnson, September 7, 1805, ibid.; Grand-Pre to RW, September 9, 1805, ibid.

37. RW to Grand-Pre, September 6, 1805, EJ; RW to JM, September 14, 1805, ibid.; RW to Lt. Col. John Ellis in Hamilton Collection, Duke University; Major Johnson to RW, September 17, 1805, GC.

38. TR to C. A. Rodney, September 30, 1805, TRP (LC); TR to [TJ], September 7, 1805, ibid.; RW to Grand-Pre, September 30, EJ; *ASP, FR*, 2:683–89.

39. LBC, 3:43–49, 51–52, 54.

40. TP, 5:485–86; Frank Lawrence Owsley Jr. and Gene A. Smith, *Filibusters and Expansionists: Jeffersonian Manifest Destiny, 1800–1821* (Tuscaloosa, Ala., and London, 1997), 16–31.

41. J. Leitch Wright Jr., *Anglo-Spanish Rivalry in North America* (Athens, Ga., 1971).

42. WC to SS, November 5, 1805, GC; LBC, 3:32–33, 80–83.

43. Edmund P. Gaines to IB, IBP; *TP*, 5:437–38, 495–96.

44. Rodney to C. A. Rodney, October 6, 1805, TRP (LC).

45. LBC, 3:58–59.

46. Owsley and Smith, *Filibusters and Expansionists*, 10–12; Drew R. McCoy, *The Elusive Republic: Political Economy in Jeffersonian America* (Chapel Hill, N.C., 1980).

47. LBC, 1:258.

7. Security and Settlements

1. JM to WC, May 1 and August 24, 1804, M40; WC to JM, May 30, 1804, EJ; *TP*, 5:317–18, 437–38.

2. TP, 9: 397–98; TR to C. A. Rodney, October 6, 1805, TRP (LC); LBC, 3:25–26, 80–83, 87–88.

3. TP, 5:54, 57; WS to Gayoso, December 22, 1798, WSP (OHS).

4. TP, 5:118–19. On the Natchez Trace, see William C. Davis, *A Way through the Wilderness: The Natchez Trace and the Civilization of the Southern Frontier* (New York, 1995); and the numerous articles by Dawson Phelps: "The Natchez Trace in Alabama," *AR* 7:22–41; "The Natchez Trace in Tennessee," *Tennessee Historical Quarterly* 13:195–203; "Travel on the Natchez Trace: A Study of Economic Aspects," *JMH* 15:155–64.

5. JW to Dearborn, May 30, 1802, Office of Secretary of War, Unentered

Letters Received of War Department, RG107, NA; *TP*, 5:215–18, 52–58; *MTA*, 166.

6. The act is in 2 *Statutes*, 82. See also Prucha, *American Indian Treaties*, 106–7; Dearborn to Cherokees, Chickasaws, and Choctaws, June 18, 1801, M15; *ASP, IA*, 1:649–50. Davies was subsequently replaced by Andrew Pickens of South Carolina.

7. Dearborn to JW, Hawkins, and Pickens, July 18, 1801, M15; *C&G, FC*, 31. The administration's attitude toward Indian Affairs is well summarized by Secretary of War Henry Dearborn in *TP*, 5:146–48.

8. *ASP, IA*, 1:648; Benjamin Hawkins, *Letters*, Georgia Historical Society, *Collections* (Savannah, 1918), 9:384. The provisions of the treaty are in Charles J. Kappler, ed., *Indian Affairs: Laws and Treaties*, 5 vols. (Washington, D.C., 1904), 2:55–58. See also *MTA*, 1:363; and *C&G, FC*, 31.

9. *TP*, 5:118–19, 152–53, 237–38; Secretary of War to JW, July 17, 1801, M370.

10. *TP*, 5:472, 185. Earlier, Sargent had estimated the cost of delivering the mail, once a month, from Nashville to Natchez to be "$1300 a year" (*MTA*, 1:140).

11. LBC, 1:222–24; *TP*, 5:211–12, 186; Henry DeLeon Southerland Jr., and Jerry Elijah Brown, *The Federal Road through Georgia, the Creek Nation, and Alabama, 1806–1836* (Tuscaloosa, Ala., and London, 1989).

12. *TP*, 5:187–88; LBC, 1:232.

13. *TP*, 5:306–7, 395.

14. Postmaster General to TJ, February 6 and August 18, 1805, TJP (LC); *TP*, 5:443, 191–92; LBC, 2:123; William Lattimore to IB, November 3, 1803, IBP.

15. *C&G, FC*, 86–87; Jamison, "Natchez Trace," 82–99.

16. Numerous references to these gangs are in GC. See also *MTA*, 391, 422–23; LBC, 2:40; *TP*, 5:224–25; Robert M. Coates, *The Outlaw Years: The History of the Land Robbers of the Natchez Trace* (New York, 1930); and *C&G, FC*, 86–93.

17. *TP*, 5:188, 221–22, 239–40; ibid., 9:57; LBC, 1:371–72; Julian P. Bretz, "Early Land Communication with the Lower Mississippi Valley," *Mississippi Valley Historical Review* 13:3–29.

18. Secretary of War to Samuel Mitchell, October 12, 1803, M370; Dawson A. Phelps, "Stands and Travel Accommodations on the Natchez Trace," *JMH* 11 (1949):1–54; LBC, 1:195–96.

19. *TP*, 5:222; Secretary of War to Silas Dinsmoor, May 28, 1805, M370; JW to Lieutenant Campbell or Officer Commanding at Tennessee River, Choctaw Line of Demarcation, December 27, 1802, M222. The same policy was to apply to the Creeks who were to reside along the proposed route from Georgia to Fort Stoddert (*TP*, 5:306–7).

20. *TP*, 5:222; Secretary of War to Dinsmoor, May 28, 1805, M370; Secretary of War to Wm H. Wooldridge, May 14, 1805, ibid.; John Pitchlynn to RW, June 4, 1806, GC; *Mississippi Messenger*, November 11, 1806; C&G, *FC*, 88; Phelps, "Stands and Accommodations," 1–54.

21. This incident has attracted the attention of numerous scholars. See Davis, *Way through Wilderness*, 277–78; Stephen Ambrose, *Undaunted Courage: Meriwether Lewis, Thomas Jefferson, and the Opening of the American West* (New York, 1996), 472–75; Dawson Phelps, "The Tragic Death of Meriwether Lewis," *William and Mary Quarterly* 13:310–16; John D. W. Guice, *By His Own Hand? The Mysterious Death of Meriwether Lewis* (Norman, Okla., 2006). For a different impression of travel conditions, see *TP*, 5:3308.

22. *Mississippi Messenger*, June 3 and October 14, 1806; *TP*, 5:679–80; ibid., 9:473–74; J. K. Love to the Secretary of War, December 9, 1807, M221.

23. TR to [?], January 2, 1806, TRP (LC); Secretary of War to Thomas M. Randolph, December 24, 1805, M370; Postmaster General to TJ, TJP (LC); *TP*, 5:398.

24. John Pitchlynn to Thomas H. Williams, July 3, 1806, GC.

25. FH, *SIBH*, 102–3; Francis Paul Prucha, *The Great Father: The United States Government and the American Indians*, 2 vols. (Lincoln, Neb., and London, 1984), 1:106–7; Prucha, *American Indian Policy in the Formative Years: Indian Trade and Intercourse Acts, 1790–1834* (Cambridge, Mass., 1962), 203–6. References to horse stealing by Indians are replete in the correspondence of the territorial governors. For instance, see Dinsmoor to CW, June 16 and November 14, 1804, GC; and CW to Dinsmoor, July 10, 1804, ibid.

26. Granger explained to the Speaker of the House that he wished to guard "against expending large sums of money in unavailing attempts to force a rapid mail through an immense wilderness intersected with streams, swamps, and marches" (*TP*, 5:510–11). On the high cost of living in Mississippi Territory, see ibid., 5:436–37. There are numerous references in personal letters to the cost of living, especially by newcomers and visitors.

27. *TP*, 9:418; ibid., 5:315, 396n, 453–54; Postmaster General to TJ, August 19, 1805, TJP (LC).

28. *TP*, 5:450–51, 317, 341–42, 352–53, 368, 450–51.

29. Ibid., 5:358, 390.

30. The act is printed in 2 *Statutes* 337–38. See also Southerland and Brown, *Federal Road*, 17–18; Postmaster General to TJ, February 6, 1805, TJP (LC).

31. *TP*, 5:443–44, 468–69, 516; ibid., 9:459–60, 471, 473–74.

32. Ibid., 5:541–2, 558; James Silver, *Edmund Pendleton Gaines: Frontier General* (Baton Rouge, 1949).

33. *TP*, 5:558, 598–602; James W. Silver, "Edmund Pendleton Gaines and Frontier Problems, 1801–1849," *JSH* 1:320–30.

34. *TP*, 5:601; George Strother Gaines, "Gaines Reminiscences," *Alabama Historical Quarterly* 26:149–56.

35. Claiborne to the President, December 10, 1804, *TP*, 9:349. For Briggs's report of his journey, see *ASP*, *Post Office*, 1:37–38.

36. *TP*, 5:395–96, 459–61, 476–78, 518–20. The act, approved April 21, 1806, is in 2 *Statutes* 397.

37. *TP*, 5:491–92, 510–11; Southerland and Brown, *Federal Road*, 24–27.

38. Benjamin Hawkins, *Letters, Journal and Writings of Benjamin Hawkins*, ed. C. L. Grant, 2 vols. (Savannah, Ga., 1980), 2:526–27; FH, *SIBH*, 172–73; Benjamin W. Griffith Jr., *McIntosh and Weatherford: Creek Indian Leaders* (Tuscaloosa, Ala., and London, 1988), 64–65.

39. James Leonard to Nimrod Doyle, n.d., enclosure in BH to Secretary of War, August 29, 1805, M221; BH to Secretary of War, September 6 and 11, 1805, ibid.; Col. Constant Freeman to JW, October 3, 1805, M221; Griffith, *McIntosh and Weatherford*, 66; BH to Secretary of War, January 2, 1805, M221.

40. *TP*, 5:601; Extract, Hawkins to the Secretary of War, December 14, 1811, M15, reel 3; George Colbert to Friend, November 20, 1811, M221; James Neelly to the Secretary of War, November 29, 1811, ibid.

41. *MTA*, 21–22, 30; *LBC*, 1:9–11; *TP*, 5:39, 241. Pickering also reported that Evan Jones, in whose care he entrusted several important dispatches to New Orleans, "went by way of Pittsburg, the Ohio and Mississippi" (SS to WS, June 30, 1799, M40). See also Horse Browse Trist to [Mrs. Trist], December 10, 1802, Nicholas P. Trist Papers, Southern Historical Collection, University of North Carolina, Chapel Hill.

42. For example, General Wilkinson reported that he had endured a "most unpleasant journey of 25 days," sailing to New York from the Balize, located near the mouth of the Mississippi River (JW to Dearborn, May 25, 1804, M221).

43. Dwight L. Smith and Ray Swick, eds., *A Journey through the West: Thomas Rodney's 1803 Journey from Delaware to the Mississippi Territory* (Athens, Ohio, 1997).

44. *PMHB* 43:209–10; *TP*, 5:357; ibid., 9:279–80.

45. Lowery, "Great Migration," 173–92; James Hall, "A Brief History of the Mississippi Territory," MHSP, 9:554–55.

46. Dunbar to John Ross, August 21, 1797, Wailes Papers (MDAH); Hamilton, "Beginnings," 178–203.

47. Hamilton, "Mississippi 1817," 266–68; Daniel S. Dupre, *Transforming the Cotton Frontier: Madison County, Alabama, 1800–1840*, (Baton Rouge and London, 1997), 11–41; *TP*, 5:684–92.

48. Alexis de Tocqueville, *Democracy in America*, 2 vols. (New York, 1945), 2:136–37.

49. Lowery, "Great Migration," 70–71. See also Avery D. Craven, *Soil*

Exhaustion as a Factor in the Agricultural History of Virginia and Maryland (Urbana, Ill., 1926); Frank L. Owsley, "Pattern of Migration and Settlement of the Southern Frontier," *JSH* 11:147–76; C&G, *FC*, 164–82.

50. *TP*, 5:154–55; TR to C. A. Rodney, May 10, 1805, TRP (LC); John Bisland to James [?], October 15, 1817, Bisland Papers, MDAH; John Bisland to William Bisland, May 5, 1817, ibid. See also Gilbert Imlay, *The Topographical Description of the Western Territory of North America* (London, 1792), 39.

51. H. B. Trist to [his wife], March 25, and April 6, 1803, Trist Papers.

52. Fortescue Cuming, *Sketches of a Tour of the Western Country . . .* (1810), in *Early Western Travels, 1748–1846*, ed. Reuben G. Thwaites, 32 vols. (Cleveland 1904–1907), 4:310.

53. C&G, *FC*, 166–69.

54. WC to C. A. Rodney, August 9, 1803, Gratz Collection, Historical Society of Pennsylvania, Philadelphia; TR to C. A. Rodney, May 20, 1806, TRP (LC) .

8. "Some Dark Mysterious Business"

1. JW to Dearborn, January 15, 1807, M221; *Mississippi Messenger*, January 20, 1807; TR to C. A. Rodney, January 20, 1807, TRP (LC).

2. There are numerous studies of the so-called "Burr Conspiracy." The standard work is still TPA, *BC*. See also Walter F. McCaleb, *The Aaron Burr Conspiracy* (New York, 1936).

3. There are several biographies of Aaron Burr. The latest is Nancy Isenberg, *The Fallen Founder: The Life of Aaron Burr* (New York, 2007). Milton Lomask's two-volume study is also valuable. The second volume, entitled *Aaron Burr: The Conspiracy and Years of Exile* (New York, 1982), is more germane to this study than the first, which is entitled *Aaron Burr: The Years from Princeton to Vice President, 1756–1805* (New York, 1979). See also Samuel H. Wandell and Meade Minnegerode, *Aaron Burr*, 2 vols. (New York, 1925); Nathan Schachner, *Aaron Burr* (New York, 1937); and Herbert Parmet and Marie B. Hecht, *Aaron Burr: Portrait of an Ambitious Man* (New York, 1967). An older but useful biography is James Parton, *The Life and Times of Aaron Burr* (New York, 1864).

4. For the election of 1800, see Elkins and McKitrick, *The Age of Federalism*, 743–50; and Edward J. Larson, *A Magnificent Catastrophe* (New York, 2007). See also LBC, 3:127; *TP*, 9:489, 731; William B. Hatcher, *Edward Livingston* (Baton Rouge, 1940); Cox, *West Florida Controversy*, 189; and TPA, *BC*, 29. For Clark's enmity toward Claiborne, see Clark to JW, May 28, 1803, M370. "Blessed are the poor," Clark wrote, "for theirs is the Kingdom of Heaven—I wish Claiborne was already in his place in it & his on earth occupied by a person better fitted for the Station."

5. TPA, *South*, 192–216; TPA, *BC*, 17–20. See also Clark, *Proofs of the Corruption of Gen. James Wilkinson*.

6. TPA, *BC*, 32–40; TPA, *South*, 271–74; LBC, 3:182, 213–14.

7. LBC, 3:216–17, 225–27, 285, 320, 328; *TP*, 9:618; TPA, *BC*, 48; Isaac J. Cox, "The Louisiana–Texas Frontier," pt. 2, *Quarterly of the Southwest Historical Association*, 16 (1913):179–85.

8. LBC, 3:192; *TP*, 9:533, 628; TPA, *BC*, 51–54.

9. Secretary of War to William Dunbar, June 11, 1806, M370; LBC, 3:375, 383–84; WC to Secretary of War, August 29, 1806, GC; TPA, *BC*, 50.

10. LBC, 3:377, 381, 386–90, 396–99; ibid., 4:15.

11. RW to Joseph Chambers, March 27, 1806, GC; John Pitchlynn to RW, June 4, 1806, ibid.; RW to JM, April 1, 1806, EJ; RW to Grand-Pre, April 8, 1806, ibid.; LBC, 328–29.

12. HT to T. H. Williams, June 5, 1806, GC; *Mississippi Messenger*, June 17, 1806.

13. RW to T. H. Williams, April 21, 1806, EJ; *Mississippi Messenger*, February 11 and June 3, 1806; ibid., April 7, 1807; *MH&NG*, June 3, 1806; *TP*, 5:456–57; Hamilton, *Law*, 308; Haynes, "Political History," 141–42; Dunbar Rowland, ed., *Encyclopedia of Mississippi History*, 2 vols. (Madison, Wisc., 1907), 2:213–14.

14. CW to Dearborn, June 6, 1806, EJ; CM to Capt Thomas Swaine, June 22, 1806, ibid.; CM to Dearborn, June 22, 1806, ibid.; Swaine to CM, July 22, 1806, GC.

15. Joseph P. Kennedy to Thomas H. Williams, June 3, 1806, GC; HT to CM, August 16, 1806, ibid.; John Caller to Thomas H. Williams, June 12, 1806, ibid.; Mead to Colonel John Caller, July 24, 1806, EJ.

16. CM to Col. Caller, July 24, 1806, EJ; CM to Capt. Swaine, August 28, 1806, ibid.; CM to John Pitchlynn, August 28, 1806, ibid.

17. LBC, 3:383–90; *TP*, 9:696–97; WC to CM, August 30, 1806, GC; *PMHB*, 44:289–90.

18. LBC, 3:397–99, 4:7–8; Jacobs, *Tarnished Warrior*, 229; TPA, *BC*, 52–53; CM to John Pitchlynn, August 28, 1806, EJ; CM to Captain Swaine, August 28, 1806, ibid.; WC to CM, August 30, 1806, GC.

19. CM to Dearborn, September 7, 1806, EJ.

20. CM to RW, September 9, 1806, EJ; CM to Dearborn, September 10, 1806, ibid.; General Orders, September 8, 1806, ibid.; William B. Shields to Capt. Benjamin Farrar, September 8, 1806, GC; *Mississippi Messenger*, September 23, 1806.

21. CM to Dearborn, September 7 and 10, 1806, EJ; CM to Maj. Thomas White, October 6, 1806, ibid.

22. JW to CM, September 12, 1806, GC.

23. *Mississippi Messenger,* September 23, 1806; CM to GP, September 23, 1806, GPP; Shields to Col. John Ellis, September 25, 1806, GC; CM to Dearborn, September 26, 1806, EJ; CM to F. L. Claiborne, September 27, 1806, ibid.

24. Colonel John Ellis to Mead, October 2 and 19, 1806, GC; Petition by Citizens of Wilkinson County to CM, October 6, 1806, ibid.

25. Lt. Sevier to CM, October 2, 1806, GC; Hugh Davis to CM, October 3 and November 11, 1806, ibid.; CM to Maj. John F. Carmichael, October 3, 4 and 27, 1806, EJ; CM to Secretary of War, October 7, 1806, ibid.; CM to Lt. Sevier, October 10, 1806, CC (MDAH); Sevier to CM, October 13 and November 3, 1806, ibid.; *Mississippi Messenger,* November 25, 1806. The charges against Carmichael, dated November 2, 1806, are in EJ.

26. CM to Secretary of War, October 7, 1806, EJ; RW to Maj. Claiborne, October 3, 1806, GC; Maj. Claiborne to CM, October 10, 1806, ibid.; *Mississippi Messenger,* October 14 and 21, 1806; TPA, *BC,* 146.

27. LBC, 4:11–14; TPA, *BC,* 138–41.

28. Wilkinson to the Secretary of War, October 4, 1806, with enclosures of correspondence with Governor Manuel Antonio Cordero, M221, reel 14.

29. JW to Secretary of War, September 27 and October 4, 1806, M221; *Mississippi Messenger,* October 28, 1806; *Natchez Herald,* November 11, 1806; JW to CM, November 12, 1806, GC; TR to C. A. Rodney, November 11, 1806, TRP (LC); JFHC, *Miss.,* 268–72; Jacobs, *Tarnished Warrior,* 230–31; Felix D. Almaraz, *Tragic Cavalier: Governor Manuel Salcedo of Texas, 1808–1813* (Austin, Tex., 1971), 14–17.

30. Depositions of Colonel Thomas Cushing and Col Thomas A. Smith, November 15, 1806, quoted in JFHC, *Miss.,* 267–68; TPA, *BC,* 148.

31. There is still much controversy surrounding this letter, known as the notorious "cipher letter," variously dated July 22 or July 27. The letter delivered to Wilkinson was likely written by Jonathan Dayton, although both he and Burr worked together on the final wording (see Lomask, *Burr: The Conspiracy,* 114–22, 163–68; the letter is quoted ibid., 116–17).

32. JW, *Memoirs of My Own Times,* 3 vols. (Philadelphia, 1816, 2, lcv). This letter is also in Burr Conspiracy Papers (LC). JW made a career peddling information to the Spaniards (see APW, *MQ,* 58–59, 103–4, 157–58; and Jacobs, *Tarnished Warrior,* 77–153). JFHC, *Miss.,* 271–72; JW to Governor Folch and Morales, January 5, 1807, M222; Lomask, *Burr: The Conspiracy,* 173–74; McCaleb, *Aaron Burr Conspiracy,* 141–45.

33. *National Intelligencer,* August 22, 1806; Lomask, *Burr: The Conspiracy,* 122–27; TPA, *BC,* 61–8;William H. Safford, *The Life of Harman Blennerhassett, comprising an Authentic Narrative of the Burr Expedition: and Containing Many Additional Facts not Heretofore Published* (Chillicothe, Ohio, 1850), 19–48, 58–61, 65–67.

34. Leslie Henshaw, "The Aaron Burr Conspiracy in the Ohio Valley," *Ohio State Archaeological and Historical Quarterly* 24:126–29; Leland R. Johnson, "Aaron Burr's Treason in Kentucky?" *Filson History Quarterly* 75:1–20; AJ, *Papers* 2:110–11, 114–15; TPA, *BC*, 145–48; Plumer, *Memorandum*, 577–78; The Secretary of War to Jackson, December 19, 1806, M370.

35. TPA, *BC*, 66–79, 88–95; APW, *Sp-Am*, passim; Thomas M. Green, *The Spanish Conspiracy* (Cincinnati, 1891); Davies to TJ, February 10, 1806, in Joseph Hamilton Davies, *A View of the President's Conduct Concerning the Conspiracy of 1806* (Frankfort, Ky., 1807), reprinted in Isaac J. Cox and H. A. Swineford, eds., *Quarterly Publication of the Historical Society of Ohio* 12 (1917):74. Jefferson received the communication on March 8, 1806 (Malone, *Jefferson: Second Term*, 237–39).

36. Samuel M. Wilson, ed., "The Court Proceedings of 1806 in Kentucky against Aaron Burr and John Adair," *Filson History Quarterly*, 10 (1936): 31–40; Davies, *View*, 102–5; TPA, *BC*, 95–96; Bernard Mayo, *Henry Clay: Spokesman of the New West* (Boston, 1937), 234–58; Robert V. Remini, *Henry Clay: Statesman for the Union* (New York, 1991), 42–44.

37. AJ, *Papers* 2:117–19; Malone, *Jefferson: Second Term*, 244–45; TPA, *BC*, 104–6; Lomask, *Burr: The Conspiracy*, 186–87; Safford, *Blennerhassett*, 85–86. On the Bastrop land claims, see *TP*, 9:469.

38. Secretary of War to Governor Edward Tifflin, November 26, 1806, M370; Safford, *Blennerhassett*, 87–94; Henshaw, "Burr Conspiracy," 131–32; TPA, *BC*, 105–7.

39. TPA, *BC*, 107–17; Safford, *Blennerhassett*, 100–105; Lomask, *Burr: The Conspiracy*, 115–17, 209; TR to C. Rodney, January 20, 1807, TRP (LC); Burr to Mead, January 12, 1807, Aaron Burr Papers (microfilm edition, ed. Mary-Jo Kline).

40. Malone, *Jefferson: Second Term*, 247–51; TPA, *BC*, 189–90; Dearborn to Wilkinson, November 27, 1806, in E. Bacon, Chairman, *Report of the Committee Appointed to Inquire into the Conduct of General Wilkinson, February 26, 1811* (Washington, 1811), 408–9.

41. *PMHB* 44:291; TR to C. A. Rodney, June 30, 1806, TRP (LC); Memorandum of TR, August 11, 1806, ibid.; TR to C. A. Rodney, September 22, 1806, ibid.

42. CM to Dearborn September 7, 1806, EJ; CM to JW, September 9, 1806, ibid.; CM to Dearborn, September 10, 1806, ibid. "My impression is," Mead wrote, "that 'all is not right'" (LBC, 4:5–6).

43. AJ, *Papers*, 2:116–17. Jackson also wrote a similar letter of warning to a congressman (Secretary of War to AJ, December 19, 1806, M370).

44. TR to C. A. Rodney, July 11, 1805, TRP (LC); *Mississippi Messenger*, November 18, 1806; JW to Col. Cushing, November 20, 1806, M222; CM to

WC, November 23, 1806, Orleans Territory Papers, RG 59, NA; Wilkinson to Mead, November 12 and 13, 1806, GC; CM to JW, November 13, 1806, EJ; CM to Territorial Legislature, December 15, 1806, JLC, 4th G.A., 1st sess. See also the council's reply, December 16, 1806, ibid.

45. TR to C. A. Rodney, November 11, 1806, TRP (LC); *TP*, 9:688–89; *PMHB* 44:294–96.

46. Memorandum, dated November 11, 1806, TRP (LC); *PMHB* 44:294–96; Gideon Granger to R. Williams, December 20, 1806, Ms M (MDAH); Hamilton, *Law*, 78–79.

47. LBC, 4:82–83; CM to F. L. Claiborne, November 23, 1806, Orleans Territory Papers; Proclamation of CM, December 23, 1806, EJ.

48. LBC, 4:37, 38–40, 46–48; TR to C. A. January 1807, TRP (LC); *National Intelligencer*, January 23, 1807; JW to Dearborn, January 10, 1807, M222.

49. LBC, 4:46–48, 63–65; JW to Dearborn, January 8 and 15, 1807, M222; TR to C. A. Rodney, January 12, 1807, TRP (LC); JW to Dearborn, January 15, 1807, M221; TPA, *BC*, 175–76.

50. CM to Legislature, December 15, 1806, JLC, 4th G.A., 1st sess.; Proclamation of CM, December 23, 1806, EJ; General Orders signed by William B. Shields, December 25, 1806, ibid.; *MHGNG*, December 23, 1806; *Mississippi Messenger*, January 6, 1807.

51. LBC, 4:66; *PMHB* 44:271; Silas Dinsmoor to John McKee, January 7, 1807, in Alabama Historical Society, *Transaction* 3:169. Rodney declared that "the story [of Burr's invasion] has become like the Boy in the Fable crying Wolf" (TR to C. A. Rodney, January 5, 1807, TRP [LC]).

52. William B. Shields to Captain Joshua Baker, January 13, 1807, EJ; Deposition of Dr. John F. Carmichael, January 18, 1807, M221 (also in Bacon, *Report*, 347–49); *PMHB* 44:302–3; TPA, *BC*, 205–6.

53. Col. Thomas Fitzpatrick to CM, January 12, 1807, GC; CM to Fitzpatrick, January 12 and 13, 1807, EJ; CM to Dearborn, January 13, 1807, ibid.

54. Fitzpatrick to Mead, January 15, 1807, GC; CM to Burr, January 15, 1807, EJ.

55. CM to Legislature, January 12, 1807, JLC, 4th G.A., 1st sess.; *Mississippi Messenger*, January 13 and 20, 1807; CM to Joshua Baker, January 12, 1807, EJ; CM to Dearborn, January 19, 1807, ibid.; Shields to Baker, January 13, 1807, ibid.; F. L. Claiborne to CM, January 14, 1807, GC; CM to "Commandant of the Squadron Stationed at Point Cupee [*sic*]," January 14, 1807, EJ; William Scott to Major John Minor, January 14, 1807, GC; CM to Scott, January 13, 1807, M221; Scott to JW, January 13, 1807, ibid.

56. Col. Woodridge to CM, January 14, 1807, GC; Burr to Fitzpatrick, January 15, 1807, ibid.; Fitzpatrick to CM, January 15, 1807, ibid.; CM to Burr, January 15, 1807, EJ; TR to C. A. Rodney, TRP (LC); Burr to CM, January 12,

M221; JFHC, *Miss.*, 279; Safford, *Blennerhassett*, 120; Lomask, *Burr: The Conspiracy*, 211–12.

57. Hamilton, *Law*, 79–80; TR to C. A. Rodney, January 26, 1807, TRP (LC).

58. [James L.] D[onaldso]n to JW, January 22, 1807, M221; JW to Dearborn, January 29, 1807, ibid.; *TP*, 5:604–6; Walter Leake to [Wilson Cary Nicholas ?], December 15, 1807, Samuel Smith Papers, Alderman Library, University of Virginia; JFHC, *Miss.*, 287–88.

59. John A. Donaldson to CM, January 20, 1807, GC; Resolution of Legislature, January 26, 1807, JHR, 4th G.A., 1st. sess.; BH to Dearborn, February 18, 1807, M221; *Mississippi Messenger*, January 13 and 20, 1807.

60. *TP*, 5:507–8; JW to Secretary of War, February 6, 1807, M221; TPA, BC, 215.

61. CM to GP, January 19 and 26, 1807, EJ; TR to C. A. Rodney, January 20, 1807, TRP (LC). .

62. CM to Dearborn, January 26, 1807, EJ; CM to JW, January 25, 1807, ibid.; JW to Dinsmoor, December 4, 1806, Burr Conspiracy Papers (LC); JW to Capt. Moses Hook, January 28, 1807, M221; LBC, 4:107–8, 121; Governor Claiborne to Governor Williams, February 10, 1807, ibid., 119–21.

63. CM to F. L. Claiborne, January 22, 1807, GC; TR to C. A. Rodney, January 20, TRP (LC).

64. *PMHB* 45:38; RW to C. A. Rodney, August 7, 1807, EJ; GP to CM, October 27, 1807, quoted in JFHC, *Miss.*, 281. See also ibid., 282–83. Misfortune continued to plague Blennerhassett. After settling in Mississippi Territory, he saw his mansion burn in 1819, after which he moved to Montreal, Canada, where he found more disappointment. He later sailed for Ireland, eventually taking up residence on the Island of Guernsey, where he died in 1831 (Safford, *Blennerhassett*, 186–202). The fate of Mrs. Blennerhassett is unknown.

65. *Mississippi Messenger*, January 27, 1807; TPA, BC, 216–17; Lomask, *Burr: The Conspiracy*, 215–16; Proclamation of Governor Williams, February 6, 1807, EJ; *ASP, MS*, 1:529–30.

66. John Graham to JM, February 8, 1807, Burr Conspiracy Papers; RW to Burr, February 13, 1807, GC; *PMHB* 44:299–302.

67. TR to C. A. Rodney, February 23, 1807, TRP (LC).

68. "United States v Col: Aron [sic] Burr" in Hamilton, *Law*, 260. Poindexter's account of the trial is in *ASP, MS*, 1:568.

69. *PMHB* 44:290–302; Hamilton, *Law*, 260.

70. *Mississippi Messenger*, February 10, 1807; JFHC, *Miss.*, 283–84; Hamilton, *Law*, 284.

71. Hamilton, *Law*, 261–63; JFHC, *Miss.*, 284.

72. William B. Shields to editor of *Messenger*, February 26, 1807, quoted in JFHC, *Miss.*, 284–86.

73. Haynes, "Political History," 145–47; Hamilton, *Law*, 81, 262–63.

74. Proclamation of RW, February 6, 1807, EJ; RW to Col. Fitzpatrick, February 10, 1807, RW Papers (MDAH); RW to Burr, February 13, 1807, GC; Report of Captain Moses Hook to General Wilkinson, February 11, 1807, M221; Extract of a letter from Judge Toulmin to Gaines, n.d., enclosure in Gaines to Dearborn, February 17, 1807, ibid; Hamilton, *Law*, 263–64.

75. Safford, *Blennerhassett*, 126–28; Evidence of Lemuel Henry, AC, 10th Cong. 1st sess., 664; RW to JM, February 23, 1807, Burr Conspiracy Papers; RW to C. A. Rodney, May 18, 1807, EJ.

76. *PMHB* 44:301–2; TR to C.A. Rodney, February 23, 1807, TRP (LC); Hamilton, *Law*, 265.

77. TR to C. A, Rodney, February 23, 1807, TRP (LC); Hamilton, *Law*, 96–98.

78. *ASP, MS*, 1:524–25; Dinsmoor to Dearborn, February 23, 1807, M221; RW to Andrew Marschalk, March 7, 1807, EJ; TPA, *BC*, 221; Lomask, *Burr: The Conspiracy*, 220; Safford, *Blennerhassett*, 126–27; JFHC, *Miss.*, 286–87. For an assessment of Ashley's character, see *PMHB* 45:36–37.

79. JW to Dearborn, February 27, 1807, M221.

80. Edmund P. Gaines to Dearborn, February 22, 1807, M221; RW to JW, March 1, 1807, M222; TPA, *BC*, 221–27. Josiah Blakely reported that when captured, Burr claimed to have "been fifteen days from Natchez" (Blakely to WC, February 20, 1807, M221).

81. *PMHB* 44:302; Ashley to Burr, n.d., enclosure in William R. Boote to Dearborn, March 20, 1807, M221; TPA, *BC*, 223; JFHC, *Miss.*, 288–89.

82. Gaines to JW, March 4, 1807, M221; TPA, *BC*, 225; *Mississippi Messenger*, March 31, 1807; Silver, "Gaines and Frontier Problems," 323.

83. Gaines to Dearborn, February 22, 1807, M221; Gaines to Wilkinson, March 4, 1807, ibid.

84. RW to Dinsmoor, March 1, 1807, GC; RW to JM, March 1, 1807, ibid.; TPA, *BC*, 225–26; Albert J. Picket, *History of Alabama and Incidentally of Georgia and Mississippi* (1851; repr., Tuscaloosa, 1962), 485–502.

9. The Williams Imbroglio

1. *Mississippi Messenger*, July 7 and November 7, 1807; RW to Burr, February 13, 1807, GC; CM to Col. Cushing, January 22, 1807, ibid.; RW to Col. Fitzpatrick, February 10, 1807, RW Papers; CM to Dearborn, January 15, 19, and 16, 1807, EJ; *PMHB* 45:50, 53.

2. *PMHB* 44:305, 45:43; Malone, *Jefferson: Second Term*, 274, 294–97.

3. William Cabell Bruce, *John Randolph of Roanoke, 1775–1833*, 2 vols. (New York, 1922), 1:303–5; TPA, *BC*, 240; Lomask, *Burr*, 2:253–55.

4. James McHenry to Pickering, February 6, 1807, Pickering Papers (MHS); *TP*, 5:509, 544–45, 550–52.

5. *TP*, 5:544–46.

6. RW to Burr, February 13, 1897, GC; CM to Dearborn, January 26, 1807, EJ; *TP*, 5:551.

7. JHR, 4th G.A., 1st sess., January 26 and 28, 1807. The governor's reply is also in this journal.

8. *TP*, 5:552.

9. Ibid., 5:528–30, 556, 563–64.

10. *Mississippi Messenger*, April 14, 1807; *TP*, 5:530, 532, 553; *PMHB* 45:38–39, 41; Hamilton, *Law*, 84.

11. *TP*, 5:530–32, 511. On the Briggs controversy, see ibid., 448.

12. Shields to GP, December 23, 1807, Shields Papers (LSU); *Mississippi Messenger*, February 10, 1807; *TP*, 5:606; Walter Leake to Wilson Cary Nicholas, December 15, 1807, Samuel Smith Papers.

13. *TP*, 5:531–32; LBC, 3: 200–201, 293–94. RW insisted that opposition to him always became "more violent" during CM's frequent visits to Natchez (*TP*, 5:578). In mid-August, TR reported that "Governor Claiborn is still here but returns in a few days" (*PMHB* 45:42). GP to Messrs. Fitzpatrick, Caller, and Joseph Sessions, JLC, 4th G.A., 1st sess., February 5, 1807; *MH&NG*, February 4, 1807.

14. A. M. Poindexter to J. F. H. Claiborne, April 4, 1860, GPP; John Poindexter to his brother George, April [?], 1803, ibid.; Lucy to her brother George, August 30, 1803, ibid. See also MS, *Poindexter*, passim; Suanna Smith, "George Poindexter: A Political Biography" (Ph.D. diss., University of Southern Mississippi, 1980).

15. *TP*, 5:529, 553.

16. Ibid., 5:529, 530, 549, 553, 558; CM to JM, May 2, 1807, GC; RW to CM, April 14, 1807, ibid.; RW to Dearborn, March 20, 1807, EJ; RW to JM, August 1, 1807, ibid.; *PMHB* 45:45; *Mississippi Messenger*, February 10, 1807.

17. *TP*, 5:550–51, 556.

18. Ibid., 5:563–67, 606.

19. Ibid., 5:604–7; *Mississippi Messenger*, July 7, 1807.

20. *TP*, 5:530, 550–52, 556; *MTA*, 483; Brigham, *American Newspapers, 1690–1820*, 1:424–26; *PMHB* 45:39, 41; *Mississippi Messenger*, May 19 and 26, June 9, 1807. F. L. Claiborne was one of the signers for Terrell and Shaw. The copy of his bond, dated June 13, 1807, is in GC.

21. *TP*, 5:556, 577; Testimony of Joshua Baker before TR, March 25, 1807, GPP; *Mississippi Messenger*, June 9, 1807; Hamilton, *Law*, 469–70. Governor Williams also revoked Baker's commission as justice of the peace in Wilkinson County (RW to Baker, May 7, 1807, EJ).

22. *TP*, 5:532–33, 589.

23. *Mississippi Messenger*, April 14 and June 3, 1807; *TP*, 5:630.

24. For the influence of newspapers in national politics, see Jeffrey L. Pasley, *"The Tyranny of Printers": Newspaper Politics in the Early American Republic* (Charlottesville, Va., and London, 2001).

25. *Mississippi Messenger*, August 4, 1807.

26. On the place of honor and dueling in southern culture, see Bertram Wyatt-Brown, *The Shaping of Southern Culture; Honor, Grace, and War, 1760s–1820s* (Chapel Hill, N.C., 2001). Andrew Jackson's famous duel with John Dickinson is covered in Remini, *Jackson and American Empire*, 136–42; For the death of Claiborne's brother-in-law in a tragic duel, see WC to IB, February 17, 1805, IBP; and *TP*, 9:393–94.

27. *Mississippi Messenger*, February 10 and August 4, 1807. In early September, William B. Shields fought a duel with Dr. James Speed in which the latter "received a slight wound in the abdomen" from which he was "rapidly recovering" (ibid., September 8 and 27, 1807).

28. *Mississippi Messenger*, August 4, 1807.

29. RW to Capt Voss, August 6, 1807, EJ; *Mississippi Messenger*, August 11 and September 15, 1807.

30. RW to F. L. Claiborne, August 16, 1807, EJ; Williams to F. L. Claiborne, September 12, 1807, ibid.; *Mississippi Messenger*, August 13 and 25, September 29, 1807.

31. Voss also resorted to the courts. He "sued the Governor for a Libel—and laid his damages at $10,000" (TR to GP, October 10 and December 23, 1807, Shields Papers [LSU]). See also *PMHB* 45:47–48; *Mississippi Messenger*, October 20, 1807.

32. HT to RW, September 11, 1807, GC; *Mississippi Messenger*, June 23 and 30, 1807.

33. *TP*, 5:581; RW to IB [November 1807 ?], IBP.

34. TR to GP, January 25, 1808, CC; *TP*, 5:573; "Kentucky" to "Scurvy Grass" in *Mississippi Messenger*, June 23, 1807; RW to Robert Tanner, June 19, 1807, EJ.

35. *TP*, 5:553.

36. RW to sheriffs of Adams and Wilkinson counties, July 21 and August 24, 1807, EJ; RW to House of Representatives, November 9, 1807, ibid.; *Mississippi Messenger*, May 26, July 28, August 4, September 1, November 5 and 12, 1807.

37. *TP*, 5:577, 580–81; *Mississippi Messenger*, November 5, 1807; D. W. Breazeale to RW, November 6, 1807, GC.

38. *TP*, 5:560–61, 564–65; Andrew Marschalk to Governor Williams, October 16, 1807, ibid., 560–61; RW to Marschalk, October 15, 1807, EJ.

39. *TP*, 5:560–62, 565.

40. TR to GP, October 10, 1807, CC; *TP*, 5:565–66; Walter Leake to W. C. Nicholas, December 15, 1807, Samuel Smith Papers.

41. *TP*, 5:567–68.

42. Ibid., 5:568–69, 570–72, 576–77.

43. Ibid., 5:569; Dunbar to RW, October 22, 1807, GC; Alexander Montgomery to RW, November 2, 1807, ibid.; TR to GP, October 10, 1807, CC; Shields to GP, December 20, 1807, Shields Papers (LSU).

44. *TP*, 5:575–76.

45. RW to IB, [November 1897], IBP; *TP*, 5:574, 579–80.

46. *TP*, 5:580–81; RW to Legislature, December 24, 1807, GC. GP earlier had instructed CM to encourage the legislature to adopt a "mild petition" to assist him in his efforts to have Williams removed (see GP to CM, October 27, 1807, GPP).

47. *TP*, 5:581.

48. Ibid., 5:587; RW address to Legislature, December 14, 1807, GC; George Humphrey to RW, November 15, 1807, ibid.; Governor's Proclamation to the Sheriffs of Jefferson and Claiborne Counties, November 19, 1807, EJ.

49. Shields to [Poindexter], n.d. [January 1808?], Shields Papers (LSU); MS copy of undated Memorial in CC. The latter manuscript is likely the memorial drafted by Mead in late 1807 but never endorsed by the territorial legislature. See also *TP*, 5:610; and Hamilton, "Politics in Mississippi Territory," 277–91.

50. Shields to GP, December 23, 1807, Shields Papers (LSU); *TP*, 5:590–92.

51. Shields to [Poindexter], n.d., Shields Papers (LSU); Rodney to C. A. Rodney, *PMHB* 45:57.

52. *TP*, 5:623.

53. Ibid., 5:573.

54. Leake to Nicholas, December 15, 1807, Samuel Smith Papers; *TP*, 5:603.

55. *TP*, 5:607; Shields to GP, [January 1808 ?], Shields Papers (LSU).

56. *TP*, 5:596–98.

57. Ibid., 5:610–12.

58. Ibid., 5:613.

59. Ibid., 5:614, 616–18; *PMHB* 45:63; Governor's Proclamation, March 1, 1808, EJ.

60. Proclamation of the President, March 4, 1808, EJ; *TP*, 5:578, 603.

10. Changing of the Guard

1. *TP*, 5:623.

2. Governor Williams to the President, February 10, 1808, *TP*, 5:611; *Mississippi Messenger*, February 4, 1808.

3. *TP*, 5:611, 634–36; *Mississippi Messenger*, February 4, 1808.

4. Williams to the Secretary of State, March 8, 1808, EJ (Williams).

5. The Secretary of State to Governor Williams, July 19, 1808, GC (Williams); Lemuel Henry to Williams, August 8, 1808, ibid.

6. RW to SS, March 8, 1808, EJ; SS to RW, July 19, 1808, GC; Lemuel to RW, August 8, 1808, ibid.; *TP*, 5:640.

7. Williams to the Secretary of State, March 8, 1808, *TP*, 5:618.

8. Williams to the President, November 16, 1808, *TP*, 5:665.

9. *TP*, 5:603, 612, 665.

10. *Mississippi Messenger*, June 23 and 30, July 7 and 14, 1808.

11. The election returns are in GC and *Natchez Weekly Chronicle*, July 27, 1808; and *Mississippi Messenger*, July 28, 1808. See also TR to GP, October 20, 1808, TRP (LC).

12. Circular Letter of George Poindexter, February 13, 1808, in *Mississippi Messenger*, March 31, 1808.

13. *Mississippi Messenger*, March 3, April 7, June 16 and 23, July 14, 1808. TR reported that a group of citizens wanted him to run for territorial delegate. They even, he claimed, promised to name him the state's first senator if he agreed (TR to C. A. Rodney, May 14, 1808, TRP [LC]).

14. *Mississippi Messenger*, July 7, 1808; *Natchez Weekly Chronicle*, July 6, 1808; W. H. Wooldridge to Williams, July 16, 1808, GC.

15. *Mississippi Messenger*, July 7 and 28, 1808; *Weekly Chronicle*, July 6, 1808; W. H. Wooldridge to RW, July 16, 1808, GC.

16. James W. Bramhan to Thomas M. Randolph and John W. Eppes, January 17, 1808, in *Natchez Weekly Chronicle*, November 23, 1808 (also photostatic copy in Mississippi Imprints [MDAH]); Bramhan to Randolph, August 5, 1807, ibid., October 26, 1808; Governor Williams to the President, January 30, 1808, *TP*, 5:602–3.

17. *Weekly Chronicle*, October 26 and November 23, 1808; *TP*, 5:602–3, 656–57, 684.

18. *TP*, 5:665; *Weekly Chronicle*, October 26, November 16, and November 23, 1808.

19. TR to GP, October [20], 1808, TRP (LC); *Weekly Chronicle*, October 26, 1808 (also in Mississippi Imprints).

20. See the exchange of notes between Bramhan and Williams, October 22 to October 25, in *Natchez Weekly Chronicle*, October 26, 1808; Public Statement of Robert Williams, n.d., ibid. For a second round of notes, see ibid., November 2, 1808. Subsequently, the governor's detractors had the entire correspondence published in pamphlet form (Haynes, "Political History," 183n).

21. *Weekly Chronicle*, October 26, November 2, 16, and 23, 1808; Haynes, "Political History," 183n; *TP*, 5:674.

22. RW to Beverley R. Grayson, October 7, 1808, EJ; RW to Theodore Stark, October 7, 1808, ibid.; *TP*, 5:655–56.

23. John Brabston to Williams, July 22, 1808, GC; Beverly R. Grayson to Williams, August 5, 1808, ibid.; Williams to Grayson, August 12, 1808, ibid.; Grayson to Williams, August 17, 1808, ibid.

24. John Brabston to RW, July 22, 1808, GC; Beverly R. Grayson to RW, August 5, 1808, ibid.; RW to Grayson, August 12, 1808, ibid.; Grayson to RW, August 17, 1808, ibid.; RW to Grayson, October 15 and 18, 1808, EJ; *TP*, 5:655; Proclamation of RW, December 19, 1808, GC.

25. *Natchez Weekly Chronicle*, October 19, 1808; Hamilton, *Law*, 149–52. See also TR's notes, ibid., 401–9, 414–18; TR to C. A. Rodney, October [20], 1808, TRP (LC).

26. Bruin to the Secretary of State, October 12, 1808, *TP*, 5:650; Resolution of the Territorial Legislature, March 1, 1808, ibid., 615.

27. Hamilton, *Law*, 150–51.

28. *TP*, 5:615, 650, 656; Hamilton, *Law*, 150–51; RW to Seth Lewis, October 14, 1808, EJ; RW to JM, October 22, 1808, ibid.

29. Hamilton, *Law*, 432–38; Proclamation of RW, October 14, 1808, EJ; RW to Seth Lewis, October 14, 1808, ibid.

30. Proclamation of Governor Williams, September 9, 1808, EJ (Williams); Governor to the Territorial House of Representatives, September 16, 1808, GC (Williams).

31. Proclamation of RW, September 9, 1808, EJ; RW to House of Representatives, September 16, 1808, GC; Williams to the Gentlemen of the House of Representatives, September 17, 1808, EJ; *TP*, 5:633, 640.

32. *Weekly Chronicle*, October 5, 19, and 26, 1808; *TP*, 5:640–44.

33. *TP*, 5:645–48.

34. *Mississippi Messenger*, April 8, 1806; Hamilton, *Law*, 210n.

35. *TP*, 5:648–50.

36. Ibid., 5:644–45.

37. *TP*, 5:640, 649, 698–701; ibid., 6:13–14; *Weekly Chronicle*, December 14, 1808.

38. George Davis had been deeply involved in the Briggs-Poindexter controversy. Davis, who had some "disagreeable qualities" such as a "Jealous temper," and Briggs had clashed repeatedly while doing the surveying of the territory. After Briggs did not appoint Davis to be one of his principal deputies for the Orleans Territory, the latter was "thrown . . . into a paroxysm of rage," and the old animosities broke out again, this time into a bitter quarrel accompanied by an exchange of recrimination. In this instance, Poindexter came to Davis's defense and turned on Briggs, ultimately forcing him to resign. Apparently Davis was trying to work back into the good graces of Williams (see *TP*, 5:482–84).

39. *Natchez Weekly Chronicle*, November 30, 1808; Haynes, "Political History," 174–75.

40. Bullock to Shields, December 16, 1808, *Natchez Weekly Chronicle*, December 28, 1808. Those attesting to the accuracy of the recorded debates were John C. Cox, Major William Vick, John B. Willis, Pierson Lewis, Clinch Gray, Charles de France, Samuel Cook, and Alexander Covington (ibid.). Later, even Henry Downs, who had voted with the Mead forces, admitted that they were correct (Parke Walton to Bullock, February 24, 1809, ibid., March 1, 1809).

41. "One George Davis" to the editors, December 22, 1808, *Natchez Weekly Chronicle*, January 11, 1809, March 25, 1809.

42. *Natchez Weekly Chronicle*, December 28, 1808, January 11, February 22, March 1 and 25, 1809; CM to GP, December 3, 1808, GPP; GP to C, December 26, 1808, ibid.

43. *Natchez Weekly Chronicle*, October 12 and December 21, 1808; GP to CM, December 26, 1808, GPP.

44. The congressional debates on Poindexter's motion are printed in *Natchez Weekly Chronicle*, January 4 and 11, 1809. See also ibid., December 21, 1808; GP to CM, December 26, 1808, GPP. Poindexter also claimed that Governor Williams had sent copies of Davis's "mutilated debates" to several members of Congress (ibid.).

45. See Memorial to the President and Congress by the Territorial Legislature, December 21, 1807, *TP*, 5:587–90; Edmund P. Gaines to the Secretary of War, April 15, 1808, ibid., 625–26; and Memorial to the President and Congress by the Territorial House of Representatives, September 19, 1808, ibid., 638–39.

46. Governor Williams reported that news of the embargo "has Created a considerable bustle with the plantering as well as mercantile interest" (Williams to the President, January 30, 1808, *TP*, 5:603). See also Memorial to the President and Congress by the Territorial House of Representatives, September 19, 1808, ibid., 638.

47. *TP*, 5:587–90, 603, 625–26, 638–39, 662–63.

48. Haynes, "Disposal of Lands," 21–23.

49. *TP*, 5:662–63, 693.

50. Ibid., 5:720–21, 739–40.

51. Williams to the Secretary of the Treasury, August 23, 1808, Executive Journal, Williams; Williams to Major Thomas Freeman, December 19, 1808, ibid.; The Secretary of the Treasury to Williams, November 5, 1808, GC.

52. RW to Gallatin, August 23, 1808, EJ; RW to Maj. Tomas Freeman, December 19, 1808, ibid.; Gallatin to RW, November 5, 1808, GC; *TP*, 6:20, 25–26.

53. GP to CM, December 26, 1808, GPP; GP to Judge [TR], January 16, 1809, Mississippi Territory, Miscellaneous Manuscripts, New York Historical Society; *Natchez Weekly Chronicle*, March 8, 1809.

54. *Natchez Weekly Chronicle*, March 8, 1809; *TP*, 5:703–4.

55. GP to CM, December 26, 1808, GPP; *TP*, 5:680–81.

56. *TP*, 5:722–23.

57. *Weekly Chronicle*, March 8, 1809; Shields to GP, March 10, 1809, Shields Papers (LSU); Hamilton, *Law*, 69.

58. Shields to GP, March 10, 1809, Shields Papers (LSU).

59. *Natchez Weekly Chronicle*, December 28, 1808; Shields to GP, March 10, 1809, Shields Papers (LSU); James, *Natchez*, 93–94.

60. *TP*, 5:661.

61. Ibid., 5:665–66.

62. Mead to Poindexter, December 23, 1808, GPP.

63. CM to GP, December 23, 1808, GPP; *TP*, 5:674.

64. *TP*, 5:682–84.

65. *Natchez Weekly Chronicle*, February 8, 1809. The governor's lengthy address to the legislature, February 9, 1809, is in GC.

66. The acrimonious debates for these short sessions are reported in *Natchez Weekly Chronicle*, February 22, March 1 and 8, 1809. See also Governor Williams to the General Assembly, March 3, 1809, GC.

67. *Natchez Weekly Chronicle*, February 8, 1809. The governor's lengthy address of February 9, 1809, is in GC. The debates are in *Natchez Weekly Chronicle*, February 22, March 1 and 8, 1809. See also Hamilton, *Law*, 85.

68. Rodney to C. A. Rodney, May 2, 1809, *PMHB* 45:182.

69. Ibid.; Hamilton, *Law*, 70.

11. Transformation of a Territory

1. William B. Hamilton, "The Southwestern Frontier, 1795–1817: An Essay in Social History," *JSH* 10 (1944):389–403. By 1797, cotton had become the staple crop of the district. William Dunbar to John Ross, August 21, 1797, Extract [by Benjamin L. C. Wailes] from Letter Books of Dunbar, (LC). See also James Hall, *A Brief History of the Mississippi Territory, in which is Prefixed a Summary View of the Country between the Settlements on Cumberland River, & the Territory* (Salisbury, N.C., 1801). Hall's *History* is reprinted in MHSP, 9:539–75. See also Hamilton, "Beginnings," 332–35.

2. The importation of foreign luxuries into Natchez was nothing new, although it increased with the rise of prosperity after 1800 (Mack Swearingen, "Luxury at Natchez in 1801: A Ship's Manifest from the McDonogh Papers," *JSH* 3:187–90; William B. Hamilton and William D. McCain, eds., "Wealth

in the Natchez Region: Inventories of the Estate of Charles Percy, 1794 and 1804," *JMH* 10:290–316). For figures on the exports of the territory and the duties collected at the port of entry at Loftus Heights, consult *ASP, Commerce,* 1:928, and *ASP, Finance,* 2:548. See also CSS, *Wailes,* 21–22; and Hamilton, "Beginnings," 222–32.

3. Christian Schultz, *Travels on an Inland Voyage,* 2 vols. (New York, 1810), 2:135; Henry B. Fearon, *Sketches of America . . .* (London, 1818), 273.

4. For an in-depth discussion of the Mississippi River boatmen, see Michael Allen, *Western Rivermen, 1763–1861: Ohio and Mississippi Boatmen and the Myth of the Alligator Horse* (Baton Rouge and London, 1990).

5. Schultz, *Travels,* 140–43, 145–46.

6. Natchez "under-the-Hill" has fascinated a number of historians and writers. The earliest descriptions are by travelers such as Christian Schultz, who was especially taken with this part of the town. *The Louisiana & Mississippi Almanack* for 1812 contains a list of the businesses along the riverfront. They included one tavern, two blacksmith shops, thirteen "Catalene shops, porter houses, &c." This portion of the town impressed a later traveler as a "Pandemonium of devils, a limbo of vanity, and a paradise of fools" (Arthur Singleton, *Letters from the South and West of the United States* [Boston, 1824], 126). For some earlier secondary accounts, see MS, *Poindexter,* 52–53; Virginia Park Malthias, "Natchez-Under-the-Hill as It Developed under the Influence of the Mississippi River and the Natchez Trace," *JMH* 7:201–21. See also Michael Francis Baird, "Frontier Post on the Mississippi: A History of the Legend of Natchez Under-the-Hill, 1800–1900" (master's thesis, LSU, 1981); and Beard, "Natchez Under-the-Hill: Reform and Retribution in Early Natchez," *Gulf Coast Historical Review* 4 (1988):29–48.

7. Schultz, *Travels,* 2:136; MS, *Poindexter,* 51n; HT, *Stat.,* 128.

8. James, *Natchez,* passim; Hamilton, "Beginnings," 354–57.

9. Cuming, *Tour,* 293–95.

10. The first play presented in Natchez took place in February 1806. By 1808, the Natchez Theatrical Association had been organized, and shortly thereafter it began a successful string of plays, pantomimes, after-pieces, and road shows (William B. Hamilton, "The Theater in the Old Southwest: The First Decade at Natchez," *American Literature,* 12 [1941]:471–85; Joseph Miller Free, "The Ante-Bellum Theatre of the Old Natchez Region," *JMH* 5:471–85; William Bryan Gates, "The Theatre in Natchez," *JMH* 3:71–74). Dancing societies existed in Natchez as early as 1801 (*Green's Impartial Observer,* February 21, 1801).

11. For example, see the advertisement in the *Mississippi Messenger,* October 15, 1805. After accepting the presidency of a dancing assembly, Judge Rodney explained that he attended "the dances to Preserve order and Decorum, but seldom dance" (TR to C. A. Rodney, November 24, 1805, TRP [LC]).

12. *Mississippi Messenger,* January 28, 1806, December 10, 1807; *Natchez Weekly Chronicle,* January 22, 1810.

13. John Bisland paid ten dollars a year as a subscription fee to James T. Bell's coffeehouse (receipt, dated November 29, 1810, Bisland Papers ([LSU]). See also *Louisiana & Mississippi Almanack* for 1813, 50; *Washington Republic and Natchez Intelligencer,* August 30, 1817; *Natchez Weekly Chronicle,* September 5, 1808, October 7, 1809.

14. Wailes, *Report,* 114; CSS, *Wailes,* 24, 30; JFHC, *Miss.,* 258–60.

15. Guy B. Braden, "A Jeffersonian Village: Washington, Mississippi," *JMH* 30:135–44; Suanna Smith, "Washington, Mississippi: Antebellum Elysium," ibid., 40:143–65. The dinners in the district were so frequent that little mention is made of them in letters or other documents. They were discussed only when some unusual event accompanied them (see, for instance, *TP,* 5:566). Judge Rodney's letters to his son are the best source for social life at the territorial capital. On one embarrassing occasion, the judge's friends threw a public dinner in his honor as a send-off for his trip to Richmond where he was to testify in the Aaron Burr trial. Unfortunately, Rodney became suddenly ill and was forced, at the last minute, to cancel his journey, but the dinner was held as scheduled (*PMHB* 45:41–42).

16. Cuming, *Tour,* 315–16; Edward Turner to B. L. C. Wailes, March 30, 1859, Wailes Papers (MDAH).

17. Entry dated September 12, 1804, Diary of Thomas Rodney (MDAH). A published version is in Laura D. S. Harrell, ed., "Diary of Thomas Rodney, 1804," *JMH* 7:111–16.

18. H. G. Hawkins, "History of Port Gibson," MHSP, 10:279–99; Cuming, *Tour,* 315–16; Henry Ker, *Travels through the Western Interior of the United States from the Year 1808 up to Year 1816* (Elizabethtown, N.J., 1816), 302; Orrin Schofield, ed., *Perambulations of a Cosmopolite: or Travels and Labors of Lorenzo Dow* (Rochester, 1842), 156.

19. Rodney reported that Joshua Baker's house, where he spent the night, "looked dirty" but he "had a clean bed." He was disappointed to find that Mrs. Baker, who like Rodney was from Delaware, had none of the "manners of Delaware about her or its neatness" (Harrell, ed., "Diary of Rodney," 115). See also Ray Holder, ed., "The Autobiography of William Winans" (master's thesis, University of Mississippi, 1936), 254–56; JFHC, "A Trip through the Piney Woods [1840–1841]," MHSP, 9:487–538. An inventory of the property of John Montgomery, which the Indians had burned, gives a good indication of the possessions of one of the wealthier frontier settlers (schedule of the property of John Montgomery, August 1, 1817, GC).

20. There are numerous references to the illegal cutting of timber from the public domain. See, for example, *TP,* 6:205–6, 543, 774. One persistent offender was known as "the notorious Burch" (ibid., 207).

21. *TP*, 5:442, 497–505, 693.

22. Tax Lists, Adams County, 1815, Records of the Territorial Auditor, RG 3 (MDAH). That year Judge Poindexter purchased 1,200 acres on Bayou Sara where he built his beautiful home (Articles of Agreement signed by GP and Moses Liddell, September 1815, ibid.). The first known letter that Poindexter dated Ashwood Place was in May 1816 (GP to Ficklin, May 16, 1816, GPP). Poindexter's first marriage was to Lydia Carter, daughter of a prominent planter (Hamilton, *Law*, 86). He later divorced her and married Agatha Chinn (MS, *Poindexter*, 137).

23. James, *Natchez*, 32, 37, 98, 145, 155, 240.

24. For the early homes of the Natchez District, see J. Frazer Smith, *White Pillars* (New York, 1941), 111–17; Edith W. Moore, "Natchez Holmes," *Natchez Democrat*, 1959, Pilgrimage Edition; and J. Wesley Cooper, *Natchez: A Treasure of Ante-Bellum Homes* (Natchez, 1957).

25. Hamilton, "Southwestern Frontier," 390–95; Hamilton, *Law*, 86; Harrell, ed., "Diary of Rodney," 111–16.

26. TR to Richard Claiborne, December 27, 1806, TRP (LC); Harrel, ed., "Diary of Rodney," 111–16; William B. McGroaty, ed. "Diary of Captain Philip Buckner," *William and Mary Quarterly Historical Magazine*, 2nd ser., 6:173–207; Hamilton, *Law*, 86; G. P. Whittington, "Dr. John Sibley of Natchitoches, 1757–1837," *LHQ* 10:468.

27. An excellent example of the wealth and leisure living of the "nabob" class is in John A. Quitman to his father, January 16, 1822, in JFHC, *Life and Correspondence of John A. Quitman*, 2 vols. (New York, 1860) 1:70–74; Quitman to Col. P. Brush, August 23, 1822, ibid., 83–86.

28. On Dunbar, see Rowland, ed., *Dunbar*, passim; F. L. Riley, "Sir William Dunbar—The Pioneer Scientist of Mississippi," MHSP, 2:85–111. Arthur H. DeRosier Jr., "Natchez and the Formative Years of William Dunbar," *JMH* 34:29–47; DeRosier, "William Dunbar: A Product of the Eighteenth Century Scottish Renaissance," ibid., 185–227. A good summary of the scientific interests in the territory is in Hamilton, "Beginnings," 332–34, 380–87.

29. For instance, the Mississippi Society was incorporated November 18, 1803 (HT, *Stat.*, 409–10; see also *Washington Republican*, June 16, 1813, June 29, 1814).

30. Other than Jefferson College, various academies opened their doors from time to time, although all of them were short-lived. Those in the western part of the territory included Franklin Academy (1806), Madison Academy (1809), Washington Academy (1811), Amite Academy (1815), Jackson Academy (1814), and Wilkinson Academy (1816). In the eastern half, schools were established much later. The few included Greene Academy (1816) and St. Stephens Academy (1816) (*Mississippi Messenger*, August 9, 1806, July 7, 1807; HT, *Stat.*, 415; Turner, *Digest*, 53, 55–60).

31. Among the various societies established during the territorial period were the Planters Society of Claiborne County, the Jacksonian Library Society at Woodville, and the Franklin Debating and Literary Society in Wilkinson County (Holmes to House of Representatives, December 12, 1809, EJ; HT, *Stat.*, 309; Holder, "Winans," 264–65).

32. The American Bible Society, which elected Governor Holmes its president, was launched in 1813 (*Washington Republican*, August 26, 1815). The session records of the Salem Presbyterian Church, February 1807 to May 1820, are in Walter B. Posey, *The Presbyterian Church in the Old Southwest* (Richmond, 1952), appendix, 129–38. For a general discussion of religion in Mississippi, see Frances Allen and James Allen Cabaniss, "Religion in Ante-bellum Mississippi," *JMH* 6:192–224; Randy J. Sparks, *Religion in Mississippi* (Jackson, Miss., 2001), 3–94.

33. The growth of the African American population can be seen in following statistics.

Year	Population	Percentage of blacks
1801	7,400	42%
1810	30,100	47%
1816	34,800	52%

(Schedule of the whole number of persons within the Mississippi Territory, 1801; Abstract of the Census . . . for 1810 in GC; *Mississippi Republican and Natchez Intelligencer*, November 20, 1816; see also TP, 6:720–30).

34. These figures are painstakingly worked out in Hamilton, "Beginnings," 266–68.

35. See the assessor's roll for 1805 and 1815 in Auditors Records (MDAH); Hamilton, "Beginnings," 268–69.

36. Hamilton, "Politics in Mississippi Territory," 277–91; Robert V. Haynes, "Territorial Mississippi, 1798–1817," *JMH* 44:283–305.

37. JFHC, *Miss.*, 144; Hamilton, "Beginnings," 215–16; Thomas Nuttall, *Journal of Travels into the Arkansas Territory, During the 1819, With Occasional Observations on the Manners of the Aborigines* (Philadelphia, 1821), 233. See also *Mississippi Messenger*, January 21, 1808.

38. The story of this famous encounter is discussed in MS, *Poindexter*, 114–16. The various documents covering the exchanges between parties are in GPP.

39. MS, *Poindexter*, 68–74, 160–68; Hamilton, "Politics in Mississippi Territory," 285–90.

40. For instance, Lorenzo Dow described this type of inhabitant as "like Sheep without a Shepherd" (Lorenzo Dow, *The Life, Travels, Labors, and Writings of Lorenzo Dow including his Singular and Erratic Wanderings in Europe and America* . . . [New York, 1881], 120). See also Kirby to TJ, May 1, 1804, TJP (LC).

41. Haynes, "Early Washington County," 183–98; *TP*, 5:320–21, 359. Toul-min deserves a good biography. For his part in the Creek conflict, see Leland Lengel, "The Road to Fort Mims: Judge Harry Toulmin's Observations on the Creek War, 1811–1813," AR 29:16–36; Cox, *West Florida Controversy*, passim.

42. For Toulmin's role as surrogate official for the Tombigbee District, see Toulmin to William Lattimore, February 1, 1806, M179. The complaints against him began as early as 1802 (Daniel Clark Jr. to James Madison, June 22, 1802, T225).

43. George Strother Gaines, *The Reminiscences of George Strother Gaines: Pioneer and Statesman of Early Alabama and Mississippi, 1805–1845*, ed. James P. Pate (Tuscaloosa, Ala., and London, 1998), 40–42.

44. One traveler predicted that St. Stephens would in "a few years . . . [become] of considerable importance to the United States" (Ker, *Travels*, 332–33). Contemporary descriptions of the Tombigbee District are less available than those of the Natchez District.

45. Kirby to Jefferson, May 1, 1804, TJP; *TP*, 5:318.

46. *PMHB* 44:180; TR to GP, February 3, 1808, GPP; CM to GP, September 1, 1809, ibid.

47. Hamilton, "Beginnings," 253–54.

48. An interesting letter from St. Stephens indicates that the Tombigbee region recovered quickly from the ravages of the Creek War (James Churchill to Wm. Churchill, March 2, 1814, James and Zelpha Churchill Papers, Duke University; *Natchez Weekly Chronicle*, September 28, 1808). There are numer-ous petitions from citizens requesting stay laws in TLR, RG4 (MDAH); *PMHB* 45:180–86.

49. Petition by Citizens of Adams County to the Territorial Legislature, n.d., TLR.

50. *Washington Republican*, April 19, 1813; August 24, 1814; October 5, 1814. "Planter" conveniently divided the two groups into one composed of creditors, speculators, shysters, lawyers, sheriffs, and law clerks and the other of honest and godly farmers.

51. Douglas C. McMurtrie, ed., *The Banking Act of 1809* (Chicago, 1936); Charles H. Brough, "History of Banking in Mississippi," MHSP, 3:317–20; Marvin Bentley, "The State Bank of Mississippi: Monopoly on the Frontier," *JMH* 40:297–308. In October 1814, the bank's board of directors assured "every person, who shall deposit specie at the Bank, that no contingency shall prevent their receiving the same in specie when demanded" (*Mississippi Republican*, October 19, 1814).

52. Resolution of House of Representatives, December 21, 1814, TLR; Peti-tion by Inhabitants of Claiborne County to the Territorial Legislature, Novem-ber, 1814, ibid.; JFHC, *Miss.*, 301.

53. John Bisland to William Bisland, May 5, 1817, Bisland Papers (LSU); *Louisiana & Mississippi Almanac* for 1813, 47.

12. Natives and Interlopers

1. James H. O'Donnell III, *Southern Indians in the American Revolution* (Knoxville, Tenn., 1973). For an excellent account of the earlier period, see the classic study by Verner W. Crane, *The Southern Frontier, 1670–1732* (New York, 1928). See also Mary Ann Wells, *Native Land: Mississippi, 1540–1798* (Jackson, Miss., 1998); Robert S. Cotterill, *The Southern Indians* (Norman, Okla. 1954), 37–56; and Greg O'Brien, *Choctaws in a Revolutionary Age, 1750–1830* (Lincoln, Neb., and London, 2002).

2. MTA, 198–200. Also consult Daniel H. Usner Jr., *Indian, Settlers, and Slaves in a Frontier Exchange Economy: The Lower Mississippi Valley before 1783* (Chapel Hill, N.C., 1992); Kathryn E. Holland Braund, *Deerskins and Duffels: Creek Indian Trade with Anglo-Americans, 1685–1815* (Lincoln, Neb., 1993); and Greg O'Brien, "The Conqueror Meets the Conquered: Negotiating Cultural Boundaries on the Post-Revolutionary Southern Frontier," *JSH*, 67 (2001): 39–72. .

3. John Walton Caughey, "Willing's Raid down the Mississippi, 1778," *LHQ* 15 (1932): 5–32; Haynes, *Natchez District*, 60–61.

4. David J. Weber, *The Spanish Frontier in North America* (New Haven and London, 1992), 275–85; Jack D. L. Holmes, "Juan de Villebeuve and Spanish Indian Policy in West Florida, 1784–1797," *Florida Historical Quarterly* 58 (1980): 387–99.

5. For instance, see the description of the Choctaw "play-off system" in Richard White, *The Roots of Dependency*, 34–68. See also J. Leitch Wright Jr., *Anglo-Spanish Rivalry in North America* (Athens, Ga., 1971), 154–70. For a good example of this strategy, see MTA, 193–94.

6. C&G, FC, 1–12.

7. The best and most thorough study of the Spanish presence in West Florida is Cox, *West Florida Controversy*, 1–187.

8. Usner, *American Indians*, 74–75; Peter H. Wood, "The Changing Population of the Colonial South: An Overview by Race and Religion, 1685–1790," *Powhatan's Mantle: Indians in the Colonial Southeast*, ed. Peter H. Woods, Gregory A. Waselkor, and M. Thomas Hatley (Lincoln, Neb., and London, 1989), 38, 72.

9. C&G, FC, 9; John A Swanton, *The Tribes of North America*, Smithsonian Institution, Bureau of American Ethnology, Bulletin 145 (Washington, 1953), 153–95; John A. Swanton, "Sun Worship in the Southeast," *American Anthropologist*, 30 (1928): 206–13.

10. White, *Roots of Dependency*, 83–87, 92–94.

11. FH, *SIBH*, 146–48; Mary Ann Wells, *Searching for Red Eagle: A Personal Journey into the Spirit World of Native America* (Jackson, Miss., 1998), 107; White, *Roots of Dependency*, 20–22.

12. FH, *SIBH*, 127.

13. Charles Hudson, *The Southeastern Indians* (Knoxville, Tenn., 1976), 120–84, 317–75; C&G, *FC*, 22; White, *Roots of Dependency*, 21–22; MDG, *Politics*, 15–16; Arret M. Gibson, *The Chickasaws* (Norman, Okla., 1971), 8–13.

14. MDG, *Politics*, 4–6; Wells, *Red Eagle*, 47; Gibson, *Chickasaws*, 19–20; Gaines, *Reminiscences*, 46.

15. FH, *SIBH*, 6–10; C&G, *FC*, 2–16. There are several early travel journals that describe the topography of the southwestern and south central parts of the United States. For instance, see John Pope, *A Tour through the Southern and Western Territories of the United States of North America* (Richmond, 1792), 24–31; Cuming, *Tour*, 284–95. See also AEJ, passim; and William Bartram, *Travels of William Bartram*, ed. Mark Van Doren (New York, 1904), 335–42.

16. C&G, *FC*, 20–22. See also Benjamin Hawkins, *A Sketch of the Creek Country in the Years 1798 and 1799*, Georgia Historical Society, *Publications*, vol. 3 (Americus, Ga., 1938).

17. MDG, *Politics*, 4–12; DeRosier, *Removal of Choctaw*, 7–9; Gibson, *Chickasaws*, 21–23.

18. For the influence of Alexander McGillivray, see James W. Caughey, *McGillivray of the Creeks* (Norman, Okla., 1938); and Cotterill, *Southern Indians*, 57–99. The most recent assessment of McGillivray is Michael D. Green, "Alexander McGillivray," in *American Indian Leaders: Studies in Diversity*, ed. R. David Edmunds (Lincoln, Neb., 1980), 41–63. On the other hand, there is no biography of George Colbert (see Gibson, *Chickasaws*, 99–100; Gaines, *Reminiscences*, 157; TP, 5:601; see also Kathryn E. Holland Braund, "The Creek Indians, Blacks and Slavery," *JSH* 57:601–36).

19. TP, 5:177; Gibson, *Chickasaws*, 74–79; MDG, *Politics*, 11–12, 38–40; FH, *SIBH*, 17–20; DeRosier, *Removal of Choctaw*, 7–9; White, *Roots of Dependency*, 64–65, 87–88. See also Greg O'Brien, *Choctaws in a Revolutionary Age, 1750–1830* (Lincoln, Neb., and London, 2002).

20. Prucha, *Great Father*, 102–8; MTA, 33–34, 206–7.

21. HT, *Stat.*, 213. For example, acting Governor West informed the legislature that the Jefferson County jail had been "lately demolished," and that the building of "a new one . . . demands the most prompt attention" (CW to Legislature, December 4, 1804, GC; see also Petition of the Justices of Peace of Adams County, August 21, 1804, ibid; John Callier [*sic*] to CW, February 26, 1805, ibid.).

22. Hudson, *Southeastern Indians*, 223–34; Prucha, *American Indian Policy in Formative Years*, 188–212.

23. Silas Dinsmoor to CW, May 17, 1804, GC; CW to David Berry, May 29, 1804, ibid.; West to Dinsmoor, May 31, 1804, ibid.; CW to Dearborn, June 2 and July 19, 1804, ibid.

24. *MTA*, 223–33.

25. Ibid., 350–51, 527–29.

26. For instance, see The Secretary of War to TJ, January 7, 1803, M127.

27. Prucha, *Great Father*, 44–60.

28. Usner, *American Indians*, 75–76; Wallace, *Jefferson and the Indians*, 220–26; *MTA*, 261, 266–67; *TP*, 4:424; 5:35–36; Pound, *Benjamin Hawkins*, 99–101; FH, *SIBH*, 14, 58–59, 93.

29. *TP*, 5:146–50; Dearborn to agents Wm Lyman, Saml Mitchell, and Wm Wells, February 23, 1802, M15; *MTA*, 94, 107–8, 155–56, 460. George S. Gaines stated that Dinsmoor's "wit and humor appeared to be inexhaustible" (Gaines, *Reminiscences*, 41). Governor Claiborne, who admired Dinsmoor greatly, described him as "an active, faithful officer & has great influence with the Choctaws" (LBC, 3:281).

30. *TP*, 5:146; *MTA*, 401; Prucha, *Great Father*, 115–18.

31. *MTA*, 416–18, 482; *TP*, 5:146–49. 176; Secretary of War to TJ, January 7, 1803, M127; Aloysius Plaisance, "The Choctaw Trading House — 1803–1822, *Alabama Historical Quarterly* 21:15–53; Usner, *American Indians*, 76; LBC, 1:84–86; Gaines, *Reminiscences*, 40, 51.

32. LBC, 2:20, Usner, *American Indians*, 76–77; Gaines, *Reminiscences*, 48–51.

33. Usner, *American Indians*, 76; Ora Brooks Peake, *A History of the United States Indian Factory System, 1795–1822* (Denver, 1954), 204–50; *TP*, 5:187.

34. L&B, 10:369–71. The activities of the Panton, Leslie & Company are well covered in William S. Coker and Thomas D. Watson, *Indian Traders of the Southeastern Spanish Borderlands: Panton Leslie & Company and John Forbes & Company, 1783–1847* (Gainesville, Fla., 1986).

35. Samuel J. Wells, "International Causes of the Treaty of Mount Dexter, 1805," *JMH* 48:177–86; *TP*, 5:212–14; Prucha, *American Indian Treaties*, 108–10; C&G, FC, 37–39.

36. Prucha, *American Indian Treaties*, 51–65; Pound, *Hawkins*, 1–98.

37. SS to WS, May 18 and August 31, 1798, M40; SS to Secretary of War, December 8, 1798, ibid.; LBC, 1:13–14, 72–73, 87–88; *MTA*, 350–51.

38. *MTA*, 20–21, 46–47.

39. Ibid., 143–44, 169–70, 178–81; *TP*, 5:59; Secretary of War to JW, January 31, 1799, JW Papers, Chicago Historical Society.

40. *MTA*, 23, 32.

41. *TP*, 5:58; *MTA*, 143–44.

42. *MTA*, 20–21, 32.

43. Ibid., 149, 195, 237; Ephraim Kirby to TJ, April 20, 1804, Ephraim Kirby Papers, Duke University Library; Kirby to Albert Gallatin, July 1, 1804, ibid.; Dinsmoor to the Secretary of War, July 17, 1811, M221.

44. *MTA*, 55.

45. Hatfield, *Claiborne*, 41–66; C&G, FC, 29–31. For a slightly different viewpoint, see Bernard W. Sheehan, *Seeds of Destruction: Jeffersonian Philanthropy and the American Indian* (New York, 1973).

46. *The Works of Thomas Jefferson*, ed. Paul L. Ford, 12 vols. (New York, 1904–1905), 9:447; L&B, 10:370; 17:374; Wallace, *Jefferson and Indians*, 206–40: Prucha, *Great Father*, 135–48; Prucha, *American Indian Policy*, 213–24; Thomas Jefferson, *Notes on the State of Virginia*, ed. William Peden (New York, 1954), 140.

47. Reginald Horsman, *Expansion and American Indian Policy, 1783–1812* (1967; repr., Norman, Okla., and London, 1992), 104–14.

48. *MTA*, 393–94, 400–3; LBC, 1:109.

49. *MTA*, 405, 407–9, 452, 460, 489, 493.

50. Ibid., 472–74, 479, 546, 553.

51. Gaines, *Reminiscences*, 41–42, 47–48.

52. Gibson, *Chickasaws*, 90.

53. Horsman, *Expansion and American Indian Policy*, 115–41; Clark and Guice, *Frontiers in Conflict*, 29–39; Prucha, *American Indian Treaties*, 105–13; C&G, FC, 31–39.

54. Prucha, *American Indian Treaties*, 106–7; 2 *Stat.*, 92; Kappler, *Indian Affairs: Laws and Treaties*, 255–56; Gibson, *Chickasaws*, 108, 148.

55. Hawkins, *Letters*, 372–73; *MTA*, 357–58, 372–73.

56. Kappler, *Treaties*, 56–58; ASP, IA, 1:651–52, 658–59; *MTA*, 363.

57. TP, 5:236–37.

58. Ibid., 5:189, 213–4; *MTA*, 484–86. See also Robert S. Cotterill, "A Chapter of Panton, Leslie and Company," *JMH* 10:475–92; Coker and Watson, *Indian Traders*, 243–72.

59. Quoted in Prucha, *American Indian Treaties*, 109. See also TP, 5:342, ASP, IA, 2:759; C&G, FC, 35–36.

60. TP, 5:213–14, 238, 343; 6:123–27.

61. Quoted in Horsman, *Expansion and American Indian Policy*, 136.

62. Usner, *American Indians*, 79–80; Kappler, *Treaties*, 85–86; C&G, FC, 36–37; TP, 5:434–35; DeRosier, *Removal of Choctaw*, 32. DeRosier attributes the delay in ratifying the treaty to Jeffersonian parsimony, but the real reason was Jefferson's displeasure with the location of the land cession (Prucha, *American Indian Treaties*, 109–10; see also ASP, IA, 1:748–49; and Richardson, comp., *Messages and Papers*, 1:434–35).

63. Horsman, *Expansion and American Indian Policy*, 136–37, 139.

13. Manifest Destiny

1. Samuel C. Hyde Jr., *Pistols and Politics: The Dilemma of Democracy in Louisiana's Florida Parishes, 1810–1899* (Baton Rouge and London, 1996), 2–5; LBC, 5:134. For descriptions of early West Florida, see AEJ, 198–238; Gilbert Imlay, *A Topographical Description of the Western Territory* (1792; repr., New York, 1969), 414–57; Bernard Romans, *A Concise Natural History of East and West Florida* (1775; repr., Gainesville, Fla., 1962).

2. Gilbert C. Din, "Spain's Immigration Policy in Louisiana and American Penetration, 1792–1803," *Southwestern Historical Quarterly* 76:255–76; Din, "Proposals and Plans for Colonization Efforts in Louisiana," *Louisiana Studies* 11:31–49; Light T. Cummins, "An Enduring Community: Anglo-Americans at Colonial Natchez and in the Felicianas, 1774–1810," *JMH* 55:133–54; Hyde, *Pistols and Politics*, 2.

3. Cummins, "Enduring Community," 140–52; Arthur H. DeRosier Jr., "Natchez and the Formative Years of William Dunbar," *JMH* 34: 29–47; Eron Orpha Moore Rowland, ed., *Life, Letters, and Papers of William Dunbar of Elgin, Morayshire, Scotland and Natchez, Mississippi: Pioneer Scientist of the Southern United States* (Jackson, Miss., 1930).

4. Hyde, *Pistols and Politics*, 3–4; Gilbert C. Din, *The Canary Islanders of Louisiana* (Baton Rouge, 1988).

5. Lawrence S. Kaplan, *Thomas Jefferson: Westward the Course of Empire* (Wilmington, Del., 1999), 142.

6. LBC, 1:346, 3:58–59, 150–51; John Hawkins Napier III, *Lower Pearl River & Piney Woods: Its Land and People* (Oxford, Miss., 1985); Thomas D. Clark, "The Piney Woods and the Cutting Edge of the Lingering Southern Frontier," in *Mississippi's Piney Woods: A Human Perspective*, ed. Noel Polk (Jackson, Miss., 1986), 64. Some of the same conditions prevailed north of Mobile (see Cox, *West Florida Controversy*, 159; and C&G, *FC*, 56–57).

7. Cox, *West Florida Controversy*, 183–87; Peter J. Hamilton, *Colonial Mobile: An Historical Study Largely from Original Sources, of the Alabama-Tombigbee Basin from the Discovery of Mobile Bay in 1519 until the Demolition of Fort Charlotte in 1821* (Boston and New York, 1898), 299. For an earlier description, see Isaac Johnson to Anthony Hutchins, August 17, 1802, JFHC Papers, Southern History Collection, University of North Carolina, Chapel Hill.

8. LBC, 3:51; Hyde, *Pistols and Politics*, 19–20.

9. LBC, 5:56–57; Hyde, *Pistols and Politics*, 20–21.

10. Cox, *West Florida Controversy*, 156–63. For the Kempers' later escapades, see William Linnard to Secretary of War, September 20, 1812, M221, and Owsley and Smith, *Filibusters and Expansionists*, 51–52, 61–63.

11. LBC, 3:25. For a slightly different interpretation, see Andrew McMi-

chael, "The Kemper 'Rebellion': Filibustering and Resident Anglo-American Loyalty in Spanish West Florida," *LH* 43:133–65. An older and somewhat outdated study is Stanley Clisby Arthur, *The Story of the West Florida Rebellion* (St. Francisville, La., 1935).

12. Hamilton, *Colonial Mobile*, 304–14. AE had found the trade at Mobile "considerable" (AEJ, 201, 210–11; see also, LBC, 5:147; John Forbes, *John Forbes Description of the Spanish Floridas, 1804*, ed. William S. Coker [Pensacola, 1979]; and David J. Weber, *The Spanish Frontier in North America* [New Haven and London, 1992], 213, 275, 276).

13. *TP*, 5:325; Hamilton, *Colonial Mobile*, 296–97, 306–14.

14. LBC, 5:134.

15. John Adair to JM, January 9, 1809, JM Papers (LC); *Messages and Papers*, 1:379; Owsley and Smith, *Filibusters and Expansionists*, 24, 30–31; Tucker and Hendrickson, *Empire of Liberty*, 157–63; Robert V. Haynes, "The Southwest and the War of 1812," *LH* 5:41–51; Turreau to Talleyrand, July 9, 1803, quoted in Adams, *History*, 3:85.

16. Cox, *West Florida Controversy*, 102–38; DH to SS, June 20, 1810, EJ.

17. L&B, 11:350–51.

18. APW, *The United States and the Independence of Latin America, 1800–1830* (Baltimore, 1941), 1–3, 38–72; LBC, 5:31–32; L&B, 12:186–87.

19. L&B, 12:186–87.

20. LBC, 4:201.

21. Ibid., 4:210; *Natchez Weekly Chronicle*, June 18, 1810; DH to Robert Smith, June 20, 1810, MTP; Cox, *West Florida Controversy*, 335–36.

22. John Lynch, *The Spanish-American Revolution, 1808–1826* (New York, 1973); Cox, *West Florida Controversy*, 312–35; C&G, FC, 49–50.

23. DH to Robert Smith, June 20, 1810, MTP. For Secretary of State Smith's reactions, see The Secretary of State to Governor Holmes, July 12, 1810, GC.

24. Robert V. Haynes, "The Road to Statehood," in *A History of Mississippi*, ed. Richard A. McLemore, 2 vols. (Hattiesburg, Miss., 1973), 1:224–25; James A. Padgett, "The West Florida Revolution of 1810," *LHQ* 21:76–102; TPA, *South*, 344–45.

25. DH to the SS, July 11, 1810, MTP; James A. Padgett, "Constitution of the West Florida Republic," *LHQ* 20:188–94.

26. C&G, FC, 53–54.

27. DH to SS, June 20, 1810, MTP.

28. DH to SS, August 8, 1810, MTP; Henry L. Favrat, "Some Causes and Conditions that Brought about the West Florida Revolution in 1810," *LHQ* 1:37–41; Journal of the First West Florida Convention, July 25–27, 1810, in West Florida Papers (LC); *Natchez Weekly Chronicle*, August 6, 1810; *TP*, 9:894–95.

29. Gov. Delassus to Messrs. Thomas Lily, John H. Johnson and Manuel Lopez, July 30, 1810, MTP; DH to SS, August 21, 1810, ibid.; TP, 9:896.

30. Journal of the West Florida Convention, WFP (LC).

31. TP, 6:115–16; Rhea to DH, September 26 and October 5, 1810, MTP; Favrat, "Some Causes and Conditions," 45–46; TPA, South, 350; Cox, West Florida Controversy, 394–95. Claiborne refers to Thomas as "the Ajax of the late Revolution" in LBC, 5:56.

32. DH to SS, September 26 and October 3, 1810, MTP; R. Davidson to Abner Duncan, September 25, 1810, enclosure in Holmes to Robert Smith, October 3, 1810, ibid.; Holmes to John Rhea, September 30, 1810, ibid.; Hugh Davis to Holmes, September 25, 1810, GC; TPA, South, 351–52.

33. LBC, 5:32; Robert Smith to Holmes, July 17, 1810, GC; Haynes, "Southwest and War of 1812," 41–51.

34. LBC, 5:31–34; TP, 9:883–84.

35. TP, 9:885.

36. John H. Johnson to DH, August 14, 1810, enclosure in DH to SS, August 21, 1810, MTP; Cox, West Florida Controversy, 364–65.

37. John Rhea to SS, October, 11, 1810, MTP.

38. DH to SS, July 11, 1810, MTP; Hugh Davis to DH, September 25, 1810, GC.

39. DH to Rhea, October 17, 1810, EJ; DH to Col. Thomas Cushing, September 26, 1810, ibid.; Holmes to Colonel Davis, September 27, 1810, ibid.; General Orders of October 1, 1810, ibid.; TP, 6:121–22.

40. ASP, FR, 3:396–98; TP, 9:903–4. The proclamation is in James D. Richardson, ed., Compilation of the Messages and Papers of the Presidents, 1789–1897, 10 vols. (Washington, 1969), 1:480–81.

41. Republican and Savannah Evening Ledger, December 20, 1810; TP, 9:901–2; ibid., 6:161–63; DH to WC, December 4, 1810, EJ; DH to Legislature, November 8, 1810, GC; TPA, South, 358–59.

42. LBC 5:34–36, 38–39; TPA, South, 356–57.

43. LBC, 5:40–41, 44–46, 51–54.

44. TP, 9:909–12.

45. LBC, 5:46–49.

46. Ibid., 5:50–51, 159–60; Skipwith to JM, December 5, 1810, WFP (LC).

47. Skipwith to WC, December 10, 1810, WFP (LC); Skipwith to [James Graham], January 14, 1811, ibid.; LBC, 5:53–56, 56–57, 208–9; TP, 9:912–13.

48. TP, 9:906, 927; C&G, FC, 54–64. .

49. TP, 6:296, 305–6; TPA, South, 364–66; Haynes, "Road to Statehood," 227, 228. The measure annexing all of the tract east of the Pearl River, west of the Perdido River, and south of the thirty-first degree of north latitude to Mississippi Territory was approved May 14, 1812 (2 Stat., 734).

50. *TP*, 9:913–14. On amnesty to deserters, see LBC, 2:94–96; and ibid., 5:352–53.

51. LBC, 5:62; Skipwith to Graham, December 23, 1810, WFP (LC).

14. The Mobile Question

1. TR to C. R. Rodney, March 31, 1806, TRP (LC); *TP*, 5:69–70.

2. Sargent completely ignored the eastern region during his first two years as governor. In fact, Sargent's first mention of this settlement was in November 1799, when he wrote John McKee, Choctaw agent, that he was "anxious for the information you promised me from Tombigby" (*MTA*, 191–92). In the following spring, Sargent planned to visit the area, and he asked General Wilkinson to furnish him with an escort for his "visit to the Tombeckbee Settlements" (ibid., 220). Although prevented from undertaking this trip by distractions in Natchez, Sargent extended county government to the region (ibid., 238–39).

3. *TP*, 5:220, 290, 317.

4. Ibid., 5:219–20, 280–81.

5. Ibid., 5:237, 317–19.

6. Ibid., 5:238.

7. Ibid., 5:290–91, 425. Sargent mistakenly used the term "district" when he was really referring to counties (see SS to WS, June 3, 1799, M40).

8. *TP*, 5:223–24, 322; C&G, FC, 58.

9. Marion Twinling and Godfrey Davies, introduction to HT, *The Western Country in 1793: Reports on Kentucky and Virginia*, ed. Twinling and Davies (San Marino, Calif., 1948), iv–x; Robert Davidson, *History of the Presbyterian Church in Kentucky* (n.p., 1847), 290–25.

10. *TP*, 5:320–22.

11. Ibid., 5:345–46, 353–55.

12. Hamilton, *Colonial Mobile*, 345; Cox, *West Florida Controversy*, passim; C&G, FC, 58–61.

13. *TP*, 5:461–64, 468–69; ibid., 6:118.

14. John D. W. Guice, "The Cement of Society," 85; Hamilton, *Colonial Mobile*, 345–46.

15. *TP*, 5:433, 438–40, 505.

16. *ASP, IA*, 1:751; *TP*, 5:434–35. The treaty, signed on November 16, 1805, is in 7 *Stat.* 98–100.

17. Petition of legislative members to CW, March 6, 1805, GC; Dinsmoor to CW, May 28, 1805, ibid.; Joseph Chambers to CW, April 30, 1805, ibid.; James Caller to Captain Edmund P. Gaines, May 18, 1809, M221; Gaines to the Secretary of War, May 27, 1809, ibid.; C&G, FC, 56.

18. *TP*, 5:733–34.

19. Ibid., 6:26–30, 36–39.

20. Ibid., 6:77.

21. Ibid., 6:79–82.

22. Ibid., 6:84–90.

23. James Caller to DH, August 21, 1809, GC; *PMHB* 45:188–9; *TP*, 6:67, 91, 98; DH to HT, September 8, 1810, EJ.

24. *TP*, 6:104–5.

25. DH to HT, September 8 and 16, 1810, EJ; DH to Colonels Caller, Carson, and Patton, September 8 and 16, 1810, ibid.

26. *TP*, 6:117, 119; DH to Colonel Sparks, September 9, 1810, EJ.

27. *TP*, 6:120–21, 129; Jonathan Longstreet to HT, October 14, 1810, JM Papers (LC); LBC, 5:37–38; Cox, *West Florida Controversy*, 421; TPA, *South*, 354.

28. *TP*, 6:132, 135, 141.

29. Ibid., 6:129, 130–31.

30. Ibid., 6:132, 135, 141.

31. HT to DH, September 16, 1810, GC; *National Intelligencer*, November 7 and 13, 1810; *TP*, 6:129.

32. HT to James Innerarity, November 15, 1810, *AHR* 2: 701–2.

33. *TP*, 6:138–39.

34. Ibid., 6:147–48.

35. Ibid., 6:138.

36. Folch to Sparks, November 13, JM Papers (LC); Folch to Holmes, November 15, 1810, GC; *TP*, 6:138.

37. *TP*, 6:140–43.

38. Ibid., 6:147, 151; ibid., 9:922; Folch to Sparks, November 20 and 29, 1810, JM Papers (LC); LBC 5:71; C&G, FC, 59; Cox, *West Florida Controversy*, 471–75.

39. *TP* 6:140; Reuben Kemper to John Rhea, December 16, 1810, WFP (LC).

40. *TP*, 6:140–43; Cox, *West Florida Controversy*, 475–79.

41. This description is taken from the following sources: *TP*, 6:140–43, 149–51, 152–57; LBC, 5:76–77, 89–90; Cox, *West Florida Controversy*, 482–86. Toulmin collected evidence against the Mobile Society during and immediately after these events (see House Files 12B–A1 in Records of the United States House of Representatives, MTP, RG 233 [NA]).

42. *TP*, 6:180; LBC, 5:111. There are numerous pleas from Governor Claiborne for their release in LBC, 160–61, 165, 173–74, 191, 211–12, 225–26, 249, 276, 344, 370–71; 6: 90, 112–13, 239–40, 267. See also *TP*, 9:926.

43. *TP* 6:152–53, 158–59; Issuance of Warrants for the Arrest of Joseph P. Kennedy, et al., December 6 and 7, 1810, House Files, 12B–A1.

44. *TP*, 6:152–57, 173–74.

45. HT to JM, February 13, 1812, House Files, 12B–A1; *TP*, 6:154–57.

46. Reuben Kemper to John McMullen, November 23, 1810, WFP (LC). See charges against Judge Toulmin, September 1811, in House Files, 12B–A1.

47. *TP*, 6:176, 266–67; LBC, 5:83, 86–87.

48. LBC, 5:73–74, 77.

49. *TP* 6:167, 176–77; LBC, 5:71–72.

50. LBC, 5:73–74.

51. *TP*, 6:167–68, 179.

52. LBC, 5:107, 232, 247.

53. Statements of R. M. Gilmer and Benjamin Smoot, February 14, 1812, House Files, 12B–A1.

54. LBC, 5:290, 396–97.

55. SS to George Mathews and John McKee, January 29, 1811, M40; SS to McKee, January 2, 1812, ibid.; SS to General Hampton and Colonel Cushing, January 14, 1811, M6; General Orders of Secretary of War, January 25, 1811, ibid.

56. *TP*, 9:922; ibid., 6:188–89; Isaac Joslin Cox, "The Border Mission of General George Mathews," *Mississippi Valley Historical Review* 12: 309–20, Cox, *West Florida Controversy*, 524–29.

57. James E. Lewis Jr., *The American Union and the Problem of Neighborhood: The United States and the Collapse of the Spanish Empire, 1783–1829* (Chapel Hill, N.C., 1998), 38. For the "No Transfer Resolution," see John A. Logan Jr., *No Transfer: An American Security Problem* (New Haven, Conn., 1961), 111–28.

58. *TP*, 9:927; Frank L. Owsley Jr., *Struggle for the Gulf Borderlands: The Creek War and the Battle of New Orleans* (Gainesville, Fla., 1981), 23; C&G, FC, 64; Hamilton, *Colonial Mobile*, 358.

59. *TP*, 6:360, 362, 368; Cox, *West Florida Controversy*, 409–15; Hamilton, *Colonial Mobile*, 358–63.

60. *TP*, 6:305, 320–21, 323, 364–65, 371–73.

15. The Creek War

1. John Sevier to Secretary of War, May 10, 1808, M221.

2. James Robertson to Secretary of War, January 22, 1809, M221; Dinsmoor to Secretary of War, October 27, 1808, ibid.; Seth Pease to the Secretary War, September 27, 1809, ibid.; *TP*, 6:27–29, 41–42.

3. *TP*, 6:5, 9, 21, 95; Governor Blount to Secretary of War, January 28, 1811, M221.

4. BH to Secretary of War, October 16, 1808, and April 18, 1811, M221; James Edington to BH, September 13, 1808; ibid.; *TP*, 6:34.

5. AJ, *Papers*, 2:190–92.

6. RW to Col. Sparks, August 8, 1808, M221; Dinsmoor to Dearborn, December 8, 1808, ibid.; JW to Dearborn, September 26, 1808, ibid.

7. James Neelly to Secretary of War, October 20, 1809, M221; J. V. Stewart to Secretary of War, November 19, 1808, ibid.; Dinsmoor to Secretary of War, May 2 and December 12, 1809, ibid.; DeRosier, *Removal of Choctaw*, 31–32.

8. *TP*, 6: 76; C&G, *FC*, 42–43; Southerland and Brown, *Federal Road*, 33–36.

9. Return J. Meigs to Secretary of War, July 4, 1812, M221; Proclamation of Dinsmoor, October 16, 1808, ibid. For a comparison with conditions in the Old Northwest, see Francis Paul Prucha, *Broadax & Bayonet: The Role of the United States Army in the Development of the Northwest, 1815–1860* (1953; repr., Lincoln, 1995), esp. 55–68.

10. David J. Weber, *The Spanish Frontier in North America* (New Haven, 1992), 279–96.

11. Usner, *American Indians*, 73–86; Dinsmoor to Dearborn, October 11, 1808, M221; BH to Secretary of War, January 6, 1811, ibid.

12. C&G, *FC*, 235–36; John Sugden, *Tecumseh: A Life* (New York, 1997), 239–40.

13. Coker and Watson, *Indian Traders*, passim.

14. JW to Secretary of War, October 1, 1812, M221; AJ, *Papers*, 2:190–94; *TP*, 6:215–16, 317; GP to CM, December 12, 1811, GPP.

15. Joseph Kent to Levn Wailes, April 2, 1812, Wailes Papers (MDAH); GP to CM, November 11, 1811, and January 25, 1812, GPP.

16. *TP*, 6:298, 302–3.

17. Ibid., 6:303–5.

18. AJ, *Papers*, 2:290–93, 307–8, 336–38; Robert V. Remini, *Andrew Jackson and the Course of American Empire, 1767–1821* (New York, 1977), 168–71; *The Correspondence of Andrew Jackson*, ed. John Spencer Bassett, 6 vols. (Washington, 1926–1930), 1:240.

19. AJ, *Papers*, 2: 337, 342–44, 349–50, 358–60, 364–65.

20. Ibid., 2:361, 368–69, 383–86; Remini, *Course of Empire*, 175–77; AJ, *Correspondence*, 1:292–93.

21. AJ, *Papers*, 2:390–92, 403–4; Robert V. Remini, *Andrew Jackson and His Indian Wars* (New York, 2001), 60.

22. Donald R. Hickey, *The War of 1812: A Forgotten Conflict* (Chicago, 1898), 72–99; Gregory Evans Dowd, *A Spirited Resistance: The North American Indian Struggle for Unity, 1745–1815* (Baltimore and London, 1992), esp. 33–36. The best studies of the two Indian leaders are both by R. David Edmunds: *Tecumseh and the Quest for Indian Leadership* (Baltimore, 1984) and *The Shawnee Prophet* (Lincoln, Neb., 1983).

23. Quoted in Gibson, *Chickasaws*, 96. See also the speech that Tecumseh supposedly gave to a joint council of Chickasaws and Choctaws in W. C. Vanderwerth, comp., *Indian Oratory* (Norman, Okla., 1971), 62–66.

24. H&B, *CW*, 40–41; Edmunds, *Tecumseh*, 146. Apparently James Neelly, the Chickasaw agent, was unaware of Tecumseh's visit (Cotterill, *Southern Indians*, 169). For favoritism toward Colbert, see LBC 1:258; Wilkinson to Dearborn, November 2, 1804, M221; FH, *SIBH*, 226; and Sugden, *Tecumseh*, 241.

25. Debo, *Choctaw Republic*, 40–41; DeRosier, *Removal of Choctaw*, 33–35; H&B, *CW*, 41–55.

26. MDG, *Politics*, 26–39; Horsman, *Expansion and Indian Policy*, 120–24; Prucha, *American Indian Treaties*, 110–11; Kappler, *Treaties*, 2:85–86; *TP*, 5:222; FH, *SIBH*, 172–73, 222–23, 227.

27. *TP*, 6:213–14, 218; *ASP*, *IA*, 1:843; Pound, *Hawkins*, 209–11; H&B, *CW*, 36–37.

28. BH to Secretary of War, May 22 and October 3, 1811, M221; Genl. Hampton to Col. Leonard Covington, July 20, 1811, M221; Hampton to Col. John Symonds, July 22, 1811, ibid.; Christian Limbaugh to Secretary of War, May 27, 1811, ibid.; Secretary of War to BH, June 27 and July 20, 1811, M15; Hopoheithle to JM, May 11, 1811, M271. See also Benjamin W. Griffith Jr., *McIntosh and Weatherford, Creek Indian Leaders* (Tuscaloosa, Ala., 1988), 65–69; Angie Debo, *The Road to Disappearance: A History of the Creek Indians* (Norman, Okla., 1941), 74–75.

29. Pound, *Hawkins*, 99–117, 183–73; MDG, *Politics*, 33–38; *TP* 5:404; FH, *SIBH*, chap. 4. See also BH to Dearborn, January 23, February 18, and June 15, 1807, M221.

30. MDG, *Politics*, 36–38; BH, *A Sketch of the Creek Country in the Years 1798 and 1799* in Georgia Historical Society, *Publications*, vol. 3 (1848) pt. 1, 51–68; Debo, *Road to Disappearance*, 66–71; Dowd, *Spirited Resistance*, 149.

31. Dowd, *Spirited Resistance*, 149–52, 154–57; MDG, *Politics*, 38–39. The Cherokees and the Choctaws even agreed to this principle in their conflicts with one another. See, for instance, The Agreement of Cherokees west of the Mississippi and the Great Medal Chiefs . . . of the Choctaws, Septembers 19, 1812, M221.

32. MDG, *Politics*, 38–41; Griffith, *McIntosh and Weatherford*, 46–47.

33. BH to Secretary of War, September 21, 1811, M221; Griffith, *McIntosh and Weatherford*, 72–73; H&B, *CW*, 42–43; JFHC, *Miss.*, 315–16.

34. FH, *SIBH*, 269; J. F. H. Claiborne, *The Life and Times of Gen. Sam Dale, the Mississippi Partisan* (1860; repr., New York, 1960), 52–53; Griffith, *McIntosh and Weatherford*, 73–74.

35. JFHC, *Miss.*, 317–18; Sugden, *Tecumseh*, 245–48; Thomas Wilkins,

Cherokee Tragedy: The Ridge Family and the Decimation of a People, rev. ed. (Norman, Okla., and London, 1986), 52–55. See also *ASP, IA*, 1:845.

36. Edmunds, *Tecumseh*, 150–51; Dowd, *Spirited Resistance*, 134, 146, 169–73; Griffith, *McIntosh and Weatherford*, 79–80; Sugden, *Tecumseh*, 246–48; Mary Ann Wells, *Searching for Red Eagle: A Personal Journey into the Spirit World of Native America* (Jackson, Miss., 1998), 150–63; MDG, *Politics*, 39–42.

37. BH to Secretary of War, January 31, 1812, M221; Deposition of Samuel Manac [Manioc], August 2, 1813, quoted in H&B, *CW*, 91–93; Edmunds, *Tecumseh*, 151–52; FH, *SIBH*, 270; JFHC, *Miss.*, 316; Griffith, *McIntosh and Weatherford*, 77–78.

38. BH to Secretary of War, February 3, March 9 and 30, 1812, M221.

39. BH to the Secretary of War, April 1 and 6, July 20, August 13, and September 7, 1812, M221; Christian Limbaugh to Secretary of War, May 14, 1812, ibid.; BH, *Letters, Journal and Writings of Benjamin Hawkins*, ed. C. L. Grant, 2 vols. (Savannah, Ga., 1980), 2:605, 617; H&B, *CW*, 85–86.

40. BH to Secretary of War, May 25, 1812, M221; Talk of Hawkins to Chiefs of Creek Nation, n.d., ibid.; Deposition of William Womack, June 5, 1812 before John Caller, ibid.; Deposition of Nathan Lott, June 6, 1812, ibid.; Deposition of Major William Lott, June 6, 1812, ibid.

41. BH to the Secretary of War, June 22, 1812, with enclosure Talk of Tustunnugee Thllucco, Speaker for Council of Chiefs, to Hawkins, June 17, 1812, M221; James Neelly to Secretary of War, April 24 and 30, 1812, ibid.; H&B, *CW*, 91–92; Debo, *Road to Disappearance*, 76; Owsley, *Struggle for Gulf Borderlands*, 14–15; C&G, *FC*, 125.

42. For the effect of the earthquake in 1811, see Henry Cassidy to Benjamin Morgan, August 31, 1812, M221; Pitman Colbert to John Ellicott, April 6, 1812, ibid. The stories about the earthquake are covered in H&B, *CW*, 67–73; JFHC, *Miss.*, 317–18; Griffith, *McIntosh and Weatherford*, 76–77; Owsley, *Struggle for Gulf Borderlands*, 13; Sugden, *Tecumseh*, 246–51; Wilkins, *Cherokee Tragedy*, 55–57.

43. AJ, *Correspondence*, 1:225n; Griffith, *McIntosh and Weatherford*, 81–82; H&B, *CW*, 104; Gaines, *Reminiscences*, 53; Robert Cooper to Thomas Johnson, April 2, 1812, M221; AJ, *Papers*, 2:298–99, 310–11.

44. Gaines, *Reminiscences*, 53–54; C&G, *FC*, 123; AJ, *Papers*, 2:316.

45. AJ, *Papers*, 2:300–303.

46. James Caller to DH, June 14, 1812, M221; John Hanes to DH, June 13, 1812, ibid.; 6:283, 297; DH to James Caller, June 23, 1812, EJ; DH to Maj. John Bowyer, June 23, 1812, ibid.; DH to BH, June 24, 1812, ibid.

47. *TP*, 6:306–7, 327; BH to Secretary of War, September 7 and November 24, 1812, M221; BH to Secretary of War, September 21, 1812, ibid.

48. *TP*, 6:307; Capt. Gaines to Secretary of War, March 11, 1817, M221; *ASP, IA*, 1:814; JFHC, *Miss.*, 318, 322.

49. *ASP, IA*, 1:839; Cotterill, *Southern Indians*, 178–79; Griffith, *McIntosh and Weatherford*, 84–85; Thomas S. Woodward, *Reminiscences of the Creek, or Muscogee Indians, Contained in Letters to Friends in Georgia and Alabama* (1895; repr., Tuscaloosa, Ala., 1939), 36.

50. *ASP, IA*, 1:841–43.

51. Ibid., 1:846, 847, 849–50; *TP*, 6:389; Griffith, *McIntosh and Weatherford*, 87–88; MDG, *Politics*, 41–42.

52. JW to HT, June 25, 1813, GC; HT to F. L. Claiborne, July 19, 1813, ibid.; Deposition of Sam Manac, August 2, 1813, H&B, *CW*, 92; FH, *SIBH*, 279–83; JFHC, *Miss.*, 321–22.

53. *ASP, IA*, 1:851; Deposition of David Tate, August 2, 1813, M221; Deposition of Sam Manac, August 2, 1813, H&B, *CW*, 93, 125–26; Wells, *Searching for Red Eagle*, 182–83; Woodward, *Reminiscences*, 97–98.

54. Extract of letter from John Innerarity to James Innerarity, July 7, 1813, enclosure in HT to Secretary of War, August 13, 1813, M221. See also Coker and Watson, *Indian Traders*, 479–80; F. L. Claiborne to Secretary of War, August 12, 1813, M221; Joseph Carson to General Claiborne, July 30, 1813, ibid.; HT to Governor Blount, July 30, 1813, ibid.; H&B, *CW*, 130–31; C&G, *FC*, 127.

55. HT to Gaines, July 19, 1813, M221; H&B, *CW*, 126; DH to HT, July 26 and 29, 1813, GC; *TP*, 6:388–89.

56. *TP*, 6:283. In mid-July, Toulmin wrote the governor that he had hoped the "danger [was] really less than was conceived" by General Wilkinson (HT to DH, July 12, 1813, GC).

57. HT to Gov. Blount, July 28 and 30, 1813, M221.

58. H&B, *CW*, 129; John Hanes to Maj. Bowyer, July 30, 1813, GC; Statement of William Pierce, August 1, 1813, M221; John Pierce to HT, July 15, 1813, ibid.; HT to Gaines, July 19, 1813, ibid.; John Pierce to DH, July 23, 1813, GC.

59. The battle is described in H&B, *CW*, 128–40. See also *TP*, 6:396–97; James Caller to DH, August 15, 1813, GC; and HT to Blount, July 30, 1813, M221. In his descriptions, General Claiborne was more generous toward Caller and his men (F. L. Claiborne to Secretary of the War, August 12, 1813, ibid.). On the other hand, the governor's aide-de-camp, John Hanes, reported that "most of our party Behaved Extremely Cowardly" (Hanes to Holmes, August 4, 1813, GC).

60. F. L. Claiborne to Secretary of War, August 28, 1813, M221; HT to Blount, July 28, 1813, ibid.; Benjamin Hicks to DH, August 21, 1813, GC; F. L. Claiborne to DH, August 4, 1813, ibid.; HT to DH, August 10, 1813, ibid.; H&B, *CW*, 140–41; Griffith, *McIntosh and Weatherford*, 97.

61. MDG, *Politics*, 42.

62. C&G, *FC*, 129–30; H&B, *CW*, 107–8, 146–48. A copy of the plan for Fort Mims is printed in Griffith, *McIntosh and Weatherford*, 103. The original is in MDAH.

63. DH to HT, July 26, 1813, GC; F. L. Claiborne to DH, August 4, 1813, ibid.; Gaines to Gov. Blount, July 23, 1813, M221; *TP*, 6:329; HT to JM, September 11, 1813, MTP; H&B, *CW*, 148–49, 150–51; C&G, *FC*, 130; JFHC, *Miss.*, 323.

64. H&B, *CW*, 150–53; Griffith, *McIntosh and Weatherford*, 102–4; Owsley, *Struggle for Gulf Borderlands*, 35–36.

65. Wells, *Searching for Red Eagle*, 195–99; H&B, *CW*, 153–76; C&G, *FC*, 130–31; Griffith, *McIntosh and Weatherford*, 104–10. For some sketchy contemporary accounts, see F. L. Claiborne to DH, September 4, 1813, GC; Lewis Sewall et al. to Secretary of War, September 4, 1813, M221; F. L. Claiborne to Secretary of War, Oct 11, 1813, ibid.; HT to JM, September 11, 1813, MTP; *ASP, IA*, 1:852–53.

66. C&G, *FC*, 131; H&B, *CW*, 157–63; JFHC, *Miss.*, 325.

67. *TP*, 6:295, 320–21; JFHC, *Miss.*, 319–20.

68. *TP*, 6:370, 379, 381; H&B, *CW*, 94–95.

69. F. L. Claiborne to DH, August 12, 1813, GC., JFHC, *Miss.*, 319; *TP*, 6:385; Holmes to the Secretary of War, August 10, 1813, ibid., 385, 393–94; DH to Flournoy, July 14, 1813, EJ.

70. DH to Col. Joseph Constant, August 5, 1813, EJ; *TP*, 6:396–98, 400–402.

71. DH to Legislature, December 7, 1813, EJ; DH to Col. Nelson, September 11, 1813, ibid.; DH to F. L. Claiborne, September 13, 1813, ibid.; *TP*, 6:399–400.

72. General Orders, September 15 and 22, 1813, EJ; JFHC, *Miss.*, 327–28.

73. John Pitchlynn to DH, September 3, 1813, GC; DH to Turner Brashears, October 8, 1813, EJ; DH to Pitchlynn, October 8, 1813, ibid.; DeRosier, *Removal of Choctaw*, 34–36.

74. General Flournoy to Secretary of War, November [8?] and December 6, 1813, M221; Flournoy to SS, December 12, 1813, ibid.; General Thomas Pinckney to Colonel Gilbert C. Russell, February 1, 1814, GC.

75. Owsley, *Struggle for Gulf Borderlands*, 43–45.

76. These developments are well covered in Remini, *Jackson and His Indian Wars*, 62–75. See also JFHC, *Miss.*, 340, 331n; HT to [JM], September 14, 1813, MTP; Colonel Russell to General Claiborne, January 12, 1814, GC.

77. Cotterill, *Southern Indians*, 184–85; Owsley, *Struggle for Gulf Borderlands*, 47–48, 57–58; C&G, *FC*, 133–34; JFHC, *Miss.*, 329.

78. JFHC, *Miss.*, 338; JFHC, *Sam Dale*, 133–36; Owsley, *Struggle for Gulf Borderlands*, 46–48.

79. Griffith, *McIntosh and Weatherford*, 126–32; H&B, *CW*, 241–56; Mrs. Dunbar (Eron) Rowland, *Mississippi Territory in the War of 1812* (1921; repr., Baltimore, 1968), 712–17.

80. F. L. Claiborne to DH, March 8, 1814, Wailes Papers (MDAH); JFHC, *Miss.*, 330–31.

81. Owsley, *Struggle for Gulf Borderlands*, 51–60.

82. The brawl in Nashville is covered in Remini, *Jackson and the Course of Empire*, 180–87; AJ, *Papers*, 2:441, 443; and Remini, *Jackson and His Indian Wars*, 62–73.

83. AJ, *Papers*, 2:444; *Nashville Whig*, November 9, 1813.

84. AJ, *Correspondence*, 1:348–50; AJ, *Papers*, 2:448–49.

85. Remini, *Jackson and His Indian Wars*, 73–74.

86. For the battle of Horseshoe Bend, see Remini, *Jackson and His Indian Wars*, 75–79; and Owsley, *Struggle for Gulf Borderlands*, chap. 7. See also DH to Col. Russell, May 12, 1814, EJ; AJ, *Correspondence*. 1:491–92; and H&B, *CW*, 275–77.

87. MDG, *Politics*, 43.

88. Kappler, *Laws and Treaties*, 2:107–10; J. Leitch Wright Jr., *Creeks and Seminoles: The Destruction and Regeneration of the Muscogule People* (Lincoln, Neb., and London, 1986), chaps. 6 and 7. For Jackson's attitude, see Remini, *Jackson and the Course of Empire*, chaps. 13 and 14.

16. Holmes Sweet Holmes

1. *TP*, 6:12–13.

2. CM to GP, September 1, 1809, CC; *PMHB* 45:184; *Natchez Weekly Chronicle*, July 1, 1809.

3. There is no published biography of Governor Holmes. Unfortunately, he left no personal papers, and the biographer must rely entirely upon his public and official papers, which are housed for the most part in the MDAH. Information about his early life is particularly sketchy. The most complete account, written by a relative, is David Holmes Conrad, "David Holmes," MHSP, 4:234–57. Two master's theses have been completed about his public career: William Boyd Horton, "The Life of David Holmes" (University of Colorado, 1935); and Frances Elizabeth Melton, "The Public Career of David Holmes" (Emory University, 1966). See also William D. McCain, "The Administration of David Holmes, Governor of the Mississippi Territory," *JMH* 19:328–47.

4. *TP*, 6:205, 325–26. For his personality, see ibid, 5:697–98, 703.

5. Conrad, "Holmes," 234–57; McCain, "Administration of Holmes," 328. For his congressional career, consult *AC*.

6. *TP*, 6:67, 75; ibid., 9:858n.

7. Ibid., 6:49–51, 526–27; *Washington Republican,* February 22, and August 12, 1815.

8. E[dward] T[urner] to Wailes, April 6, 1859, Wailes Papers (MDAH). The demise of the Federalist Party is traced in a number of excellent studies: George Dangerfield, *The Awakening of American Nationalism, 1815–1828* (New York, 1965), 1–35; Robert Allen Rutland, *The Presidency of James Madison* (Lawrence, Kans., 1990), 183–213; Shaw Livermore Jr., *The Twilight of Federalism: The Disintegration of the Federalist Party, 1815–1830* (Princeton, 1962); and George Dangerfield, *The Era of Good Feelings* (New York, 1952).

9. The latest study of the Monroe administration is Noble F. Cunningham Jr., *The Presidency of James Monroe* (Lawrence, 1996). See also Ammon, *Monroe,* 396–545; Charles Sellers, *The Market Revolution: Jacksonian America, 1815–1846* (New York, 1991); and Dangerfield, *Era of Good Feelings,* 95–104, 175–414.

10. TR to GP, June 27, 1809, Shields Papers (LSU); HT to Samuel Postlethwait, October 21, 1811, CC; *Washington Republican,* May 10, 1815.

11. *Natchez Weekly Chronicle,* April 12, 1809; *PMHB* 45:180; GP to CM, November 11, 1811, CC; Joseph Kent to Levin Wailes, Wailes Papers (MDAH); J. Leitch Wright Jr., *Anglo-Spanish Rivalry in North America* (Athens, Ga., 1971), 173.

12. Edmunds, *Tecumseh,* 150; Wells, *Searching for Red Eagle,* 156–57; Remini, *Jackson and His Indian Wars,* 62–79.

13. Addin Lewis to DH, September 22, 1814, GC; Owsley, *Struggle for Gulf Borderlands,* 62–79; Arsene Lacarriere Latour, *Historical Memoir of the War in West Florida and Louisiana in 1814–15* (1816; repr., Gainesville, Fla., 1964), vii–viii; David S. Heidler and Jeanne T. Heidler, *Old Hickory's War: Andrew Jackson and the Quest for Empire* (Mechanicsburg, Pa., 1996), 40–42.

14. AJ, *Papers,* 2:416. Toulmin agreed with Jackson (*Mississippi Messenger,* August 17, 1814).

15. Owsley, *Struggle for Gulf Borderlands,* 95–119; Remini, *Jackson and the Course of Empire,* 234–43; HT to [DH], February 2, 1814, GC.

16. Remini, *Jackson and the Course of Empire,* 242–45, 247–48; William S. Coker, "How General Jackson Learned of the British Plans before the Battle of New Orleans," *Gulf Coast Historical Review* 3 (1987):84–95; Hickey, *The War of 1812,* 206.

17. Robert V. Remini, *The Battle of New Orleans* (New York, 1999).

18. JFHC, *Miss.,* 342–46; Address of Secretary Nathaniel R. Ware to Legislature, November 7, 1815, JHR, 9th G.A., 1st sess.; *Washington Republican,* January 4 and November 11, 1815.

19. C&G, *FC,* 207–13.

20. There are various references, too numerous to cite, to these matters in the official correspondence of Governor Holmes in the MDAH.

21. Proclamation of DH, May 21, 1813 and April 14, 1815, GC; *TP*, 6:334–35.

22. Marschalk to DH, June 21, 1811, GC; Thomas Malone to DH, October 18, 1811, ibid.; HT to DH, June 10, 1811, ibid.; William Henry to DH, October 15, 1812, ibid.; Jefferson County Inhabitants to DH, ibid.; Gabriel Moore to DH, April 16, 1811, Gratz Collection (Historical Society of Pennsylvania); Daingerfield to Joseph Johnston, May 18, 1812, EJ; *TP*, 6:289.

23. HT to DH, August 10, 1813, GC; Josiah Blakeley to DH, September 19, 1814, ibid.; Petition by Inhabitants of Franklin County, July 8, 1815, ibid.; Captain Stephen McBroom to DH, March 1, 1811, ibid.; Daingerfield to Toulmin, May 11, 1812, EJ; DH to the Secretary of War, January 30, 1814, ibid.; JHR, 8th G.A., 1st sess., December 11, 1813; *TP*, 6:22–23.

24. DH to Anthony Campbell, August 10, 1813, EJ; Campbell to DH, August 22, 1813, GC; Deposition of Phillip Hill, August 11, 1813, ibid.; Proceedings of Court Martial of Samuel Montgomery, October 19, 1812, ibid.

25. DH to Joseph Briggs, January 6 and July 1, 1813; January 19, 1814, EJ; DH to Malone, November 8, 1813, ibid.; DH to Joseph Briggs, January 19, 1814, ibid.; Briggs to DH, July 26, August 9 and 15, 1813, GC.

26. DH to Montfort Calvit, May 12, 1811, EJ; Testimony of Natchez Lawyers, February 11, 1811, GC; Petition by Citizens of Natchez to DH, July 27, 1813, ibid.; Testimony of Stephen Carter, July 27, 1813, ibid.

27. DH to Peter P. Pollard, July 29, 1813, EJ; F. L. Turner to DH, February 8, 1811, GC; Testimony of Henry Bulen, July 27, 1813, ibid.; Petition by Citizens of Natchez to DH, July 27, 1813, ibid.

28. John Stafford to DH, September 17, 1813, GC; W. H. Beaumont to DH, August 26, 1811, ibid.

29. George H. Nixon to DH, August 2, 1813, GC; J. K. Cook to DH, August 19, 1813, ibid.; *Mississippi Republican*, August 17, 1813.

30. Peter Perkins to DH, November 15, 1814, GC; Neal Smith to DH, February 23, 1814, ibid.; DH to Robert Andrews, September 30, 1812, EJ; JFHC, *Miss.*, 238–30, 340.

31. DH to Flournoy, August 11, 1813, GC; DH to Thomas Hinds, August 9, 1813, ibid.; DH to Flournoy, November 3, 1813, EJ; DH to Hinds, November 9, 1813, ibid.; JFHC, *Miss.*, 327–28, 337–38; C&G, *FC*, 137. Hinds had married into the powerful Green family of Jefferson County and was a brother-in-law of Cato West (JFHC, *Miss.*, 228).

32. Genl. Claiborne to DH, October 1, 1812, GC; Lt. Col. John Wood to Genl. Claiborne, September 25, 1812, ibid.; DH to Flournoy, September 12, 1813, EJ; DH to Secretary of War, March 12, 1814, ibid.; DH to Captain Downs, May 2, 1814, ibid.; Address, DH to Legislature, January 20, 1814, GC.

33. Petition by "Exempts of Claiborne County," August 21, 1813, GC; James

Archer to DH, September 17, 1813, ibid.; F. L. Claiborne to DH, July 22, 1813, F. L. Claiborne Papers, Ms M (MDAH); Major Nathaniel Power to DH, August 23, 1813, GC; John Nugent to DH, July 12, 1813, ibid.; J. G. Richardson to DH, August 23, 1813, ibid.; James Archer to DH, August 22, 1813, ibid.; H. Harmon and P. A. Vandom to DH, August 23, 1813, ibid.; DH to Daniel Burnet, August 20, 1813, ibid.; *TP*, 6:328; JFHC, *Miss*, 326.

34. *TP*, 6:299, 328–29; Samuel Stockett to DH, December 27, 1814, GC.

35. John Ford to DH, November [3], 1813, GC; Jordan Morgan to DH, June 18, 1814, ibid.; B. Hicks to DH, January 10, 1814, ibid.; DH to Cornet James I. Mitchell, September 12, 1813, EJ; DH to Lt. Col. George Nixon, August 6, 1813, ibid.; Governor Holmes to Territorial Legislature, November 3, 1812, ibid.

36. John Ford to DH, July, 22, 1813, GC; F. L. Claiborne to DH, July 25, 1813, ibid.; R. Roache to DH, January 1, 1814, ibid.; DH to James Mitchell, September 12, 1813, EJ; JFHC, *Miss.*, 340. See also Mrs. (Eron) Rowland, *Jackson's Campaign*, 180–82; *TP*, 6:526.

37. James A. Maxwell to DH, November 11, 1813, GC; G. H. Nixon to DH, April 2, 1814, ibid.; Samuel Stockett to DH, August 18, 1813, ibid.; Ensign Benjamin Shields to DH, October 18, 1813, ibid.; Samuel Ross to Holmes, April 7, 1814, ibid.

38. Silas Hillson to DH, June 29, 1813, GC; Petition by Jefferson County Troop of Horse to DH [recd. September, 1813], ibid.; T. P. Bradish to DH, September 13, 1813, ibid.; Wm. Bruce to DH, June 22, 1813, ibid.; DH to John B. Taylor, August 28, 1813, EJ.

39. *Washington Republican*, August 25, 1813.

40. DH to HT, September 3, 1813, EJ; DH to JW, October 6, 1812, ibid.; DH to Flournoy, September 12, 1813, ibid.; DH to Flournoy, August 30, 1813, GC; DH to legislature, November 8, 1814, ibid.; *TP*, 6:385, 388–89, 396, 397–98, 400–402, 435.

41. DH to Secretary of War, September 29, 1812, GC; F. L. Claiborne to DH, September 4, 1813, ibid.; DH to Ralph Regan, October 18, 1803, ibid.; DH to Flournoy, September 6, 1813, EJ; DH to Lt. Col. Fleming, October 18, 1813, ibid.; HT to [SS?] September 11, 1813, Hamilton Collection, Duke University; DH to Flournoy, September 11, 1813, EJ; JHR, 8th G.A., 1st. sess., January 14, 1814; ibid., 8th G.A., 2nd. sess., November 28, 1814; DH to White Turpin, December 20, 1815, Wailes Papers, (MDAH); *Washington Republican*, July 28, 1813.

42. *Address of Doct. William Lattimore, to the Electors of the Mississippi Territory, on the Subject of the Approaching Election of Delegate to the Congress of the U States*, pamphlet in MDAH; *TP*, 6:636–37. Hunt's claims are in *ASP, PL*, 3:165–66.

43. *Mississippi Republican*, March 23 and May 11, 1814. The act is in 3 *Stat*

116–20. See also C. Peter Magrath, *Yazoo: Law and Politics in the New Republic, the Case of Fletcher v. Peck* (Providence, R.I., 1966); and *TP*, 6:509.

44. The proclamation is in Richardson, *Messages and Papers*, 1:572–73. See also *TP*, 6:513–14, 597, 618, 631–32. Secretary of the Treasury to Meigs, December 15, 1815, *TP*, 6:618; Toulmin to Lattimore, December 28, 1815, ibid., 631–32. Toulmin asked the president, "how can a jury be found in Monroe County to convict a man of *intrusion*—where every man is an intruder" (ibid., 641). The residents received news of the "Bill contemplating an indulgence . . . with *much rejoicing*" (ibid., 666–67).

45. MS, *Poindexter*, 28, 61–83; JFHC, *Miss.*, 361–75.

46. For the Duncan controversy, see written notation on the back of A. L. Duncan to Poindexter, n.d. [1805?], GPP. On the Poindexter-Hunt affair, see W. C. Mead to Captain Ebenezer Bradish, June 6, 1811, CC. A manuscript copy of the rules for this duel can be found ibid. See also W. C. Mead to GP, September 15, 1811, ibid.; GP to CM, December 12, 1811, ibid.; Richard Poindexter to his brother George, November 25, 1811, ibid.; MS, *Poindexter*, 114–16.

47. Unfortunately, there is no biography of this important figure in early territorial politics. On the printing of the first laws, see William B. Hamilton, ed., "The Printing of the 1799 Laws of the Mississippi Territory," *JMH* 2:88–89.

48. *TP*, 5:452, 630, Haynes, "Political History," 161–79; *Washington Republican*, October 13, 1813; Hopkins to GP, May 8, 1811, CC; JFHC, *Miss.*, 375; MS, *Poindexter*, 113–16.

49. GP to CM, January 4, February 3 and 22, 1813, CC; John W. Walker to GP, December 23, 1812, ibid.; Shields to GP, January 3 and November 30, 1812, ibid.; Shields to GP, November 23, 1812, Shields Papers (LSU); *TP*, 6:351–52. The Senate confirmed Poindexter as territorial judge on March 3, 1813 (*Executive Journal of the Senate*, 2:329, 333). He took the oath of office before Governor Holmes on June 11, 1813 (EJ).

50. *Washington Republican*, April 27 and 28, May 4, 11, and 18, June 30, 1813; *Natchez Mississippi Republican*, April 28, 1813. The election returns are in GC.

51. The correspondence concerning the Poindexter-Marschalk feud was later collected and published, possibly by friends of Poindexter. The only extant copy is in MDAH, but the first few pages, including the title page, are missing. Further reference to this pamphlet will be to "Castigator" pamphlet, which is in Poindexter, Personal File (MDAH). See Castigator to Poindexter, October 8, 1814, "Castigator" pamphlet, 8–10. Mead, who at this time was Speaker of the territorial House of Representatives, admitted suppressing the two petitions (CM to GP, October 8, 1814, ibid., 39–40; see also *Washington Republican*, May 3, November 17 and 23, 1814).

52. GP to DH, October 6, 1814, CC; JFHC, *Miss.*, 376–77; *Washington Republican*, November 16, 1814.

53. *Washington Republican*, November 9 and 23, December 21, 1814; *Mississippi Republican*, November 30, and December 14, and 21, 1814. See also "Castigator" pamphlet, 31–32, 35–59.

54. DH to Col. John McKee, December 16, 1814, EJ; *Mississippi Republican*, January 18, 1815.

55. JFHC, *Miss.*, 379–81; "Castigator" pamphlet, 72–79; *Washington Republican*, January 11, 1815.

56. Carroll to GP, January 22, 1815, CC; Burr Harrison to GP, July 11, 1815, ibid.; GP to Samuel Brown, June 27 and July 4, 1815, ibid.; GP to Thomas G. Percy, July 3, 1815, ibid.; John Beckly to GP, September 28, 1815, ibid.; J. W. Hamilton to GP, February 14, 1815, ibid.; John Lowry to GP, July 4, 1815, ibid.; *Mississippi Republican*, July 26, 1815; *Washington Republican*, February 1 and 8, 1815.

57. JFHC, *Miss.*, 379–80. The articles of separation between GP and Lydia, dated April 3, 1815, are in GPP. For Lydia's reactions to the separation, see Eliza I. Cosby to GP, May 29, June 26, and December 16, 1815, CC.

58. JFHC, *Miss.*, 377–78; Petition to DH, [1815], GC; GP to Judge Simpson, October 27, 1816, ibid.; "Castigator" pamphlet, 87–93. A manuscript copy of *Marschalk v. Shields* is in GC.

59. *TP*, 6:360, 364–65; DH to HT, July 3, 1813, EJ.

60. *TP*, 6:129, 322, 379.

61. Ibid., 6:365, 371–73, 618–19. This issue is thoroughly discussed in Hamilton, *Law*, 91–105.

62. *TP*, 6:325–26, 365.

63. Ibid., 6:363, 366–67, 431–36, 438–39; *Washington Republican*, March 8, 1815.

64. *TP*, 6:616–25.

65. Ibid., 6:371–73, 425–26, 434.

66. HT to D H, June 21, 1813, GC; *TP*, 6:324, 326; JHR, 8th. G.A., 1st sess., December 11 and 17, 1813; Petition by Brightwell to House of Representatives [December 1813], GC; Report of the House Committee on Privileges and Elections [December 1813], ibid.; Toulmin to Speaker of House Daniel Burnet, December 21, 1813, ibid.; *Washington Republican*, December 15, 1813, January 21, 1814.

67. HT to DH, May 30, and June 5, 1815, GC.

68. HT to DH, August 7, 1815, GC.

69. *Washington Republican*, May 10 and 17, 1815. See also three undated petitions in Legislative Records, RG 4 (MDAH). The election results are in *Washington Republican*, May 31, 1815.

70. *Washington Republican*, March 17, 1815.

17. Statehood

1. Peter S. Onuf, *The Origins of the Federal Republic: Jurisdictional Controversies in the United States, 1775–1787* (Philadelphia, 1983); Peter S. Onuf, *Statehood and Union: A History of the Northwest Ordinance* (Bloomington and Indianapolis, 1987); Peter S. Onuf, "Territories and Statehood," *Encyclopedia of American Political History*, ed. Jack P. Greene, 3 vols. (New York, 1984), 3:1283–304. The ordinance is reprinted in Onuf, *Statehood and Union*, 60–64; and in *TP*, 2:40–49. See also Risjord, *Jefferson's America*, 144–45, 189.

2. Jack Ericson Eblen, *The First and Second United States Empires: Governors and Territorial Government, 1784–1912* (Pittsburgh, 1968), 213–36.

3. *TP*, 6:508; *Washington Republican*, April 12, 1815.

4. Haynes, "Political History," 233–34; C&G, *FC*, 207–12.

5. *TP*, 5:290–92, 733–37; ibid., 6:3–4, 331–32.

6. *TP*, 6:242, 253–54, 339.; Proclamation of Governor Holmes, August 1, 1812, EJ; GP to CM, January 25, May 24, November 15, and December 14, 1812, GPP; CM to GP, January 3, 1812, ibid.; Joseph Kent to Levin Wailes, April 2, 1812, Wailes Papers (MDAH).

7. GP to CM, May 24, 1812, GPP; C&G, *FC*, 218; 2 *Stat* 734.

8. *TP*, 6:332–33, 358–59.

9. Ibid., 6:339–41.

10. *TP*, 6: 337, 347–51; James Monroe to Governor Mitchell, December 8, 1812, M40.

11. *TP*, 5: 142–46; ibid, 6:485, 744–46; *Washington Republican & Natchez Intelligencer*, April 16, 1817.

12. *Report of the Committee to whom was Referred from the House of Representatives, The Bill 'To enable the people of Mississippi Territory to form a Constitution and State Government,'* in MDAH. See also Laura D. S. Harrell, ed., "Imprints toward Statehood," *JMH* 29: 430–32; *Washington Republican & Natchez Intelligencer*, February 19, 1817.

13. *TP*, 6:106–8, 231–32, 409–10, 481–82, 494–95, 501–3, 550–52.

14. C&G, *FC*, 210; Dupre, *Transforming the Cotton Frontier*, 11–13, 31–41; *Washington Republican & Natchez Intelligencer*, May 29, 1816.

15. *TP*, 6:484–87.

16. Lattimore to Burnet, October 25, 1814, GC; *Washington Republican*, November 23, 1814, September 17, 1817; *Washington Republican & Natchez Intelligencer*, April 9 and 23, 1817.

17. Lattimore to Burnet, November 4, 1814, GC; *Washington Republican*, April 13, May 17, July 20, September 17, November 23 and 30, 1814; *Washington Republican & Natchez Intelligencer*, April 17, 1816; ibid., April 9 and 23, 1817; *TP*, 6:593–94.

18. *Washington Republican*, May 17, 1815; *Washington Republican & Natchez Intelligencer*, May 29, 1816 and February 26, 1817.

19. TP, 6:507, 719, 720; *Washington Republican & Natchez Intelligencer*, February 19, 1817; Harrell, ed., "Imprints," 433.

20. TP, 6:655–56; *Washington Republican & Natchez Intelligencer*, February 19, 1817.

21. TP, 6:44–46, 492–93; *Washington Republican & Natchez Intelligencer*, February 19, 1817.

22. Lattimore to Burnet, October 25, 1814, GC; *Washington Republican*, November 23, 1814; *Washington Republican & Natchez Intelligencer*, April 9–23, 1817.

23. TP, 6:489–91, 636–37: ASP, PL, 2:891–93; *Report of the Committee on Public Lands* . . . [1816], printed pamphlet in MDAH. Appended to the above pamphlet is a "List of British grants filed with the register of the land office at Washington, Mississippi Territory." Hunt filed for twenty-four claims, totaling 174,465 acres.

24. *Washington Republican*, April 13 and May 18, 1814, and April 26, 1815; TP, 6:580–82.

25. Harrell, ed., "Imprints," 435–37; *Report of the Committee on Public Lands, on the Petition of sundry inhabitants*, [1816?], in MDAH.

26. Hamilton, "Beginnings," 64; *Washington Republican*, July 20, November 23, 14, and 16, 1814; TP, 6:451; MS, *Poindexter*, 120–21.

27. *Washington Republican*, February 22, and April 5, 1815.

28. TP, 6:708–17.

29. Ibid., 6:748–49, 763–74; *Washington Republican & Natchez Intelligencer*, February 5, 19, 1817.

30. TP, 6:731–35, 744–46; Petition by House of Representatives to Congress, December 4, 1816, TLR; *Washington Republican & Natchez Intelligencer*, April 9, 16, and 23, 1817; AC, 14th Cong., 2nd sess., 358–60.

31. AC, 14th Cong., 2nd sess.1282–84; Haynes, "Road to Statehood," 246; Richard A. McLemore, "The Division of Mississippi Territory," *JMH* 5:79–82; Hamilton, "Mississippi 1817," 278–81.

32. *Washington Republican & Natchez Intelligencer*, April 23, 1817; *Mississippi Republican*, September 17 and 24, 1817.

33. Thomas Hinds attributed the enabling act with "crushing at once the hopes of us indivisible politicians." Mead, he reported, was "in the dumps" (Hinds to GP, March 26, 1817, CC). For Poindexter's position, see *Washington Republican & Natchez Intelligencer*, July 19, 1817. See the remarks of Lattimore about "designing men" who opposed the boundary line in *Mississippi Republican*, September 24, 1817; and *Washington Republican & Natchez Intelligencer*, May 14, 21, and 28, 1817.

34. R. H. Gilmer to DH, May 28, 1817, GC; *Mississippi Republican*, September 17, 1817.

35. The best studies of the Constitutional Convention of 1817 are Winbourne Magruder Drake, "The Framing of Mississippi's First Constitution," *JMH* 29:301–27, and "Constitutional Development in Mississippi, 1817–1865" (Ph.D. diss., University of North Carolina, 1954), 67–93. Although there is no extant copy of the journal that was printed in 1817, a later edition is in the MDAH (see *Journal of the Convention of the Western Part of the Mississippi Territory begun and Held at the Town of Washington on the Seventh Day of July, 1817*). The journal, as first published in 1831, is reprinted in William F. Winter, ed., "The Journal of the Constitution Convention of 1817," *JMH* 29:443–504. Brief sketches of some members of the convention are in Dunbar Rowland, "Mississippi's First Constitution and Its Makers," MHSP, 6:79–90.

36. Winter, ed., "Journal," 448–49; Drake, "Framing of Constitution," 308–9; MS, *Poindexter*, 145–46; Joseph Johnson to William Johnson, July 3, 1817, William Johnson Papers (MDAH).

37. This committee initially had twenty members, but an additional one was added later (Winter, ed., "Journal," 450–56, 468, 500–501; Drake, "Framing of Constitution," 309; John Bond to DH, July 5, 1817, GC).

38. Winter, ed., "Journal," 482–83; Drake, "Framing of Constitution," 317–18.

39. Hamilton, *Law*, 65–115; Drake, "Constitutional Development," 14–20. The Constitution of 1817 is in Francis Newton Thorpe, comp., *The Federal and State Constitutions, Colonial Charters, and Other Organic Laws of the States, Territories, and Colonies Now or Heretofore forming the United States of America*, 7 vols. (Washington, 1909), 4:2029–31.

40. *Mississippi Republican*, September 17, and 24, 1817, January 19, and February 2, 1818; *Washington Republican & Natchez Intelligencer*, July 26, 1817; Winter, ed., "Journal," 459–64.

41. Drake, "Framing of Constitution," 315; Winter, ed., "Journal," 475; TP, 6:805.

42. Drake, "Framing of Constitution," 324–27; MS, *Poindexter*, 153–59; Richard A. McLemore and Nannie P. McLemore, "The Birth of Mississippi," *JMH* 29:261–69.

43. Quoted in Chilton Williamson, *American Suffrage: From Property to Democracy, 1760–1860* (Princeton, N.J., 1960), 210.

44. *Mississippi Republican*, September 17, 1817; AC, 15th Cong., 1st sess., 25, 446.

Index

419